LIBERAL VALUES

Benjamin Constant and the Politics of Religion

In *Liberal Values*, Professor Rosenblatt presents a study of Benjamin Constant's intellectual development into a founding father of modern liberalism, through a careful analysis of his evolving views on religion. Constant's life spanned the Enlightenment, the French Revolution, Napoleon's rise and rule, and the Bourbon Restoration. Rosenblatt analyses Constant's key role in many of this era's heated debates over the role of religion in politics, and in doing so, exposes and addresses many misconceptions that have long reigned about Constant and his period. In particular, Rosenblatt sheds light on Constant's major, yet much-neglected work, *De la religion*. Given that the role of religion is, once again, center-stage in our political, philosophical and historical arenas, *Liberal Values* constitutes a major and timely revision of our understanding of the origins of modern liberalism.

HELENA ROSENBLATT is Professor of History at Hunter College and The Graduate Center of The City University of New York.

IDEAS IN CONTEXT 92

LIBERAL VALUES

Benjamin Constant and the Politics of Religion

IDEAS IN CONTEXT

Edited by QUENTIN SKINNER and JAMES TULLY

The books in this series will discuss the emergence of intellectual traditions and of related new disciplines. The procedures, aims and vocabularies that were generated will be set in the context of the alternatives available within the contemporary frameworks of ideas and institutions. Through detailed studies of the evolution of such traditions, and their modification by different audiences, it is hoped that a new picture will form of the development of ideas in their concrete contexts. By this means, artificial distinctions between the history of philosophy, of the various sciences, of society and politics, and of literature may be seen to dissolve.

The series is published with the support of the Exxon Foundation.

A list of books in the series will be found at the end of the volume.

LIBERAL VALUES

Benjamin Constant and the Politics of Religion

HELENA ROSENBLATT

CAMBRIDGE
UNIVERSITY PRESS

CAMBRIDGE UNIVERSITY PRESS
Cambridge, New York, Melbourne, Madrid, Cape Town, Singapore, São Paulo, Delhi

Cambridge University Press
·The Edinburgh Building, Cambridge CB2 8RU, UK

Published in the United States of America by Cambridge University Press, New York

www.cambridge.org
Information on this title: www.cambridge.org/9780521898256

First published 2008

Printed in the United Kingdom at the University Press, Cambridge

A catalogue record for this publication is available from the British Library

Library of Congress Cataloguing in Publication Data

Rosenblatt, Helena
Liberal values : Benjamin Constant and the politics of religion / Helena Rosenblatt.
p.   cm. – (Ideas in context ; 92)
Includes bibliographical references and index.
ISBN 978-0-521-89825-6 (hardback)
1.   Constant, Benjamin, 1767–1830 De la religion considérée dans sa source, ses formes
et ses développements.   2. Religions.   3. Religion – Philosophy.   4. Religion
and politics.   I. Title.   II. Series.
BL80.3.R67   2008
200.92–dc22
2008018125

ISBN 978-0-521-89825-6 hardback

To Marvin, Eric and Annika

Contents

Acknowledgements

Although it is hard to believe, I began thinking about this book almost ten years ago. The idea to work on Benjamin Constant came originally from Larry Dickey, who also offered invaluable guidance and encouragement along the way. I will always be grateful for his intellectual generosity and scholarly example.

It was fortuitous that, about nine years ago, I contacted Professor William Harris of Columbia University, to ask him for some professional advice. I would like to thank him not only for so graciously responding, but for informing me about the opportunities that a fellowship at the National Humanities Center might provide, and for encouraging me to apply. My year in North Carolina was absolutely crucial to this book and to my academic career. I am grateful to the Center's extraordinary staff, and also to the fellows of 2000–1, who made it an ideal environment in which to work. In particular, I would like to thank Carla Hesse, Tom Laqueur, Jeremy Popkin, Timothy Tackett and Helen Chenut for the many kindnesses they extended to me that year, and for all our wonderful discussions. My stay in North Carolina was greatly enhanced by the presence of Steven Vincent and Tony Lavopa, who have since become dear friends.

In 2002, I joined the faculty of Hunter College and the Graduate Center, CUNY. Without the warm welcome of my colleagues there, and without the guidance of Barbara Welter, the Chair of Hunter's History Department, my transition to teaching would not have been such a smooth and happy one. Barbara has been unfailingly supportive of my endeavors, for which I am deeply grateful. At the Graduate Center, I owe special thanks to Richard Wolin and Jack Diggins for their collegiality and support.

Material drawn from my book was presented at the annual meetings of the French Society for Historical Study, the Benjamin Constant Association, the Western Society for French Historical Society and the American Political

Science Association. I was also invited to share parts of my research with the New York City Intellectual and Cultural History Seminar, and the Intellectual History Seminar at the National Humanities Center. Harrick Chapman and Edward Berenson kindly asked me to present papers at two separate conferences hosted by the Maison Française at NYU. Early on in my project, I was offered the opportunity to present my work in Patrice Gueniffey's seminar at the Ecole des Hautes Etudes en Sciences Sociales in Paris. I am grateful to the organizers of all these events for their interest in my research and to the participants for their precious feedback.

I am happy to express my appreciation for several grants (PSC-CUNY 34, 35, 36, 37) that helped pay for research trips to Switzerland, and a Hunter College Presidential Travel Award that allowed me to participate in a conference there. Portions of chapters four and five have appeared elsewhere. For permission to reproduce them in slightly different form, I am grateful to the editors of the *History of European Ideas* and the *Annales Benjamin Constant.*

Over the years, I have benefited greatly from conversations about Constant with many friends and colleagues. Besides the people already mentioned, I would like to thank particularly Stephen Holmes, Jerry Seigel, Mel Richter and Aurelian Craiutu. I am, of course, especially grateful to those who read the entire manuscript and offered me their sage advice: Larry Dickey, Steven Vincent, Tony LaVopa, Jeremy Jennings, Bryan Garsten, Jack Diggins and Anne Hofmann.

Research for this book was conducted at several libraries, but by far the most important was the Bibliothèque publique et universitaire de Lausanne at Dorigny. It is, without a doubt, one of my favorite places in the world. Besides its cordial and efficient staff, it houses the Institut Benjamin Constant, which, thanks to my friends, Etienne and Anne Hofmann, has become my intellectual home away from home. My gratitude to them is immeasurable.

Personal debts are the deepest. As always, my husband has been my most enthusiastic and steadfast supporter. At a pivotal moment in this project, around year five, when I was beginning to show serious signs of procrastination, he urged me to stop hesitating and get on with the writing. When the manuscript was complete, he read it scrupulously several times, helping me to untangle my thoughts and clarify my prose. Throughout, he has been my sparring partner, intellectual sounding board and a fellow-fan of Benjamin Constant. His constant love and support, as well as that of my children, is why I dedicate this book to them.

Note on translations

Unless otherwise indicated, all translations are the author's own.

Abbreviations

ABC	*Annales Benjamin Constant*, 1980–, Lausanne: Institut Benjamin Constant
B&R	B. Constant and R. de Constant, *Correspondance, 1786–1830*, ed. A. and S. Roulin (Paris, 1955)
C&Ch	B. Constant and I. de Charrière, *Correspondance, 1787–1805*, ed. J.-D. Candaux (Paris, 1997)
DA	G. de Staël, *De l'Allemagne*, ed. S. Balayé (Paris, 1968)
DLR	B. Constant, *De la religion considérée dans sa source, ses formes et ses développements*, ed. T. Todorov and E. Hofmann (Arles, 1999)
JI	B. Constant, *Journaux intimes* (1804–1807), in OCBC, série I, *Œuvres*, vol. VI or *Journal intime* (1811–1816), in OCBC, série I, *Œuvres*, vol. VII
KK	G. de Staël, Ch. de Villers, B. Constant, *Correspondance*, ed. K. Kloocke *et al.* (Frankfurt am Main, 1993)
OCBC	B. Constant, *Œuvres complètes*, ed. P. Delbouille, K. Kloocke *et al.* (Tübingen, 1993–)
PB	"Lettres de Benjamin Constant à Prosper de Barante," *Revue des Deux Mondes*, vol. XXXIV (1906)
PoP 1806	B. Constant, *Principles of Politics Applicable to All Governments*, ed. E. Hofmann, trans. D. O'Keeffe (Indianapolis, 2003)
PoP 1815	B. Constant, *Principles of Politics Applicable to All Representative Governments*, in PW
PhM	*Philosophical Miscellanies translated from the French of Cousin, Jouffroy, and B. Constant*, ed. G. Ripley (Boston, 1838)
PW	B. Constant, *Political Writings*, ed. B.-M. Fontana (Cambridge, 1993)
SCU	B. Constant, *The Spirit of Conquest and Usurpation and their Relation to European Civilization*, in PW

Introduction

Recent years have witnessed a remarkable revival of interest in the thought of Benjamin Constant. Long recognized for his literary masterpiece *Adolphe*, it is now his political writings that are attracting attention. A steady stream of paperback editions are appearing on the market, college textbooks increasingly include references to him, and, recently, a US Supreme Court judge drew inspiration from him in a book on the US constitution.[1] Along with a rapidly growing body of scholarship, this Constant renaissance is reaffirming Constant's stature as a founding father of modern liberalism. In fact, many people today regard Constant as *the* most important liberal thinker between Montesquieu and Tocqueville.

Oddly, however, Constant's present fame rests on a partial and skewed reading of his philosophy, since it ignores his lifelong interest in, and copious writings on, religion. Today, few people even know that Constant began doing research for a book on religion at the age of eighteen and that he pursued this endeavor throughout his life until he finally published it as the five-volume *De la religion considérée dans sa source, ses formes et ses développements* (1824–1831). But Constant wrote much more on religion than that; he wrote newspaper articles and essays on religion; he wrote chapters on religion for his other books; he made speeches about it and gave lectures on it – and yet all of this is somehow missing from the accounts that we have of his liberalism.

This book is an attempt to redress this omission. It tells the story of Constant's transformation into an original political thinker. It recounts his education in Scotland and Germany, his introduction to French politics under the Directory, his battles under Napoleon, and his apotheosis as a liberal leader during the Restoration. But this book also

---

[1] S. Breyer, *Active Liberty: Interpreting Our Democratic Constitution* (New York, 2005), pp. 3–6.

tells the story of Constant's evolution from a somewhat flippant admirer of the materialist *philosophe*, Helvétius, into a sincere and mature defender of religion, and a self-described Protestant. I argue that these two things, Constant's political evolution and his religious evolution, are inextricably connected. One cannot understand or properly evaluate Constant's mature liberalism without understanding his views on religion.

The stress on Protestantism may surprise modern readers, but it certainly would not have surprised Constant's contemporaries. Whether they were on the right, like Louis de Bonald, Joseph de Maistre, or Felicité de Lamennais, or on the left, like the Idéologues, Industrialists, and Saint-Simonians, Constant's political adversaries and allies understood him to be a *Protestant* thinker. They would not have needed to be reminded about his major book on religion, or about his many speeches, articles, and essays on the topic. Not being constrained by the disciplinary boundaries of modern scholars, Constant's contemporaries understood that his Protestantism was integral to his liberalism.

Constant himself would have been surprised, and disappointed, to know that his posthumous reputation rests more on his novel *Adolphe* than it does on his writings on religion. Personally, he regarded *De la religion* as his most important undertaking and achievement. Over a period of several years, he called this book "the only interest, the only consolation of my life"[2] and "the book that I was destined by nature to produce."[3] At times it seems that his whole persona was wrapped up in his book. To his friend, Prosper de Barante, Constant once wrote, "The only thing remaining of me is my book."[4]

Over the past two centuries, however, Constant's interest in religion and the importance he accorded to it have been obscured, leaving a seriously distorted view of his liberalism. The erasing of the religious dimension of Constant's liberalism has much to do with Marxism, and its grip on twentieth-century scholarship. In his *The Eighteenth Brumaire of Louis Bonaparte*, Marx famously dismissed Constant as a mere "mouthpiece" of "bourgeois society,"[5] and somehow, this derogatory and simplistic depiction stuck. In fact, however, the distortion of Constant's views began much earlier and is more complicated. It is the result of his opponents, on both the left and the right, who belittled or ignored his

---

[2] JI, April 8, 1804, p. 102.   [3] JI, December 6, 1806, p. 480.   [4] PB, p. 557.
[5] *The Marx–Engels Reader*, ed. R. Tucker (New York, 1978), p. 595.

writings on religion.[6] This is in large part why, to this day, he is often caricatured as an enthusiastic celebrant of *laissez-faire* capitalism, or as a great defender of the individual's right to private "pleasures," and thus serves as convenient foil for community and value-minded republicans.[7] Recent theorists, whether political, literary, or feminist, who continue to ignore his religious writings, have done little to overturn the image of Constant that has been handed down over the years. Failing to address his religious concerns, they have perpetuated a distorted and truncated picture of this founding father of modern liberalism.[8]

As the French historian Maurice Agulhon once remarked, "Having concentrated too much on the struggle between classes, we have managed to forget that the life of our country a century ago was – or, at least, was also – characterized by a 'war of religions'."[9] This book is an effort to return Constant to a historical context in which religious affiliations and religious commitments were at least as important as class.

PREVIOUS SCHOLARSHIP ON CONSTANT AND RELIGION

I do not wish to suggest that Constant's writings on religion have been neglected altogether. Several older studies do exist, but they are rather poor in quality and also outdated. Early treatments tend to be preoccupied with describing Constant's character, often with the aim of rehabilitating the reputation he had acquired for cynicism and immorality.[10] By proving that Constant had an interest in religion, the authors hoped to prove that he had morals. Moreover, those scholars interested in the religious side of Constant's *œuvre* have tended to focus on just one narrow issue: did he undergo a religious conversion?[11] Stated another

---

[6] On this, see my "Why Constant? A Critical Overview of the Constant Revival," *Modern Intellectual History*, 1, 3 (2004), pp. 439–453 and also my forthcoming essay "Eclipses and Revivals: The Reception of Constant in France and America" in the *Cambridge Companion to Constant*.

[7] See, for example, A. Boyer, "De l'actualité des anciens républicains," in S. Chauvier (ed.), *Libéralisme et républicanisme* (Caen, 2000), pp. 37–8; Ph. Pettit, *Republicanism: A Theory of Freedom and Government* (Oxford, 1997), pp. 17–18; Q. Skinner, *Liberty before Liberalism* (Cambridge, 1998), pp. 60, 117; and R. Whatmore, *Republicanism and the French Revolution: An Intellectual History of Jean-Baptiste Say's Political Economy* (Oxford, 2000), pp. xiii, 5, 199.

[8] A. Laurent defends and admires Constant as a *laissez-faire* liberal in his *La philosophie libérale: Histoire et actualité d'une tradition intellectuelle* (Paris, 2002).

[9] From M. Agulhon's preface to J. Lalouette, *La Libre Pensée en France, 1848–1940* (Paris, 1997), p. 12.

[10] H. Evans, "Les idées et les sentiments religieux de Benjamin Constant," unpublished Ph.D. dissertation, Université de Bordeau Faculté des lettres, 1958; M. Saltet, *Benjamin Constant historien de la religion* (Geneva, 1905); D. Berthoud, *Constance et grandeur de Benjamin Constant* (Lausanne, 1944).

[11] H. Hogue, *Of Changes in Benjamin Constant's Books on Religion* (Geneva, 1964).

way: between his juvenile infatuation with Helvétius and his later, more favorable comments about Christianity, did Constant find God?

Among such studies, aimed at evaluating the exact nature of Constant's personal religious beliefs, the most scholarly and thorough is certainly Pierre Deguise's *Benjamin Constant méconnu*.[12] Deguise argues convincingly that Constant was never a militant atheist; rather, he was a lifelong agnostic, whose various experimentations with religion on the personal plane never amounted to a full-blown religious conversion. Henri Gouhier makes a similar argument in his *Benjamin Constant: devant la religion*.[13] Other important work has focused on the sources for Constant's *De la religion*, highlighting his indebtedness to German theology, philosophy, and historiography. Kurt Kloocke is a pioneer in this domain and James Lee has shed additional light on the matter.[14] My footnotes bear witness to how much my own work has benefited from theirs.

Nor do I wish to suggest that Constant's Protestantism has been entirely overlooked. Scattered references to his Protestant "tendencies" can be found sprinkled in the scholarship. Bianca-Maria Fontana, for example, refers to the "Protestant matrix" of Constant's ideas, and even his "strong Protestant bias" and "deep Calvinist instinct."[15] George Armstrong Kelly points to the importance of Constant's "Protestant descent and culture."[16] However, what is still missing from the scholarship is an explanation of what this actually means in the historical context of post-Revolutionary France. What kind of Protestant was Constant, and how did his views on religion inform his political thought?

It is striking what a different image of Constant emerges when one pays attention to his writings on religion. According to Pierre Deguise, Constant's religious writings show him to have been "above all a moralist."[17] More recently, James Lee has also stressed Constant's

---

[12] (Geneva, 1966); see also Frank Paul Bowman, "La révélation selon Benjamin Constant," *Europe*, 46, 467 (March, 1968), pp. 115–125.

[13] (Paris, 1967).

[14] K. Kloocke, *Benjamin Constant: Une biographie intellectuelle* (Geneva, 1984), and J. Lee, "The Moralization of Modern Liberty," unpublished Ph.D. dissertation, University of Wisconsin–Madison, 2003. Mention should also be made of P. Thompson, *La religion de Benjamin Constant: Les pouvoirs de l'image: essai de mise en perspective d'une situation* (Pisa, 1978), which is, however, virtually impenetrable.

[15] B.-M. Fontana, *Benjamin Constant and the Post-Revolutionary Mind* (New Haven, CT, 1991), pp. 109, 103, 7.

[16] G. A. Kelly, *The Humane Comedy: Constant, Tocqueville, and French Liberalism* (Cambridge, 1992) p. 72.

[17] Deguise, *Benjamin Constant méconnu*, p. 265.

preoccupation with the "moral destiny" of mankind,[18] while Catherine Carpenter has referred to Constant's veritable "*obsession* with morality."[19] Having read *De la religion*, Jean Starobinski has also noticed Constant's deep moral concerns and even his "desire for re-Christianization."[20] Indeed, taking Constant's religious views seriously forces one to jettison the notion that he wished above all to protect the material interests of the rising bourgeoisie, or the individual's right to unobstructed "private pleasures." It reminds us that liberal support for state neutrality in the realm of religion should not be equated with moral indifference or a lack of concern for morals. As we shall see, in Constant's case, the very opposite was true.

As of yet, however, there has been little sustained attempt to integrate Constant's ideas on religion and his ideas on politics so as to show how they interrelate and in fact feed on each other.[21] This is what my own study seeks to do. To do it properly requires paying attention to his evolving historical context, because Constant's ideas did not take shape just as a result of his readings and his studies, but were equally a response to his changing religious and political environment. Constant was not only a political theorist; he was also a political actor thoroughly immersed in the battles of his day. For this reason, I reconstruct the main political-religious debates of his time, using them to clarify Constant's positions and to shed light on his distinctive brand of liberalism. From the Enlightenment to the Revolution, through the reign of Napoleon, and on to the Restoration, the context changed dramatically, but religion was always a main focus for Benjamin Constant.

---

[18] Lee, "Moralization," p. 21.

[19] C. Carpenter, "Ethics and Polytheism in Constant's Early Writings: The Influence of Hume, Smith and Gillies," ABC, 29 (2005), p. 73, my emphasis.

[20] J. Starobinski, *Blessings in Disguise; or, The Morality of Evil*, trans. A. Goldhammer (Cambridge, MA, 1993), p. 25.

[21] Exceptions to the rule are G. Dodge, *Benjamin Constant's Philosophy of Liberalism: A Study in Politics and Religion* (Chapel Hill, NC, 1980); Fontana, *Benjamin Constant*; E. Hofmann, "Histoire politique et religion: essai d'articulation de trois composantes de l'oeuvre et de la pensée de Benjamin Constant," *Historical Reflections*, 28, 3 (Fall, 2002), pp. 397–418; and Kelly, *Humane Comedy*. While valuable, these works only scratch the surface.

CHAPTER I

Constant's education: the French, Scottish, and German Enlightenments

CHILDHOOD

Unfortunately, very little evidence about Constant's early childhood and religious education remains. We know that he was born in Lausanne on October 25, 1767 and was baptized in the Calvinist church of Saint-François about two weeks later; but thereafter information is scarce. Benjamin's mother, who died in childbirth, came from a French Protestant family who had emigrated to the Pays de Vaud for religious reasons. Benjamin's father, Juste de Constant, was a Swiss army captain attached to a regiment in the service of the United Provinces. During his early childhood, Constant was placed in the care of various female relatives and his father's young housekeeper and mistress, Marianne Magnin. A prayer dating from these years, which Benjamin probably wrote himself, suggests at least a rudimentary exposure to religion.[1] In any case, the Protestantism prevalent in Lausanne during his childhood was of a liberal and undogmatic variety similar to the rational theology being preached in Geneva.[2] And Juste seems not to have been very concerned about this part of his son's education. A letter written to Marianne in 1772, when Benjamin was six years old, suggests a "reasonable," almost Deist attitude towards religion and church attendance. "You are a bit too difficult," writes Juste,

You want that one preaches to you as one would in the city. Sermons should be proportioned to the intelligence of those who are listening. Anyway, one goes to church only to offer one's hommage to the Supreme Being and this hommage should be in the heart and independent of the exterior cult.[3]

---

[1] "Prière au créateur du monde," in OCBC *Œuvres* I, p. 56.

[2] J. G. A. Pocock, *Barbarism and Religion* (Cambridge, 1999), esp. vol. I, chs. 2–3; on Calvinism in eighteenth-century Geneva, see H. Rosenblatt, *Rousseau and Geneva: From the First Discourse to the Social Contract, 1749–1762* (Cambridge, 1997), esp. pp. 10–29, 34–37.

[3] As quoted by G. Rudler, *La jeunesse de Benjamin Constant (1767–1794): Le disciple du XVIIIe siècle, utilitarisme et péssimisme, Mme de Charrière d'après de nombreux documents inédits* (Paris, 1908), p. 73.

In 1774 Juste decided to take personal control of his son's education, and to bring him along on a series of military assignments in Belgium and Holland. Over the next few years, Benjamin was supervised by a succession of exceptionally inappropriate and badly chosen private tutors. One of these, according to Constant's own recollections, was a self-proclaimed atheist with whom he shared lodging in a brothel. To say the least, this was a rather unconventional education, and not especially conducive to piety. In all likelihood, the young boy received no formal religious training at all. Instead, he was left very much to his own devices and, to a considerable extent, was self-taught in most subjects. According to his autobiography, he learned Greek by himself at the age of five. Thus Henri Gouhier is undoubtedly right to speculate that whatever religious education Constant might have received as a young boy, it "surely did not rekindle in him the faith of his ancestors."[4] On the contrary, Constant later recounted that at the tender age of nine, he was spending eight to nine hours a day alone, reading not only novels but "all the irreligious books that were then in fashion ... from the works of La Mettrie to the novels of Crébillon."[5]

A precursor to the Marquis de Sade, Claude Prosper de Crébillon (1707–1777) was the author of erotic novels depicting the libertine values of the French aristocracy, while Julien Offray de La Mettrie (1709–1751) was a radical materialist and the author of a book provocatively entitled *Man a Machine* (1748). To refer to these two authors was thus to conjure up the most extreme and scandalous side of the French Enlightenment. And the "irreligious books" that Constant devoured as a young boy apparently made a profound impression on him. Constant later recalled that during his youth he had thoroughly "imbibed the philosophy of the eighteenth century and especially the works of Helvétius."[6] Helvétius was, of course, another "bad boy" of the French Enlightenment. Widely reputed to have been an atheist, he was the author of virulently anti-clerical and materialist books. Constant's own recollections thus suggest that, while still a youth, he had been won over to what he would later derogatorily refer to as the "dogmatic incredulity"[7] of the French Enlightenment.

At the age of fourteen, as Benjamin began to show unmistakable signs of intellectual promise, his father decided that a more serious and

---

[4] H. Gouhier, *Benjamin Constant: devant la religion*, (Paris, 1967) p. 31.
[5] *Ma vie*, in OCBC *Œuvres* III, 1, p. 304.   [6] *Ma vie*, in OCBC *Œuvres* III, 1, p. 314.
[7] DLR, pp. xv, 1, 566.

systematic course of study should be chosen. Although he had been astonishingly lax in his parental supervision and careless in his choice of tutors, Juste did make sure to choose a Protestant environment for his son's studies. Several Protestant universities were considered. Oxford University was deemed a possibility, but Benjamin was too young. Eventually, it was decided that he attend the University of Erlangen in Bavaria. There, he apparently "studied fervently"[8] for about a year, although we do not know exactly which subjects he pursued. What we do know is that he got into trouble for something that he would later refer to as "extravagances" and that invariably involved women, gambling, and/or duelling. Thus, his father quickly removed him and soon the decision was taken to send him off to the University of Edinburgh, where he arrived on July 8, 1783, still only sixteen years old.

EDINBURGH

For a brilliant young man with budding literary talents, Edinburgh was an excellent choice. The city and its university had a well-deserved and European-wide reputation as a dynamic center of learning. Thanks in part to figures of great renown, such as David Hume, Adam Smith, and William Robertson, Edinburgh was widely regarded as a "hotbed of genius."[9] The faculty of the university was excellent and the students diligent. In his journal, Constant wrote that "working was in fashion among the young men in Edinburgh,"[10] and that it was there that he first acquired "a real taste for study."[11] That the environment was conducive to serious learning is confirmed by the memoirs of his friend and fellow-student, James Macintosh, who claimed that "it is not easy to conceive a university where industry was more general, where reading was more fashionable, [and] where indolence and ignorance were more disreputable."[12]

Scholars investigating Constant's early years have tended to focus on his psychological make-up. The temptation to psychoanalyze the man who would write one of the best psychological novels of all time, *Adolphe*, has all too often proved to be irresistible. Meanwhile, considerably less attention has been paid to the intellectual work Constant might have

---

[8] *Ma vie*, in OCBC *Œuvres* III, 1, p. 310.
[9] A good introduction to eighteenth-century Scotland and Edinburgh is D. Daiches, P. Jones, and J. Jones, (eds.), *The Scottish Enlightenment 1730–1790: A Hotbed of Genius* (Edinburgh, 1996).
[10] *Ma vie*, in OCBC *Œuvres* III, 1, p. 310.   [11] JI, p. 238.
[12] J. Mackintosh, *Memoirs of the Life of the Right Honourable Sir James Mackintosh*, ed. R. J. Mackintosh (London, 1835), vol. II, p. 29.

done as a young man, and particularly to the exciting new ideas that he encountered in Edinburgh. This is unfortunate because, whatever his emotional or psychological state at the time, it is likely that he fully imbibed the intellectual and cultural atmosphere of Edinburgh during the almost two years that he would later describe as "the happiest of my life."[13]

Someone raised on the "irreligious" books of the French Enlightenment, and smitten by the radical anticlericalism of Helvétius, certainly would have reacted to the very special intellectual and religious climate that reigned in Edinburgh, which was then a leading center of the Scottish Enlightenment. While in France the relationship between key *philosophes*, like Helvétius, and the established Catholic Church was deeply hostile, the situation in Scotland was quite different. There, the Enlightenment was principally the work of moderate Protestant clergymen and took place *within* the churches themselves. Many key thinkers of the Scottish Enlightenment, men like William Robertson (1721–1793), Hugh Blair (1718–1800), Adam Ferguson (1723–1816), and John Home (1722–1808), had been educated for careers in the church and thereafter rose to positions of prominence within the church and/or the university. "In no other country," writes Richard Sher, "were the principles of the Enlightenment . . . so openly and enthusiastically espoused by the leaders of the established church."[14]

The friendly relations between the Enlightenment and religion in Edinburgh meant that a special kind of Protestantism pervaded the city's intellectual environment. The Moderates, who controlled both the church and the university when Constant was there, held exceptionally liberal views when it came to intellectual freedom and religious tolerance. Convinced of the benefits brought to society by learning, polite sociability, and moderation, they had abandoned the austere Calvinism of their forefathers and espoused a more tolerant and self-consciously enlightened religion. They turned away from traditional questions of dogma, such as sin, election, and predestination, and focused more on issues of practical morality. This, they thought, would be more effective in helping men and women lead virtuous and happy lives.

The most famous preacher in Edinburgh at the time, Hugh Blair, was also Professor of *Belles Lettres* and Rhetoric. His fame extended far beyond Scotland, and his five-volume collection of sermons were among

---

[13] *Ma vie*, in OCBC *Œuvres* III, 1, p. 310.
[14] R. Sher, *Church and University in the Scottish Enlightenment: The Moderate Literati of Edinburgh* (Princeton, NJ, 1985).

the most popular English-language works of his time. A great admirer of both the moral philosophy of Francis Hutcheson and the polite sociability of the *Spectator*, Blair's lectures and sermons extolled the "sense of humanity" that he took to be the "distinguishing virtue" of his age. "For what purpose," asked Blair, "did God place thee in this world, in the midst of human society, but that as a man among men thou mightest cultivate humanity; that each in his place might contribute to the general welfare."[15]

As one scholar puts it, the enlightened Protestants of Edinburgh were "world-affirming" by nature and espoused a culture of improvement.[16] Perhaps most importantly, they were firm believers in progress and were personally committed to furthering it. Such an attitude led them to develop a strong interest in history and to focus more on the social and political effects of religion than on its intrinsic truth. It was to history that they turned in order to decipher God's plan for the continuing improvement of mankind. In fact, it has been said that the Scots were "obsessed with history," so that the concepts of progress, development, and change are ever-present in their writings.[17] To them, history illustrated the many advantages brought to mankind by religion. In his sermon "The Importance of Religious Knowledge to the Happiness of Mankind," Blair described Christianity as essentially a socializing and humanizing force: it "forms [men] for Society. It civilizes Mankind. It takes the Fierceness of their Passions, and wears off the Barbarity of their Manners."[18]

Perhaps the most representative of these Enlightenment trends within Scottish Calvinism was William Robertson. Like Blair, Robertson was at the height of his prestige and influence while Constant was in Edinburgh. Robertson was not only a clergyman and leader of the Moderate faction within the Scottish church; he was also University principal. Moreover, he was an internationally renowned historian, whose *History of Scotland* (1759), *History of the Reign of the Emperor Charles V,* (1769), and *History*

---

[15] Quoted by D. Daiches, "The Scottish Enlightenment," in Daiches, Jones and Jones (eds.), *The Scottish Enlightenment 1730–1790*.

[16] I. Clarke, "From Protest to Reaction: The Moderate Regime in the Church of Scotland, 1752–1805," in N. T. Phillipson and R. Mitchison (eds.), *Scotland in the Age of Improvement* (Edinburgh, 1996), p. 205; see also S. Brown, "William Robertson (1721–1793) and the Scottish Enlightenment," in S. Brown (ed.), *William Robertson and the Expansion of Empire* (Cambridge, 1997), p. 9.

[17] Daiches, "The Scottish Enlightenment," p. 9.

[18] H. Blair, "The Importance of Religious Knowledge to the Happiness of Mankind" (Edinburgh, 1750), quoted by Sher, *Church and University*, p. 63.

of America (1777) earned him well-deserved comparisons with Voltaire, Hume, and Gibbon. Like other Enlightenment historians of his day, Robertson took a keen interest in the transforming effects of social and cultural forces. To him, history illustrated the benefits brought to man by the expansion of commerce, and the related virtues of learning, toleration, and polite sociability. As a clergyman and church leader, Robertson also believed in the many advantages brought to civilization by Christianity. In his sophisticated and nuanced conception of history, religion worked hand-in-hand with social and material factors to promote progress over time.

But Robertson's optimism about Christianity's influence on the world did not mean that he was insensitive to the considerable harm done by both superstition and intolerance. On the contrary, Robertson deplored both the "absurd fictions"[19] and "ridiculous"[20] rites, as well as the fanaticism and bigotry, that had accompanied religion throughout history. He showed little sympathy for the "scrupulous observance of external ceremonies"[21] that some Christians regarded as the heart of religious practice, and which in his mind only served to undermine true religion. The point was: if *properly understood*, Christianity was a reasonable and eminently useful religion that promoted progress, encouraged virtue, and civilized men gradually over time. "Genuine Christianity," whose precepts were "mild" and "humane," was as "rational" and "sublime" in its doctrines as it was "pure" and "simple" in its worship.[22] To Robertson, religion and society worked together to promote progress in a consensual, mutually sustaining way. And with the "enlargement and maturity of the human understanding" came improved ways of conceptualizing religion.[23]

Unfortunately, there is very little available evidence as to Constant's specific course of study at Edinburgh. However, we do know that, while he was there, William Robertson was University principal, Hugh Blair was Professor of *Belles Lettres* and Rhetoric, Adam Ferguson was teaching moral philosophy, and Dugald Stewart was lecturing in mathematics. These are only a few of the most famous exponents of the Scottish

---

[19] W. Robertson, *The Situation of the World at the Time of Christ's Appearance, and its Connexion with the Success of his Religion, Considered* (Edinburgh, 1759), p. 23.

[20] W. Robertson, *History of the Reign of the Emperor Charles V* (New York, 1838), p. 516.

[21] W. Robertson, "View of the Progress of Society in Europe, with Respect to Interior Government, Laws and Manners," in *History of the Reign*, p. 16.

[22] Robertson, *The Situation of the World*, p. 23.

[23] W. Robertson, *History of America* (London, 1796), p. 392. For more on this idea, see I. Clarke, "From Protest" and N. Phillipson, "Providence and Progress: An Introduction to the Historical Thought of William Robertson," in Stewart Brown (ed.), *William Robertson and the Expansion of Empire* (New York, 1997).

Enlightenment to whom Constant was exposed and under whom he may even have studied. Moreover, we know that Constant specialized in history, both in and outside of the classroom. Evidence shows that he enrolled in a lecture course of the historian Alexander Fraser Tytler. According to Dennis Wood, who has studied Tytler's lecture notes, Tytler's view of history was typically "whiggish" and displayed a "pronounced Christian bias." The particular course that Constant probably attended began with the civilization of ancient Egypt and covered topics like the "Origin of Idolatry and Polytheism" and the "Institution of the Priesthood and its Connection with the Regal Dignity." As Wood has suggested, Tytler may have been the spark that ignited Constant's idea of writing his own history of religion.[24]

Although we cannot be sure that Constant read Robertson while at Edinburgh, it is hard to believe that he could have remained unaware of the Scottish historian's point of view – especially since it infused the entire intellectual atmosphere. Moreover, among Constant's most intimate friends during this period was Malcolm Laing (1762–1818), the future historian, whom Constant describes in his journal as being "one of the best developers [*continuateurs*] of Robertson."[25] Constant's other closest friends during this period, John Wilde (*c.* 1763–1840) and James Macintosh (1765–1832), also shared a deep interest in history, a trait typical of the Scottish Enlightenment.

It was John Wilde who proposed Constant for membership in the Speculative Society, one of Edinburgh's many debating clubs. Club activities revolved around lectures and discussions of interrelated historical, political, and moral or religious themes. As a member from the fall of 1783 to the spring of 1785, Constant frequently joined in the debates. Apparently, his friends were favorably impressed by his participation. In his memoirs, Mackintosh remembers Constant fondly, noting that "[h]e was much esteemed" in the Speculative Society and that his appearances there "did him great credit."[26] Constant, too, would proudly recall his performance in Scotland: "I distinguished myself as a writer and orator."[27]

Surviving records further indicate that Constant was actively involved in debates on religion. For example, on March 16, 1784, he introduced a

---

[24] D. Wood, "Constant in Edinburgh: Eloquence and History," *French Studies*, 40 (April 2, 1986), pp. 150–166.

[25] *Ma vie*, in OCBC *Œuvres* III, 1, p. 310. Laing wrote a *History of Scotland* which was published in several editions.

[26] Macintosh, as quoted by Wood, "Constant in Edinburgh," p. 158.

[27] *Ma vie*, in OCBC *Œuvres* III, 1, p. 310.

debate on the question "Ought Universal Toleration to be Allowed?" and on November 23, 1784 he gave a speech on "The Influence of Pagan Mythology on Manners and Character."[28] These sorts of questions, approaching religion from the social and political point of view, were of course among the central preoccupations of the Scottish Enlightenment. But Constant's positions seem to have been those of a contrarian, a trait that he would come to develop into a fine art. A portrait, penned by his friend John Wilde, suggests that Constant was an irreverent "atheist," who liked to defend the relative virtues of paganism over Christianity:

an Atheist professed, he maintains at the same time the cause of Paganism, and while he spurns Jehovah cringes before Jupiter, while he execrates the bigotry and laughs at the follies of superstitious Christians, yet makes the vices of adulterous Deities the subject of his panegyric and prostitutes his genius to support the ridiculous mummeries of its Priests.[29]

This description also highlights Constant's sarcastic and flippant side, which became a trademark of his later years.

PARIS

In April 1785, Constant left Edinburgh abruptly. Once again, he was obliged to leave a university because of "extravagant" behavior; this time it was his accumulated gambling debts. Thus, Constant's formal education came to an end. It was only a few months later, however, while on a brief trip to Brussels, that he conceived the research project that would consume much of his life: a history of polytheism. He later described what were his original motivations:

Nourished by the principles of eighteenth-century philosophy, and above all, by the works of Helvétius, I had no other thought than to contribute to the destruction of what I was calling prejudices. I had seized upon an assertion by the author of *De l'Esprit* which claims that the pagan religion is much preferable to Christianity.[30]

It seems fairly obvious, then, that Constant's exposure to the Scottish Enlightenment had not cured him of his aversion for Christianity, nor his infatuation with Helvétius. He had not been won over by the ideas of the Scottish Enlightenment. On the contrary, he seems to have been

---

[28] Wood, "Constant in Edinburgh."
[29] C. P. Courtney, "Isabelle de Charrière and the 'Character of H. B. Constant': A False Attribution," *French Studies*, 36, 3 (July 1982), pp. 282–289.
[30] *Ma vie*, in OCBC *Œuvres* III, 1, pp. 314–315.

convinced that paganism was superior to Christianity and he wished to write on religion in order to help destroy what he dismissed as mere "prejudices."

For three years after leaving Edinburgh, Constant traveled around Europe, sometimes in the company of his father, sometimes alone. During these unsettled years, two extended stays in Paris must have made a great impression on him. The first was in the summer of 1785; the second was for seven months in 1786–1787.

The contrast between Paris and Edinburgh was certainly extreme. In France, the Enlightenment had taken a virulently anti-Christian turn and was distinguished by its profoundly anticlerical character. Key *philosophes*, like Voltaire, made it their life's work to "écrase[r] l'infâme" and by mid-century their writings had succeeded in putting the Catholic Church very much on the defensive. Moreover, by the last years of the Old Regime, criticism of the Church was coming not only from anticlerical *philosophes* like Voltaire and Helvétius, members of what Robert Darnton has referred to as the "High Enlightenment"; increasingly, anticlerical attacks were coming from the more radically subversive, and sometimes atheist, world of the "literary underground."[31] During the 1780s, this "Grub street," as it is also called, was literally exploding, flooding the market with violently anticlerical *libelles*. In such writings, the Catholic clergy was depicted as corrupt, greedy, and sexually lascivious parasites who were deliberately exploiting the people's ignorance and gullibility for their own selfish ends. According to this point of view, there was clearly nothing "useful," "reasonable," or "civilizing" about Christianity.

In response, the Church engaged in an increasingly desperate struggle for survival.[32] Recognizing very little difference between the productions of the High and Low Enlightenment, it counter-attacked by subsidizing the publication of hundreds of books, pamphlets, and sermons condemning the Enlightenment wholesale. The *philosophes* were accused of wanting to destroy all religion, and along with it, all morality and even society itself. According to Charles-Louis Richard's *Exposition de la doctrine des philosophes modernes*, a pamphlet published in 1785, the *philosophes* were deliberately trying to annihilate not only the Catholic religion but "every idea of duty, of obligation, of law, of conscience, of

[31] R. Darnton, *The Literary Underground of the Old Regime* (Cambridge, MA, 1982).

[32] D. McMahon, *Enemies of the Enlightenment: The French Counter-Enlightenment and the Making of Modernity* (Oxford, 2001).

justice and injustice, of vice and virtue."[33] Journals and newspapers such as the *Année littéraire*, the *Journal historique et littéraire* and the *Journal ecclésiastique* joined in, denouncing the *philosophes* in equally sweeping terms. Indeed, spokesmen for the Catholic Church described their struggle in violent and apocalyptic language. Thus, during the final years of the Old Regime, the atmosphere in Paris became increasingly polarized between *philosophes* and *anti-philosophes*. On both sides, there was a reductive and Manichean tendency to depict society as a battleground between good and evil, *philosophes* and *anti-philosophes*, the Enlightenment and the Christian religion.

Thanks to his father's intercession, Constant's home in Paris was with Jean-Baptiste Suard (1733–1817), where a very different sort of climate reigned. Suard was the very model of the moderate *philosophe* and even a "symbol of civility."[34] He believed in the virtues of polite sociability and civilized conversation. Diderot, who knew him well, described Suard as "considerateness itself."[35] In his home, Enlightened *philosophes* of very different views, such as Condorcet, Mirabeau, Garat, the abbé Morellet, and de la Harpe, to mention only a few, could engage in a free and cordial exchange of opinions. In fact, Suard seems to have made a point of making friends with people with whom he did not agree. On the issue of religion, for example, he personally favored the beliefs of English Protestants like Clarke and Newton, but this did not stop him from being on more than cordial terms with both Holbach and Helvétius.[36]

It was no doubt of some importance that Constant's host was an admirer of Scottish thought. Suard is known to have referred to Edinburgh as "*the* great school of philosophy." Therefore, Constant's Scottish education would have commended him to Suard, and may even have served as a bond. Indeed, in his correspondence with Suard, Juste de Constant made sure to write about his son's studies at Edinburgh. Juste may very well have known that Suard was a close personal friend of David Hume, eventually becoming known as Hume's greatest champion in France. Suard was also an admirer of William Robertson.[37] Apparently, it was in response to Hume's suggestion that Suard came to translate some

[33] As quoted by McMahon, *Enemies*, p. 30.
[34] D. Gordon, *Citizens without Sovereignty: Equality and Sociability in French Thought, 1670–1789* (Princeton, NJ, 1994), p. 143.
[35] Ibid.
[36] D.-J. Garat, *Mémoires historiques sur la vie de M. Suard, sur ses écrits, sur le XVIIIe siècle* (Paris, 1820), pp. ix–xi, 169, 210, 215.
[37] For a recent discussion of Robertson, see also Pocock, *Barbarism*, vol. II, pp. 258–305.

of Robertson's most famous historical works, notably his *History of the Reign of the Emperor Charles V*. In fact, Suard's induction into the Académie française in 1774 was very much based on the reputation he had acquired from translating Robertson's *History of America*. Thus, in the entourage of Suard, Constant had occasion, once again, to consider not only the Scottish Enlightenment, but also the broader question of the relationship between religion and progress.

It has been suggested that his stay in Paris in the company of Suard and his friends might have reinforced Constant's "dogmatically materialist and atheistic cast of mind."[38] This is unlikely. It is more probable that exposure to the Suard circle added nuance and complexity to Constant's views on religion and prompted a greater appreciation for the Protestants of Edinburgh. First, although it is true that the Enlightenment in France was more anticlerical than it was elsewhere, few French *philosophes* actually advocated the eradication of religion altogether. In fact, most of them were Deists and had a more nuanced view of religion than Church apologists at the time acknowledged. French *philosophes* tended to agree that some form of religion, however false, was necessary for the maintenance of public order and morals. Second, they knew that there were different ways of being "Christian," and, on the whole, believed that some ways were better than others. Many, if not most, French *philosophes* viewed Protestantism in a relatively favorable light, as a more enlightened, more reasonable, and more useful religion than Catholicism. This helps to account for the favorable reception they gave to the writings of Robertson.

PROTESTANTISM AND THE ENLIGHTENMENT

The idea that there were close connections between the Enlightenment and Protestantism was often asserted by friends and foes of both. Enlightened Protestants proudly claimed that the Reformation had played a crucial role in the spiritual and intellectual emancipation of mankind. Certainly, William Robertson believed this. In fact, his view of history displayed a pronounced Protestant bias, a bias that was recognized by his admirer and translator, Suard.[39] Robertson spoke of "that happy

---

[38] D. Wood, *Benjamin Constant: A Biography* (New York, 1993), p. 68. See also Rudler, *La jeunesse de Benjamin Constant*, p. 176.

[39] J.-B. Suard, "Avertissement du traducteur," in *Histoire du règne de l'empereur Charles-Quint, Précédée d'un Tableau des progrès de la Société en Europe, depuis la destruction de l'Empire Romain jusqu'au commencement du seizième siècle* (Amsterdam, 1771), p. 6.

reformation," calling it "the most beneficial that has happened since the publication of Christianity,"[40] and crediting it with having improved the manners and morals of Europeans immeasurably. In contrast, he viewed Catholicism as retaining too many "superstitious" and "illiberal" rites. A special problem was that "all its institutions and ceremonies must be *immutable* and *everlasting*," so that even in "enlightened times" like their own, the Catholic Church continued to observe "rites which were introduced during the ages of darkness and credulity."[41]

French *philosophes* often wrote as though they favored Protestantism over Catholicism. In Catholicism there were simply too many ceremonies and rites, doctrines and mysteries, priests and hierarchies, while Protestantism seemed to be a much simpler, more straightforward, and more moral religion. The *philosophes* criticized the Catholic practice of celibacy as unnatural and harmful to population growth and deplored monasticism as a useless, even parasitical institution. They regarded what they saw as the overabundance of religious holidays and ornate rituals in Catholicism as nothing but unnecessary and wasteful interruptions of the working week. To French *philosophes*, Protestantism appeared to be a less irrational, less reactionary, and less obstructionist form of religion, one more able to promote all their favorite reforms. Protestantism was a religion more conducive to civic virtue.[42] Moreover, in their campaign against religious "fanaticism" and intolerance, the *philosophes* could quite naturally be drawn to defend French Protestants, who had for so long been subjected to religious persecution by political and religious authorities. This is precisely what happened in the famous Calas Affair (1762):[43] by using his talents and reputation, Voltaire intervened in a very public way to overturn the verdict and clear the name of a Protestant man who had been unjustly convicted of murdering his own son. In the abundance of literature surrounding the case, Catholic bigotry and intolerance were regularly contrasted with the quiet innocence and patience of the Protestants.

Perhaps most important for many *philosophes* was the idea that Catholicism divided man's loyalties and thereby interfered with good government. Obedience to a foreign leader and an exaggerated concern

---

[40] Robertson, *History of the Reign*, p. 124. [41] Ibid., p. 516, emphasis added.
[42] G. Adams, *The Huguenots and French Opinion, 1685–1787: The Enlightenment Debate on Toleration* (Waterloo, Ontario, 1991); see also B. Poland, *French Protestantism and the French Revolution: A Study in Church and State, Thought and Religion, 1685–1815* (Princeton, NJ, 1957); E. I. Perry, *From Theology to History: French Religious Controversy and the Revocation of the Edict of Nantes* (The Hague, 1973).
[43] D. Bien, *The Calas Affair* (Princeton, NJ, 1960).

with the afterlife split a person's allegiances in ways deemed harmful to society. This idea was famously expressed by Rousseau in his *Social Contract* (1762). The problem with Catholicism, he wrote, was that it subjected citizens to "contradictory duties"; it gave men "two sets of legislation, two leaders, and two homelands."[44] Protestantism did not pose this problem: "it was the only religion in which the laws can maintain their dominion and the leaders their authority."[45] Such arguments would have disposed *philosophes* favorably to Protestantism, since the idea that religion should be under state control was common among them. Indeed, noticing the Erastianism of key *philosophes*, J. G. A. Pocock has recently gone so far as to define the entire Enlightenment project as essentially "a series of programs for strengthening civil sovereignty" and reducing that of Christian churches.[46] Voltaire undoubtedly spoke for many *philosophes* when he argued that

It is an insult to reason and to the law to say these words: civil and ecclesiastical government. You must say civil government and ecclesiastical regulations; and none of these regulations must be made by anything other than the civil authorities.[47]

High-profile Protestants living in Paris would, in all likelihood, have confirmed the relatively positive view of Protestantism held by *philosophes*. One could, for example, consider Jacques Necker, the self-made man from Geneva who rose to become one of the richest bankers in Europe and finance minister to Louis XVI. Constant would get to know him well. Throughout his turbulent career, Necker refused to convert to Catholicism despite the obvious advantages it would have meant for his career. Known as an enlightened reformer, and a friend of public opinion,[48] Necker wrote several hugely successful books on politics and finance. Notably, he also wrote and published two books on religion, in which he defended the very "reasonable" and tolerant variety of Christianity he himself professed. Necker's wife, Suzanne, the daughter of a Protestant minister, ran a successful salon, which was attended by such

---

[44] J.-J. Rousseau, *On the Social Contract*, in *The Basic Political Writings*, ed. and trans. D. Cress (Indianapolis, IN, 1987), p. 223.
[45] J.-J. Rousseau, *The Geneva Manuscript*, in *On the Social Contract*, ed. R. Masters (New York, 1978), p. 201.
[46] J. G. A. Pocock, "Conservative Enlightenment and Democratic Revolution: The American and French Cases in British Perspective," *Government and Opposition*, 24, 1 (1989), p. 84 and his *Barbarism*.
[47] Voltaire, *Political Writings*, ed. D. Williams (Cambridge, 2000), p. 198.
[48] On Necker's relationship to public opinion, see L. Burnand, *Necker et l'opinion publique* (Paris, 2004).

Enlightenment luminaries as Suard, Grimm, Marmontel, Abbé Raynal, and, occasionally, even Diderot and d'Alembert. A practicing Protestant like her husband, Suzanne Necker welcomed Catholics and even atheists into her home for frank and cordial discussions on a broad range of topics. Her kind of religion – moral, tolerant, and enlightened – was one that many *philosophes* could appreciate.

For perhaps an even better understanding of what it meant to be Protestant in eighteenth-century Paris, one might consider the leaders of the Protestant community there. Protestant ministers like Court de Gébelin (1719–1784) and Rabaut de Saint-Etienne (1743–1793) came to Paris to represent French Protestants before both the government and enlightened opinion. Both men were not only ministers, but also the sons of prominent ministers; and both had been educated at the Protestant Seminary of Lausanne. Arriving in 1763, Court de Gébelin's express mission was to promote religious toleration; he remained in Paris for about twenty years. When he died in 1784, Rabaut Saint-Etienne continued his work. Their long struggle was rewarded in 1787, when the Edict of Toleration was finally passed.

Historians are unanimous in their assessment of the kind of religious instruction Protestants like Court de Gébelin and Rabaut Saint-Etienne would have received at the Seminary in Lausanne. For one, they would have been poorly instructed in theology.[49] The trend for some years had been to de-emphasize the teaching of orthodox doctrines concerning matters such as original sin, salvation, and Christ's divinity. Instead, seminary students were taught what historians now derisively refer to as a "lukewarm" and "spiritually impoverished" form of Protestantism, far removed from the ideas of John Calvin. So anemic was the level of theological instruction that it seems that many newly consecrated pastors came out of the Seminary largely indifferent on the matter. Above all, they wished to avoid what they regarded as "obscure," "incomprehensible," and "nonessential" dogmas in their own preaching in order to accord more time to the teaching of sound morals.[50] Surviving sermons from the period testify to this widespread tendency among French Protestants in the eighteenth century. As theologians, these graduates of the Lausanne Seminary were apparently "not much";[51] the instruction they received had, in effect, rather turned them into Protestant moralists with a strong belief in human dignity and the educability of man. Despite their

---

[49] See, for example, D. Robert, *Les églises réformées en France (1800–1830)* (Paris, 1961), and F. Kuhn, "La vie intérieure du protestantisme sous le premier empire," *Bulletin de l'histoire du protestantisme français*, 51, 2 (February, 1902), pp. 57–73; also R. Mandrou *et al.*, *Histoire des protestants en France* (Toulouse, 1977).

[50] Kuhn, "La vie intérieure."   [51] Robert, *Les églises réformées*, p. 17.

long oppression by intolerant laws, they seem even to have shed any deep hostility towards Catholicism. Rabaut Saint-Etienne's father, a famous Protestant leader in his own right, expressed this attitude well: "reasonable Catholics," he wrote, "are Protestants without even knowing it."[52]

Court de Gébelin and Rabaut Saint-Etienne are outstanding representatives of a general trend within eighteenth-century French Protestantism. As pastors, they espoused a very "reasonable" religion, something that was so weak on dogma and so strong on morals that it resembled natural religion. Rabaut Saint-Etienne stated categorically that the Christian religion was really "only natural religion ... *confirmed* by Jesus Christ."[53] It is not surprising, then, that both men gave considerable latitude to human reason in defining the content of their belief. Court de Gébelin asserted that true religion should above all be "reasonable and useful":

In order to decide if we must believe the articles of faith that the Christian religion teaches, it is necessary ... to assure oneself first of all of their conformity with reason and then their certainty. Finally, in order to practise Christian morality, one must first see if it is reasonable and really useful to men.[54]

Rabaut Saint-Etienne would certainly have agreed with this, since he favored "a simplification of religion" that would make it both more understandable to common people and more palatable to *philosophes*.[55] Everything "accessory" to religion should be discarded, so that people might focus on the true goal of man, which was a life of virtue and sound morals. What Rabaut really wanted was an end to all the useless theological quarrels and "a return to the Christianity of Jesus Christ."[56]

The summation of this very reasonable theology was the catechism commonly used by the Protestants of Paris.[57] It was a catechism composed by the Genevan minister, Jacob Vernes, a friend and disciple of Jean-Jacques Rousseau. According to Vernes, dogmas that were "obscure," "incomprehensible," and "nonessential to faith," only served to "divide churches and promote intolerance" and thus on all accounts should be avoided. Instead, Vernes espoused a doctrine that "conformed to reason" and which therefore was "well-suited to make individuals and societies happy."[58] Although this

---

[52] As cited by Robert, *Les églises réformées*, p. 17.   [53] Ibid., p. 10, emphasis added.

[54] As cited by D. Robert, "Court de Gébelin et les églises," *Dix-huitième siècle*, 17 (1985), p. 182.

[55] As cited by A. Dupont, *Rabaut Saint-Etienne, 1743–1793: Un protestant défenseur de la liberté religieuse* (Geneva, 1989), p. 33.

[56] Ibid.

[57] See M.-C. Pitassi, "Le catéchisme de Jacob Vernes ou comment enseigner aux fidèles un 'christianisme sage et raisonnable,'" *Dix-huitième siècle*, 34 (2002).

[58] As quoted by Kuhn, "La vie intérieure."

catechism seems to have been popular with enlightened Parisian Protestants, a Catholic writer, noticing its utter neglect of dogma and surprising optimism about human nature, assessed it to be nothing but "the purest elixir of socinianism."[59]

Protestants of a later period, as well as twentieth-century historians, regretting the disappearance of the "old Calvinist spirit" and disapproving of theological "indifference," have been critical of these developments within eighteenth-century Protestantism. To such critics, the enlightened form of Protestantism professed in France during the eighteenth century was almost entirely devoid of dogma and thus really "didn't amount to much."[60] This, however, was exactly what the *philosophes* liked about it. They appreciated Protestants for championing a simpler, clearer, more tolerant, and, in their minds, more morally efficacious religion, a religion that was undoubtedly closer to the Deism that many of them themselves espoused.

Court de Gébelin and Rabaut Saint-Etienne also went to great lengths to represent the Protestant cause. They aggressively sought contacts and friends in Parisian high society. They were outgoing and sociable at a time when such qualities were particularly highly prized. They were intellectually curious, deliberately cultivating friendships not only in places close to power but in the scientific and intellectual community as well. Beginning in 1768, Court de Gébelin devoted himself to research, and, only a few years later, published his multi-volume *Le Monde primitif analysé et comparé avec le monde moderne*. With the stated goal of promoting "universal harmony" between all peoples and all religions, he tried to prove that there existed only one primordial language common to all men and one common religion, born in Egypt and based on man's observation of nature and the heavens. Through an allegorical reading of ancient fables, he attempted to show that all religious cults throughout history were just residues of this one perfect, primitive religion. Court's book won universal acclaim; leading luminaries like Diderot, Franklin, Turgot, and d'Alembert purchased copies, as did several government ministers and royal family members. In 1780 and again in 1781, Court received prizes from the Académie française in recognition of his scholarly work.[61] When he died in 1784, he was thus not only a well-known Parisian representative and spokesperson of all French Protestants, but also a distinguished historian and scholar of religion. Rabaut Saint-Etienne, who obviously shared his predecessor's

---

[59] M. de Beaufort, quoted by Kuhn, "La vie intérieure," p. 66.   [60] Kuhn, "La vie intérieure."
[61] Recounted by P. Schmidt, *Court de Gébelin à Paris (1763–1784): Etude sur le protestantisme français pendant la seconde moitié du XVIIIe siècle* (St. Blaise, 1908).

scholarly and enlightened attitude towards religion, as well as his love of science and learning, wrote a deeply respectful eulogy.[62] Rabaut himself was so thoroughly imbued with the thought of the Enlightenment that, in his writings, "one finds more easily Locke, Condillac, Montesquieu, Rousseau, Voltaire than Calvin."[63] No wonder, then, that the *philosophes* found his Protestantism so congenial.

Both Court de Gébelin and Rabaut Saint-Etienne also joined masonic lodges at a time when Freemasonry attracted some of the most enlightened and intellectually curious minds in France.[64] Court de Gébelin joined the prestigious Parisian lodge, the Nine Sisters, and became its secretary. This particular lodge recruited many of its members from the salon of the widowed Madame Helvétius; *philosophes* like Turgot, Condorcet, Franklin, Cabanis, Garat, and Volney were regulars. On April 7, 1772, when Voltaire joined, it was Court de Gébelin and Benjamin Franklin who introduced him to the members; then, during the initiation ceremony, Court read a fragment of his *Monde primitif*.[65] All this made him a kind of ideal "bridge-person between the Protestant community of France and the *philosophe* milieu in Paris."[66]

When Rabaut Saint-Etienne took over from Court in 1784, he was able to build on established friendships; this, no doubt, served him well in the long and drawn-out negotiations that finally resulted in the Edict of Toleration. A friend of Jefferson and Lafayette, Rabaut would go on to become an important deputy in the Constituent Assembly, where he worked to ensure the inclusion of a strong statement protecting freedom of conscience and worship in the Declaration of the Rights of Man.

The cordial relations between *philosophes* and Protestantism were of course noticed by the Catholic Church. The Church itself often made an explicit connection between Protestantism and the Enlightenment, claiming, for example, that the *philosophes* inherited their subversive ideas from the Protestant reformers.[67] In their attacks on the *philosophes*, Catholic apologists often used language very similar to that used for years against Protestants. Thus, the *philosophes* were frequently referred to as "*prétendus* savants" or "*prétendus* philosophes," the way Protestants had

---

[62] Dupont, *Rabaut Saint-Etienne*, p. 50.   [63] Mandrou, *Histoire*, p. 235.

[64] On the links between Protestantism and Freemasonry, see D. Ligou, "Franc-maçonnerie et protestantisme," *Dix-huitième siècle*, 17 (1985), pp. 41–51.

[65] Recounted by Schmidt, *Court de Gébelin à Paris*, ch. 6.

[66] Robert, "Court de Gébelin," p. 179.

[67] A. Hofmann, "The Origins of the Theory of the *Philosophe* Conspiracy," *French History*, 2, 2 (1988), pp. 152–172.

for long been labeled *"prétendus réformés."* And like Protestants, the *philosophes* were accused of fostering dangerous sectarianism that threatened not only religion but the state as well.

In answer to the argument that Protestantism was a simpler and more enlightened form of religion, Catholics replied that Protestantism was really only a half-way house to Deism or even atheism. Once individuals were allowed to question the dogmas and traditions of the Church, they were on the slippery and dangerous slope of irreligion. At its very core, they argued, Protestantism really meant the defiance of authority and, as such, was profoundly destabilizing to the social and political order. Through doctrines such as freedom of inquiry, Protestantism encouraged individual dissent, while its organizational structure was favorable to republicanism. The notion that Protestantism was somehow politically subversive was, of course, vehemently denied by the leaders of the French Protestant community, who were in fact obsequious in their professions of loyalty to the French king.[68] But the stigma of rebelliousness, cultivated by Catholics, remained. Thus, it was on the grounds of their supposed "republican principles" and the perception that they were the natural "enemies of hierarchy and the habits of monarchy" that Louis XV refused to grant Protestants toleration throughout his reign.[69]

Most scholars agree that, at this point in his life, Constant was both an atheist and an admirer of Helvétius. Although based on very little evidence, this conclusion may be true. At the very least, however, pairing the label "atheist" with a casual reference to Helvétius oversimplifies Constant's views on religion. After all, Helvétius was no ordinary atheist, if he was one at all. In *De l'homme* he made it perfectly clear that his real target was the Catholic Church rather than religion in general. It was the "sacerdotal body" of the Catholic Church that obstructed progress and deliberately exploited people's ignorance for its own selfish ends. Catholicism, Helvétius wrote, is a "human invention" devised by the Church to serve as "an instrument of its avarice and pride." Here Helvétius was only expressing what many *philosophes* believed: the true problem with a "sacerdotal" religion like Catholicism was that it interfered with good government by splitting people's allegiances and priorities and by encouraging wasteful, backward, and superstitious practices. For as long as such a Church was

[68] Dupont, *Rabaut Saint-Etienne*, p. 34, recounts that his sermon in honor of Louis XVI's coronation was so fawning that it angered people in his congregation.

[69] J.-L. Soulavie, *Mémoires historiques et politiques du règne de Louis XVI* (Paris, 1801), vol. I, p. 171, as quoted by G. Adams, "Monarchistes ou républicains," *Dix-huitième siècle*, 17 (1985), p. 83.

able to control people's minds, the civil authority would be impeded in its pursuit of much-needed reforms. Notably, the solution proposed by Helvétius in *De l'homme* was not the eradication of religion *per se*; rather, he recommended the placing of "the spiritual power" in the hands of "an enlightened magistrate." For Helvétius, "the union of the temporal and spiritual power in the same hands" was "indispensable."[70]

In Helvétius' view, not all established religions were equally repressive and obstructionist. Historically, one of the least harmful had been the pagan religion. Because it was "without dogmas" and did not require an abundance of priests, it was naturally "humane and tolerant." Since it did not involve so many costly festivals, it was also more economical. But most significantly, the pagan religion never got in the way of the civil authority's law-making efforts; because of its relationship with the state, it would never obstruct the work of a "patriotic legislator." Thus it had "none of the inconveniences of popery." Interestingly, for similar reasons, Protestantism was preferable to Catholicism. Helvétius proffered that

> The Lutherans and Calvinists of Germany are better governed and happier than the Catholics, and the Protestant Cantons of Switzerland are more rich and powerful than the Papist Cantons. The Reformed Religion thus contributes more directly to the public happiness than the Catholic.[71]

In other words, from the social and political point of view, the Protestant religion was superior to Catholicism. It was more supportive of the secular aims of the Enlightenment and was more likely to facilitate, rather than obstruct, an enlightened magistrate's reform efforts.

One should keep in mind the above when considering Constant's professed admiration for Helvétius. There can be little doubt that Constant shared the general tendency of the Enlightenment to view Protestantism in a more favorable light than Catholicism. His upbringing, schooling, and exposure to the Suard circle in Paris would all have encouraged it.

BRUNSWICK

In 1788, at the urging of his father, Constant took up a post as chamberlain at the court of the Duke of Brunswick-Wolfenbüttel, where he remained until August 1794. It was while in Brunswick that he first heard about the outbreak of the Revolution in Paris. Constant followed the news with great interest.

---

[70] C.-A. Helvétius, *De l'homme* (Paris, 1989), vol. I, note 45, p. 136.   [71] Ibid., pp. 112, 133–134.

A series of letters written to his friend and perhaps lover, Isabelle de Charrière, constitutes our principal source for this period in Constant's life. From them, we know that he greeted the Revolution with enthusiasm. The letters show that during its early phases Constant regarded himself a "democrat"[72] and believed that "common sense . . . is against any other system."[73] In fact, as late as June 1794 he was still defending the Revolution, although he worried about its excesses.[74] "To occupy the middle ground is to take up a worthless position," he wrote; "at this juncture it is more worthless than ever. That is my profession of faith."[75]

Constant's letters to Charrière also reveal that he quickly became bored and felt isolated at the court of Brunswick. His periodic expressions of pessimism and hopelessness have prompted some to believe that he was suffering from an emotional and/or intellectual crisis. Contributing to his emotional distress was a failed marriage to a lady at court,[76] which ended in 1794. Throughout the correspondence, Constant displays a singular talent for psychological self-analysis and self-critique, a quality for which he would later become famous. His letters give us a precious window into the current state of his religious beliefs and his continuing quest for meaning, one that would periodically compel him to grapple with religion on a deeply personal plane.

"I feel more than ever the nothingness of all things," Constant wrote Charrière in June 1790,[77] following up in December with: "The life that I'm leading exhausts me . . ."[78]

We are like watches that have no dial . . . and whose cogs, endowed with intelligence, turn until they are worn without knowing why and always telling themselves: because I turn I have a goal . . . this idea seems to me the most brilliant and profound piece of folly that I have heard, and certainly preferable to the Christian, Muslim or philosophical follies.[79]

In January 1791, he summed up his feelings of depression and related them to his inability to be anything other than agnostic:

Unable to believe in the mysterious and unproven promises of a religion that is in many respects absurd, and seeing no reason for hope in a philosophy that

---

[72] Letter no. L, September, 17, 1792, in C&Ch, p. 167.
[73] Letter no. LVII, May 17, 1793, ibid., p. 179.
[74] K. S. Vincent, "Benjamin Constant, the French Revolution, and the Origins of French Romantic Liberalism," *French Historical Studies*, 23, 4 (Fall 2000), pp. 607–637.
[75] Letter no. CXLII, June 7, 1794, in C&Ch p. 344.   [76] Minna von Cramm (1758–1823).
[77] Letter no. XXXVII, June 4, 1790, ibid., p. 131.
[78] Letter no. XLI, December 10, 1790, ibid., p. 141.
[79] Letter no. XXXVII, June 4, 1790, ibid., p. 132.

consists merely of words, I see here on earth only a great deal of unavoidable suffering ... very few pleasures ... and at the end of it all, sooner or later, nothingness.[80]

In one particularly telling letter, Constant confesses:

My life is sadder than ever without my having any particular reason to be unhappy. I feel disconnected from everything, with no interests, no moral bonds, no desires, and fed up and disgusted [*à force de satiété et de dégoût*], I am often ready to do stupid things.[81]

At times, Constant seems genuinely to regret his lack of faith. He explains that he is unable to find solace in "Christian follies" and finds "all forms of religious-day dreaming"[82] equally vapid and useless. But this is not something that he is happy about.

I am neither credulous nor incredulous, moral nor immoral; I see no proof, no probability that there is a God; although I swear to you I would very much like for there to be one. It would change my whole existence and would give me prospects [*des vues*] and a goal.[83]

At other times, he could be quite humorous about his lack of religion:

Oh, how I would like to believe what I don't believe! ... I would volontarily have my nose and ears cut off in order to be convinced, but I fear that without ears and without a nose, I would be incredulous despite myself, as I am now.[84]

MAUVILLON, THE NEW GERMAN THEOLOGY AND
THE IDEA OF PROGRESSIVE REVELATION

Under these circumstances, it was fortunate that Constant met and got to know Jakob Mauvillon (1743–1794). Their friendship helped to dispel Constant's boredom and pull him out of his depression. Mauvillon came from a French Protestant family that had immigrated to Germany a generation earlier. A man with broad intellectual interests, he had taught mathematics and military architecture at the Collegium Carolinum in Kassel. He had also served as the ghostwriter of Mirabeau's *De la monarchie prussienne sous Frédéric le Grand* and had translated both Raynal's *Histoire des deux Indes* and Turgot's *Réflexions sur la formation et distribution des richesses* into German. A political radical with ties to the

---

[80] Letter no. XLIV, January 21, 1791, ibid., p. 150.
[81] Letter no. XLIX, July 6, 1791, ibid., p. 164.
[82] Letter no. XLI, December 10, 1790, ibid., p. 140.
[83] Letter no. XLIX, July 6, 1791, ibid., p. 165.   [84] Rudler, *La jeunesse de Benjamin Constant*, p. 430.

Illuminati and Freemasonry, Mauvillon shared Constant's sentiments about the Revolution.[85] In the staid and isolated atmosphere of Brunswick, the two men were quite naturally drawn together and a bond developed.

Mauvillon did more than cure Constant's boredom. He did something that would have profound consequences for Constant's evolution as a political and religious thinker: he introduced Constant to key thinkers of the German Enlightenment and, more specifically, to their liberal Protestant theology. Mauvillon was an admirer of Kant and had a deep interest in religion; in fact, he was something of an expert on the Protestant theology of the Aufklärung. When Constant met him in Brunswick, he had already published several essays on religion, as well as a major book, *Das einzige wahre System der christlichen Religion*. In this book, he engaged with many vital theological issues, grappling in particular with the ideas of religious innovators like Johann Salomo Semler (1725–1791), the so-called Neologists,[86] and G. E. Lessing (1729–1781). Thanks in large part to Mauvillon, Constant borrowed 114 books in the Göttingen library and immersed himself in German Protestant theology.

In some important ways, the ideas to which Constant was now exposed were a repetition of what he had already learned in Edinburgh. In other words, they were the standard fare of the Protestant Enlightenment. Like their Scottish counterparts, the German Aufklärer were on good terms with Christianity. Most of them were more interested in reforming their religion than they were in attacking it. Also like the Scots, they were interested in history and progress, believing that Christianity was integral to both. This time, Constant's exposure to the Protestant Enlightenment had a powerful effect. The liberal Protestant theology of Germany fundamentally reoriented Constant's thinking about religion, causing him to give up his early infatuation with paganism, and to adopt a more overtly Protestant perspective. We know this from a precious manuscript that he left behind; entitled "l'Esprit des religions," it shows a remarkable competence in German theology.[87]

[85] My information on Mauvillon comes from J. Lee, "The Moralization of Modern Liberty," unpublished Ph.D. dissertation, University of Wisconsin–Madison (2003) pp. 261–264; K. Kloocke, *Benjamin Constant: Une biographie intellectuelle* (Geneva, 1984), pp. 53–58; and K. Kloocke, "Le concept de la liberté religieuse chez Benjamin Constant," ABC, 10 (1989), pp. 25–39.

[86] The classic source remains K. Aner, *Die Theologie der Lessingzeit* (Hall, 1929).

[87] K. Kloocke, "Religion et société chez Benjamin Constant," in L. Jaume (ed.), *Coppet, creuset de l'esprit libéral: Les idées politiques et constitutionnelles du groupe de Madame de Staël* (Paris and Aix-Marseille, 2000), p. 123.

Although there were considerable differences between the ideas of
Semler and those of the Neologists and Lessing, they all agreed on several
points. First, they took a strong interest in history and were believers in
progress. Second, they were proponents of a non-dogmatic, tolerant, and
humanistic form of Protestantism that held moral improvement to be
man's ultimate and God-given goal. Third, they all subscribed to the
notion of "progressive revelation,"[88] an idea which would have a
profound and lasting impact on Constant.

Scholars now agree that what German enlighteners like Semler and his
followers were trying to do was to reconcile the Enlightenment with
Christianity – in essence, this meant to *update* Protestantism so as to keep
it relevant to the modern world. They thought that old-fashioned
orthodoxy had become too staid, formulaic, and dry to be morally useful.
History provided them with the arguments they needed. Adopting and
reworking the well-known principle of accommodation,[89] they seized
on the idea that "religion," which they held to be moral, timeless, and
true, was something different from "theology," which was bound to a
particular time and place, and therefore could be false. For them, religion
was something more than a prescribed set of doctrines or an established
form of worship, fixed once and for all. Rather, it was something akin to
an elemental drive that, over the course of history, took on a number of
variable forms. In Semler's thought and in that of his followers, Christianity became an evolving religion, a religion which was, and was meant
to be, *improving* over time – thereby retaining its capacity to serve as an
agent of human progress.

Integral to this notion of a perfectible Christianity was the idea of
"progressive revelation," a theory articulated by Semler, before it was
rendered famous by Lessing, one of Mauvillon's favorite authors. The
theory of progressive revelation held that God, in his infinite wisdom, did
not dispense his revelation to man all at once. Rather, he dispensed it in
stages, in effect accommodating his teaching so as to accord with man's
evolving capacity to understand it. In his "The Education of the Human
Race" (1780), Lessing argued that history revealed mankind's growing
maturity in religious matters. Progressive revelation was what was driving
this gradual process of moral and religious education. "What education is

---

[88] There are hints of the notion in Scottish thinkers, but I have not found it as pronounced as in
German thinkers.
[89] S. Benin, *The Footprints of God: Divine Accommodation in Jewish and Christian Thought* (Albany,
NY, 1993) and P. Reill, *The German Enlightenment and the Rise of Historicism* (Berkeley, CA, 1975),
esp. pp. 162–171.

to the individual man," Lessing wrote, "revelation is to the whole human race."[90] To Lessing, "positive religions" should be seen as stages in the steady advance of humanity from infancy to maturity. Judaism was thus a "step" in the right direction; it was ideally suited for man in a state of "childhood."[91] It proposed rewards and punishments that he could understand and appreciate. New Testament Christianity was another step in the gradual improvement of mankind; it was perfectly adapted to the child who had now become a "youth" and could understand more sophisticated forms of rewards and punishments. After these two revelations, Lessing looked forward to a coming "third age," which would bring mankind even nearer to perfection and moral adulthood. Each step in the process brought "nobler and worthier motives for moral action," progressively educating man in both reason and morality. Eventually, Lessing predicted, man would "do right because it *is* right," and not because of any "arbitrary rewards" promised him.[92]

CONSTANT'S "THE SPIRIT OF RELIGIONS"

The manuscript Constant left behind dating from the 1790s shows him engaging the thought of what he refers to as the German "neologists" or "innovators."[93] In it, Constant tells the story of the dramatic transformations Prussia had undergone in the realm of religion, due to some rather controversial state policies. Sixty years ago, Constant explains, a "dogmatic spirit" reigned among Lutherans and Calvinists in Germany. Both denominations of Protestantism were intolerant on principle. This, Constant adds, was a manifest contradiction since the Reformation itself had been justified on the grounds of the "inalienable right that each individual has to choose the manner he thinks is best to please his God." Nevertheless, because of a contradiction that was as "absurd" as it was "cruel," early German Protestants denied others the religious liberty that they wanted for themselves.[94]

---

[90] G. Lessing, "The Education of the Human Race," in *Lessing's Theological Writings*, ed. and trans. H. Chadwick (Stanford, CA, 1983), p. 82.

[91] Ibid., pp. 84–85.

[92] Ibid., pp. 93, 97, 92, 96. On Lessing's view of progressive revelation, see H. E. Allison, *Lessing and the Enlightenment: His Philosophy of Religion and its Relation to Eighteenth-Century Thought* (Ann Arbor, MI), pp. 52–53.

[93] "D'une nouvelle espèce de rapports que les Théologiens modernes voudroient introduire dans la Religion." Bibliothèque cantonale et universitaire de Lausanne, Fonds Constant.

[94] Ibid., p. 2.

Things changed dramatically when Frederick the Great (1712–1786) ascended the throne and embarked on a state policy of religious toleration. Constant recounts that the Prussian king even invited French *philosophes* to Berlin and allowed them to attack religion with impunity. Prussian theologians were thrown on the defensive and scrambled to defend their religion. Some of these theologians, Constant explains, quickly realized that the most unassailable part of the Christian religion was its morals. Thus, in an effort to defend themselves and their religion, they began to abandon various dogmatic positions and to focus, rather, on morals.

The situation may very well have stayed this way had Frederick the Great's successor, Frederick William II (1744–1797), not decided to abandon the policy of religious toleration and embark on a diametrically opposite course. Constant recounts that Frederick William liked to surround himself with "Rosicrucians, alchemists, Catholics & Orthodox [Lutherans]." Despite their differences, they all agreed that Prussia's liberal course with regard to religion should be reversed. Thus, they joined the king in what Constant describes as an outrageous attempt to "command opinions and rule over the thoughts of their people." The Edict of 1788[95] was passed. Henceforth, any deviations from "ancient doctrine" would be strictly forbidden.[96]

The point that Constant was eager to make was that Frederick William II's reactionary religious policies had unanticipated consequences and, in the end, were counter-productive. They were a shock to the liberal theologians, who had always seen themselves as defenders of religion. Now, suddenly, due to state policy, they were treated as its enemies. In self-defense, the liberal Protestant theologians began to advocate complete freedom of religion. They became fullyfledged proponents of progress, freedom of thought, and enlightenment. Having originally not pushed for religious liberty, and having suffered because of it, they now committed themselves entirely to this "sublime goal" and fought hard to defend the "religious rights" of man. The German theological innovators came to the realization that religion should not and could not be subjected to any constraint whatsoever. Religious persecution was as "unjust"

---

[95] Issued by the Prussian minister for ecclesiastical affairs, Johann Christoph von Wollner, this edict aimed to protect Lutheran orthodoxy against the "enlighteners." It forbade any Lutheran minister from teaching anything not contained in the official books and placed all educational establishments under the strict supervision of orthodox clergy.

[96] "D'une nouvelle espèce," p. 7. Kloocke ("Le concept," p. 29) thinks that Constant may even have witnessed personally this battle of Protestant liberals against the Prussian reaction.

as it was "ridiculous"; indeed, it was even "illusory," since governments "had no authority over consciences."[97]

Constant expressed special admiration for those German theologians who "discard[ed] the whole dogmatic and miraculous part of Christianity" and turned it, rather, into "a moral doctrine." He admired their attempt to "purify" religion. He liked their view that man was "perfectible" and that "God's intention [was] that he perfects himself." Constant was also favorably impressed by the theory of progressive revelation. To the liberal German theologians, Constant noted, revelations are only a "means of improvement that God gives to man." God "proportions" his revelations to "the state in which man finds himself." Revelation, Constant seems to agree, should not be seen as something immutable or timeless. Rather, it is something that one must allow to "march" along with Enlightenment, thus allowing it to purify itself by successively ridding itself of various accretions, like miracles, prophecies, and mysteries. The Jewish revelation was good for the period in which it appeared; but the Jews were soon ready for a purer, higher form of religion. The Christian religion was also good for the period in which it appeared. Likewise, the Reformation suited a certain epoch. Now, however, was "the moment for another" reformation. Protestantism, Constant concluded, also needed to be improved and purified: "We can do without the dogmatic side of religion. We should therefore discard it."[98]

Constant's manuscript shows that he very much appreciated the views of the German innovators. Their system had "great advantages." It was both "gentle" and "consoling"; moreover, it "avoid[ed] the grossest absurdities" that many people "*called* the Christian Religion." Constant was particularly impressed by their idea that religion "must be perfected"; by employing this principle, the German Protestants allowed "free reign to Enlightenment," and "consecrate[d] the sacred principle of toleration." In sum, the perspective of Protestant Germany's theological innovators had become Constant's favorite "system." "I prefer it to all others," he wrote, "I would like for it to supplant them."[99]

On the personal plane, however, the Germans' ideas still presented some problems. Constant's intellectual appreciation of the new theologians did not mean that he suddenly discovered faith and became a believer. There remained disturbing, unanswered questions, "difficulties" that he could not ignore. Why, for example, would a powerful and benevolent God create a being as imperfect as man, and then make his

---

[97] Ibid., pp. 10, 9.   [98] Ibid., pp. 10, 11, 12, 12, 14, 16.
[99] Ibid., pp. 16, 17, emphasis added.

improvement so complicated and laborious? Why would God dispense enlightenment piecemeal? Why would he allow religion to be so disfigured by man? Why would he allow Christianity to be turned into nothing but "a collection of errors, of superstitions," thereby enabling the subjection of humankind "under the most degrading and cruel yoke" for countless years? Could God not foresee that this is what would happen? Could He not prevent it? These troubling questions, which appear at the end of Constant's manuscript, made it impossible for him to accept entirely the new German theology, even though he thought it the best "system" he had encountered so far.[100]

Letters to Isabelle de Charrière indicate that Constant was making substantial progress on his book on religion while at Brunswick. On May 23, 1794 he informed her that "I am working hard on my big book, and it's coming along. There are thirty-seven chapters completed of which I'm not displeased, but it's hellishly difficult."[101] By July 21, he reported that his manuscript was over 600 pages long, "and that's just the first part." He projected being able to finish it during the next year and would publish it in order to "test whether my readership likes it"; his "reader-ship," in all likelihood, would consist of "a few *philosophes* scattered here and there, friends of tolerance and liberty."[102]

It is worth noting that after his encounter with Mauvillon and the new German theology, Constant had favorable things to say about Christianity. His, however, was not an unequivocal approval. "I am not unaware of the good Christianity has produced," he wrote, but then added: "if only Heaven had allowed for the list to be longer!" Towards the end of his manuscript, he reveals that despite his lingering questions and various objections, "the Christian religion, such as these venerable men would like to establish it ... seems to me to be a system made for man, an ennobling system, consoling and purifying." There were, for him, however, some overriding constraints. Whichever "system" one endorsed, it must never be promoted at the expense of toleration and intellectual freedom. It must not be allowed to endanger "the first of our goods," which is "the independence of our thought."[103] What the Prussian story proved was that governmental interference in the realm of religion was not only harmful but also counter-productive. In Brunswick, and through his exposure to liberal German theologians, Constant thus hit upon what would be a central principle of his mature liberal philosophy – that there should be complete freedom of

---

[100] Ibid., pp. 19, 24, 26.   [101] Letter no. CXXXIX, May 23, 1794, in C&Ch, p. 335.
[102] Letter no. CXLVI, July 21, 1794, ibid., p. 355.   [103] "D'une nouvelle espèce," p. 26.

opinion and belief, and that such freedom was conducive to both intellectual and moral progress. Thanks to the German theologians, his book would no longer be so much *against* religion as it would be *for* religious liberty.[104]

It is clear that Constant's research on religion was done with one eye trained on France. During his stay in Germany, he followed with great interest the unfolding revolutionary events in France. He also appears to have kept himself well informed about *French* attitudes towards religion. We know, for example, that in 1788 he was thinking about writing a refutation of Jacques Necker's *De l'importance des opinions religieuses*, although he apparently abandoned the project.[105] And in 1794, Constant wrote an essay on the National Convention's decree on religion, passed on 18 Floreal Year II, instituting the cult of the Supreme Being. Although the essay is lost, Constant left precious hints about it in a letter to Charrière. The "absurd" decree designed by Robespierre put Constant in "a bad mood," he wrote. He found it "ridiculous" and "worrying."[106] One thing is certain: Constant's thoughts on religion were, from the outset of his project, inextricably connected with his thoughts on the Revolution, government, and politics. While working in German libraries and with German sources, he remained very much concerned with political developments in France.

Indeed, Constant's manuscript on religion reflects his tendency to think about religion and politics simultaneously, and to consider their parallels and interconnections. Thus, in the midst of a discussion of the difficulties he perceives in the German theological system – in particular, its somewhat naive optimism about all the good things brought to the world by Christianity – Constant suddenly makes an analogy to current political events in France. He notes that the revolutionaries are being blamed for the Terror, which is something, in all probability, they could not have foreseen. By the same reasoning, Constant asks, should not God be blamed for what *He* did not foresee, in other words the perversion of religion in the hands of men? "Reason, like justice," writes Constant, "ought to be the same in religion as in politics." For fifteen centuries of Christian history, he adds, "each year has had its 10th of August, its 2nd of September and its 6th of October." If one judged God the way one was

---

[104] K. Kloocke, "Les écrits de Benjamin Constant sur la religion: quelques réflexions hermeneutiques et méthodologiques," in *Huit études sur Benjamin Constant, Cahiers de l'Association internationale des études françaises,* 48 (1996), p. 396.

[105] Letter no. XVI, March 9, 1788, in C&Ch, p. 70.

[106] Letter no. CXXXIX, May 23, 1794, ibid., pp. 334–336.

judging the French revolutionaries, God would receive "a very rigorous sentence" indeed.

Constant left Brunswick an admirer of the new German Protestant theology. Christianity, for him, was no longer simply a set of superstitions and "prejudices" retarding human progress. Rather, it could also be a system of thinking that allowed for and encouraged progress. Indeed, under conditions of intellectual freedom, widespread toleration, and governmental non-interference, the Christian religion could be a powerful instrument in mankind's intellectual and moral development. When speaking of the "Christian religion," it should be emphasized that the German theologians obviously favored Protestantism, since they regarded it as the highest form Christianity had attained so far, and because it alone recognized what Constant referred to as the "inalienable right that each individual has to choose the manner he thinks is best to please his God." What we do not know from Constant's surviving writings from this period is how he thought – or *if* he thought – that this liberal Protestant "system" might be applied to France. What could be done, and what should be done, in a country whose population was predominantly Catholic? It was a question with which Constant would grapple in the years to come.

MADAME DE STAËL

Constant met Madame de Staël (1766–1817) for the first time on September 18, 1794. The brilliant daughter of Louis XVI's controversial finance minister, Jacques Necker, she was then a renowned figure in her own right. By the time she met Constant, she had already obtained notoriety as a salonnière and was a published author. The two would have much to talk about – and not just about politics, but also about religion. At their very first meeting, Constant showed Madame de Staël the manuscript of "L'esprit des religions," and she was much impressed by it.

Madame de Staël's religious upbringing had been starkly different from that of Constant. Although both were Swiss Protestants, de Staël had been taught early on to respect and admire her religion. Scholars agree that she had received a "solid" religious education,[107] some say even a "strictly Protestant"[108] one. Her father, Jacques Necker, descended from a long line

[107] S. Balayé, *Madame de Staël: Lumières et liberté* (Paris, 1979), p. 13.
[108] P. Kohler, *Madame de Staël et la Suisse* (Payot, 1916), p. 35; see also P. Cordey, "Madame de Staël et les prédicants lausannois," *Cahiers staëliens*, NS, 8 (1969), pp. 7–21; H. Perrochon, "Les sources suisses de la religion de Mme de Staël," in *Madame de Staël et l'Europe, Colloque de Coppet* (Paris, 1970).

of pastors, while her mother, Suzanne Curchod, was the daughter of a pastor as well. As a result, Germaine was raised on the Bible, the catechism of Osterwald,[109] and various books of piety carefully selected by her mother.

But the Necker household was an enlightened one, and the Protestantism they imparted to Germaine was of the liberal variety current in both Geneva and Paris at the time. Priding itself on being "reasonable," it rejected both "superstition" and "fanaticism" and stressed moral and benevolent behavior over dogma. Thus, Germaine was raised to see no contradiction between enlightened values and religious ones, but rather to see them as inextricably connected.[110] All of this would have resonated with Constant, who had just imbibed the liberal Protestant theology of Germany.

Madame de Staël would certainly have endorsed the lessons he had learned in Germany. She would have encouraged Constant to look favorably on religion – to see Christianity not just as a collection of "prejudices" needing to be rejected, but rather as something consoling, uplifting, and positive for morals. It has been noted that the religion Germaine absorbed as a young girl had a certain "Rousseauean" coloration to it; according to R. Mortier, it was "a religion of the heart ... a faith without dogmas and miracles."[111] Clearly, this variety of religion was no longer the Calvinism of Calvin, yet Madame de Staël would describe herself, in at least one of her writings, as "a good Calvinist."[112] Hers was a reasonable, tolerant, and sentimental religion of the heart, deeply influenced by Rousseau, whose "Profession of Faith of the Savoyard Vicar" de Staël celebrated in one of her earliest writings as a "masterpiece of eloquence in its sentiments ... and metaphysics."[113]

Due to her wealth, connections, and powerful intellect, Madame de Staël was poised to become a significant player on the Parisian intellectual scene. Meeting her was probably the single most important event in Constant's life. He was instantly seduced by her mind and conversation, and fell desperately in love. On the intellectual plane, de Staël appears to have been equally impressed; but her heart took longer to conquer. The evening of

---

[109] Jean-Frédéric Ostervald (1663–1747), famous theologian from Neuchâtel, one of a triumvirate of important Swiss liberal Protestant theologians responsible for "post-orthodoxy."

[110] See also J. Giblein, "Note sur le protestantisme de Mme de Staël," in *Bulletin du protestantisme français* (Paris, 1954).

[111] R. Mortier, "Philosophie et religion dans la pensée de Mme de Staël," *Rivista de letterature moderne e comparate* (September–December 1967), p. 135.

[112] *Des Circonstances actuelles qui peuvent terminer la Révolution et des principes qui doivent fonder la république en France*, ed. L. Omacini (Geneva, 1979) p. 229.

[113] "Lettres sur J.-J. Rousseau," in *Œuvres de jeunesse*, ed. S. Balayé and J. Isbell (Paris, 1997), p. 73.

their first encounter, she wrote to her lover, the Swedish diplomat Adolphe de Ribbing, "I found here this evening a man of great wit called Benjamin Constant. He is . . . not very handsome but exceptionally intelligent."[114]

Eventually de Staël succumbed to Constant's advances; they became lovers and most likely had a daughter together,[115] although Constant's paternity was never openly acknowledged. Over the years, their love life was tumultuous and, at times, tortuous. There were numerous arguments, break-ups, reconciliations, highs and lows. Remarkably, however, throughout their rocky romance, their intellectual complicity remained firm. Indeed, they became lifelong intellectual partners. Together they co-authored and/or collaborated on many books and projects essential to the foundations of modern liberalism.

From the outset, Madame de Staël encouraged Constant's research into religion. Impressed by his manuscript, she wrote Ribbing: "I have genuinely praised him for his work entitled *L'Esprit des religions*, in which he truly shows a talent equal to Montesquieu."[116] In January 1795, Constant moved closer to Madame de Staël, and in May he accompanied her to Paris, where they arrived on May 25, 1795. Immediately, Constant was taken up by the whirlwind of political events, and he set aside, temporarily, his book on religion.

[114] G. de Staël, *Correspondance générale*, vol. III, part 1, ed. J. J. Pauvert, notes and commentary by B. Jasinski (Paris, 1962), p. 117–118.
[115] Albertine, who would eventually marry the Duc de Broglie.
[116] *Correspondance*, vol. III, part 1, October 22, 1794, p. 158.

CHAPTER 2

The crucible of the Directory years

THE SEE-SAW POLICY OF THE DIRECTORY

Although, upon arriving in Paris, Constant put aside his book on polytheism, religion would never be far from his mind during the Directory years. Religion was one of the government's most pressing problems and one of the period's most contentious issues. Within governing circles and intellectual elites, heated debates took place on the nature and political value of Catholicism, with key theorists and politicians arguing over its compatibility or incompatibility with a republican regime. In the end, the Directory's failed religious policies were a principal cause of its ignominious decline and fall. Constant's experiences during these years taught him much that would inform his liberal philosophy and his writings on religion.

When Constant and Madame de Staël arrived in Paris, they could not have failed to notice the changing political mood. With the removal of Robespierre, the political pendulum had swung to the right. After six years of revolutionary upheaval, culminating in the trauma of the Terror, the propertied and educated classes of Paris longed for peace and a return to order. Only a few days before the couple's arrival, the last *sans-culottes* uprising of the Revolution had been put down. Large crowds of hungry men and women from the working-class districts had invaded the Convention's meeting hall demanding "bread and the Constitution of 93." This time, however, they had elicited little sympathy from the government, which countered with a swift and harsh repression. In the minds of more well-to-do Parisians, these final revolutionary *journées* served only to revive bad memories of street violence and mob-rule. Thus they accelerated the reaction against everything associated with the radical phase of the Revolution.

Constant's republican sympathies remained strong in 1795, although they had been tempered somewhat since the days of Brunswick when he described himself as a "democrat" and had even defended Robespierre. Through Madame de Staël, and her salon in the Swedish Embassy, Constant was now introduced to key "Thermidorians," or the main political players in the city, men like the Vicomte de Barras (1755–1820) and the Abbé Sieyès (1748–1836). The principal topic of discussion during those summer months was the need for a new constitution. The constitution of 1793, conceived during the most radical phase of the Revolution, called for Universal Manhood Suffrage and recognized both a right to subsistence and a right to insurrection. In the more conservative climate, it was thought that popular participation in the decision-making process should be restricted. The deputies dominating the Convention sought a political settlement that would put an end to the political disturbances, while protecting what they regarded as the main accomplishments of the Revolution.

In August 1795, the new constitution was approved. Boissy d'Anglas' inaugural speech affirmed the widespread belief that France should be "governed by the best," that is, by "people with property." For the sake of law and order, then, the constitution limited the right to hold office to the wealthiest taxpayers. Moreover, all references to social rights were removed and a "declaration of duties" was added.

Constant supported what was, in the context of its times, a centrist and moderate republican position. He shared the Thermidorians' desire to "end the Revolution," while safeguarding its principal reforms. In his earliest political writings, Constant became a spokesman for what has rightly been called the *juste milieu*, a position somewhere between royalism and Jacobinism. He defended the new constitution and steadfastly worked to promote "the strengthening of the republic."[1]

But Constant and his Thermidorian allies were more than aware that a new constitution alone could not solve France's many problems. The government faced major hurdles. The economy was in shambles and the country was still at war, both at home and abroad. With brigands roaming the country, there was a general sense of lawlessness. At the same time, the machinery of government was so weakened and inefficient that it was nearly impossible to govern. All of these problems were compounded by a poor harvest and particularly vicious winter in 1795–1796.

Of the Thermidorians' numerous problems, perhaps the most daunting was the bitterly divided political landscape. On the radical left were

---

[1] *De la force du gouvernement actuel de la France et de la nécessité de s'y rallier*, in OCBC *Œuvres* I, p. 328.

irreconcilable neo-Jacobins disappointed by the end of the Terror. These were joined by Babouvists calling for the abolition of private property and the wholesale leveling of social, economic, and political differences. On the extreme right were die-hard royalists and angry *emigrés* plotting the overthrow of the regime. Somewhere in the middle were the vast majority of the French population, tired of incessant change and disillusioned by politics. To many, the Revolution had come to mean only violence, insecurity, and chaos. Exhausted and apathetic after years of revolutionary turmoil, this "inert mass" of people, to use Constant's words,[2] was unlikely to give more than half-hearted support to the new regime. Indeed, there was a growing sense that the country at large was turning counter-revolutionary. Adding to the uneasiness of the government were disturbing reports that a Catholic revival was underway.

The government was painfully aware of its narrow base of support and vulnerability. Its survival strategy, however, was ultimately counter-productive. Unable to accept the political realities of their predicament, the Thermidorians adopted what has been described as an "ostrichlike attitude."[3] Instead of accommodating themselves to the reality of organized political opposition, and to what was, in essence, an emerging party politics, they tried to remain above it. Their policy consisted in a "see-saw policy [*politique de bascule*]," in other words, a series of alternating blows aimed against the royalists or the neo-Jacobins, depending upon which of these constituted the most immediate political threat. And while the government repeatedly resorted to electoral manipulation and other unconstitutional means to stay in power, it stigmatized any oppositional movement as a "faction" subversive to the republic. Despite the well-intentioned efforts of people like Constant and Madame de Staël, who tried to rally moderates to the new Republic, in the long run the Directory managed only to increase the numbers of its enemies.

CATHOLICISM AND THE NEED FOR "REPUBLICAN INSTITUTIONS"

Unfortunately, Thermidorian leaders exhibited the same shortsightedness and rigidity when it came to religion. This was especially tragic, since the divisive religious situation was probably the most important challenge

---

[2] Ibid., p. 339.
[3] I. Woloch, *The New Regime: Transformations of the French Civic Order, 1789–1820* (New York, 1994), p. 101.

that they faced. By all accounts, the Revolution's policies towards the Church had been a colossal failure. The expropriation of the Church by the National Assembly in 1789, the Civil Constitution of the Clergy of 1790,[4] and then the oath of loyalty imposed on the clergy, had served only to polarize the country and radicalize the Revolution. Large sections of the population had been angered by these policies and had turned against the Revolution. The violent and anarchic dechristianization campaign at the height of the Terror had only made matters worse. By 1795, the leadership and organization of the French Church was utterly destroyed, as thousands of priests had been imprisoned, killed, or forced into hiding or exile. Churches across the country had been vandalized and/or closed, and the regular practice of Catholicism had been disrupted for years.

However, despite the havoc wrought upon the Catholic clergy, and the state of "semi-anarchy"[5] that reigned, the Directory soon had to face an extraordinary predicament: a religious revival was underway. Deprived of their traditional clergy, and forced into secrecy, French Catholics did not abandon their faith, but found new and often creative ways of worshiping.[6] And, by 1795, with the winding down of the Terror, there was a growing optimism that restrictions on religious observance would be lifted. Indeed, many people mistakenly interpreted the fall of Robespierre as a sign that the churches would be reopened and freedom of religion respected.

French Catholics, however, were to be bitterly disappointed. While the Thermidorians may have been political moderates, they certainly were not moderate when it came to Catholicism. Many had been among the most determined dechristianizers and retained a deep personal aversion for the Catholic Church. Boissy d'Anglas, himself a Protestant, spoke for many in his government when he called Catholicism "an auxiliary of despotism." "Intolerant and dominating," it was "the accomplice of

---

[4] Passed in July 1790, the Civil Constitution of the Clergy was designed to rationalize the structure of the Church and place it under the control of the state. Diocesan boundaries were redrawn and bishops and parish priests became salaried officials of the state, to be elected by their local populations. All of this was done without prior consultation with either the French Church or the pope.

[5] A. Dansette, *Histoire religieuse de la France contemporaine: De la Révolution à la Troisième République* (Paris, 1948) p. 137.

[6] S. Desan, *Reclaiming the Sacred: Lay Religion and Popular Politics in Revolutionary France* (Ithaca, NY, 1990) and O. Hufton "The Reconstruction of a Church, 1796–1801," in G. Lewis and C. Lucas (eds.), *Beyond the Terror: Essays in French Regional and Social History, 1794–1815* (Cambridge, 1983), pp. 21–52.

all the crimes of kings."[7] So, while they repudiated the Terror, Thermidorian leaders did not repudiate anticlericalism and were very slow to dismantle existing antireligious legislation. When they finally did grant religious freedom, it was obvious that they did so reluctantly. They acted out of a conviction that heavy-handed tactics against religion were counter-productive. On the floor of the Convention, Boissy d'Anglas accused priests of "stupefying humankind," but he conceded that it was pointless to try to "extirpate error by force."[8] More gentle policies against Catholicism were needed.

The Law of Ventôse (February 21, 1795) is a perfect illustration of the Thermidorians' contradictory, disingenuous, and ultimately ineffec-tual strategy towards religion. Ostensibly, the law recognized freedom of religion and promised state neutrality in all religious matters. Hence-forth, churches would be allowed to reopen. In practice, however, the law withdrew the funding that France's Constitutional Church depended upon for its survival. Church property nationalized during the Revolu-tion was not returned, and the use of public buildings for religious ceremonies remained restricted. Communes were forbidden from col-lectively buying or renting buildings for religious purposes, from taxing their inhabitants to build them, and from accepting endowments for the support of worship. No wonder that many people saw the Law of Ventôse as yet another attempt to debilitate the Catholic Church financially.

Other aspects of the law were similarly contradictory and frustrating for Catholics. While the Law of Ventôse recognized the right to freedom of conscience, it also restricted religious expression. The law prohibited the celebration of religious ceremonies in public or even the public dis-play of religious symbols. In practice, this meant that no outdoor pro-cessions, no bell-ringing, and no statues, crosses, or inscriptions would be allowed. Priests could not wear habits in public, or even announce church services. This, clearly, was not "neutrality" with regard to religion; rather, it was a transparent attempt to force religion out of the public sphere, and, more specifically, to stop Catholicism from regaining its former strength.

But the Thermidorians miscalculated the popular mood and, in the end, their policies proved counter-productive. Despite the restrictions

---

[7] As quoted in A. Latreille, J.-R. Palanque, E. Delaruelle and R. Rémond, *Histoire du catholicisme en France: La période contemporaine* (Paris, 1962), vol. III, p. 127.

[8] Dansette, *Histoire religieuse*, p. 139.

and impediments to worship, the Catholic revival gained momentum. Apparently, the liberalizing decrees, starting with the Law of Ventôse, had an energizing effect on the population. Newspapers reported that chapels in Paris and throughout the country were reopening to throngs of worshipers. Services had to be held in private oratories and hired rooms, because there was not enough space to accommodate the crowds.[9]

The religious revival disturbed the government deeply. Especially alarming was the growing sense that it was allied to political reaction. As early as March 1795, the conservative Mallet du Pan somewhat wishfully observed: "in re-creating Catholicism, the Convention is re-creating Royalists."[10] An indication of this was the steady decline of France's Constitutional Church, made up of those priests who had accepted the Civil Constitution of the Clergy in 1790 and had sworn an oath of allegiance to the constitution. Despite the valiant efforts of its leader, Abbé Grégoire, to rebuild this church after Thermidor, French Catholics were leaving it in droves. They preferred to transfer their allegiance to the "non-juring" priests, in other words, to those who had refused to take the oath, and who were now returning to France in growing numbers. Constitutional priests themselves began retracting their oaths and joining the non-juring clergy, whose prestige and influence steadily rose. In addition to this, the government was receiving reports that, in reopened Catholic churches accross France, purchasers of nationalized Church lands were being denounced and prayers were being recited for the royal family. It was in an attempt to draw these counter-revolutionary forces closer together and to offer them encouragement, that the new claimant to the throne, Louis XVIII, issued the Verona Declaration (June 24, 1795). Ruling out any compromise with the Revolution, he promised to completely restore France's "ancient constitution," including the Roman Catholic Church. In a circular to French bishops, he urged Catholic leaders in France to work hard to promote not only the Catholic religion, but also the "monarchical spirit." He asked the bishops to emphasize the "intimate connection that exists between Throne and Altar." Religious leaders should teach French men and women that Catholicism could not long survive without monarchy and that the two depended upon "their mutual support."[11]

[9] N. Aston, *Religion and Revolution in France 1780–1804* (Washington, DC, 2000), p. 283.
[10] As quoted by G. Lefebvre, *The Thermidorians & the Directory*, trans. R. Baldick (New York, 1964). p. 69.
[11] As quoted in *Histoire du catholicisme*, p. 142.

Under these circumstances, it is not surprising that the Thermidorians continued to view the Catholic revival with deep suspicion and fear. Unfortunately, however, they dealt with it in the same way they handled political dissent: with contradictory and ultimately unsuccessful policies. Ostensibly, the new constitution recognized both freedom of religion and the separation of church and state. A few weeks after its proclamation, however, a decree on the exercise of worship codified earlier impediments to religious practice. It also subjected all religious gatherings to police surveillance and obliged all priests to take another oath of loyalty to the state. Meanwhile, repressive and punitive laws against emigrés and non-juring priests stayed in place. Abbé Grégoire was correct when he observed that these policies only served to further alienate the French people from their government.

For Thermidorians, however, the politics of the ongoing religious revival only confirmed what they had always believed: Catholicism and the Revolution were fundamentally incompatible. Moreover, it provided incontrovertible proof that the Revolution was losing the battle for the hearts and minds of the people. Obviously, a new government and a new constitution alone could not provide France with the stability it so desperately needed. The country lacked the requisite political culture. Not long after arriving in Paris, Constant expressed this republican commonplace when he wrote that the success of a republican regime depended not only on its constitutional "forms," but also on its citizens' "convictions."[12] It was precisely these "convictions" that were missing in France.

In fact, revolutionaries and counter-revolutionaries agreed that France lacked the political traditions, habits, and values necessary to sustain a republican constitution. This led royalists to argue for a return to the pre-Revolutionary monarchy, a system they regarded as better suited to French *moeurs*. So said Louis de Bonald (1754–1840), who would soon emerge as the evil genius of Ultraroyalism. Giving a nod of approval to the counter-revolutionary rebels of the Vendée, Bonald declared that the French had a special "national character" making them unsuited for republican regimes. Trying to change their deeply ingrained customs and habits would be like attempting to build "an edifice of snow on burning soil."[13]

---

[12] *De la force*, in OCBC *Œuvres* I, p. 342.
[13] L. de Bonald, *Théorie du pouvoir politique et religieux*, ed. C. Capitan (Paris, 1966), pp. 100–101.

Nevertheless, this is, of course, precisely what the post-Thermidorian government tried to do. Believing that the constitution was doomed to failure without the requisite political and religious culture, they embarked on an ambitious campaign to transform French *moeurs*. In other words, despite its professed goal of "ending the Revolution," the Thermidorian government continued unabated a project conceived at the height of the Revolution: national "regeneration" would dechristianize the country. Naturally, the Thermidorians wanted to avoid the violent coerciveness of the Terror and, in particular, the anarchic excesses of the dechristianization campaign. They preferred the gentler, better organized, and, they hoped, more effective methods of civic instruction and moral indoctrination. However, they had not given up on the goal of turning Frenchmen into civic-minded citizens, which, in their minds, meant detaching them from their religion. It was the pace and the methods that changed, rather than the goal itself.

Fostering moral reform involved the government in a new and deeper intervention into France's cultural life.[14] 1795 saw the formation of a National Institute of Science and Arts, with a "class of moral and political sciences," which took a lead in the planning.[15] Decreed from above, the correct moral principles were meant to pass to the people through a new and comprehensive system of public education. Primary schools would offer children not only "instruction," that is, necessary skills like reading, writing, and arithmetic, but also "education," which referred to the all-important principles of morality and citizenship. Significantly, the subject of religion would be replaced by the study of the constitution and republican morals.

The project of national regeneration did not end with the education of children. As one prominent advocate noted: "*all* the generations display prejudices, vicious habits, with an equal need of Enlightenment and virtues."[16] Thus it was decided to continue the project inaugurated during the most radical phase of the Revolution, namely government sponsorship of public holidays and national festivals expressly designed to inspire

[14] On public instruction during Thermidor, see B. Baczko, *Ending the Terror: The French Revolution after Robespierre*, trans. Michel Petheram (New York, 1994); R. R. Palmer, *The Improvement of Humanity: Education and the French Revolution* (Princeton, NJ, 1985), pp. 208–236; and C. Hesse, *Publishing and Cultural Politics in Revolutionary Paris 1789–1810* (Berkeley, CA, 1991).

[15] On the National Institute, see F. Azouvi, "L'Institut national: une encyclopédie vivante?," in F. Azouvi (ed.), *L'Institution de la raison: La Révolution culturelle des Idéologues* (Paris, 1992); R. Hahn, *The Anatomy of a Scientific Institution: The Paris Academy of Sciences, 1666–1803* (Berkeley, CA, 1971); M. Staum, *Minerva's Message: Stabilizing the French Revolution* (Buffalo, NY, 1996).

[16] P.C.F. Daunou, *Essai sur l'instruction publique*, (Paris, 1793).

civic virtue. The government would also subsidize the publication and distribution of the "good" books needed to propagate appropriate moral values. Essentially, the overarching goal was to turn the French population into the Thermidorians' vision of virtuous citizens.

Given their commitment to fostering civic virtue, it is somewhat ironic that the Thermidorian and Directory governments ended up with reputations for corruption and immorality. For a long time, scholars simply dismissed the Directory as a morally bankrupt, "shameless regime" composed of selfish politicians bent only on safeguarding their own class interests.[17] Recently, however, a more sympathetic view has emerged, one that emphasizes the Thermidorians' devotion to furthering key revolutionary ideals.[18] Several studies have revealed the Thermidorians' commitment to civic education and their employment of "republican institutions" to further this goal.

Whatever their intentions, however, one should not lose sight of the fact that much of their project was designed and implemented with an obvious disdain, and a flagrant disregard, for the express wishes of the French people. This is particularly true when it came to religion. Realizing that they lacked the political support to remain in power, the Thermidorians purposely turned to non-political ways to "republicanize" the nation. They set about strengthening their republic not by encouraging political participation or electoral activity, which they felt would work against them, but rather by molding the minds of the French masses, masses who, they thought, had shown themselves to be irrational and self-destructive. This was the true meaning of their frequent references to "republican institutions" during this period.

No wonder, then, that their program of national "regeneration" reminded so many people of the Terror; there was, in fact, a clear link between the two.[19] When forced to defend their plans and policies, the Thermidorians often resorted to the same arguments made by Robespierre. Revolutionaries before, during, and after Thermidor shared the same belief in moral *dirigisme*, a confidence in the state's ability to train

---

[17] See, for example, A. Vandal, "A Shameless Regime," in F. Kafker, J. Laux, and D. G. Levy (eds.), *The French Revolution: Conflicting Interpretations* (Malabar, FL, 2002), p. 357.

[18] Baczko, *Ending the Terror*; J. Livesey, *Making Democracy in the French Revolution* (Cambridge, MA, 2001); Woloch, *The New Regime*; D. Coleman, "The Foundation of the French Liberal Republic: Politics, Culture and Economy after the Terror," unpublished Ph.D. dissertation, Stanford University, 1997; A. Jainchill, "Republicanism and the Origins of French Liberalism, 1794–1804," unpublished Ph.D. dissertation, University of California at Berkeley, 2004.

[19] M. Ozouf, "Revolutionary Religion," in F. Furet and M. Ozouf (eds.), *A Critical Dictionary of the French Revolution*, trans. A. Goldhammer (Cambridge, MA, 1989), p. 566.

people's minds and mold their morals. Thus, Jean-Jacques Rousseau's famous line in the *Discourse on Political Economy* was frequently heard during this period: "If it is a good thing to know how to use men as they are, it is better still to turn them into what one needs them to be."[20] In these matters, the Thermidorians differed from their predecessors not in their greater liberalism, but in their *increased* desire for system and organization.[21]

Abbé Grégoire's newspaper often complained that the Thermidorians had a strong "desire to impose their opinions." This was why they engaged in such "incessant talk of republican institutions." For Grégoire, there was something "laughable" about their efforts to republicanize the nation. He thought it ridiculous to try to impose a cultural "uniformity" and "force thirty million men into the same mold." Grégoire felt certain that the government's efforts would fail. He warned that the cause of liberty was not served by the demand for republican uniformity; in truth, uniformity was a "symptom of slavery." Displaying a liberalism rare for the times, Grégoire tried to convince Thermidorians that "the social order ... gets its harmony from the very diversity that shocks you."[22]

In their goal to regenerate and republicanize the nation, the Thermidorians received valuable support from a group of intellectuals sympathetic to the new regime. These were the so-called "Idéologues," men like the Comte de Volney (1757–1820), Pierre-Jean-Georges Cabanis (1757–1808), Destutt de Tracy (1754–1836), Dominique-Joseph de Garat (1749–1833) and Pierre-Louis Roederer (1754–1835), who were powerful within the National Institute. It was the Idéologues' "science of morals" that lay behind the proposed educational reforms.[23] They shared the Thermidorians' belief that "republican institutions" should be enlisted to reform national mores. Given the deplorable state of French political culture, the Idéologues saw it as imperative for the government to step in and to foster the desperately needed republican values. According to Tracy, this was how best to strengthen the Republic and to purge democracy of its "inconveniences." This was how to render the French masses "free but

---

[20] J.-J. Rousseau, *Discourse on Political Economy*, in *The Basic Political Writings*, ed. and trans. D. Cress (Indianapolis, 1987), p. 119.
[21] M. Ozouf, *Festivals and the French Revolution*, trans. A. Sheridan (Cambridge, MA, 1988), p. 120.
[22] *Annales de la religion*, vol. 1 (1795), pp. 3, 5.
[23] On the Idéologues, see C. Welch, *Liberty and Utility: The French Idéologues and the Transformation of Liberalism* (New York, 1984); J. Simon, *Une Académie sous le Directoire* (Paris, 1885); F. Picavet, *Les Idéologues* (Paris, 1891); F. Azouvi (ed.), *L'Institution de la raison: La Révolution culturelle des Idéologues* (Paris, 1992); and Staum, *Minerva's Message*.

calm." It was important, he thought, to "direct their judgement by indoctrinating them."[24]

In many ways, the Idéologues were the intellectual heirs and continuators of Enlightenment *philosophes* like Helvétius and Condorcet. Indeed, two of their favorite meeting places were the salons of the widowed Madame Helvétius and of Sophie de Condorcet. Moreover, their cultural project had strong anti-Catholic overtones. The Idéologues' fondest hope was that the schools, festivals, books, and symbols designed and promoted by them would gradually wean the population off the Catholic religion, seen by them as the epitome of ignorance and superstition.

The Idéologues were certainly not shy about their anti-Catholicism. The textbooks, manuals, and moral catechisms that they endorsed continuously linked Catholicism with both fanaticism and tyrannical government. Their journal, the *Décade philosophique*, was full of articles describing Catholicism as an irrational, obscurantist, and reactionary force.[25] In contrast, they described their own moral philosophy as a "physical and geometric *science*." It was a science and not a religion because it was based on empirically provable facts about human nature. Tracy defined it as "a science that we construct, like all others, from the results of experience and reflection."[26] Heirs to the sensationist philosophy of Condillac (1714–1780), the Idéologues held that all knowledge came from the senses and that any effective moral system must be based on fundamental human drives like self-interest and the pleasure–pain principle. As Cheryl Welch has shown, the Idéologues subscribed to "an egoistic model of human nature"; they saw men as physical beings with certain basic needs and an overriding desire for happiness.[27] To moralize men effectively, one had to work with their needs and direct their desires.

The Idéologues were continuators of the *philosophes* in another way, and this was the confidence they placed in the state as moral educator. Tracy spoke for all of them when he claimed that "Law-makers and government" (rather than priests) were "the true preceptors" of mankind.[28] The Revolution seems not to have shaken the Idéologues' confidence in the ability of good laws and state-sponsored institutions to

---

[24] As quoted by L. Jaume, *L'Individu effacé ou le paradoxe du libéralisme français* (Paris, 1997), p. 30.
[25] J. Kitchin, *Un journal "philosophique": La Décade (1794–1807)* (Paris, 1965).
[26] As quoted by Staum, *Minerva's Message*, p. 121, my emphasis.
[27] Welch, *Liberty and Utility*, p. 14.   [28] As quoted by Palmer, *The Improvement of Humanity*, p. 4.

shape human behavior; in some ways, that faith seems even to have increased. Thanks to the special circumstances of post-Thermidorian France, the Idéologues saw themselves as having been granted a unique opportunity to apply the principles of Helvétius.[29] In his *De l'esprit* (1758) and *De l'homme* (1772), Helvétius had proposed that the "happiness of the greatest number" could be obtained by harmonizing "personal and general interest." In the same vein, the Idéologues hoped to use legislation and public education to enlighten the French population's self-interest so that it accorded with the interest of the nation. This, they thought, was the only way to pursue real reform.

CATHOLIC COUNTER-ARGUMENTS

The Catholic and right-wing press vehemently rejected this Thermidorian–Idéologue agenda. Agreeing that French *moeurs* were in a deplorable state, they maintained that only religion could moralize and stabilize the country. For the sake of peace and order, a fully restored Roman Catholicism was urgently needed. Abbé Grégoire insisted that a morality based on "egoism" and self-interest would never work. Without religion, even the family would fall apart, since "there [would be] no guarantee of the faithfulness of wives, the obedience of children, or the honesty of servants."[30] In *La Quotidienne*, the more conservative Catholic journalist Gallais agreed that there simply was no substitute for religion:

it is its principles that, more universal than those of opinion, more repressive than those of fear, and more evident than those of the public interest, should guide the legislators, and teach men, along with the disinterestedness of virtue and the courage of truth, the rights and duties of all without exception.[31]

The arguments in defense of Catholicism were often flagrantly utilitarian. Catholics and political conservatives repeatedly claimed that the most important lesson taught by religion was respect for the privileges of the rich. In his *De la religion considerée dans ses rapports avec le but de toute législation* (1795) Joseph Fiévée put this argument plainly:

Suppose there were no God. What reason would a poor man have not to murder a rich man, if he thought he could get away with it?[32]

[29] Staum, *Minerva's Message*, p. 124.
[30] As quoted by C. Welch. I have altered her translation a little bit.
[31] *La Quotidienne*, 9 Messidor III (June 27, 1795), as quoted by J. Popkin, *The Right-Wing Press in France, 1792–1800* (Chapel Hill, NC, 1980), p. 111.
[32] As quoted by Popkin, *The Right-Wing Press*, p. 110.

In fact, some high-profile advocates of Catholicism were unconcerned whether or not the upper classes were non-believers, as long as the poor remained Catholic. Gallais, for instance, saw no problem in the so-called "double-truth" doctrine: Catholicism for the masses and *philosophie* for their superiors. Approvingly, he cited Gibbon to show that Roman rulers had upheld the traditional religion even after they had become non-believers: in Rome, "the robe of a pontiff often covered an atheist." Jeremy Popkin has characterized these views, common in the right-wing Catholic press of the time, as "cynical religious utilitarianism."[33]

CONSTANT DURING THE DIRECTORY

When Constant and Madame de Staël arrived in Paris, their moderate republicanism drew them into the Thermidorian orbit. Like the Thermidorians, Constant and de Staël wanted to protect the Revolution's principal gains while preventing a slide into either Jacobin dictatorship or royalist reaction. Soon, Constant was on friendly terms with the Idéologues, and began to write in defense of the government.

In the context of the virulent and bitterly polarized political climate, Constant's stance has rightly been described as moderate. Staking a centrist position equidistant from what he referred to as "anarchy" on the one hand and "despotism" on the other, Constant warned people that extremists on both sides risked precipitating a civil war and a return to Terror. He admonished those irreconcilables on the right whose "implacable memories" of past injustices were causing them to stir up counter-revolutionary passions. At the same time, he counseled those on the left to abandon certain "revolutionary habits," especially the dangerous idea that one could "revolutionize on behalf of virtue [*révolutionner pour la vertu*],"[34] in other words, impose morality by force. Constant invited moderates of all stripes to rally behind the Directory in order to "help consolidate liberty and make the Republic flourish."[35] One could even say that in his first major political pamphlet, *De la force du gouvernement*, Constant exhibited an early predilection for liberal principles: he denounced those who would resort to "arbitrary" rule and stipulated that "the great art is to govern with force, but to govern little."[36]

At this point, however, Constant's liberalism was only embryonic, and it is important to recognize that, when it came to its religious

---

[33] Ibid., p. 116. [34] *De la force*, OCBC *Œuvres* I, p. 376. [35] Ibid., p. 342. [36] Ibid., p. 362.

policies, the regime he was defending was hardly moderate or liberal. Its continued support of restrictive measures against Catholics, combined with its strong endorsement of national "regeneration" through "republican institutions," were rightly seen by many as a continuation of dechristianization by different means. And Constant certainly shared the tendency of his republican and Idéologue friends to define themselves in opposition to Catholicism. His first writings in Paris show that he was quite willing to employ the standard anticlerical and anti-Catholic polemics favored by the regime. For example, in his letter "A Charles His,"[37] he lumped "Catholicism and royalism" together as the Republic's main threat. Constant suggested that the French people were confronted by a straightforward choice between "subjection" and "liberty," "superstition" and "enlightenment," and "a return to the eleventh century" and "the promises of the nineteenth."[38]

The intent behind Constant's first major political pamphlet, *De la force du gouvernement*, was to shore up the Directory at a time of growing disaffection. Once again he saw the unfolding crisis in terms of clear alternatives: "It is a matter of choosing between the stupefication [*abrutissement*] of man and his rehabilitation, between superstition and enlightenment, between the eleventh century and the nineteenth."[39] He also expressed disdain for what he referred to as Catholic "theocracy," which he contrasted with the onward march of history.[40]

Constant's jabs at Catholicism were common among Idéologues; however, at the very least, they oversimplified a complicated situation. Moreover, they very likely offended many Catholics, who considered themselves neither unenlightened nor superstitious and who were growing impatient with the regime's anti-Catholic policies, several of which were clearly violating its own constitution. Knowingly or unknowingly, Constant was ignoring an undisputable fact: many in France thought Catholicism and the Revolution perfectly compatible, at least during the early stages of the Revolution.

More specifically, Constant's reified view of religious politics could not account for someone like Henri Grégoire, the leader of France's Constitutional Church, for whom "liberté, égalité, fraternité" were inherently

---

[37] This, Constant's first published text, appeared in *Le Républicain français* on July 24, 1795. Charles-Antoine His (1769–1857) was a founder of the *Moniteur universel*, and launched *Le Républicain français* in 1792. See Mauro Bauberis' introduction in OCBC *Œuvres* I, pp. 291–293.
[38] "A Charles His, rédacteur du *Républicain français*. Juillet 1795," OCBC *Œuvres* I, p. 295.
[39] *De la force*, OCBC *Œuvres* I, p. 380.   [40] Ibid., p. 350.

Christian, and even Catholic, values.[41] While Constant was writing his early pamphlets, Grégoire was desperately trying to rebuild his beleaguered church, and bitterly complained that the government's religious policies were harming, not helping his cause. As early as December 21, 1794, on the floor of the Convention, Grégoire had bravely pleaded for the right of all Frenchmen to practice their chosen religion. "Freedom of religion exists in Turkey, but not in France," he had complained. Depriving people of this freedom was not only unjust and "tyrannical," but also counter-productive, since harassing people's religions only provoked their hostility. French legislators should know that "whether an individual is baptized or circumcised, whether he invokes Allah or Jehova ... is outside of the domain of politics."[42]

Now, during the Directory, Grégoire's newspaper, the *Annales de la religion*, repeated his liberal argument: by obstructing the people's right to practice their religion freely, the new regime was overstepping the legitimate bounds of government. Freedom of religion was a "sacred" right protected by the "social contract." Grégoire's newspaper further maintained that the Catholic religion posed no danger to the Republic or its principles; they were entirely compatible as long as governments "knew how to remain within the bounds of their competence."[43]

At this juncture, however, Constant expressed little enthusiasm for such liberal arguments. Rather, he chimed in with his Idéologue and republican friends: Catholicism was, by definition, a grave threat to the Republic. A petition submitted by Constant to the Council of 500 provides further insight. Referring to Catholicism, Constant wrote: "Fanaticism is still menacing France." The real problem, he noted, was that "fanaticism" was not easily combated head-on; it "cannot be fought by authorities with success, or by atheism without danger." This principle, in other words, that the state could not forcibly nullify beliefs, was an argument dear to members of the current government. Moreover, it had been made by Robespierre in his famous speech justifying the Cult of the Supreme Being on May 7, 1794, and by many others since. What they meant was that more gentle policies against Catholicism were

---

[41] See Dale Van Kley, "The Abbé Grégoire and the Quest for a Catholic Republic," in J. and R. Popkin (eds.), *The Abbé Grégoire and His World* (Dordrecht, 2000).

[42] As quoted by A. Latreille, *L'Eglise catholique et la Révolution française: Le pontificat de Pie VI et la crise française (1775–1799)* (Paris, 1946), vol. I, p. 199, emphasis added. On Abbé Grégoire, see A. Sepinwall, *The Abbé Grégoire and the French Revolution: The Making of Modern Universalism* (Berkeley, CA, 2005).

[43] *Annales de la religion*, vol. 1 (1795), p. 15.

needed. However, in his petition, Constant added a new twist to the old argument. Catholicism could not simply be abolished; rather, it should be replaced by a religion more friendly to republicanism. Proposing a more subtle solution to the current problem, Constant suggested that the French government should encourage Protestantism to take root in the country.[44] This could be done simply by allowing more Protestants to acquire French citizenship.

Constant put forward several reasons to support his petition. He argued that Protestants would bring their money to France, thereby helping the economy to grow. He claimed that they were hardworking people with "simple mores," who would therefore help to promote a culture of industry. Perhaps most importantly, Constant contended that admitting more Protestants into France would have advantageous intellectual and political effects. He claimed that, historically, Protestantism had always been "conducive to ideas." As we have seen, this was a fairly widespread belief during the Enlightenment, when many people held Protestantism to be more favorable to all the progressive and reforming ideas *philosophes* held dear. Constant further claimed that, contrary to Catholics, Protestants would contribute usefully to the political culture because they were naturally "favorable to liberty." He cited Montesquieu in support of the claim that Protestantism was inherently "conducive to republicanism." Constant also delved into history, reminding the authorities that long before the Revolution, French Protestants had been the first to propose that France be turned into a republic. Traditionally, such arguments had of course been used by Catholics *against* Protestants; now, in the changed political climate, Constant used them in their favor. Finally, Constant contended that in addition to the economic, intellectual, and political benefits they would bring to France, Protestants would also encourage the proliferation of sects, which was an excellent thing. "The cults should be multiplied," Constant explained, because you "paralyze superstition by dividing it."[45]

In making these arguments on behalf of Protestant immigration, Constant seems to have assumed that the Directory held relatively favorable views towards Protestantism. Like everyone else, he knew that French Protestants had strongly supported the Revolution from

---

[44] "Aux citoyens représentans du peuple composant le Conseil des Cinq-cents," OCBC *Œuvres* I, pp. 395–399.

[45] My quotations are from "De la restitution des droits politiques aux descendans des religionnaires fugitifs," OCBC *Œuvres* I, pp. 407–411.

the beginning. After all, one of the great accomplishments of the Revolution had been the Declaration of the Rights of Man and Citizen, which made Protestantism legal and granted Protestants full political rights for the first time in French history. Understandably, French Protestants voiced no objections to the Civil Constitution of the Clergy, which had alienated so many Catholics. In fact, many Protestants welcomed the decline in prestige, wealth, and influence of the Church that had oppressed them for so long, and expressed themselves openly to that effect.

In contrast, Pope Pius VI had vehemently denounced both the Declaration of Rights and the Civil Constitution of the Clergy. His brief *Quod Aliquantum*, of March 10, 1791, declared that the effect of such legislation would be "to annihilate the Catholic religion, and along with it the obedience due to kings." The pope singled out for special rebuke article 10 of the Declaration of Rights, which guaranteed freedom of religion; he called it a "monstrous right" and part of a nefarious plot to destroy Catholicism. Meanwhile, a popular manual for Catholic missionaries contained instructions for priests to fight against "the false and pernicious maxims that have been called rights."[46]

Many French Catholics appear to have concluded that the Civil Constitution of the Clergy was something essentially "Protestant" in inspiration. For them, the decision to nationalize the Church's property and to suppress religious vows seemed ominously similar to actions taken by Henry VIII at the beginning of the English Reformation. The election of parish clergy by the local laity also seemed close to Calvinist practices. Those Constitutional Catholics who did swear the oath often referred to the New Testament and to the early Church Fathers to support their decision. Thus, they were accused of "Protestantizing" Catholicism by those who refused the oath. It seems that many Catholics even feared that the Civil Constitution of the Clergy and the oath were part of a secret Protestant plot.[47] The head of the Constitutional Church, Abbé Grégoire, was accused of having a "Protestant soul."[48]

---

[46] *Manuel pour les missionnaires of M. Coste* (1799), as quoted by B. Plongeron, "L'Eglise et les déclarations des droits de l'homme au XVIIIe siècle," *Nouvelle revue théologique*, 191 (May–June, 1979). The *Manuel* went through three editions by 1801.

[47] T. Tackett, *Religion, Revolution and Regional Culture in Eighteenth-Century France: The Ecclesiastical Oath of 1791* (Princeton, NJ, 1986), pp. 218–220.

[48] Sepinwall, *Abbé Grégoire*, p. 46. Sepinwall shows that the abbé was, in fact, greatly influenced by Protestantism early on.

CRITICS OF THE DIRECTORY'S RELIGIOUS POLICIES

Louis de Bonald

When it came to the confluence of Protestantism with republican principles, Constant evidently agreed with Louis de Bonald, the emerging theorist of counter-revolution. In his *Théorie du pouvoir* (1796), Bonald perceived a "striking relationship" between "certain political opinions" and "certain religious opinions." But here the two men's agreement ceased. To Bonald, the Protestant Reformation had "only been a cause of trouble." Not only was it responsible for the French Revolution, but it continued to be the cause of France's ongoing problems. Every religion "correspond[ed] to a particular form of government" and Catholicism was best suited to monarchy. Bonald reasoned that this was why the Directory was out to "destroy" Catholicism. With its "hypocritical" decrees, it was making "a secret effort to establish the religion that [was] most analogous to its [own, republican] principles."[49] As we have seen, Bonald was not altogether wrong.

Jean-François de La Harpe

In fact, the Directory was frequently accused of being disingenuous in professing support for religious freedom. Having defended the regime and derided Catholicism, Constant was accused of both hypocrisy and of having his own brand of anti-religious "fanaticism." One of the most biting critiques came from Jean-François de La Harpe (1739–1803), a poet and literary critic who had embraced the religious revival and become a Catholic apologist. As a young man, La Harpe had been an aspiring *philosophe* and protégé of Voltaire; however, after a period of imprisonment during the Terror, he had shed his irreligion and support for the Revolution.[50] La Harpe accused the Thermidorians of unconscionable duplicity. They continuously *spoke* of religious freedom while carrying on the persecution of Catholics. Zeroing in on Constant's defense of the government in his *De la force du gouvernement actuel*, La Harpe charged him with not only ignoring, but deliberately disobeying, the express wishes of the French public. And this was how the Revolution,

---

[49] L. de Bonald, *Théorie du pouvoir politique et religieux*, ed. C. Capitan (Paris, 1966), pp. 54, 218, 116.
[50] On La Harpe's conversion and final years, see A. Jovicevich, *Jean-François de la Harpe, adepte et renégat des lumières* (South Orange, NJ, 1973).

supposedly "made for the people," behaved! Angered by Constant's referral to Catholicism as "fanaticism," La Harpe retorted that the only fanaticism existing was the "fanaticism of irreligion" being inflicted on the people by the government. Clearly, Constant and his colleagues were still "infected" by "the execrable revolutionary spirit." Repeating arguments often heard in the conservative press, La Harpe accused the Thermidorians of being irresponsible, since religion was the essential glue holding society together. By attacking Catholicism, they were creating a state of anarchy in the country, which was dissolving all social bonds and all moral order. It was ridiculous that the Thermidorians professed to be so concerned with public morality when it was their accursed *philosophie* that was destroying it.[51]

Jacques Necker

Catholic royalists and reactionaries were not alone in criticizing the Directory's religious policies. Another censor was Madame de Staël's father, Jacques Necker. In 1788, while momentarily out of favor with the king, he had published his *De l'importance des opinions religieuses*, which, as we recall, Constant had planned to refute while he was in Brunswick. In that text, Necker had warned French intellectuals and governing elites of the dangers of their growing irreligion. Governments needed to be "seconded" by religion, he argued, and it was a dangerous illusion to imagine that they could survive without it. To attack religion, which had become so fashionable in the eighteenth century, was to sap society of its very foundations. According to Necker, society's survival depended on the cultivation of the right moral sentiments, and this was what the Christian religion did. Although Necker was himself a Protestant, he defended the importance and value of Catholicism in France. Writing around the time of the 1787 Edict of Toleration, Necker hoped that an enlightened and tolerant form of Catholicism would give France the social and political support it so clearly needed.[52]

Now, eight years later, Necker repeated essentially the same argument in *De la révolution* (1796). He lashed out against both the dechristianization campaign undertaken during the radical phase of the Revolution,

---

[51] J. de La Harpe, *Du fanatisme dans la langue révolutionnaire, ou De la persécution suscitée par les barbares du dix-huitième siècle, contre la religion chrétienne et ses ministres* (Paris, 1797), pp. 8, 41.

[52] A. Encrevé corrects some errors in previous interpretations of Necker's religious views in "La Réception des ouvrages de J. Necker sur la religion, d'après sa correspondance privée," in *Jacques Necker (1732–1804): Banquier, ministre, écrivain.* (Geneva, 2004), pp. 73–130.

and the Directory's ill-advised "neutrality" towards religion. Despite their professed support for the principle of religious toleration, he accused the Thermidorians of really wanting the "debasement"[53] of the Catholic Church. Tragically, they refused to understand that without their support of Catholicism, *all* religion in France would eventually disappear, with disastrous repercussions for society. Such reckless policies would invariably lead to more authoritarian forms of government, because, in Necker's estimation, only despotism could contain an irreligious people. Their unreasonable obsession with Catholicism rendered the Thermidorians incapable of comprehending that there was no contradiction between the existence of a state-sponsored "dominant religion" and the principle of religious toleration. France could have a national (that is Catholic) church and religious toleration as well.

Such arguments did not sway the Directory and its supporters, who were increasingly anxious about the alliance being forged between activist Catholics and counter-revolutionary royalists. It was becoming clear that the strategy of their enemies on the right was to promote counter-revolution by legal means. Their object was to use constitutional freedoms to gain control of the Republic; thereafter, they would overturn the constitution and restore the monarchy along with its ally, Catholicism. There can be little doubt that many counter-revolutionaries viewed the resurgence of Catholicism as an aid to their cause.

Constant's second major political pamphlet, *Des réactions politiques*, repeated his counsel of moderation. He regretted the poisonous politico-religious climate, and condemned the immoderate and unjust attacks on the government. A large quantity of "incendiary or perfidious pamphlets" were stirring up harmful passions and preventing political reconciliation and stabilization. Above all, however, he advised the government not to take revenge on its enemies. Constant thought that it was his responsibility, and that of other authors who could influence public opinion, to combat the counter-revolutionary resurgence in their writings.

When it came to the question of religious toleration, Constant defended himself and turned the accusation of hypocrisy against his accusers. If people like La Harpe were sincerely disturbed by religious persecution, then certainly Constant would sympathize with them and even offer them his support. Religious persecution was as "unjust" as it was "absurd." The problem was, however, that Catholic apologists

---

[53] J. Necker, *De la Révolution française*, in *Œuvres Complètes de M. Necker publiées par M. le Baron de Staël, son petit fils* (Paris, 1820–21), vol. X, p. 214.

invoked the "sacred right of toleration" only to embarrass and weaken the government. All their rhetoric about toleration was only a ploy to "re-establish religious prejudices."[54] The truth was that La Harpe, and others like him, were working to restore the "triple edifice of royalty, nobility and priesthood,"[55] which would overturn all the freedoms acquired by the Revolution.

A second edition of *Des réactions* came out in May 1797, and along with it Constant published a new essay called *Des effets de la Terreur*. He now directed his fire at those on both sides of the political spectrum who were arguing that the Revolution could not have been accomplished without the Terror. To Constant, this was wrong-headed. The radical phase of the Revolution, and its violence, had served no positive purpose whatsoever and were indefensible from any point of view. "The terror was *not* necessary to save the republic," he insisted, and "the republic was saved *despite* the terror,"[56] not because of it. The implications were that defenders of the Revolution should stick to peaceful, legal, and non-arbitrary means, and moderates should not be swayed by arguments deliberately contrived to discredit the Revolution.

Joseph de Maistre

It was in the context of renewed hopes for a restoration of throne and altar, that Joseph de Maistre published his now famous *Considerations on France*. Maistre would soon emerge as an eminent spokesman and theorist for counter-revolution. One of his main reasons for writing was that he wished to respond directly to Constant's *De la force du gouvernement*, whose support of the Directory had infuriated him.[57] Maistre's *Considerations* offered a sweeping indictment of the Enlightenment and the "satanic" Revolution that it had spawned. To Maistre, the true causes of the Revolution, including the Terror, were ideological. The blame should be placed squarely on the shoulders of the *philosophes*, whose arrogant attacks on Christianity had provoked the wrath of God. And despite Thermidor, Maistre saw the battle as not yet over. What the present generation was witnessing, he wrote, was "one of the greatest spectacles

---

[54] *Des réactions politiques*, OCBC *Œuvres* I, p. 472.   [55] Ibid., p. 472.
[56] *Des effets de la terreur*, OCBC *Œuvres* I, p. 519.
[57] V. Vermale, "Les origines des *Considérations sur la France* de Joseph de Maistre," *Revue d'histoire littéraire de la France*, 33, (1926), pp. 521–529.

ever beheld by human eyes ... the fight to the death between Christianity and philosophism."[58]

Interestingly, however, Maistre traced the problem of "philosophism" back beyond the eighteenth-century Enlightenment. Like Bonald and a whole contingent of Catholic and royalist writers in existence even before the Revolution,[59] he located the origins of the evil as far back as the sixteenth century. The poisonous seed of violence and revolution had been planted by none other than Martin Luther and his diabolical Protestant Reformation:

it is from the shadow of a cloister that there emerges one of mankind's very greatest scourges. Luther appears; Calvin follows him. The Peasants' Revolt; the Thirty Years War; the civil war in France; the massacre of the Low Countries; the massacre of Ireland; the massacre of the Cévennes; St Bartholomew's Day; the murders of Henry II, Henry IV, Mary Stuart, and Charles I; and finally, in our day, from the same source, the French Revolution.[60]

It was therefore in unequivocal terms, and for interconnected religious and political reasons, that Maistre proclaimed it "the duty of every good Frenchman ... to work untiringly to direct public opinion in favour of the king."[61] To restore the king was to combat both the Enlightenment and its progenitor, Protestantism.

THE "SECOND DIRECTORY" AND THE RENEWED CAMPAIGN FOR "REPUBLICAN INSTITUTIONS"

As feared, the spring and summer elections of 1797 were won by royalists and moderate republicans hostile to the regime. Faced with the real possibility of a "legal" counter-revolution, three members of the Directory, La Révellière-Lépeaux, Paul Barras, and Jean-François Reubel, took emergency measures to save the Republic: on 18 Fructidor (September 4, 1797), they called on the army to seize power. The two other directors, Carnot and Barthélemy, were purged. Fifty-three deputies were deported; the election results in forty-nine departments were annulled; thirty-two journalists were arrested; and forty-two newspapers banned.[62]

---

[58] J. de Maistre, *Considerations on France* ed. and trans. R. Lebrun (Cambridge, 2000), p. 45.
[59] McMahon, *Enemies*, pp. 45, 77–78, and n. 116, pp. 216–217.   [60] *Considerations*, p. 27.
[61] Ibid., p. 74.
[62] D. M. G. Sutherland, *The French Revolution and Empire: Quest for a Civic Order* (Malden, MA, 2003), p. 286.

Overt religious persecution by the government returned immediately. It openly declared priests "unfit tó educate you in the principles of purified virtue" and decreed that, henceforth, "philosophical and universal morality must be the exclusive basis of republican instruction." A law of 19 Fructidor Year V (September 5, 1797) reinstated stiff penalties for non-juring priests and imposed a new oath of "hatred of royalty" on the entire clergy. By administrative decree, 1400 priests were deported to Guyana, where nearly 200 of them died. More zealous than ever, intellectuals close to the government pressed for the "republican institutions" they felt were needed to combat Catholicism. To them, the election results were incontrovertible proof that France's moral and intellectual culture was infected by royalism and Catholicism, which were two sides of the same coin.

While supporters of the regime argued over the best way to turn subjects into citizens, they all agreed that the Catholic religion was, at best, an obstructionist and, at worst, a counter-revolutionary force. This partly explains why the so-called Second Directory inaugurated what has been called "a new era of persecution"[63] against Catholicism. Although it was less bloody than the Terror, it was just as cruel and destructive. Churches were closed, sometimes vandalized and demolished. Confiscated religious property was sold off at a fraction of its value. Albert Mathiez once remarked that "there was never a government in France more hostile to Catholicism than the Directory."[64] Denis Woronoff describes its persecution of the Church as a "war of extermination."[65]

Contradicting his often-repeated commitment to the rule of law and abhorrence for arbitrary measures, Constant supported the coup of Fructidor. Like others, he had become convinced that monarchists were preparing to overthrow the Republic and restore the Old Regime. In a speech delivered at the *Cercle constitutionnel* a little more than a week after the coup, Constant defended the actions of the three directors. This was no longer the time for vacillation, he declared. It had been a dangerous illusion to imagine that proponents of monarchy and aristocracy could be trusted to accommodate themselves to the Republic and to play by its rules. The painful truth was that only true republicans could be counted on to support and defend the Republic. "Two nations share the soil of

---

[63] A. Latreille, J.-R. Palanque, E. Delarvelle, and R. Rémond, *Histoire du catholicisme en France: La période contemporaine* (Paris, 1962), vol. 2, p. 148.
[64] A. Mathiez, *La Révolution et l'Eglise* (Paris 1910), p. 219.
[65] D. Woronoff, *La République bourgeoise 1794–1799 de Thermidor à Brumaire* (Paris, 1972), p. 142.

France," Constant claimed, a "nation of free men," and a "mob of slaves."
If you gave to the latter even the smallest share of power, France would
soon be "debased" and "corrupted."[66] The government could no longer
afford to prevaricate or compromise, allowing enemies of the Republic to
undermine it from within.

Despite these bombastic declarations, Constant was sickened by the
turn of events. Alongside his statements of support for the *coup*, he made
some contradictory comments that bear witness to his abiding discomfort
with arbitrary rule and the recourse to violence. Both he and Madame de
Staël deeply regretted the repression and persecution that followed the
coup. Shaken by the events taking place around him, Constant tried to
come to grips with the Republic's disappointing lack of popular support.
"Fourteen hundred years of royalty" had created "a mutilated," "tired," and
"faded" generation of Frenchmen and women with "shrunken" souls.
Tragically, their moral degeneration played right into the hands of counter-
revolutionary forces, since all the "ignoble passions," such as "pride,"
"cupidity," "vengefulness," and "superstition" caused people to rally to the
idea of a king.[67]

What could be done to address this tragic situation? Constant was
convinced that the main problem was a moral one: France lacked
republican values. In order to solve it, the only thing that would work was
"the moral force of institutions." Constant noted with regret that the
present generation was being corrupted by the power of "fashion,"
especially by the nefarious fashion for royalty that was gaining ground. It
was essential that this trend be "smothered" before it caused irreparable
harm and, for this, "regenerating institutions" were needed. These
institutions would foil "noble pride" and prevent the aristocracy from
acquiring influence; at the same time, they would popularize republicanism. In order to tap "the power of conviction," republican institutions
should celebrate liberty with "pomp and splendor," in other words, with
festivals and ceremonies promoting the virtues of republicanism.[68]

It is not surprising that the directors rewarded Constant for his
support by appointing him to an administrative post.[69] In some ways,

---

[66] "Discours prononcé au Cercle constitutionnel pour la plantation de l'arbre de la liberté, le 30
fructidor an V [September 16, 1797]," in OCBC *Œuvres* I, p. 554.

[67] Ibid., p. 553.   [68] Ibid., pp. 552, 556, 557, 553, 557, 552, 557.

[69] On this episode, see E. Tambour, "Benjamin Constant à Luzarches," *Revue de l'histoire de
Versailles et de Seine-et-Oise* (Feb.–Nov., 1906), pp. 333–335 and M. Déchery, "Benjamin Constant
à Luzarches," in D. Verrey and A.-L. Delacrétaz (eds.), *Benjamin Constant et la Révolution
française, 1789–1799* (Geneva, 1989).

Constant's speech at the *Cercle constitutionnel* sounds like an ideal "job talk" from someone applying for a position in the administration. After having purchased a piece of property in the canton of Luzarches in November 1796, Constant had become domiciled there the following February and had then stood for election. Though his attempt at elective office failed, the Directory now made him president of the canton. Of note is a letter written to the Directory in support of Constant's nomination by a citizen from Luzarches. In it, he explained that "the public spirit" of Luzarches had recently been "fanaticized" by non-juring and royalist priests. Luzarches desperately needed a president, who, "by his enlightenment and republicanism could cure the people of their errors." No person was better suited for this job than Benjamin Constant.[70]

As president of Luzarches, Constant became an agent of the Directory and thereby acquired first-hand experience with the "republican institutions" he apparently admired. One of his principal roles was to enforce the ten-day calendar and to preside over the festivals associated with it. By 1797, these were principally what were being referred to by the term "republican institutions."[71] By then, the Directory's ambitious plans for most other institutions, such as a new public education system, had been scaled down, due mainly to a lack of funds. Supporters of the Directory were hoping that the festivals and ceremonies associated with the calendar would accomplish the much-needed "transfer of sacrality"[72] from Catholicism to the Republic. They would serve the dual purpose of extirpating "fanaticism" in the population and inculcating republican values.

Evidently, Constant took his duties as president of Luzarches seriously. In his inaugural address, he asked people to rally behind the Republic and the government. Constant promised to execute strictly the law of 19 Fructidor against non-juring priests. But he also promised not to interfere with priests who behaved like "good citizens," in other words, who did not participate in any "manoeuvres contrary to republican principles," and restricted themselves to their "purely spiritual functions."[73]

---

[70] Letter of Le Flamand, cited by Déchery, "Benjamin Constant à Luzarches," p. 159.

[71] I. Woloch, "'Republican Institutions,' 1797–1799," in C. Lucas (ed.), *The French Revolution and the Creation of Modern Political Culture*, vol. II: *The Political Culture of the French Revolution* (Oxford, 1988).

[72] Ozouf, *Festivals*, p. xi.

[73] "Discours d'installation prononcé à Luzarches le 23 brumaire an VI [November 13, 1797]," in OCBC *Œuvres* I, p. 576.

Records show that, as president of Luzarches, Constant presided over approximately seventeen republican festivals, celebrating such things as agriculture, youth, old age, and marriage. On each occasion, he was obliged to write and deliver a speech; unfortunately, none of these speeches has survived. Constant's responsibilities also included informing people of new laws and decrees, performing marriages, announcing local births and deaths, and generally to distribute a republican and moral instruction. Some commentators have seen a humorous and even ridiculous side to this. Others, however, focus on the more ominous aspects of Constant's administration: they criticize him for extreme anticlericalism. On September 14, 1797, Constant wrote a letter to the ministry of police requesting that a certain priest be kept away from Luzarches. Subsequently, the priest was deported to Guyana where he, along with many other Catholic clergymen, died as a result of the harsh conditions.[74] In Constant's defense, the letter he wrote specifically requested that the priest be removed, not persecuted. Nevertheless, later in life, he deeply regretted having written it at all.

It seems clear that combating resurgent Catholicism was one of Constant's chief duties as president of Luzarches. He believed Catholicism was conducive to monarchist sentiments and inherently reactionary. He reported his efforts to republicanize the canton to his superiors in Paris. On one such occasion, he recounted a confrontation he had had with a priest, who objected that a statue of liberty, which was being used in a republican ceremony, was being left in his church. It was common practice and, indeed, a deliberate part of the Directory's religious policy, to use churches for republican festivals. Constant reported that along with the priest, "a large portion of the population" had demanded that the statue be removed. He had forcefully resisted their entreaties and had told the priest that under no circumstances would the statue be removed. The Republic "did not recognize any cult," he had explained, and just because it "deigned to allow citizens to celebrate their [religious] ceremonies," they should not infer from this that they had any more rights than just that. Constant had then given the priest "a serious warning about his future conduct."[75]

The signatures of Constant and two other officials appear on another report from Luzarches. Evidently, upon his arrival, Constant had found

---

[74] The best source on this is P. Deguise, "Benjamin Constant a-t-il été dénonciateur? L'affaire Oudaille," *Mercure de France*, 343 (Sept.–Dec., 1961), pp. 75–92.

[75] As quoted by H. Grange, *Benjamin Constant: Amoureux et républicain, 1795–1799* (Paris, 2004), p. 280.

the canton "perverted by reaction." Along with his co-signatories, he recounted that he had worked as hard as possible to "raise public spirit" and, in particular, to enforce the republican calendar. Constant's efforts had apparently encountered considerable opposition, especially from priests. According to the report, priests were trying to regain influence in the canton, and this Constant's administration was "fighting with all [its] might." They were doing everything in their power to ensure that all laws were being "scrupulously observed" and that the Republic was being "honored."[76]

Constant's activities in Luzarches have drawn criticism from scholars, some of whom have accused him of inconsistency in his political principles, or worse. According to E. Tambour, Constant's actions as an agent of the Directory did not exactly conform to his supposedly liberal doctrines.[77] Likewise, Jean Baelen criticizes Constant for being more of a "budding despot"[78] than an advocate of liberalism. And more recently, Henri Grange has referred to Constant as an "apparatchik" of an essentially dictatorial regime.[79] These criticisms are certainly justified; Constant himself soon came to regret some of what he did during this period. However, as Etienne Hofmann has argued, Constant was not yet a liberal in the true meaning of the word. His political principles were "germinating"[80] and, like many of his intellectual allies, he was deeply worried about counter-revolution.

Rather than dismissing this period as a momentary aberration in an otherwise distinguished career, or using it to embarrass Constant, it might be better to see it as a crucial moment in Constant's political evolution. Being forced to impose "republican institutions" on an apathetic and increasingly hostile population must have been a disheartening and extremely frustrating experience for him, especially for a man already sensitive to public spirit and morals and who had a strong personal distaste for arbitrary measures and violence. It may even have reinforced the lessons of Prussian history he had acquired at Brunswick: intervention by a government in religious matters was counter-productive.

Constant's experiences with "republican institutions" were not dissimilar to those of other public officials throughout France. On a weekly

---

[76] Ibid., pp. 280–281.
[77] See E. Tambour, *Etudes sur la Révolution dans le Département de Seine-et-Oise* (Paris, 1913), pp. 276–399.
[78] J. Baelen, *Benjamin Constant et Napoléon* (Paris, 1965), p. 41.
[79] Grange, *Benjamin Constant*, p. 281.
[80] E. Hofmann, *Les "Principes de politique" de Benjamin Constant: la genèse d'une oeuvre et l'évolution de la pensée de leur auteur, 1789–1806* (Geneva, 1980), p. 94.

basis, officials of the Directory were forced to confront and coerce their constituents who, most commonly, reacted with indifference, disdain, or outright hostility. In the words of Isser Woloch, "nothing created so much friction between the regime and population, and so discredited the republic, as the campaign to replace Sunday observance with the décade." In most places, the effort to impose the fête décadaire was a "recurrent exercise in futility."[81] Moreover, even though deputies and officials like Constant denied it, the enforcement of the republican calendar did contradict the principle of freedom of religion that was supposed to be protected by the constitution. Constant and other Directory officials could not avoid noticing the uncomfortable truth that ordinary citizens and Constitutional priests were being "disturbed" for their religious opinions, in clear violation of article 354 of the constitution. Moreover, the imposition of "republican institutions" throughout the country was triggering widespread disobedience and resentment of the government.

THEOPHILANTHROPY

While Constant experienced first hand the workings of "republican institutions" during the Directory, he must also have become familiar with Theophilanthropy, another state-sponsored project designed to wean the French people off Catholicism. This new religion was the creation of a small group of men strongly influenced by Freemasonry. Essentially, Theophilanthropy was an institutionalized form of Deism. During the Directory, it gained the adherence and support of several influential people, such as the economist Dupont de Nemours, the writer Bernardin de Saint-Pierre and M.-J. Chénier, the poet. But most significantly, it obtained the support of the director Louis Marie La Reveillère-Lépaux (1753–1824).[82]

La Reveillère-Lépaux became convinced that Theophilanthropy could be a useful antidote to Catholicism and a valuable prop to his regime; therefore, after the coup of Fructidor, the new religion received government protection and financial support. By the end of 1798, there were sixteen places of worship in Paris and Theophilanthropic centers were cropping up across the country. Constant admired La Reveillère greatly, as is shown by a letter dated June 11, 1796, in which Constant calls him

---

[81] Woloch " 'Republican Institutions,' " p. 382.
[82] The best source remains A. Mathiez, *La Théophilanthropie et le culte décadaire 1796–1801* (Paris, 1903).

"the purest, most moral, most friendly to liberty, and most brilliant man that I have ever seen in government [*en place*] anywhere in the world."[83]

In a speech delivered to the National Institute on 12 Floréal Year V (May 1, 1797), La Reveillère-Lépaux explained the reasoning behind the new religion. He began by restating a principle on which everybody could agree: "institutions are the firmest support of constitutions." According to La Reveillère, however, there should be three, not two, types of institutions, all designed to cultivate healthy morals and strengthen the republic. The national festivals and civil ceremonies associated with the republican calendar were not enough; France also needed a religion. While educated persons might be able to do without it, this was not true of "the people." In fact, it was crazy to think that the "cold calculations of reason" could suffice "to keep men ... on the path of virtue."[84] Moreover, without some religious direction, the people would be drawn to the "grossest superstitions" peddled by charlatans preying on their vivid imaginations. One simply could not abandon the masses to the "vagueness" of their own ideas; rather, one had to give them one or two dogmas and a cult that lent support to crucial moral and political principles.[85]

The dogmas of the new religion should be "of an extreme simplicity." A profusion of ceremonies, such as existed in Roman Catholicism, only caused worshipers to neglect their real duties towards God and their obligations to "family, neighbors [and] country." Too many ceremonies also "shrank the mind" and made men "haughty" and "disdainful." Moreover, excessive fuss about "the exterior practices of devotion" allowed priests to pose as necessary intermediaries between man and God, thereby acquiring undue wealth and influence. According to La Reveillère-Lépaux, the ideal republican religion should have no priests, or at least "no sacerdotal body," claiming a special relationship with God, since this turned people into "stupid and credulous executors" of the wishes of the priests. All that was needed to ensure a truly "useful cult" was "a couple of dogmas": the existence of a God who rewards virtue and punishes vice, and the immortality of the soul. When a constitution was republican and itself based on "simple and clear principles," so should be the religion that sustained it. However, if there were to be no religion at all, he warned his

---

[83] Letter no. 457, "Benjamin Constant à la comtesse Anne-Marie-Pauline-Andrienne de Nassau,"11 juin 1796, in OCBC *Correspondance générale* III (1795–1799), p. 189.
[84] *Réflexions sur le culte, sur les cérémonies civiles et sur les fêtes nationales lues à l'Institut national, le 12 floréal an V* (Paris, Year VII), p. 8.
[85] Ibid., p. 8.

predominantly Idéologue audience, "the entire edifice of your morals will crumble, because you will have built it on sand."[86]

La Reveillère had harsh words for Roman Catholicism. By its essence, Catholicism was "an auxiliary of despotism," unreasonable, antisocial, and animated by "the spirit of domination, exclusion and cruelty." Since the Revolution, it had become driven by "the most frantic desire for revenge" and "fury at having been humiliated." However, Catholicism could not simply be abolished without providing the people with a reasonable replacement. If no alternative was provided, Catholicism might find a way to rise out of its own ruins. Its efforts to do precisely that was the principal cause of "all the frictions" the Directory was experiencing. Hence the critical need for a substitute religion.[87]

Interestingly, La Reveillère had good things to say about Protestantism. Everywhere, the Protestant religion proved that a simple and reasonable cult was more useful to society than an ornate and "pompous" one like Roman Catholicism. If you compared Catholic countries to Calvinist ones, La Reveillère argued, you would immediately find in the latter

happier households, wives more chaste and thrifty, husbands more tender and hard-working, children more adored and more respectful, [as well as] sounder reasoning, a more cultivated country, in other words, a more active, industrious, charitable, better and more contented people; much more public spirit and a real love of country.

La Reveillère also thought Protestant ceremonies much better and more effective than Catholic ones. He agreed with those who claimed that you need ceremonies "in order to catch the eye of the people" and "to fix" their attention. But he believed that it was more important to strike at the *heart* rather than at the eyes, and, for this, no "pompous" ceremonies such as existed in Catholicism were needed. Rather, you reached people more effectively with "sweet and penetrating" moral doctrines and "simple, noble and touching songs," in other words, by "methods that charm, persuade, encourage and contain" people. Thereby, one promotes what religion is really about: "to make men good and just." By way of example, La Reveillère told a story about his own two young daughters, who had been allowed to observe and compare a Catholic and a Calvinist ceremony. At the Catholic service, the nine- and six-year-olds had just been "amused"; but at the Calvinist service, their impressions had been "profound." The "decency," "exact order," "touching prayers and purely

[86] Ibid., pp. 9–10.   [87] Ibid., p. 11.

moral discourse," conveyed in a simple and unadorned temple by an austerely dressed minister, produced in the two girls "such a moving effect that they broke down in tears: their mother and I did as well." La Reveillère felt certain that the positive result of such a religious gathering was truly "incalculable."[88]

In the end, Theophilanthropy failed to establish itself as a successful alternative religion. After some initial success, the number of its adherents dwindled. Napoleon formally closed its remaining churches only a few years later.

LESSONS OF THE DIRECTORY, WILLIAM GODWIN AND *DES CIRCONSTANCES ACTUELLES*

The Directory years were crucial ones for Constant's evolution into a first-rate political thinker. The failure of the Directory's see-saw politics marked him deeply, as did its inability to foster a republican culture and a new religion. The attempt to turn Catholic subjects into virtuous and civic-minded citizens proved to be ineffective and even counter-productive. Government intervention in the private lives of individuals only provoked their resentment. Constant's realization of this helps to explain his attraction, during the closing years of the Directory, to the political theories of William Godwin (1756–1836).

Others in France refused to give up on the revolutionary project of establishing a republic of virtue. After the Fructidor coup of 1797, a neo-Jacobin movement began gaining force in France, scoring important electoral gains in April 1798. Despite another government coup and clampdown, in which the neo-Jacobin newspapers and clubs were closed and 127 of their deputies-elect purged, they again succeeded in making electoral gains during the spring of 1799. The new deputies then began passing laws eerily reminiscent of the emergency decrees of the Terror.

These events only heightened awareness of the Directory's abject failure to generate support for itself. Attacked from all sides, the government appeared doomed. It was in this context that Madame de Staël wrote her *Des circonstances actuelles* and Constant translated into French William Godwin's *An Enquiry Concerning Political Justice*. Although neither project was published, they testify to the significant evolution in both thinkers' political views and the urgent new message they wished to disseminate to the reading public.

---

[88] Ibid., pp. 12–14.

It is appropriate to treat these important, though neglected, works as a joint endeavor. Experts agree that the final years of the Directory were a high-point in the couple's intellectual complicity and reciprocal influence.[89] As Marcel Gauchet has noted, "so intimate were their intellectual relations of this Thermidorian period that it is often difficult to tell them apart."[90] Constant collaborated particularly closely with Madame de Staël on *Des circonstances*; his annotations are all over her manuscript.[91] In it, she mentions William Godwin's name several times most approvingly, linking him with Condorcet on the one hand, and Constant on the other.

There were several reasons why Constant and Madame de Staël would have regarded William Godwin as a kindred spirit. First, he offered an unequivocal endorsement of the ideals of the Enlightenment at a time when those ideals were increasingly coming under attack. *Political Justice* expressed Godwin's firm belief that human beings are not only rational but also capable of infinite moral improvement. "There is no characteristic of man," Godwin wrote, "which seems at present at least so eminently to distinguish him, or to be of so much importance ... as his perfectibility."[92] Progress, Godwin believed, was not just possible but even inevitable; the truth would ultimately prevail. Such ideas were designed to offer encouragement to beleaguered moderates and proponents of the Enlightenment in France. And Godwin's political credentials were beyond dispute; an early supporter of the French Revolution, he was already a famous representative of British Jacobinism by the time he wrote *Political Justice*.

This, however, would have been only part of Godwin's appeal to Constant and de Staël. For along with his unquestionable faith in reason and progress, came timely warnings about government intervention in the life of a nation. In fact, one of the express purposes of *Political Justice* was to refute the idea that governments should occupy themselves with promoting the religious, republican, or moral values of its citizens.

---

[89] See B. Jasinski *L'engagement de Benjamin Constant: amour et politique, 1794–1796* (Paris, 1971); a child presumed to be their daughter, Albertine, was born on June 8, 1797.

[90] M. Gauchet, "Constant," in F. Furet and M. Ozouf (eds.), *A Critical Dictionary of the French Revolution*, trans. A. Goldhammer (Cambridge, MA, 1989) p. 924.

[91] L. Omacini, "Benjamin Constant, correcteur de Mme de Staël," *Cahiers staëliens*, NS, 25 (1978), pp. 5–23. See also L. Omacini and R. Schatzer, "Quand Benjamin Constant travaille sur les papiers de Mme de Staël: le cas de la 'Copie' des *Circonstances actuelles*," in F. Tilkin (ed.), *Le Groupe de Coppet et le monde moderne: Conceptions – Images – Débats. Actes du VIe Colloque de Coppet* (Liège, 1998), pp. 59–82.

[92] W. Godwin, *An Enquiry Concerning Political Justice, and its Influence on General Virtue and Happiness*, in OCBC *Œuvres* II, 1, p. 397.

Godwin stated categorically that it was wrong to think that it was "the duty of governments to watch over the manners of the people." Not only was it wrong; it was "absurd" to put one's faith in "the political patronage of opinion." Denouncing what he called the "inquisitorial spirit of regulations," Godwin argued that when it came to moral and intellectual progress, state interference was bound to be ineffective, even counter-productive. It was easy to *command* men to be just and good; but it was "a hopeless task" to make such commands work. Moreover, such "mistaken guardianship" by the state ultimately produced only "torpor and imbe-cility" in the population.[93]

Godwin did not deny the importance of morals to the healthy func-tioning of a just society. "Nothing can be more unquestionable," he wrote, "than that the manners and opinions of mankind are of the utmost consequence to the general welfare." His point, however, was that "it does not follow that government is the instrument by which [manners and opinions] are to be fashioned." "Truth and virtue" should be allowed to "fight their own battles." They did not need to be either "nursed" or "patronized" by "the hand of power." Enlightenment and virtue would best be served "[w]herever government is wise enough to maintain an inflexible *neutrality*" and resist taking sides in intellectual disputes.[94]

The first thing government officials and intellectual elites should learn was patience. They should respect the natural course of history and not allow their policies to get too far ahead of the state of the population's enlightenment. This is what Godwin meant when he suggested, "[l]et us not vainly endeavor by laws and regulations to anticipate the future dictates of the general mind, but calmly wait till the harvest of opinion is ripe." Perhaps even more pointedly, he added "[l]et no new practice in politics be introduced, and no old one anxiously superseded, till called for by the public voice."[95]

Here, then, was a man who shared not only Constant's and Madame de Staël's deep commitment to Enlightenment values and to the underlying principles of the Revolution, but who also provided much-needed clarity and incisive judgements on an issue of particular relevance to them: the relationship between a country's political institutions and the state of its moral and intellectual development. Godwin helped crystallize in their minds what had recently gone so very wrong in France.

There were, however, large portions of Godwin's treatise with which neither Madame de Staël nor Constant could agree; one issue was the

---

[93] Ibid., pp. 665, 668, 675, 678, 674, 671.   [94] Ibid., pp. 666, 668, 681.   [95] Ibid., p. 670.

belief that private property, marriage, and even the institution of government itself would disappear over time. It was probably such radical ideas that ultimately convinced Constant to abandon publishing his translation. But reading Godwin during the chaotic and disheartening years of the Second Directory no doubt clarified and confirmed its painful lessons: "the idea of teaching virtue through the instrumentality of government" was futile.

Madame de Staël's realization that "republican institutions," so vaunted by the government and its supporters, were in fact counter-productive can be found in *Des circonstances actuelles*. In it she expresses her desire to "end the Revolution" and achieve a lasting political peace. This can only happen, she argues, if the government puts an end to arbitrary measures and intrusive regulations. Reflecting on the course of the Revolution, and the causes of the Terror, de Staël contends that in 1792 a republic had been instituted before the public was ready. Problems inevitably arise, she continues, when a country's system of government and laws are in advance of the "public spirit." In 1792, the French population was ready to adopt a "tempered monarchy," but not a republic based on "democratic principles." Fundamentally misguided about the "march of the national spirit," republicans demanded "republican institutions" and public education to create the citizenship it needed. Once again, these institutions were forced upon a people not ready to accept them.[96]

Madame de Staël agreed that the right morals were needed to underpin a republic. However, after reflecting on the Revolution, she wished to warn those still animated by a "revolutionary spirit" reminiscent of the Terror. Thus, she included several eloquent passages on the dangers of "fanaticism"; in particular, she denounced the "fanatics of *liberty*" as being especially "despotic" as well as "cruel." No doubt, she also wished to make a larger point, relevant not only to neo-Jacobins but also to more moderate republicans. Modern men want peace and privacy most of all. They desire things like "justice," "security," and "rest." They are primarily concerned with "the desire to acquire a fortune, and the need to preserve it." Under such circumstances, it is not possible to expect the same type of patriotism and the same level of commitment from modern citizens as from citizens of the ancient republics. It is wrong to try to enforce an anachronistic kind of liberty on the population against its will. In modern times it is crucial to "respect each individual's private sphere [*le cercle de*

---

[96] *Des circonstances*, pp. 5, 276.

chacun]."[97] This argument anticipates the one Constant would later make famous in his essay "The Liberty of the Ancients Compared with that of the Moderns" (1819).

Madame de Staël proffered that "no habit is born on command"; you simply cannot force the French people to become virtuous. Institutions like the republican calendar, the republican festivals, and many other revolutionary laws and measures, had been imposed by the government against the people's will. The crucial point that members of the political elite needed to comprehend was that "no habits of liberty" could be generated by government "commandments"; avant-garde institutions applied from above simply did not work. Even well-meaning revolutionaries could make the mistake of putting the cart before the horse. Legislation should flow from public opinion, rather than attempt to create it; instructing and enlightening public opinion was the work of writers and thinkers, not the government.[98] In Madame de Staël's reasoning, "Enlightenment must *precede* institutions" for them to be just and effective. Finally, no person should be confused: there could be no representative government where law is allowed to precede the desires of public opinion. Government leaders and sympathetic intellectuals should practice patience; they should wait until such time that an enlightened public itself requests the republican institutions it has learned to desire, and then creates these establishments "under the protection [but not the compulsion] of its government." It was to this that de Staël was referring when she wrote that it was "the *philosophes* [who] made the Revolution [and] it is they who will end it." Writers could enlighten public opinion far more quickly and effectively than any "public education" imposed by government.[99]

When it came to religion, Madame de Staël believed, like her father, that it was necessary to ensure good morals in society. Religion was especially valuable in a republic like France that respected principles such as political equality and popular sovereignty, since "the more influence you give to individual wills in a nation, the more you need a way to moralize the masses." Also like her father, de Staël regretted the radical turn taken by the Revolution against the Catholic Church. There were a thousand ways to reduce the influence of Catholicism, but "they chose

[97] Ibid., pp. 256, 22, 111.
[98] Ibid., pp. 277, 278: "All legislative acts must proceed from the thought of the *philosophe*, adopted by public opinion."
[99] Ibid., pp. 276, 277, 273.

the only one that tortured people without achieving the goal." Sadly, the revolutionaries managed to attack not just Catholicism, "but all idea of religion, all idea of morality, and thus all social bonds." They made the mistake of not proceeding gradually; they should have enlightened people "by degrees," gently teaching them the "absurdity of dogmas" and directing them towards "simpler and loftier ideas."[100]

Madame de Staël agreed with the goal of reducing the influence of French Catholicism, but disagreed with the methods chosen by the revolutionaries. At this point in time, she seems not to have had a problem with state interference with religion, although she would soon change her mind. In 1798, she thought it entirely within the competence of state legislators to combat a religion deemed unsuitable to their chosen form of government:

> Representative monarchies can only succeed absolute monarchies with a change in dynasty; republics can only succeed monarchies by a change in religion.

Thus, she thought it sensible that the French Republic should use "all the encouragements at its disposal," along with the help provided by "public opinion," to propagate a new religion suitable to the new regime.[101]

This was also why Madame de Staël thought very highly of Theophilanthropy. To her, it was the most "philosophical," "political," and "moral" institution yet created by the Republic. It allowed for reasoning, emphasized natural religion, and did not depend on the "blind belief" so characteristic of Catholicism. In this regard, the doctrine of Theophilanthropy was "perfect." Undeniably, however, Theophilanthropy was not working; it was not catching on with the people. Madame de Staël surmised two main reasons for this. First, Theophilanthropy lacked the ceremonies necessary to "strike at the imagination of the people." For a religion to be successful, it had to exhibit a certain amount of "splendor." Second, Theophilanthropy was perceived to be a "political tool"; therefore, many people simply refused to accept it as a legitimate religion.[102] This was why de Staël proposed another solution to the religious problem facing France, a solution that has been accorded very little attention by scholars, and has not been taken seriously by modern readers. Somewhat surprisingly, she suggested that Protestantism be made the new state religion of France.

Protestantism had all the benefits of Theophilanthropy, de Staël argued, and none of its disadvantages. It had "antique origins"; it had no church hierarchy; it was not dependent on a foreign power; and its

---

[100] Ibid. pp. 223, 227, 228.   [101] Ibid., pp. 227, 229.   [102] Ibid., pp. 229, 230, 231, 232, 234.

ministers were modestly remunerated. Moreover, Protestant ministers were useful and enlightened contributors to the community. They were "husbands, fathers and citizens." Most significantly, Protestantism was becoming more enlightened by the day:

Every day, the most enlightened ministers among the Protestants are removing all that remains of dogma in their belief. Many of them are socinians, that is they differ from theophilanthropists only in their specific adoption of the excellent morals developed in Scripture. It is a book that they prefer; it is no longer a god made man whose words they implicitly accept. With these changes growing stronger every day, Protestants and theophilanthropists, or to abbreviate, deists, are getting closer in their principles.[103]

According to Madame de Staël, Protestantism was the best religion for France at the present time. Protestantism contained within it a mechanism for continuous reform; it allowed for changes to occur over time, changes that progressively would remove "all that remains of dogma." Protestants were also "friends of liberty and equality," due not only to the organization of their churches and governing bodies, but also to the innumerable battles they had fought over the years against Catholics, hierarchy, and despotic political doctrines. However, whether they chose Theophilanthropy or Protestantism, it was imperative that the French be given a religion of state. Madame de Staël insisted that she was not advocating intolerance, and that she "hated persecution with all [her] heart." But she wanted republicans to understand that instituting a substitute cult "was the only way to destroy the influence of the Catholic religion."[104]

It is unclear whether Constant agreed with de Staël's call to endorse Protestantism as France's state religion. It is highly likely, however, that he agreed with her central premise: the replacement of Catholicism by Protestantism would lead to an improvement in France's political, intellectual, and moral culture. Both of them reasoned that Protestantism, due to the simplicity of its dogmas and ceremonies, its morality, and its lack of priestly authority or coercion, was the highest point of perfection religion had so far reached in the history of mankind. Notably, also, Protestantism contained within itself the ability to improve over time.

In any case, Madame de Staël soon abandoned the idea of a Protestant state religion and Constant never explicitly endorsed the idea, at least not in writing. As an essay written in 1799 shows, by then his most pressing concern had become the dangers of state authority. Constant's text was a

[103] Ibid., pp. 231, 232, 230–231.   [104] Ibid., pp. 230, 234, 232.

response to Boulay de la Meurthe's *Essai sur les causes qui, en 1649, amenèrent en Angleterre l'établissement de la République*, which had come out a month before. Boulay de la Meurthe's book used the history of the English Civil War to warn France of the dangers of Jacobin excesses. Constant, however, saw royalists and reactionaries as a more serious problem, and took the opportunity to warn of this counter-revolutionary danger. He feared that a restoration would be like a new revolution, probably bloodier than the first.

But the interest-value of this 1799 essay lies elsewhere: it marks a fundamental change in Constant's way of thinking. He now openly condemned the Directory for its arbitrary and coercive rule. "Our problems," he claimed, "stem from the dictatorial powers granted to authority." There should be no more coups, no more coercive laws, no more arbitrary measures. These were the things that had caused "the degradation of the public spirit." The French people were exhausted by the endless revolutionary "convulsions" they had been made to experience and these upheavals were the real cause of their increasing servility and apathy. "What people want today," Constant emphasized, was "rest." What they needed was security, order, and confidence that their institutions would foster "a regular and progressive improvement." The people desired nothing too precipitous or radical. The revival of public spirit demanded the cessation of arbitrary and dictatorial methods of government and freedom for enlightened opinion. Only then would it be possible to "really form a people."[105]

Under no conditions, however, should these words be interpreted to mean that Constant had changed his mind about Catholicism, or that he did not wish for his native Protestantism to somehow replace Catholicism as the majority religion of France. On the contrary, almost simultaneously with this essay, Constant once again voiced his preference for Protestantism in a letter to the French authorities (May 17, 1799). In it, he trumpeted the merits of deputies from Geneva, and concluded:

I would refer to the opinion of citizen Reveillère-Lépeaux, in his speech read at the National Institute in Germinal of the year II, to affirm that the Protestant cult is much more republican than the Catholic cult.[106]

The question for Constant was not *whether* France needed to be cleansed of Catholicism and reformed, but *how* this could be effectively

---

[105] *Des suites de la contre-révolution de 1660 en Angleterre*, in OCBC *Œuvres* I, pp. 675, 677, 679.
[106] "Annexe" to Letter no. 607 "Benjamin Constant à Nicolas-Louis François de Neufchâteau," May 17, 1799, in OCBC *Correspondance générale* III, p. 418.

accomplished. All previous revolutionary attempts to displace it had proven ineffective and counter-productive; France remained a religious and predominantly Catholic country. How could France be reformed? The intellectual and political elite pondered this question as the Directory gave way to Consulate.

CHAPTER 3

Napoleon, or battling "the new Cyrus"

NAPOLEON AND THE CATHOLIC REVIVAL

In her last book, *Considérations sur la Révolution française*, published posthumously in 1818, Madame de Staël reflected on the religious mood of France at the time of Napoleon's ascension to power. Observant Catholics, she reasoned, had only modest demands in 1799. Principally, they yearned for a reversal of the Revolution's legal impediments to worship. They wanted their priests no longer to be persecuted and forced to swear oaths. They wanted the government to stop "interfer[ing] ... with the religious opinions of anyone." The Consulate would have satisfied public opinion, Madame de Staël thought, if it had simply adopted the same degree of toleration that existed in America.[1]

It was a tragedy for France that this is not what happened. A rare opportunity had been missed to put the country on the road to intellectual and moral progress. Madame de Staël placed the blame squarely on the shoulders of the First Consul, Napoleon Bonaparte, who had other, more personal, ambitions. Privately indifferent to religion, Bonaparte believed only "in his own fortune" and practiced "the cult of himself." More importantly, he had a "natural penchant for despotism" and wished "to prepare the way for his arrival on the throne." Bonaparte wanted a clergy the way one might want "servants ... titles ... decorations."[2] To this end, he reasoned that a restored Catholic Church would be particularly useful.

Modern scholarship has by and large confirmed Madame de Staël's assessment.[3] A consummate opportunist, Napoleon's goals were essentially

[1] G. de Staël, *Considérations sur la Révolution française*, ed. J. Godechot (Paris, 2000), p. 373.
[2] Ibid., p. 374.
[3] G. Ellis, "Religion According to Napoleon: The Limits of Pragmatism," in N. Aston, (ed.), *Religious Change in Europe, 1650–1914* (Oxford, 1997), pp. 235–255. For an excellent account of the development of Bonaparte's thinking on the religious question see also O. Chadwick, *The Popes and European Revolution* (Oxford, 1961), pp. 467–469.

political and pragmatic. "In religion," he once remarked, "I see not the mystery of the Incarnation, but the mystery of social order."[4] In 1799, he was acutely aware of the fragility of his own power. The coup that brought him to power had only been possible because of the army's support; now, he needed to acquire other allies and disarm the domestic opposition. A deal with Rome thus offered substantial political advantages. Besides, reports from the police and prefects were confirming that the Catholic revival was in full swing.[5]

Bonaparte was also well aware that the Revolution had divided and weakened the Church. In 1799, the rump of Abbé Grégoire's constitutional church was having little success in rebuilding itself, while the refractory church was steadily gaining in strength. Both sides looked hopefully to Bonaparte and even courted his favor, urging him to heal the schism and bring Catholicism back to France. For Bonaparte it was a perfect opportunity to enhance his standing. On the one hand, during the negotiations he could play his feuding Catholic constituents off against each other, thus winning a favorable outcome for himself; on the other, by signing an agreement with the Pope, he would satisfy large segments of the population and be seen as reuniting France.

Although it took until September 1801 for a final settlement with the Pope to be ratified, and a further seven months for this "Concordat" to be publicly celebrated, Bonaparte began taking conciliatory steps towards the papacy almost immediately upon his ascension to power. A series of edicts were passed in November and December 1799 removing many impediments to Catholic worship. Church buildings not yet sold off were returned and Sunday services were allowed to resume. The revolutionary calendar was required only for official purposes, and the number of official revolutionary festivals was reduced. The oath of hatred to royalty required of all priests was abolished, replaced by a much simpler and less controversial one promising loyalty to the constitution. More of the emigré clergy now felt free to return to France. While bell-ringing and outdoor religious ceremonies remained illegal for some time, Bonaparte also ended the official commemoration of the execution of Louis XVI, and released a number of priests from jail. When the Pope died, Bonaparte ordered solemn obsequies for him and quickly signaled his willingness to work with his successor, Pius VII.

---

[4] *The Mind of Napoleon: A Selection from his Written and Spoken Words*, ed. and trans. J. Ch. Herold (New York, 1955), p. 105.
[5] L. Madelin, *Le Consulat et l'empire* (Paris, 1932–3), p. 91.

In a speech in Milan Cathedral a few months later, Bonaparte's new attitude towards the Church became crystal clear. Before the assembled Italian clergy, he now openly criticized the "cruel policy of the Directory" towards religion. He claimed that a society could not survive without religion; it would be "like a vessel without a rudder," constantly "agitated" and never at peace. Among the religions, Bonaparte favored Catholicism, for it was the only one that could simultaneously ensure the people's "real happiness" and "secure the foundations of a good government." He promised to "protect and defend" it in every way he could.[6]

Many in the French intellectual elite were alarmed by these actions and statements, which gave further momentum to the Catholic revival. As for the long-frustrated Catholics and counter-revolutionaries, they now felt emboldened to express their opinions openly. Some people hoped that what had happened in England after the death of Cromwell would happen in France, in other words that Bonaparte would be the "General Monck" who brought back the monarchy. Others entertained no such hopes, but preferred Bonaparte's government to its predecessors and wished that he would move gradually in a monarchical direction. Bonaparte himself seems to have been in no hurry to declare his long-term intentions. In the meantime, royalist sentiments appeared with increasing frequency in Catholic journals.

Until this time, most overt attacks on the Revolution had come from abroad. Joseph de Maistre and Louis de Bonald had launched their broadsides from outside the border and were still fairly unknown in France. Now, however, centers of anti-revolutionary propaganda began cropping up inside the country. The daily newspaper *Journal des débats* is one example, the new *Mercure de France* another, and the revived *Année littéraire* a third. Towards the end of 1800, La Harpe returned to Paris from exile and resumed his famous lectures at the Lycée. In the atmosphere of the early Consulate, he and other "apostles of prejudice," as the still combative *Décade philosophique* called them,[7] enjoyed considerable success. They let loose a furious barrage against the Revolution and the Enlightenment.

One of their favorite arguments was to equate the Terror with the Revolution and to blame the *philosophes* for both. With their arrogant attacks on tradition, and irresponsible dreams about change and

---

[6] Quoted by J.-O. Boudon, "Bonaparte et la réconciliation religieuse," in *Terminer la Révolution?: Actes du colloque . . . 4 et 5 décembre, 2001* (Paris, 2003), p. 156.

[7] Kitchin, *Un journal "philosophique,"* p. 73.

reform, the *philosophes* had accomplished the complete overturning of the social order, in the process triggering all the misdeeds and excesses of the Revolution. What history proved, and the *philosophes* carelessly denied, was that human nature was fatally flawed. All men were innately disposed to evil and had only a very limited capacity to reason. The record was clear: experience confirmed what Catholic theologians and moralists had been saying for centuries. Human beings needed to be contained; they needed boundaries, "bridles," and "brakes" to keep them from endangering themselves and society. What the Enlightenment disdainfully referred to as "prejudices" or "obstacles" to progress were the very restraints mankind needed to provide social cohesion, stability, and order.

Another favorite topic in the Catholic press was the corruption and moral degeneration plaguing France. The *Journal des débats* printed articles cataloguing a litany of moral vices gripping society. It lamented the "execrable cupidity" of all the "usurers," "speculators," "stock-jobbers," and "*nouveaux riches*," who were making obscene amounts of money in a time of war. It regretted the ever-growing variety of entertainments, spectacles, balls, and concerts that were being designed expressly to amuse such people. If the moral profligacy of the *nouveaux riches* was an urgent problem, so was the irrational behavior and degeneracy of the poor. The *Journal des débats* expressed its dismay at the carefree attitude of so many people, the rampant "spirit of dissipation" and the "prodigality" that were infecting all classes of society. It particularly deplored the greed, the "thirst for profits," and the "ostentatious display" of the age. "Egoism," "dissipation," and a "blasé" attitude were everywhere to be found. Children were being brought up without any religious values; suicide was on the rise.[8] The Catholic press insisted that the government take action against the deteriorating situation.

Of course the larger purpose for such articles was to support a full restoration of Catholicism, which alone could cure France's problems. The Catholic press saw the root of the predicament as a moral one and the cure was religion. Here again, the *philosophes* were attacked. It was their relentless critique of authority and, in particular, their vicious attacks on religion that were to blame for France's ills. While striking out against the Enlightenment and the Revolution, these conservative authors often paid court to Bonaparte, congratulating him for putting an end to the anarchy and re-establishing order. Calling him an "agent of

---

[8] *Journal des débats et loix du pouvoir législatif, et des actes du gouvernement*, 30 Pluviose, Year VIII, and surrounding dates, accessed on Gallica, electronic resource, Bibliothèque nationale de France.

Providence," they urged the First Consul to further reconnect France with its ancient traditions.

Interestingly, while they attacked the Enlightenment, Catholic apologists continued to employ rationalist and utilitarian arguments to promote their cause. They emphasized the indispensability of Catholicism as a means of moral indoctrination and social control. As the former *philosophe* now-turned-Catholic-apologist Rivarol claimed, the "truth" of religion was less important than its "necessity": irreligion was a "terrible luxury," he remarked, and one that France could ill afford. The Revolution provided incontrovertible proof that Catholicism was needed to maintain social and political order. It preached the crucial values of humility, patience, and obedience to authorities. It taught people to accept inequalities and to shun "innovation and diversity." Deeply marked by the turmoil of the Revolution, Rivarol proclaimed "the highest good in the social domain" to be "immobility." It was the Catholic religion that guaranteed this immobility, by producing "the miracle of obedience."[9]

ENLIGHTENED RESPONSES AND THE PLAN TO "PROTESTANTIZE" FRANCE

Scholars who write about the Concordat normally do not discuss Madame de Staël's *De la littérature* (1800) or Jacques Necker's *Cours de morale religieuse* (1800). Instead, they focus on Bonaparte's long and arduous negotiations with the pope. They make reference to the Catholic resurgence and to the political pressures affecting Bonaparte. Sometimes they mention the extreme hostility to the reinstatement of Catholicism expressed by key Idéologues such as Volney, Dupuis, or Destutt de Tracy. History books thereby tend to reduce Napoleon's options to only two: either he could reinstate Catholicism, and thus please a large portion of the French population, or he could not reinstate Catholicism, and thus please the anti-Catholic Idéologues.

The truth, however, is that the situation leading up to the Concordat was more complicated. During the early period of the Consulate, there seemed to be several possibilities in the realm of religion, some of which may sound outlandish today. While many people were clamoring for the

---

[9] A. de Rivarol, *De la philosophie moderne*, 2nd edn, n.d., n.p., accessed on Gallica, electronic resource, Bibliothèque nationale de France, pp. 42, 37, 20, 35.

reinstatement of Catholicism, others were hoping that the government instead might favor a liberal form of Protestantism, or at least an enlightened and "Protestantized" version of Catholicism. They hoped that Napoleon's regime would implement a reform of French Catholicism, and thus promote a religion more suitable to republican and modern values. Believing that the people were backward and superstitious, in large part due to the pernicious influence of Catholicism, they argued that France needed a religion more conducive to progress. It is in this context that Madame de Staël's *De la littérature* and Jacques Necker's *Cours de morale religieuse* should be seen. Father and daughter were trying to convince intellectual and political elites that a simple restoration of Old Regime Catholicism would be a serious mistake; instead, the opportunity should be taken to effect a kind of religious reformation.

Madame de Staël's *De la littérature* was a spirited response to the plethora of anti-Enlightenment, anti-Revolution, and pro-Catholic arguments circulating in France. Her dream of Protestantizing the country was still alive. Written while in the company of Constant at Coppet, near Geneva, and published during the early Consulate, de Staël's book reflects the couple's growing fears of Catholic reaction and their deep concerns about the direction in which Bonaparte was taking France. Soon after the book's appearance, Constant published a glowing review of it, unambiguously endorsing de Staël's point of view.[10] *De la littérature* stirred up quite a controversy and was a great publishing success. It went through several reprints before the end of the year, whereupon de Staël published a revised edition that responded to her critics.

De la littérature vehemently defended the Enlightenment. Its author reasserted her faith in the irreversibility of historical progress and the perfectibility of humankind. Catholic apologists and critics of the Revolution should understand that it was impossible to stop "the natural progress of the human mind."[11] However, Madame de Staël agreed with their assessment of the lamentable state of French morals. In fact, moral corruption was a problem that she and Constant had been worrying about for some time. Constant's writings during the Directory warned of the "shrunken souls" and "degraded spirits" of the men of post-Revolutionary France. Such men seemed only interested in the search for

[10] "Compte rendu de *De la littérature*, de Mme de Staël," in OCBC *Œuvres* III, 2, pp. 905–916.
[11] G. de Staël, *De la littérature*, ed. G. Gengembre and J. Goldzink (Paris, 1991), p. 410.

an "excess of pleasure,"[12] which played right into the hands of the counter-revolutionaries, by making people servile and dependent. And the problem seemed only to intensify with time. Likewise, in her *Circonstances actuelles*, Madame de Staël had complained of the "unheard-of corruption" that had taken over France.[13] Now, in *De la littérature*, she bemoaned "our present degradation,"[14] noting that money had become everyone's obsession and that "bad taste," "crude language," and "a revolting vulgarity" were everywhere to be found.[15] "What we need today," she asserted, "is a lever against egoism; all the moral force of each man is focused on his self-interest."[16]

While Constant and de Staël agreed with the counter-revolutionaries on the state of moral decay, they vehemently disagreed about its causes. The origin of the problem lay neither in the Revolution nor in the Enlightenment; rather, it was due to centuries of subjugation by a repressive political and religious system that had retarded France's development. France was immoral because it was intellectually and morally immature. Tragically, the derailment of the Revolution by the Terror had only aggravated the underlying problem. Violent and arbitrary rule had instilled fear in the population, causing people to turn inwards, making them intellectually submissive, politically despondent, cynical, and selfish. But Madame de Staël was adamant: none of this could be blamed on the Enlightenment. On the contrary, as Benjamin Constant pointed out in his review, *De la littérature* proved that "the perfecting of man's intellectual faculties always tends towards moral improvement."[17]

De Staël also had some distinctive things to say about Christianity. In the battle over the moral causes and effects of the Revolution, the role of Christianity had become a hotly contested issue. People on different sides disagreed about the very definition of Christianity, and what its "essence" or "spirit" was. While the counter-revolutionaries and anti-*philosophes* associated Christianity's fundamental message with social immobility, intellectual obedience, and political subservience, Madame

---

[12] "Discours prononcé au Cercle constitutionnel pour la plantation de l'arbre de la liberté, le 30 fructidor an V [September 16, 1797]," in OCBC *Œuvres* I, quoted in chapter 2, p. 60. On Constant's early concerns about morals and character, see K. S. Vincent, "Benjamin Constant, the French Revolution, and the Problem of Modern Character," *History of European Ideas*, 30 (2004), pp. 5–21.

[13] De Staël, *Des Circonstances*, p. 235.   [14] De Staël, *De la littérature*, p. 87.   [15] Ibid., p. 306.

[16] As quoted by J. Isbell, *The Birth of European Romanticism: Truth and Propaganda in Staël's "De l'Allemagne," 1810–1813* (Cambridge, 1994), p. 131.

[17] "Compte rendu," in OCBC, *Œuvres* III, 2, p. 905.

de Staël connected it with social progress and intellectual emancipation. Speaking glowingly of the benefits of Christianity, she contended that "the Christian religion, in the era of its establishment was absolutely indispensable to civilization" and "developed the faculties of the mind."[18] She now openly expressed her preference for Protestantism, which she held to be the purest, most moral, and therefore most suitable form of Christianity for France.

"The Reformation," Madame de Staël declared, "was the period in history that most effectively advanced the perfectibility of the human species." In countries where the Reformation had become firmly established, its salutary effects on morals were easy to see. In contrast to Catholicism, the Protestant religion "contains no active germ of superstition" and "gives to virtue all the support it needs." It does not hinder philosophical inquiry, while it "maintains efficiently the purity of morals."[19] Perhaps most important of all, Protestantism favored critical reflection and thus the faculty of judgement.[20] The crucial point de Staël and Constant wanted to make was that you promote sound morals not by preventing philosophical inquiry, but by promoting it. This was why Protestantism was a better religion for France than Catholicism: the answer to the dilemma was more enlightenment, not less.

It was certainly no coincidence that immediately after *De la littérature* was published, Jacques Necker came out with his own book on religion. In 1788, he had tried to warn France's intellectual elite about the dangers of irreligion. In 1796, he had lambasted the Directory's attacks on religion. Now, in 1800, his three-volume collection of sermons, *Cours de morale religieuse*, offered substantial support for his daughter's position. Displaying a more pronounced Protestant coloration than his first book on religion, Necker's *Cours de morale* argued once again that religion was essential to the moral health of France. Indeed, religion was "perhaps more necessary in France than anywhere else." But the type of religion Necker favored, it was now easy to see, was not Old Regime Catholicism. Rather, he championed a "simple, reasonable and pure" religion that would lend support to liberty. He espoused a religion that was "majestic in its simplicity," one that rejected "all superstitious ceremonies, all luxurious sacrifices."[21] Any contemporary educated enough to

---

[18] De Staël, *De la littérature*, p. 164.   [19] Ibid., p. 212.
[20] On this, see H. Rosenblatt, "Madame de Staël, the Protestant Reformation, and the History of 'Private Judgement,'" ABC, 31–32 (2007), pp. 143–154.
[21] J. Necker, *Cours de morale religieuse* (Geneva, 1800), vol. I, pp. xxxix, xxii, xi; vol. III, p. 211; vol. I, p. xxi.

read his book would have recognized these code words for Protestantism. In fact, Necker's book reads like a collection of liberal Protestant sermons, although they border on Deism in their lack of attention to dogma.[22] Necker was proffering a reformed strain of Christianity upon which, he hoped, all Enlightened men and women might agree.

Unsurprisingly, *De la littérature* was favorably received in Enlightened circles; Fauriel gave it a good review in the *Décade philosophique*. Equally unsurprising are the attacks it received in the conservative and Catholic press. The *Journal des Débats* claimed that two thousand years of human history proved Madame de Staël's idea of indefinite perfectibility to be nothing but a foolish myth. The *Mercure de France* denounced the notion as a dangerous fantasy; history proved, rather, that "since the century of Louis XIV . . . we have been travelling incessantly *backward*." The journal lamented Madame de Staël's predilection for the ideas of William Godwin, whose obvious goal was to "overturn all social institutions."[23] To the Catholic press, Madame de Staël's absurd obsession with perfectibility posed a continuing threat to the social and political order.

On the other hand, Necker's book was described as a sorry mix of philosophy and religion. Everything in it was "monotonous, sad and cold." According to the *Mercure*, Necker's very "Protestant" approach to religion was bound to fail because he could not strike the right tone. As was typical of Protestants, his writing was too "cold" and "dry."[24] Nevertheless, the author of the review praised Necker for the *goal* he was obviously striving for, which was to "reunite all Christian churches."[25] It was for this reason that his *Cours de morale* avoided dogma and focused instead on morals.[26] But once again, Necker's attempt, though laudable, was bound to fail, because it was too Protestant for France. By way of contrast, the *Mercure* spoke glowingly of a soon-to-be released book by Chateaubriand. Chateaubriand would be successful where Necker was

---

[22] The best treatment of Necker's religious views is now Encrevé, "La Réception des ouvrages de J. Necker," pp. 73–130.

[23] *Mercure de France*, Messidor, Year VII, p. 20.

[24] *Mercure de France*, 1 Frimaire, Year IX, pp. 333, 335.   [25] Ibid., p. 340.

[26] All of this helps us to understand why Necker's books on religion have been so differently interpreted by modern scholars. Modern readers have been puzzled by Necker's ideas and tone, having a hard time evaluating his work as either pro-Protestant, pro-Catholic, or simply Deist. His first book of 1788 can be seen as a gentle defense of Protestantism and a suggestion that French Catholicism reform itself *in a Protestant direction*, while his *Cours de morale* is a slightly more open endorsement of Protestant values at a time when Bonaparte had just assumed power and there were still several options for a religious settlement being considered.

not, the *Mercure* predicted, because Chateaubriand knew how to focus on "attaching the soul" rather than "forcing conviction." In order to successfully reach the audience, "he appeals to sentiment, and not argumentation." Chateaubriand understood that "the more mysterious a religion is, the more it conforms to human nature." Protestantism just could not touch the emotions or sway the imagination the way Catholicism did.[27]

On the relative merits of Protestantism over Catholicism, the National Institute joined the fray, in more or less subtle ways. In the fall of 1801, it announced an essay competition on the question "By which causes did the spirit of liberty develop in France, since Francis I until 1789?" First prize was given to an essay that strongly endorsed the Reformation, identifying it as a critical factor in the progress of liberty around the world. The essay described Luther as "a genius" and credited Lutheranism with introducing "a new order of things" which improved the political system of Europe immeasurably. Before the Reformation, the author contended, "the French nation languished in ignorance," the priesthood conspiring with the monarchy to "deceive the people" by keeping them in "ignorance and therefore in slavery." Protestant dogma was "more compatible with the principles of civil liberty," and caused a "universal fermentation" that had favorable political effects. In particular, Protestants were responsible for introducing a "system of equality" to France and a "republican" form of government "more analogous to their principles and their morals [*moeurs*]."[28] The clear political message was that if France was to remain a republic, Protestantism, not Catholicism, should be encouraged by the government.

CHARLES DE VILLERS

It was during this tense year of 1801, when the value of religion was being so hotly debated, along with the comparative strengths and weaknesses of Protestantism and Catholicism, that a relatively unknown interlocutor named Charles de Villers (1765–1815) walked on to the intellectual stage.[29]

---

[27] *Mercure de France*, vol. XLV, 25 Germinal, Year X, pp. 120, 121, 123.

[28] *Discours qui a remporté le prix d'Histoire proposé par l'Institut national de France, décerné dans sa séance publique du 15 vendémiaire an 9 sur cette question: Par quelles causes l'esprit de liberté s'est-il développé en France, depuis François Ier jusqu'en 1789? Par le citoyen Nicolas Ponce* (Paris, Year IX), pp. 9, 10, 6, 7, 10, 23.

[29] L. Wittmer, *Charles de Villers 1765–1815: Un intermédiaire entre la France et l'Allemagne et un précurseur de Mme de Staël* (Geneva, 1908) and R. A. Crowley, *Charles de Villers: Mediator and Comparatist* (Berne, 1978).

Born in France and raised a Catholic, Villers had emigrated to Germany during the Revolution. In Göttingen, he had been won over to enlightened Protestantism and had become a convert to Kant's philosophy. Indeed, in Villers' thought, these two things – enlightened German Protestantism and Kant's philosophy – merge together, becoming at times indistinguishable.

Villers was deeply concerned about the intellectual, moral, and political trends in France, which he, like others, saw as interrelated. Enlightened German thought helped him to identify everything he thought had gone wrong in France. A critical component of the problem was the hostility towards religion expressed by the French Enlightenment and its offspring, Idéologie. Villers wanted to inform the French reading public of the more sensible German perspective, and thus to help them out of their intellectual and moral impasse.

In 1801, Villers published *Philosophie de Kant, ou principes fondamentaux de la philosophie transcendentale*. He dedicated his book to the National Institute, hoping thereby to attract the attention of the Idéologues. Addressing "the enlightened and thinking part" of the French population, he implored them to "change their [intellectual] direction." In reality, the book was less an exposition of Kant's philosophy than a series of Kant-inspired reflections on the miserable state of the Idéologues' "new French metaphysics." By introducing France to "Kant's philosophy" and, more specifically, to a Kantian perspective on religion, Villers hoped to cure the Idéologues of their Condillacian empiricism, as well as their irrational hostility to religion, which he thought was causing serious moral harm.

In some ways, Villers' critique of the Idéologues resembled that of a Catholic apologist. He deplored the fact that the Idéologues had been so blinded by their "hatred of priests," that they had brazenly and irresponsibly tried to eradicate Christianity without any concern for the moral consequences. They had then tried to replace it with their "superficial" and "inane" morality of self-interest. Villers called the Idéologues' principles immoral and "degrading." They paralyzed and stifled man's conscience, leading people to commit incalculable evils and crimes. Villers even blamed the French Enlightenment for fostering "Jacobinism" and thus engendering "all the crimes of the French Revolution."

Thereafter, however, Villers' argument ceased to resemble that of a Catholic counter-revolutionary and showed, instead, his indebtedness to the German and Protestant Enlightenment. What neither the *philosophes* nor the Idéologues understood, he wrote, was that every religion was composed of two different parts – an inner core and an outer shell. What the French *philosophes* had thought of as "religion" was really only its outer shell, in other words its "exterior form." However, every religion also had an inner core or moral center. This was the voice of conscience or "the indestructible sentiment of justice." Every religion was necessarily made up of both, the way a human being was composed of a body and a soul. Tragically, the French *philosophes* had mistakenly thought that one could discard the outer form while retaining its inner essence. By attacking Catholicism so viciously and irresponsibly, they had unwittingly delivered a fatal blow to French morals as well.

In France's present situation, Villers thought it impossible to revive Catholicism. France's old religion had been "erased" from too many people's hearts. In fact, it was impossible to predict whether *any* form of Christianity might still be able to germinate and thrive. It was simply too soon to tell. But if Christian beliefs were somehow to make a comeback, Villers hoped they would be "recalled in their purity"; in other words, he wished that French Catholicism would be reformed. In the meantime, after the havoc wrought by the Revolution and the degrading moral philosophy of the Idéologues, France desperately needed a "new philosophy" to "restore moral order." Intellectual elites needed to work together to bring back "self-respect," to cultivate "human dignity," and to remind people of their "conscience" and "duties."[30] Villers felt certain that Kant's philosophy could do this for France.

Villers' essay does not seem to have made a big impact on French intellectuals. He certainly did not persuade Idéologues to give up their morality of self-interest and to embrace Kantianism instead. Many people in France found Kant's philosophy overly metaphysical. Admirers of the French Enlightenment thought it too abstract and formalist to be practical; moreover, it was expressed in an abstruse terminology that was hard to understand. Therefore, despite Villers' valiant attempts at clarification and dissemination, Kant's ideas had little resonance.

There were, however, two people who did understand Villers' appropriation of Kantian philosophy: Benjamin Constant and Madame de Staël. Familiar with Kantian ideas since his years in Brunswick, Constant was actually one of the very first in France to read and appreciate the German philosopher. Furthermore, he had studied the New Theology of

---

[30] C. de Villers, *Philosophie de Kant, ou principes fondamentaux de la philosophie transcendentale* (Metz, 1801), pp. 154, 163, 154–155, 167.

the most enlightened German Protestant theologians and the idea of progressive revelation.[31] So, when Constant met Villers in 1803, they had much to talk about. Soon they made plans to collaborate on the dissemination of German philosophy in France and formed a close and lasting friendship.

But it was Madame de Staël and Charles de Villers who first became friends and intellectual allies. Villers initiated the relationship by means of a letter, dated June 1802, in which he introduced himself and declared his profound admiration for her "excellent book," *De la littérature*. He begged her to ignore her critics, the "frivolous Parisians," and their "pitiful absurdities."[32] In reply, de Staël thanked him warmly and informed him that she liked his book on Kant. She praised Villers for having the clarity that Kant lacked and for correctly identifying the problems with Idéologie. "I am in absolute agreement with you about the consequences that you draw from the system that makes everything depend on sensations," she wrote, adding that Idéologie "degrade[s] the soul instead of elevating it."[33] Considering these comments, it seems more than likely that reading Villers' essay on Kant helped de Staël distance herself from her earlier Idéologue principles and to reinforce her predilection for the liberal and Protestant principles she expressed in *De la littérature*.

BONAPARTE'S DECISION

Unconvinced by the arguments favoring Protestantism, Bonaparte continued to negotiate with the papacy, although he tried to keep his efforts secret. "My policy," he told his Council of State in August of 1801

> is to govern people as the majority wish to be governed ... It was by making myself a Catholic that I won the war in the Vendée, by making myself a Moslem that I established myself in Egypt, by making myself an ultramontane that I turned men's hearts towards me in Italy. If I were to govern a nation of Jews I would rebuild the Temple of Solomon.[34]

---

[31] As early as 1794, he had had serious conversations about Kant's categorical imperative with Isabelle de Charrière and had even engaged in a public debate about it in 1797. See F. Azouvi and D. Bourel, *De Königsberg à Paris: La réception de Kant en France (1788–1804)* (Paris, 1991) and H. Rosenblatt, "Reinterpreting Adolphe: The Sexual Politics of Benjamin Constant," *Historical Reflections*, 3, 3 (Fall 2002), pp. 341–360.

[32] Letter no. 1, "Charles de Villers à Madame de Staël," June 25, 1802, in KK, pp. 15, 17.

[33] Letter no. 2, "Madame de Staël à Charles de Villers," August 1, 1802, in ibid., p. 21.

[34] As quoted by E. E. Y. Hales, *Napoleon and the Pope* (London, 1962), pp. 156–157.

For Napoleon, religion was obviously a political tool, one that he would use to unite and pacify the Catholics in France. He also wanted to curtail the Church's opposition to his regime and to destroy the influence of emigré bishops.

Late in life, while in exile on Saint Helena, Napoleon reflected on the different political pressures he had been under while negotiating the Concordat. "When I was at the helm of affairs," he recalled,

I already had some set ideas on the major elements that held society together; I had weighed the importance of religion; I was persuaded, and I was resolved, to re-establish it.[35]

Napoleon also recalled the resistance he had encountered over his plans to reinstate Catholicism. Surprisingly, in his governing councils, he had been advised to promote Protestantism instead.

In fact, evidence shows that a substantial segment of the political and intellectual elite during the early Consulate hoped that France might be "Protestantized" rather than "re-Catholicized."[36] The memoirs of Antoine-Clair Thibaudeau, for example, recount a conversation between the First Consul and one of his counselors of state on the topic of religion. Although the Council of State was hostile to the Concordat, the counselor agreed with Bonaparte that religion was useful to society. Priests, however, were entirely another matter. To re-establish a clergy beholden to a "foreign prince" would be to create a "rival power" in the state. The counselor warned Bonaparte not to forget that the pope was "a clever enemy," whose principal interest was to expand his power in France. "Never before," insisted the counselor, had the situation been more favorable to a "great religious revolution." Bonaparte had "a unique opportunity": "You only have to say the word and papism is ruined, and France becomes Protestant."

To make sure that he understood correctly, Bonaparte asked whether he was really being asked to "do the opposite of Henry IV." Yes, the counselor replied. If there must be a "dominant cult," then make it Protestantism. But Bonaparte disagreed. He was worried that it would divide the country and cause interminable quarrels. Anyway, why should he further aggravate the priests and disappoint the population? Instead, his strategy would be to "organize" the Church and "discipline" the clergy so that neither could do any harm. He knew that opting for Catholicism would disappoint enlightened intellectuals, but he reasoned that they

---

[35] E. de las Cases, *Le Mémorial de Sainte-Hélène*, ed. M. Dunan (Paris, 1951), vol. II, p. 195.
[36] Robert, *Les églises réformées*, pp. 49–50.

would not pose a long-term problem, since they were, in reality, "indifferent" to religion.[37]

Other documented conversations recount that Bonaparte received Protestant delegates kindly, and even flattered them. To one, he confessed his regret that France "had missed the opportunity [in the sixteenth century] of establishing the Protestant religion." Francis I should have converted to Lutheranism, Bonaparte reasoned, and saved France a lot of trouble. Indeed, he wished that "the whole world would be Protestant." But it was now too late to reform France.[38]

In the end, therefore, Bonaparte rejected the idea of making Protestantism France's national religion and rebuffed the "Protestantization" of French Catholicism. Contemplating this decision on Saint Helena, Bonaparte pondered what opting for Protestantism would have meant:

> I would have created two just about equal parties in France, when I didn't want any parties at all; I would have brought back all the quarrels over religion, when the goal of all enlightened thinking of the century and my own was to make them completely disappear.[39]

As usual, Bonaparte's motive was political and pragmatic. He wanted to unite the country and avoid encouraging religious sectarianism. But as de Staël later remarked, what he really wanted was to "prepare his ascension to the throne." For this, Catholicism was better.

The final draft of the Concordat was a compromise; each side gained and lost something. However, for Constant, Madame de Staël, and their political allies, the restoration of Catholicism in France was an unmitigated disaster. To them, Catholicism was a retrograde religion that lent support to despotic government and bred the wrong kind of thinking and values. Any accord that allowed priests and popes to retake control of the hearts and minds of the French people was a step in the wrong direction.

Many of them had supported Bonaparte's *coup d'état* initially. Indeed, some of them had even participated in it, believing that only Bonaparte could end the anarchy and bring back stable, orderly government. Somewhat naively, they had thought that the new regime would contribute to their own intellectual and political agendas, that Bonaparte would found a republic governed by philosophers like themselves. Therefore, it was with dismay and disappointment, and a sense of personal betrayal, that these former supporters watched Bonaparte begin

---

[37] A.-C. Thibaudeau, *Mémoires sur le Consulat 1799–1804* (Paris, 1827), pp. 153–156.
[38] Robert, *Les églises réformées*, p. 49.   [39] Las Cases, *Le Mémorial de Sainte-Hélène*, p. 195.

his negotiations with Rome. At a meeting of the Institute, the Idéologue Volney, who had been on good terms with Bonaparte, became so cross that he "lit into Bonaparte to his face." When Bonaparte tried to explain the reasons for the Concordat, reminding Volney that all of France was calling for the restoration of Catholicism, Volney indignantly replied "and if they asked for the restoration of the Bourbons, would you do that for them too?" Furious, Bonaparte kicked Volney in the stomach. Intellectuals like Volney no doubt sensed that the Concordat would mark the end of their intellectual dominance over the French government. It would also signal a major step in the "monarchization" of France and, related to this, the turning of "citizens into subjects."[40]

Back in December 1799, thanks to the intercession of Sieyès, Constant had obtained a seat on the Tribunate, one of Bonaparte's three legislative bodies. Opposition to the Concordat was almost unanimous there. Like many others, Constant had approved of Bonaparte's coup, but he was also among the first to warn against the dangers of dictatorship. This may explain why he was put under police surveillance as early as 1800. By then, it was already becoming clear to him that France's biggest threat was no longer counter-revolution; rather, it was the very personal and modern rule of Bonaparte. Constant's first speech as a tribune identified him as an opponent of Bonaparte's regime. Over the next two years, he consistently fought its steps towards dictatorship in what has been described as a "little war" against Bonaparte.[41] It was as a tribune that Constant got his first taste of parliamentary politics, at which he would eventually excel.

The twelve speeches that Constant gave as a tribune show that he intervened on a wide range of issues; in particular, he denounced the government's abuse of power. Constant was present during the most tense moments surrounding the Concordat's signing and ratification during the summer of 1801. He was there when, as a gesture of defiance and disapproval, the Legislative Body elected as its president the renowned atheist, Charles-François Dupuis, author of the flagrantly antireligious *Origine de tous les cultes*, and a week later, when the Senate chose the Constitutional bishop Henri Grégoire, an outspoken critic of the Concordat, to represent it at a special audience with the First Consul. To forestall this opposition, Bonaparte purged both the Tribunate and

---

[40] The title of chapter X in Sutherland, *The French Revolution and Empire*.
[41] B. Jasinski, "Benjamin Constant tribun," in E. Hofmann (ed.), *Benjamin Constant, Mme de Staël et le groupe de Coppet: Actes du deuxième Congrès de Lausanne et du troisième Colloque de Coppet* (Oxford, 1982), pp. 63–88.

the Legislative Body. In January 1802, Constant and approximately twenty other tribunes were eliminated. After that, the Tribunate accepted the Concordat by a vote of 78 to 7 and the Legislative Body by 228 to 21.

PORTALIS ON THE UTILITY OF RELIGION

In a speech before the Legislative Body on April 5, 1802, Bonaparte's Minister of Religious Affairs, Jean-Etienne-Marie Portalis,[42] explained the reasoning behind the Concordat so as to allay its critics' fears. In pragmatic language, he advanced an instrumentalist view of religion expressly designed to appeal to skeptics. The unavoidable fact, he declared, was that the French people were begging to have their religion restored. Under the circumstances, the wisest course was simply to give it to them. This, Portalis insisted, was one of the lessons learned from the Revolution: religious persecution was counter-productive. Another lesson learned was that it is very difficult for governments to change people's minds about religion. It was easier to pass laws than to alter people's opinions.

According to Portalis, the "multitude" *needed* religion. It was silly to ignore this, and make decisions for the whole nation based on the intelligence of a few educated men living in cities. Far away from these cities lived an immense population that Portalis believed was basically "impossible to enlighten," but that needed to be governed. Ordinary French men and women did not just follow their reason; they also followed their hearts. Indeed, they were more susceptible to "impressions" than to "principles." Without "the bridle of religion," this major portion of the population "would know only tragedy and crime."[43]

Given the fact that a religion was necessary, the only question left to decide was which religion. To Portalis, it was evident that it had to be Catholicism. First, he reasoned, you could not "make a religion" the way you "make a law." Faith was impossible to command. A good maxim of state was therefore to avoid trying to change an established religion that was deeply rooted. Second, the rites, mysteries, and dogmas of Catholicism were particularly well suited to the minds of the multitude. A "purely intellectual" religion (by which Portalis probably meant Theophilanthropy, or perhaps Deism or liberal Protestantism) could never

---

[42] J.-L. Chartier, *Portalis: Le père du Code civil* (Paris, 2004).

[43] *Discours Prononcé par Cen Portalis, orateur du Gouvernement, dans la séance du Corps législatif du 15 germinal an X, sur l'organisation des cultes* (Paris, Year X), p. 17.

work with the masses. By providing an acceptable level of mystery, Catholicism appealed to the masses, while preventing them from becoming overly superstitious. It was a perfect barrier against the "torrent of more or less false opinions that the delirium of human reason" had a tendency to invent.

Portalis assured his audience that a restored Catholicism would not be given too much power. It would be made a "protected" religion, not an "exclusive" or a "dominant" one. Other religions would be tolerated. Moreover, "public order" and state "security" mandated that religious institutions not be left to themselves. Religious affairs were a matter of "high state policy"; therefore, one had to ensure "a reasonable supervision of all cults." The state should "direct" the religions so as to maximize their "public usefulness."[44]

It is hard to tell how many people were won over by Portalis' arguments; but the die had been cast. Only a few months earlier, Bonaparte had signaled that he would tolerate no dissent by purging the Tribunate. Now, he tightened the vice of censorship and ruled in an increasingly authoritarian way. In any case, Bonaparte felt strong enough to proceed without the support of the Idéologues and their intellectual allies. The people of France were easier to please. Popular religiosity was booming, as was Bonaparte's popularity. In August 1802, he made himself First Consul for Life; two years later, he crowned himself Emperor with the blessing of the Pope.

THE CONCORDAT AND THE ORGANIC ARTICLES

It is true that Bonaparte refused to have Catholicism declared the state religion of France and did not grant it any exclusive constitutional privileges. He safeguarded the rights of Protestants and Jews to exercise their religions, and, in doing so, effectively put an end to the French confessional state. Jean Bauberot calls this the "first threshold of laicization in France."[45]

It is unlikely, however, that Constant would have viewed it this way in 1801. The Concordat gave Catholicism legal recognition and a considerable prestige as the religion of "the majority of the French" and the consuls. Henceforth, not only would it be practiced freely and openly in

---

[44] Ibid., pp. 17, 7, 11, 27, 33, 28, 33.
[45] J. Baubérot, *Histoire de la laïcité en France* (Paris, 2000), p. 25.

France, but it would also be "protected" by the state. In a very real sense, then, religion left the private sphere to which it had been relegated during the Directory, and re-entered the public realm. As Portalis argued, religion returned to being a "matter of state." Once again, the government undertook to pay the salaries of bishops and priests. It authorized the restoration of cathedral chapters and diocesan seminaries, and gave Catholics the right to create pious foundations.

Crucially, however, the Pope was forced to agree to the sale of confiscated Church lands, and to accept the redrawing of ecclesiastical boundaries. In reinstituting Catholicism, Bonaparte had no intention of giving the pope extensive powers in France. While Bonaparte acknowledged that religion was necessary, he insisted that this religion be in the hands of government. He regarded religion much like his deputy, Paul-Louis Roederer, did, that is as "a necessary auxiliary to government."[46] Thus, there was the need to "organize" the French clergy and to "discipline" it so that it could never become a "rival power" in the state.[47] On the issue of the appointment of clergy, the Pope and Bonaparte reached a compromise. To end the schism between the Constitutional Church and the non-juring clergy, both men agreed to ask all bishops, whether Constitutional or non-juring, to renounce their sees. New bishops were then to be nominated by the First Consul and confirmed by the pope. Lay elections of clergy, instituted during the Revolution, would end immediately; bishops and parish priests would once again be appointed from above, a hierarchical system that Bonaparte preferred. In fact, since French bishops were given the exclusive right to appoint their parish priests, the Concordat actually reinforced the hierarchical structure of church governance. Bonaparte seems to have reasoned that his control of the bishops also gave him control of the priests. The final concession he obtained from the Pope spoke volumes as to who was in control and to whom allegiances must ultimately be sworn: the entire French clergy were made to take an oath of loyalty to the regime, and public prayers for the well-being of the Consulate would be recited at the end of every Mass.

Bonaparte's desire to turn the Catholic Church into a useful "auxiliary" is made even more clear by the so-called "Organic Articles" that were appended to the Concordat just before it was announced. Without even consulting the pope, Bonaparte added seventy-seven articles, substantially expanding his own power at the pope's expense. Henceforth, no papal

[46] P.-L. Roederer, *Œuvres du Comte P.-L. Roederer* (Paris, 1853–1859), vol. III, p. 335.
[47] Thibaudeau, *Mémoires*, p. 152.

bulls or other communications would be published in France without government permission. Papal representatives would be required to have government authorization before engaging in any missions on French soil. Separately, Bonaparte curtailed the French Church's freedom of action by placing it under strict state supervision. Convocations of national councils needed prior government approval. The clergy was obliged to denounce all crimes to the police. They were also required to preach obedience to the government, and, in particular, to Bonaparte's conscription laws.

The Concordat with its Organic Articles did not just concern Roman Catholicism. The articles officially recognized French Protestantism and made provisions for paying salaries to French pastors as well as priests. For this, the 480,000 Calvinists and 200,000 Lutherans of France would be forever grateful to Bonaparte. However, elements of his "organization" and "discipline" of their churches, imposed without any real discussion or negotiation with the Protestant population, eventually drew criticism. One problem was that only Lutherans and Calvinists were given official recognition. Any other Protestant confession would only be *tolerated* by the state as long as it did not "disturb the public order." Secondly, Bonaparte imposed a hierarchical form of organization and adminis- tration on French Protestants that suited his designs, but that subverted traditional Calvinist practices and thus eventually irritated the Reformed community. Thirdly, his system made it very hard for Protestant churches to expand and develop. It recognized only one church per 6,000 parishioners and allowed only a fixed number of pastors. Any additional pastors required special government authorization. Finally, the Articles decreed that no "doctrinal or dogmatic decision" and no "formula [of confession]" could be promulgated without government approval, and that no "change of discipline" could be made without prior authorization. In effect, Bonaparte paralyzed the Protestant churches, severely curtailing their ability to govern themselves, to evolve over time, and to proselytize and gain converts.

Nevertheless, at least initially, Protestants welcomed the Organic Articles and lent their support to Bonaparte's regime. They were grateful for the unprecedented recognition and acceptance they received, and for the government funds that helped them to rebuild and reopen their churches. Bonaparte's motives were, of course, essentially political. Lacking any real interest in either theology or ecclesiology, he just wanted a clergy that he could control and that would help bolster his regime. Like Catholic priests, Protestant pastors now became salaried servants of the state; as such, they were required by law to lead their congregations in prayers for the prosperity of the French Republic and the consuls. As Madame de Staël bitterly remarked, Bonaparte wanted a clergy "the way one wants butlers or servants."[48]

It is likely that the average Frenchman hardly noticed the concessions made to Protestantism. To most people, the Concordat appeared as a huge victory for Catholicism. In reality, however, Bonaparte was the primary beneficiary. On Easter Sunday, 1802, the Law of Cults was solemnly promulgated in Paris. The same day, Napoleon ratified the Peace of Amiens that brought an end to the war with England. With pomp and ceremony, the leaders of the Consulate met in the cathedral of Notre Dame. There, a Mass was celebrated, a Te Deum sung, and a sermon delivered by the same archbishop who had presided at the coronation of Louis XVI. Church bells, which had not been rung for ten years, were heard in Paris. Catholics throughout France celebrated, while Idéologues looked on in horror.

FRIENDS AND FOES OF THE CONCORDAT: FROM THE *GÉNIE DU CHRISTIANISME* TO *DELPHINE*

The publication of Chateaubriand's *Génie du Christianisme* was perfectly timed to coincide with the celebrations of the Concordat, and could not have served Bonaparte's purposes better. After his return from exile, Chateaubriand had joined a neo-monarchist group led by Louis de Fontanes (1757–1821). Fontanes and his allies rallied to Bonaparte's regime in the hope that he would transform France into a Christian monarchy. To them, the Concordat was just a first step in this direction. A spectacular publishing success, the *Génie* promoted their religious and political agenda, and quickly became the symbol of the Catholic revival. It was also a direct and provocative attack on the critics and opponents of Bonaparte's religious policies, including the antireligious Idéologues as well as pro-Protestant thinkers like Madame de Staël and Benjamin Constant. One of Chateaubriand's main goals in writing the *Génie* was to counter Madame de Staël's enlightened and Protestant arguments.

The *Génie du Christianisme* is an emphatically Catholic book. Although Chateaubriand refers repeatedly to "Christianity," or to "the Christian Religion," it is obvious that he means Catholicism. And the Catholicism that he professes is neither enlightened nor modernized. To the contrary,

---

[48] De Staël, *Des considérations*, p. 374.

his book consistently expresses nostalgia for a bygone type of Catholicism, an idealized ancestral religion that never really existed, but that is beside the point. Over the course of hundreds of pages, Chateaubriand celebrates the aesthetic values and sheer poetry of "Christianity," while idealizing all of its traditions, mysteries, rites, and doctrines.

Chateaubriand's book was clearly not just a celebration of "Christianity"; it was also a promotion of Catholicism over Protestantism. It was no accident that the entire sixteenth century is labeled a "barbarous" century.[49] Nor is it by chance that Chateaubriand refers derisively to the disorder produced by religious "schism" and "heresy." "It is natural," he writes, "that schism leads to incredulity and that atheism follows heresy ... After Calvin came Bayle and Spinoza."[50] Finally, the book lambasts the notion of perfectibility. Thus, in a very real sense, Chateaubriand's *Génie du christianisme* was a refutation of de Staël's *De la littérature*.

As the journal *Mercure* had promised several months before, Chateaubriand deliberately chose not to use a rational language designed to *persuade* or *convince* his readers through argumentation. This would have been the "Protestant" way of doing things. Instead, Chateaubriand appealed to his readers' senses and sentiments. Human beings did not need rational proofs of religion, he contended; all they needed was to trust their own instincts and intuitions. Nor were they obliged to *understand* Catholicism; they only had to appreciate its beauty and poetic power. Any sincere person who opened his eyes, ears, and heart to Catholicism would immediately feel its power. Nothing was better suited to human nature. Chateaubriand ridiculed the idea that anything other than Catholicism could work with the French masses; moreover, he proffered that it would be cruel to deprive people of the consolations that only their ancestral religion could provide:

Let philosophy, which, after all, cannot penetrate the minds of the poor, content itself with inhabiting the salons of the rich, [but] let it at least allow the cottages their religion.[51]

After hundreds of pages of effusive praise for Catholicism, its traditions and structures, came what surely was a main point of the book. Repeating arguments often made in the Catholic press and echoing sentiments recently expressed by Portalis, Chateaubriand celebrated the *usefulness* and

---

[49] R. Chateaubriand, *Génie du christianisme*, ed. M. Regard (Paris, 1978), p. 643.
[50] Ibid., p. 467. [51] Ibid., p. 1090.

indispensability of Catholicism for the maintenance of public order. His statement provides a jarring contrast with the rest of the book and was designed, no doubt, to appeal to those with a more practical cast of mind:

> In the present state of society, could you repress an enormous mass of peasants – free and far away from the eye of the magistrate; could you, in the faubourgs of a large capital, prevent the crimes of an independent populace without a religion that preaches duties and virtue?[52]

Chateaubriand's message was stark: destroy Catholic worship, "and you will need a police, prisons, and an executioner in every village."[53]

The publication of *Génie du christianisme* was treated as a great literary event and the book was enormously successful. Reviews were overwhelmingly favorable; while praising Chateaubriand, they often took the opportunity to mock Protestantism, the Enlightenment, and rationalism, all of which were held to be inextricably connected. The *Moniteur universel*, official journal of the regime, republished a glowing review by Fontanes, indicating the *Génie's* usefulness to the government. The following year, Chateaubriand dedicated a second edition to Bonaparte. In "your destiny," the author gushed, "one cannot help but recognize the hand of Providence." In May 1803, Chateaubriand was named First Secretary of the French Embassy in Rome.[54]

Opponents of the Concordat fought back as best they could, although now they had to be careful not to attack Bonaparte or his government directly. The Institute immediately proposed as the subject for its next essay competition the question "What was the influence of Luther's Reformation on the political situation of the different states of Europe and on the progress of Enlightenment?" The announcement of the topic was timed to coincide with the publication of the *Génie du christianisme* and Portalis' announcement of the imminent passage of the Law on Cults. Thus, for the second time in two years, the National Institute posed a question that involved an assessment of Protestantism's relationship to Catholicism and historical progress. Of course, the Institute's views were already clear. Once again, the Institute would award first prize to an essay that extolled the intellectual, moral, and political effects of the Reformation.

---

[52] Ibid., p. 1089.   [53] Ibid.
[54] The fact was, however, that the book was not really a blanket endorsement of Bonaparte's policies. In many places in the *Génie*, Chateaubriand links Christianity with freedom, equality, the end of slavery, and the resistance to despotism.

The Idéologue journal *Décade philosophique* ran a lengthy review of the *Génie* that spanned three issues. It was written by its most talented literary critic, Pierre-Louis Guinguené (1748–1816); a virulent critic of Catholicism, he had previously defended radically anticlerical works. Guinguené had been Head of Public Instruction during the Directory and thereafter was elected to the Tribunate along with Constant. Like Constant, he distinguished himself as a critic of Bonaparte's regime. For this, he too was expelled in January 1802.

The main point of Guinguené's review was to repeat that Catholicism was fundamentally incompatible with a modern republic of reasonable men. Guinguené was especially keen to illustrate that Chateaubriand's religious ideals supported the politics of counter-revolutionaries. Faithful to the Idéologue perspective, Guinguené portrayed Catholicism as an utterly regressive religion, subversive of enlightened and republican values. Interestingly, however, Guinguené did not here portray himself as hostile to "Christianity." He conceded that it had rendered great services to humankind, and even suggested that it could still have favorable effects, particularly on morals. But for that to happen, Christianity had to return to its spirit and to its primitive character; in other words, Catholicism had to be reformed. Guinguené distinguished between "real piety"[55] and the silly and superstitious form of religion trumpeted by Chateaubriand.

Constant read and admired this review. In a letter to Fauriel, Constant praised Guinguené for the "moderation" of his tone and for his fairness. Clearly, Guinguené had been moved by "the force of truth, the love of philosophy and the Republic."[56] But these responses to Chateaubriand's book paled in comparison with Madame de Staël's novel *Delphine*, which came out in December 1802 and created as big a stir as the *Génie*. Through a tale of love and death, centered on an extraordinary woman, Madame de Staël delivered a thinly disguised political-religious message. Moreover, she did it by using the language of sentiments – by touching the hearts of her readers, rather than through academic argumentation.

Born a Catholic, Delphine is introduced to enlightened principles by her guardian, and becomes the practitioner of an enlightened type of religion. Having been taught to liberate herself from common prejudices by thinking for herself, she becomes fiercely independent, spontaneously

---

[55] *Coup-d'oeil rapide sur le Génie du christianisme, ou quelques pages sur les cinq volumes en-8* (Paris, 1802). This text comprises three articles that appeared in the *Décade philosophique*.

[56] Letter no. 958, "Benjamin Constant à Claude-Charles Fauriel," July 17, 1802, in OCBC *Correspondance générale* IV (1800–1802), p. 478.

generous, and extremely loyal to her friends. The story recounts her struggle with, and ultimate defeat by, the stultifying forces of tradition and convention, many of which have to do with Old Regime Catholicism allied with reactionary aristocratic values. Madame de Staël's liberal and pro-Protestant sentiments are more than evident throughout. While the superstition and bigotry of the Catholic Church are condemned, a very liberal Protestantism, close to Deism, is endorsed. The novel defends divorce, denounces monastic vows, and ends in a suicide.

The preface to *Delphine* explains de Staël's disagreement with the likes of the Idéologues, who disparage religion, and the likes of Chateaubriand, who espouse a dogmatic belief:

The great religious ideas – the existence of God, the immortality of the soul, and the union of these splendid hopes with morality – are so inseparable from all noble emotion, all musing and tender enthusiasm, that it would seem impossible to me for any novel, any tragedy, in sum any work of the imagination, to move people without their help ... But nothing is more opposed to imagination, just as it is thought, *than the dogmas of any sect* whatsoever.[57]

Thus, although de Staël appreciated "great religious ideas," she specifically distinguished them from "dogmas." What she favored were those religious ideas that were "understood by all men" and that could "speak to all hearts."[58]

Madame de Staël did not confine her critique of Napoleon's regime to its support for Catholicism. While Bonaparte was inviting emigrés back to France and regarded England as France's greatest enemy, the novel was clearly anti-emigré and showed great admiration for the English and their institutions. While Bonaparte reinstituted slavery in the colonies, de Staël painted slave-owners in a bad light. Interestingly, she spoke well of Germans, who were "distinguished by their enlightenment," and whose literature was as yet to be appreciated by the French. Throughout *Delphine*, stark contrasts are made between enlightened, generous, and emancipatory values and regressive, mean, and oppressive ones. Her friend Simonde de Sismondi (1773–1842) described this aspect of the novel well: "one of the principal actions of the novel [was] to make prejudices and liberal ideas collide."[59] For emphasis, de Staël dedicated her novel to the "France of silence and Enlightenment, to the future rather than to the past."

---

[57] G. de Staël, *Delphine*, trans. A. H. Goldberger (Dekalb, IL, 1995), p. 7, emphasis added.
[58] Ibid.
[59] As quoted by S. Balayé, "*Delphine*, roman des Lumières: pour une lecture politique," in Ch. Mervaud and S. Menant (eds.), *Le Siècle de Voltaire: Hommage à René Pomeau* (Oxford, 1987).

Delphine was tremendously successful: fifteen editions appeared between 1802 and 1820, and ten more between 1830 and 1883. It was also highly controversial, triggering some unusually violent and mean-spirited criticism from the Catholic press.[60] Joseph Fiévée (1767–1839), already known for his misogynist diatribes against de Staël, and now a secret adviser to Bonaparte, accused *Delphine* of being "a woman against nature." A flagrant Deist, her religion was so anemic, so personal and facile that, in the end, it was not a religion at all. Others joined Fiévée in denouncing the novel as fundamentally irreligious, immoral, and thus dangerous. Bonaparte soon made it known that de Staël would no longer be welcome in Paris, although he waited until October 15 before issuing an official decree to that effect.

Constant reacted to the occasion with a brilliantly sarcastic review;[61] while defending Madame de Staël, he derided her critics for their baseness, stupidity, and hypocrisy. Heaping ridicule on the enemies of Enlightenment, he denounced their anti-philosophic crusade using military metaphors that were not only biting, but also timely. He singled out for special rebuke the notion that *Delphine* might be an irreligious and thus immoral book. Clearly, Madame de Staël's critics were deliberately ignoring the difference between religion and dogma; only thus could they accuse the book's main character of lacking in religion. It was obvious that they were defending neither religion nor morality, but the power of priests. Mocking their hypocrisy, and using language dripping with sarcasm, Constant replied:

At a time when we are very religious, people have not failed to reproach Delphine for not having a religion; but, in fact, she does have religious ideas, though not properly speaking a religion. Or better yet, she believes in the religion of God and not the religion of priests . . . So why look for a fight on this issue? Is it not to proclaim that one cares less about the interests of morality and religion than one does about the interests of the priesthood?[62]

Another admirer of *Delphine* was Charles de Villers. In May 1803, he wrote Madame de Staël a long, exuberant, and complimentary letter.

---

[60] Critical reviews appeared in *Journal des débats*, the *Mercure* and the *Journal de Paris*. See the issue of *Cahiers staëliens* (26–27, 1979) dedicated to "La Réception de *Delphine*," and especially S. Balayé's article "Un emissaire de Bonaparte, Fiévée critique de Madame de Staël et de *Delphine*" (pp. 99–116). See also S. Balayé, "*Delphine* de Madame de Staël et la presse sous le Consulat," *Romantisme*, 51 (1986), pp. 39–47.

[61] On this, see S. Balayé, "A Propos de Benjamin Constant lecteur de *Delphine*," *Cahiers staëliens*, 26–27 (1979).

[62] OCBC *Œuvres* III, 2, p. 934.

Reminding her of his "infinite esteem" for *De la littérature*, he now compared her talents to Rousseau's. Again, he begged her to ignore her critics, "the obscure clique of hypocrites at the *Mercure* and the [*Journal des*] *Débats*," whose opinions he dismissed as "malicious stupidity." Villers reported that some of the hostility generated by the book was due to her favorable view of Protestantism; he added that he could hardly imagine their reception of his forthcoming essay on Luther.[63]

Villers was referring to the essay he had submitted to the National Institute's essay competition in March 1803. It not only won first prize, but launched a heated debate that would go on for several years. Although Villers had not managed to convert many members of the Institute to his brand of Kantianism in 1801, only a few years later, leading members of the Institute clearly thought that showcasing his views on the Reformation might deliver an important political message. In honoring him, they chose someone who was basically favorable to religion and critical of the Idéologues' sensationalism and utilitarianism. And yet Villers was also critical of Catholicism, which he regarded as a retrograde religion unable to promote the values a modern society so clearly needed. An altered context required a new strategy.

To Villers, the Reformation should be ranked among those world historical events "that have contributed the most powerfully to the progress of civilization and Enlightenment." For several centuries Europe had been submerged in a state of "stupor" and "apathy." The "spirit of Christ" had been lost, and a reformation was sorely needed. When it came, this Reformation gave "a new impetus" to everything, not just to religion.

In fact, Villers was not so interested in discussing religion *per se*. He expressed little if any interest in Martin Luther's theology. He mentioned no specific dogmatic controversies satisfactorily resolved by Lutheranism. Instead, he distilled what he regarded as the true import of the Reformation, in other words, its moral, intellectual, and political effects. Most importantly, the Reformation was about "intellectual emancipation." "In its principle," Villers claimed, "the Reformation was nothing else but the act by which reason declared itself free and emancipated from the yoke of arbitrary authority." Through the Reformation, the human spirit was liberated from the "exterior constraint imposed by hierarchical despotism" and the "inner constraint of apathy" caused by "blind superstition." Thanks to the movement inaugurated

---

[63] Letter no. 8, "Charles Villers à Madame de Staël," May 4, 1803 in KK, pp. 44–55. See also Letter no. 10, "Charles de Villers à Madame de Staël," June 24, 1803, ibid., pp. 54–56.

by Luther, man left his prior state of "tutelage" and began to use his faculties with more "freedom" and "energy." As minds became more "scrutinizing," morals improved.[64]

Inevitably, an event of such magnitude would have not only moral, but also political repercussions. Due to the Reformation, "one dared to think, reason, examine that which previously allowed only for a blind submission." What started as a simple blow to the ecclesiastical system thus "brought about a considerable change in the political situation." People's minds were "opened to new political ideas"; they became more receptive to ideas conducive to liberty. Freedom in the intellectual and religious realm fostered freedom in the political.[65]

Villers believed that, in their inner core, the "spirit" of all religions was exactly "the same." These were the moral laws and duties that are "engraved on all human hearts." But religions, he noted, are composed of more than inner spirit. They also have "an exterior form," in other words, they manifest themselves historically as specific doctrines and practices. Repeating the point made in his earlier essay on Kant, Villers declared that this "exterior" aspect of religion was meant to evolve over time. Here, Villers' Kantianism and his exposure to the enlightened German notion of progressive revelation becomes particularly evident. Like Kant, Villers believed that there was an important distinction between what Kant referred to as "pure religious faith," which had to do with moral dispositions, and was natural and universal, and "ecclesiastical faith," which had to do with the senses, and was grounded in empirical and historical conditions. Ecclesiastical faith was the "vehicle" for pure religious faith. According to Kant, for a church to be true, it had to recognize this, and allow its doctrines and practices to evolve over time.[66]

Inspired by Kant and the new German theology, Villers argued that as people evolve and become enlightened, they will prefer simpler forms of religion. The more they develop their intellectual faculties at the expense of their senses, the less they will want elaborate ceremonies and rituals. The historical trend or "march" of religion was therefore to become ever simpler, "more austere and more intellectual" over time. All of this conformed with "the beautiful concept of the perfectibility of our species" which was why the Protestant religion was a higher form of religion than

---

[64] Ch. de Villers, *Essai sur l'esprit et l'influence de la Réformation de Luther. Ouvrage qui a remporté le prix sur cette question proposée dans la séance publique du 15 germinal an X, par l'Institut national de France: "Quelle a été l'influence de la réformation de Luther sur la situation politique des différens Etats de l'Europe, et sur le progrès des lumières?"* (Paris, 1804), pp. 226, 3, 298, 358, 284.

[65] Ibid., pp. 3, 226.   [66] Ibid., pp. 25, 26.

Catholicism. Protestantism kept "the living spirit of religion alive" by contributing to mankind's goal of "gradual cultivation" and the "constant improvement" of man's institutions, both political and religious.[67]

In the end, Villers' essay was of course as much about France and Catholicism as it was about Germany and the Reformation. On every point that he raised, he offered Protestant Germany as an alternative to France. If German Protestantism favored progress through its encouragement of intellectual freedom, moral responsibility, and political liberty, French Catholicism offered regression by encouraging intellectual bondage, moral despondence, and authoritarian rule. In fact, Villers put into words what many people had been thinking for some time, in particular, Madame de Staël and Benjamin Constant. Due to Catholicism, France remained intellectually and morally immature.

By awarding Villers' essay on the Reformation the first prize, the National Institute sent an unmistakable political message. The government's promotion of Catholicism was both religiously and politically regressive. It went against the natural course of history, which, for them, was towards greater liberty and enlightenment. The Institute showed how very much its members disapproved of Bonaparte's deal with the papacy, and how worried they were about the future of intellectual and political freedom in France.

CONSTANT'S TRIP TO GERMANY

For Madame de Staël, the hostile reception of *Delphine* spelled disaster. Only a few months earlier, her father had published his *Dernières vues de politique et de finances*. Interpreting Madame de Staël's novel as yet another attack from the same family, Bonaparte formally decreed de Staël's exile on October 15, 1803. The same day, she wrote to Villers to let him know that she would spend the winter in Germany.

Actually, de Staël had been planning a trip to Germany for some time; already in August 1802, she had told Villers that she was studying German. She was convinced that only in Germany could she find "new ideas and profound sentiments." "Like you," she wrote, "I believe that the human spirit seems to travel from country to country and is at present in Germany."[68] His career in politics forestalled, Constant decided to return to his book on religion and accompany her. On their way, they took the

---

[67] Ibid., pp. 298, 284, 21, 24.
[68] Letter no. 2, "Madame de Staël à Charles de Villers," August 1, 1802, in KK, p. 21.

opportunity to visit Villers in Metz. Although they originally planned only a short stopover, they enjoyed his company and conversation so much that they stayed for two weeks.

Now, it was Constant's turn to befriend Villers. The two shared many intellectual interests, a common outlook, and a fondness for Madame de Staël. Together, they could discuss their research on religion and history, and talk about Kant and Germany's new Protestant theology. During these two weeks, Villers no doubt discussed his views on Luther and the Reformation. So when some months later, he sent Constant a published copy of his *Essai sur l'esprit et l'influence de la Réformation de Luther*, Constant would have been familiar with its arguments. In his letter of thanks to Villers for his "excellent book," Constant describes his great pleasure, not just in being able to read the finished work, but also in knowing that the Institute had "dared to be just" in awarding Villers its first prize. Thanks to Villers, Constant now had the "courage to continue" his own work on religion.[69]

From surviving manuscripts of this period and Constant's *Journal intime* (begun in Weimar in 1804), it is possible to get a picture of Constant's state of mind at this point in time. Despite his frustration with events in France, he retained his faith in historical progress. He continued to believe in the forward "march of humankind," or what he also referred to as the "march of liberty." Over the course of history, there were momentary reverses and an occasional "retrograde impulsion"; but, soon thereafter, the forward "march" of history would resume. He believed that "everything in nature has its march. Men follow it, accelerate it, or retard it, but they can't escape it." Indeed, "all human things" participate in the "progress of civilization"; if religion has its forward "march," so have "equality" and the "fondness for political liberty." The future will be more enlightened, egalitarian, free, and moral than the past.[70]

His writings from this period suggest that Constant not only believed in progress, but also considered the belief itself as valuable. Viewing history in a broader perspective and recognizing the larger trends at work provided an effective remedy to the disappointment one feels at difficult moments. This was also why Constant thought it important to propagate the idea of progress. People needed to know of history's inexorable

---

[69] Letter no. 29, "Benjamin Constant à Charles de Villers," 26 May 1804, ibid., p. 91.
[70] "Fragments d'un essai sur la perfectibilité de l'espèce humaine," OCBC *Œuvres* III, 1, pp. 441, 443, 451, 370.

advance so that they might align themselves with the right historical forces. They should be made to understand the march of history, thus avoiding "useless resistance," "wrong-minded efforts," and "horrible calamities." Both the "winners" and the "losers" of history needed to be properly educated in long-term historical trends to know how best to act. "Everyone has an equal need to be instructed in the outcome."[71]

Constant's journal indicates that his visit to Germany in 1803–4 was an extremely fertile period for his thinking about religion; while there, he worked intensively on the book that would become *De la religion*. Spending most of his time in Weimar, Constant met prominent German intellectuals like Goethe, Schiller, Wieland, the Schlegels, and Schelling. His journal records his numerous conversations and his exposure to influential German texts such as, for example, Herder's *Ideen zur Philosophie der Geschichte der Menschheit*. From German scholarship, Constant drew not only a myriad of distinctive ideas and facts, but also crucial conceptual tools that he would apply to his own work. Perhaps most significantly, Constant once again imbibed the influence of Germany's liberal Protestant theologians. Again, he was exposed to the notion of "progressive revelation," the idea that religion was "perfectible" and destined to improve over time. This was an idea to which he had been exposed in Brunswick in the company of Jakob Mauvillon, and that recently had been restated by Charles de Villers.

Although Constant published nothing on religion during this period, his journal contains the concept that religions, in tune with general historical trends, are subject to progress over time. On September 16, 1804 he writes that after asserting "certain basic principles," his book will describe the "natural march of religious ideas."[72] Additionally, early drafts of an essay published only in 1829 indicate his belief that religious ideas were meant to "develop progressively" in accordance with the needs of each epoch.[73] One draft begins by proclaiming the moral superiority of Protestants over Catholics. The main difference between the two, Constant argues, is not just that there are fewer dogmas in Protestantism. The critical distinguishing factor is that Protestantism recognizes "the right that each person has to examine what he must believe."[74]

[71] Ibid., pp. 368, 445, 446.   [72] JI, September 16, 1804, p. 213.
[73] "Fragments," in OCBC *Œuvres* III, 1, p. 444.
[74] As quoted by Deguise, *Benjamin Constant méconnu*, p. 62.

THE SENTIMENT/FORM DISTINCTION

Another significant development documented in his journal is Constant's acquisition of a critical component of his mature religious thought: the distinction between religious "sentiment" and religious "forms." Constant's diary entry on February 18, 1804 records that he has had a fruitful discussion with the German poet Christoff Martin Wieland and that he approves of a distinction made between "religious sentiment" and "positive religions." This is a distinction that he must be sure to "retain."[75] Understandably, scholars have seized upon this as a crucial moment in Constant's intellectual evolution, since his fully developed theory of religious progress would revolve around this distinction.[76]

While Constant's conversation with Wieland may have been stimulating, the idea that religion was a matter of "form" and "sentiment" had become relatively commonplace in France by 1804. Rousseau's Savoyard Vicar in *Emile* (1762) differentiated between religion as "inner sentiment" and "exterior cult." Thereafter, both Protestant and Catholic apologists were quick to seize on religious "sentiment" as the essence of religion, while they also insisted that it needed to take concrete shape in an "exterior cult" or "form."[77] That religious sentiments were somehow natural to man, and that they could serve as a means with which to moralize him, was widely acknowledged during the French Revolution by key politicians, such as Robespierre, Necker, La Reveillère-Lépeaux, and Portalis.[78] Therefore, one should not exaggerate the importance of this moment in Constant's intellectual development. Constant did not need to go to Weimar to discover either the notion of "religious sentiment" or the idea of positive "forms." Neither did he need to go there for the idea of progressive revelation, as was pointed out above. Rather, his conversation with Wieland helped crystallize in his mind the somewhat

---

[75] JI, February 18, 1804, p. 71.

[76] Kloocke thinks the sentiment/form distinction comes from Kant, and that Constant may have acquired it already in Brunswick (see "Religion et société," p. 124), but J. Lee emphasizes its connection with the conversation with Wieland in "An Answer to the Question: What is Liberalism? Benjamin Constant and Germany," ABC, 29 (2005), p. 132. Constant never used the sentiment/form distinction before then. See also Lee, "Moralization," which accentuates its "distinctively German lineage" (p. 223) and affirms that it comes from Wieland and Herder (p. 214).

[77] On this see H. Rosenblatt, "The Christian Enlightenment," in T. Tackett and S. Brown (eds.), *The Cambridge History of Christianity*, vol. VII: *Enlightenment, Revolution and Reawakening (1660–1815)* (Cambridge, 2006), pp. 283–301.

[78] Livesey, *Making Democracy*, p. 51, calls "sentiment" the most important republican term during the 1790s.

disparate thoughts and concepts that he had been mulling over for some time.

Several scholars have highlighted Constant's extensive reliance on German sources for his book on religion.[79] Indeed, most of the research was done in Brunswick (1794), Weimar (1803–4) and Göttingen (1812–13). In Germany, Constant found excellent libraries, an abundance of works of erudition unavailable in France, and, perhaps most crucially, an atmosphere conducive to scholarship in religion. German Protestants had found a way to overcome a divisive rift that existed in France; they had found an ability to combine philosophy and religion in a synthesis that was respectful of both. Constant attributed this to the founding principle of their religion: "the application of free inquiry to religion." This was why works by German Protestants tended to be "very liberal in their principles."[80]

While Germany was undoubtedly a valuable source for Constant, one should bear in mind that throughout this period he always kept one eye trained on France and kept himself informed. A journal entry from September 5, 1804 records that he had read the *Mercure*'s biting critique of Villers' essay on the Reformation. Its virulence caused Constant to ponder the enormous changes in France's political and religious climate. During the most radical phase of the Revolution, when religion was being brutally attacked, Catholics could only contemplate modest demands; they would have been grateful simply for an abatement of their perse-cution and would have appreciated the book Constant was writing. Now, however, activist Catholics had become arrogant and aggressive. They were even "preaching despotism and superstition, without bothering to disguise their intentions."[81] Constant was shocked by the "fury" of Villers' critics. Regrettably, France was now allowing such men to become numerous and self-confident.

Constant's journal entry confirms that his book on religion was intended to contribute to *French* debates on religion and politics, and that these were connected in his mind. His journal further shows that he was mindful of the dictates of French public opinion, noting, for example, that present circumstances were unfavorable to his book and that he must wait for better times. The only thing that could be done now was "to defend Protestantism ... while *concealing* its principle of free examination."[82]

---

[79] In particular, K. Kloocke and J. Lee.   [80] JI, Ibid., March 27, 1804, p. 94.
[81] Ibid., September 5, 1804, p. 204.   [82] Ibid., my emphasis.

Constant made several positions clear in these journal entries. The first was his abiding distaste for dogmatic or "positive religions." Another was his approval that "the Protestant religion in Germany is every day becoming more of a sentiment than an institution." Happily, German Protestantism was casting off its "forms," "symbols," and "ceremonies" and admitting "only gentle ideas and a sensible morality."[83] In contrast, Constant regretted the wrong-headed French discourse on religion. The debate revolved around a false choice between Catholicism and Protestantism:

One is led to believe that it is all about knowing what to choose from Protestantism and what from Catholicism, when there was every reason to believe that we were rid of them both.[84]

For Constant, Protestantism was an improvement upon Catholicism, but it was only a stage which was meant to enable further improvements over time.

Although Constant continued to dislike "positive" religions, the concept of "sentiment" allowed him to adopt a more favorable attitude towards religion in general. The "forms" could be regressive, but this was not necessarily true of religious "sentiment." He now realized that it was possible to reject dogmatic religions and at the same time avoid "the brutality of atheism."[85] In February 1804, he recorded that he did not want to make his book "directly irreligious"; "[T]here is in irreligion something vulgar, hackneyed and repugnant to me."[86] Around the same time, Constant came to realize that he, himself, was not devoid of certain religious sentiments or feelings. On February 19, 1804, he confided: "I have my own corner of religion. But it is all about sentiment, vague emotions: it cannot be reduced to a system."[87] By November 1804, Constant could even reflect on the eighteenth century's peculiar, and, in his mind, unfortunate attitude towards "received prejudices":

What a strange philosophy, in truth, was that of the eighteenth century, poking fun at itself and others, setting out to discredit not only received prejudices, not only the consoling or moral ideas that could have been separated from them, but also mocking its own principles, taking pleasure in sparing nothing from ridicule, in degrading and cheapening everything! When you read the works of that period carefully, you are surprised neither at what came after nor its consequences today. They were men who lived for the moment, limiting their existence and influence to that moment, writing only to encourage the next

[83] Ibid., February 4, 1804, p. 59.　[84] Ibid., September 5, 1804, p. 204.
[85] Ibid., February 18, 1804, p. 71.　[86] Ibid., February 19, 1805, p. 330.　[87] Ibid.

generation in selfishness and degradation, a generation which has certainly
profited from their lessons.[88]

RETURN TO PARIS AND THE DEBATE ON A NATIONAL RELIGION

Upon his return to Paris in December 1804, Constant found Franco-papal
relations at a highpoint. Earlier the same month, on December 2, the Pope
had presided over Napoleon's coronation as Emperor in Notre Dame
Cathedral. The Pope remained in France for almost six months, his
popularity soaring. Described as a triumph, his visit further stimulated the
Catholic revival and lent considerable prestige to Napoleon. This was
indeed a honeymoon period for Napoleon and the Catholic Church; it
was a time when their collaboration effectively restored something like a
Christian monarchy to France. From Constant's point of view, however,
everything that he, Madame de Staël, and their allies had feared was
coming true. An increasingly authoritarian regime was using a retrograde
religion to legitimize and strengthen its power. Furthermore, it was rapidly
becoming impossible for anyone to offer effective resistance to Napoleon,
due to his use of censorship and the changing mood in France.

Even before the Pope's visit, the tightening bond between the Church
and Napoleon had emboldened some Catholics to press for changes in
church–state relations. They argued that the Concordat had not gone far
enough towards reinstating Catholicism and that it was time to recognize it
officially as France's "dominant" or "state" religion. The theologian
Mathieu Mathurin Tabaraud (1744–1832) declared that revolutionary policies towards the Church had been entirely wrong-headed at their inception
and should be corrected once and for all. The National Assembly had been
mistaken when it listened to Rabaut Saint-Etienne's arguments for religious
toleration and had recognized Protestantism's right to exist. In Tabaraud's
mind, "philosophy and the Protestant religion" had then joined together to
"destroy" Catholicism, using the pretext of religious toleration. In reality, he
argued, religious toleration led only to "absolute religious indifference," in
other words, Deism. To prevent this calamity, Catholicism should be
proclaimed France's national religion.[89]

With the news of the Pope's impending visit for the coronation,
expectations rose that Napoleon would indeed take additional steps in
favor of Catholicism. The Pope himself raised the issue several times in

[88] Ibid., November 21, 1804, p. 260
[89] M. Tabaraud, *De la nécessité d'une religion de l'état* (Paris, 1803), p. 2.

the negotiations before his trip.[90] Then, suddenly, the Archbishop of Besançon, Claude Le Coz, seized the initiative and sent what can only be described as a very cheeky letter to the Protestant pastors of Paris. He bluntly proposed that France's Catholic and Protestant churches join together in one church. He urged Protestant leaders to take advantage of the opportunity presented by the Pope's upcoming visit. Since "religion and the fatherland" would soon act in concert to proclaim Napoleon Emperor, was this not the right moment for Catholics and Protestants to unite? "See our arms extended to receive you," he beseeched them, "see our hearts burning with fraternal charity."[91]

In responding, the leading Protestant pastor of Paris, Paul-Henri Marron (1754–1832), chose his words carefully. In a speech expressing gratitude for the Concordat and Organic Articles delivered in April 1802, he had earlier praised Napoleon publicly for maintaining a "balance" between the "various forms" of Christianity existing in France.[92] Marron had expressed his hope that religion would bring the French people together, and that no mere "difference of [religious]opinion," nor "nuance of rites" would "trouble the harmony of hearts."[93] Now, in answer to the Archbishop's entreaty, Marron professed wholehearted agreement with the principle of Christian union. He claimed to have been pressing for it himself, and that this was the reason he had been using Jacob Vernes' ecumenical catechism.[94] However, Marron cautioned against any "act of authority"[95] to accomplish this goal and disagreed with the Archbishop's manner of proceeding. By offering no doctrinal concessions to Protestants, all the Archbishop was really doing was inviting Protestants to convert to Catholicism. This was not the path to a *rapprochement*.

In any case, Marron was pessimistic about the possibility of coming to terms on doctrine. He had come to believe that a "perfect uniformity of opinion in matters of faith" was "an impossible thing." This being the case, French Protestants and Catholics should give up trying to agree on dogma. Rather, they should move towards a unity "not of ideas, but of affection." Religious freedom and mutual toleration were the best policies for French Christians; the French should learn to tolerate "simple

---

[90] A. Latreille, *Napoléon et le Saint-Siège: 1801–1808, l'ambassade du cardinal Fesch à Rome* (Paris, 1935), pp. 366, 370, 389.

[91] Letter from Mgr. L'Archevêque de Besançon (November 8, 1804), reproduced in *Détails, historiques*, (Paris, 1806) pp. 152, 155.

[92] P.-H. Masson, *Discours sur le rétablissement de la religion; prononcé dans le temple des protestants de Paris, le Dimanche 5 floréal, an X* (April 25, 1802) p. 19.

[93] Ibid., p. 15.   [94] Letter by P.-H. Marron, reproduced in *Détails*, p. 166.   [95] Ibid., p. 167.

nuances of opinion [and] differently modified rites."[96] It is a remarkable testimony to the liberal and undogmatic variety of Protestantism being preached in France at the time that this leading Protestant minister could refer to dogmatic differences between Catholics and Protestants as "simple nuances of opinion."

The pastors Rabaut-Pomier and Mestrezat responded similarly to the Archbishop's letter. They agreed that reunion would *in principle* be a good thing, but were quick to add that "public opinion"[97] had to be fully behind it. In the meantime, freedom of religion and mutual toleration were the most sensible policies; they would ensure peaceful cohabitation by Catholics and Protestants, and have additional social benefits. Here again, the arguments made by Protestant ministers sound surprisingly secular. The existence of several Christian denominations would have advantageous moral effects, the pastors argued, because it would promote "mutual surveillance" between the sects and thereby stimulate "virtuous and civic emulation."[98]

Writing in a similar vein, another Protestant pastor noted that differences of "religious opinions" would always exist among Christians. Such differences were the inevitable result of "the development of [man's] intellectual faculties." In answer to the Archbishop, he replied that it was unrealistic to think that Protestants would suddenly agree to become Catholics in order to promote Christian unity. There had to be some other basis. In any case, Christianity was not really about "the subtleties of an obscure metaphysics"; nor was it about the mere "details of faith" or "nuances" of opinion. What really mattered to Christians was something about which they could all agree, something related to *morals* – "the sentiments of the heart." This was also why freedom of religion was so crucial, and why it would eventually bind Christians together. It was imperative to have patience, to let freedom of religion take effect, and to allow "Enlightenment" to spread. This was the only real way of promoting Christian unity.[99]

It was in the context of these discussions about Christian union that Constant's friend, Charles de Villers, published a new edition of his award-winning *Essay on Luther*. In so doing, he reminded the reading public of what he regarded as the positive effects of the Reformation. Villers' new preface underscored his agreement with French Protestants

---

[96] Ibid., pp. 169, 170, 167.
[97] Letter by Rabaut-Pomier and Mestrezat, reproduced in *Détails*, p. 172.   [98] Ibid., p. 175.
[99] Letter by M. Molines, reproduced in *Détails*, pp. 179, 181.

on the question of religious unity. To Villers, the Reformation's promotion of the "spirit of free inquiry" had instigated a flow of moral and political benefits. It was this principle of free inquiry that allowed religions and societies to improve over time. Therefore, what was essential was not so much the pursuit of religious *unity* as the putting in place of a mechanism that would allow for freedom of inquiry and the progressive evolution of religion. Villers' preface suggested that the current talk of unity was somewhat irrelevant to the most pressing matter at hand.

Not surprisingly, Villers' publication aroused furious responses from French Catholics and triggered a debate that would go on for several years. A review in the *Journal des débats* was particularly nasty: it accused Villers of "ignorance," "imbecility," "ineptitude," and "bad faith."[100] Protestant newspapers hastened to defend him. In the name of "decency" and "outraged truth," the *Citoyen français* praised "the incontestable merits" of Villers' essay. Villers himself responded, expressing particular outrage at the accusation that he lacked patriotism because of his stance on Protestantism.[101]

A public "Letter to M. Charles de Villers" summarized some of the Catholics' principal arguments. According to its author, Villers had misrepresented the "spirit of Christianity" when he associated it with the Protestant Reformation rather than with Catholicism. The true spirit of Christianity and the "goal of Jesus" was not "freedom of inquiry"; rather, it was "the establishment of *unity* in the human family." By shattering this unity and giving birth to "a multitude of sects," the Protestant Reformation had been the cause of "trouble" all across Europe. Repeating age-old arguments, Villers' critic accused Protestantism of fostering "the spirit of independence," "republicanism," and "democratic" inclinations, all of which did not prevent it, "by a singular contradiction," from also being conducive to "despotism."[102]

Another one of the letter's repackaged accusations against Protestantism was that it fostered selfishness. In his *History of the Variations of the Protestant Churches* (1688), the Catholic polemicist Jacques-Benigne Bossuet (1627–1704) frequently used the term "self-love [*amour-propre*]"

---

[100] On the hostile reception given to Villers' essay, see Wittmer, *Charles de Villers*, pp. 218–228 and *Le Citoyen français, journal politique, commercial, littéraire*, etc., no. 1739 (11 Fructidor, Year XII), p. 3.

[101] *Le Citoyen français*, no. 1739, p. 3. See also *Le Publiciste*, 30 Messidor, Year XII (July 19, 1804), p. 4. Villers responded in *Le Publiciste*, Fructidor, Year XII (August 29, 1804), p. 4.

[102] L. M. P. Tranchant de Laverne, *Lettre à M. Charles Villers relativement à son Essai sur l'esprit et l'influence de la Réformation de Luther* (Paris, 1804), pp. 5, 29, 24, 25, 28, 61.

to characterize Protestantism. In fostering "the spirit of independence," and ostensibly encouraging "private judgement," Bossuet argued that what Protestants were really doing was putting their love of self before the love of God.[103] Villers' respondent now modernized this argument to tap into contemporary fears. The "essence" of Protestantism, he claimed, was materialism; its direct effect was "to attach men to temporal goods." Although he professed to admire the "commercial, manufacturing, and productive genius" of Protestants, he was also certain that the end result of all of their activity would be to encourage "egoism" in the population. The industry fostered by Protestantism "favored the taste for exclusive pleasures" and encouraged men to turn inwards; thus, the overall effect of Protestantism was "to concentrate man in himself." Under its influence, men became "selfish, calculating and cold." For all these reasons, the Reformation could not possibly advance civilization as Villers claimed; rather its influence was clearly to retard it.[104]

There is no evidence that Napoleon ever seriously entertained the idea of proclaiming a unified state religion during this time. Instead, he deliberately designed his coronation as an ecumenical event. Presidents of the Reformed churches' consistories were invited and a pastor from Geneva delivered a speech on their behalf. Of course, the Pope presided over the most important part of the ceremony. Indeed, most Frenchmen, not privy to the discussions on Protestantism, probably saw the coronation as a victory for Catholicism; it testified to the great prestige and singular importance of the Roman Catholic religion in France.

Napoleon had every reason to be pleased with the cooperation he was receiving from the Catholic Church. Almost all French bishops attended his coronation and support for his regime, among the high clergy, was nearly unanimous. Indeed, most bishops openly demonstrated their loyalty to the Emperor, calling for prayers for his armies' continued success and thanksgiving upon the birth of his son. Thus, Napoleon's strategy appeared to be working. Under the circumstances, there was no longer cause for concern over the opposition of priests. They were "behaving very well and were a great help."[105] The tightening alliance between political

---

[103] L. Dickey "Saint-Simonian Industrialism as the End of History: August Cieszkowski on the Teleology of Universal History," in M. Bull (ed.), *Apocalypse Theory and the Ends of the World* (Oxford, 1995), p. 187.

[104] Laverne, *Lettre*, pp. 50, 51, 52, 32.

[105] Latreille *et al.*, *Histoire du catholicisme en France*, vol. III, p. 192.

and religious institutions culminated in the Imperial Catechism of 1806. Designed for use throughout France, it contained the following lines:

Question: Are there special reasons why we should have a particular loyalty to Napoleon I, our emperor?

Answer: Yes there are; for God raised him up in difficult times to re-establish the public practice of the holy religion of our ancestors, and to protect it. He restored and preserved public order by his deep and active wisdom; he defends the state by the strength of his arm; he has become the Lord's Anointed by the consecration he received from the Sovereign pontiff, the head of the Church Universal.

Question: What ought one to think of those who fail in their duty towards our emperor?

Answer: According to the Apostle Saint Paul they are resisting the order established by God Himself and making themselves worthy of eternal damnation.[106]

Looking back at this early period, Napoleon's Minister of Religion, Portalis, recalled that French bishops had "distinguished themselves" by their helpfulness. Especially when it came to military conscription, they had allowed it to be carried out "much faster and with fewer obstacles" than ever before.[107] In fact, French bishops became some of the most vocal apologists for Napoleon's reign. Their pastoral letters accentuated his role as restorer of religion. They often glorified him with the name "new Cyrus" in memory of the Persian king who, in 538 BC, allowed the Jews to re-enter Palestine. Moreover, from 1803 on, the theme of war was omnipresent in the writings of French bishops, who elaborated a veritable "theology of war" in support of Napoleon's strategy of conquest. Their discourse frequently referred to great war heroes and founders of dynasties, such as Alexander the Great, Augustus, and Clovis. All of this evoked thoughts of a holy war or crusade. Napoleon's wars were presented as just wars, undertaken in order to defend a sacred cause.[108]

Meanwhile, some prominent Catholics had not given up the hope of unifying all Christian churches under the banner of Catholicism. In articles published in the *Mercure de France* on July 2 and August 1, 1806, Louis de Bonald invited Napoleon to accomplish the "re-absorption" of French Protestants into the French Catholic Church. Anxious to refute

---

[106] Cited in Hales, *Napoleon and the Pope*, pp. 89–90.

[107] "Rapport du ministre des cultes, Portalis, à l'empereur," January 28, 1806, as quoted by J.-O. Boudon, *Napoléon et les cultes* (Paris, 2002), p. 141.

[108] J.-P. Bertho, "Naissance et élaboration d'une 'théologie' de la guerre chez les évêques de Napoléon (1802–1820)," in J.-R. Derré *et al.* (eds.), *Civilisation chrétienne: Approche historique d'une idéologie* (Paris, 1975).

the ideas of Villers in particular, Bonald argued that religious divisions created "a state of death," while religious unity was the "one great need of civilized society." He felt certain that it would be relatively easy for the Catholic Church to reabsorb Protestants, since their theology had been considerably "softened" in recent times. In any case, Protestantism was bound to disappear soon, since the "political unity" towards which Europe was moving under Napoleon would inevitably lead to religious unity as well. This was good news, since everybody knew that Catholicism was much better suited to monarchical government than Protestantism.[109]

But soon Catholics were not the only ones to clamor for a national religion. Protestants would play the same game and take the initiative towards a Christian reunion. After Napoleon's coronation, his relations with the Pope began to deteriorate and, over time, became tense and acrimonious. A main source of friction was the Emperor's expansionist foreign policy and his insistence on extending the reach of his Napoleonic Code. By 1808, he had occupied the papal states and reduced the Pope to a virtual prisoner. The following year, Napoleon simply annexed the papal states to the French Empire. The Pope responded by excommunicating him.

The worsening Franco-papal relations presented a unique opportunity for politically astute French Protestants. They seized the moment by proposing their own projects for reunion. In 1806, the Protestant jurist, Liquois de Beaufort published a *Projet de réunion de toutes les communions chrétiennes*. Referring derisively to the Pope as "that criminal pontiff," Beaufort urged Napoleon to consider something akin to a "second concordat," this one with distinctly Protestant overtones. Beaufort insisted that the Reformation had not been properly understood; in reality, its "principal goal" had been "the reunion of the spiritual and temporal powers" in the hands of the sovereign. The timing was auspicious for Napoleon to place himself at the head of a reformed national church. This would add to his glory and ensure that his administration "would never be thwarted by a foreign sovereign's will." The reunion of the Christian churches would in effect create a "national religion," which would foster the "national virtues and morals" that France needed.[110]

---

[109] L. de Bonald, "De l'unité religieuse en Europe," in *Œuvres complètes*, vol. X: *Mélanges littéraires, politiques et philosophiques* (Geneva, 1982), pp. 229–283.

[110] *Projet de réunion de toutes les communions chrétiennes ... par M. de Beaufort, Jurisconsulte* (Paris, 1806), pp. 22, 28, 24, 7, 25, 48.

Similar motives inspired the Protestant leader Rabaut *le jeune* (1746–1808) to publish *Détails historiques.*[111] In it, Rabaut recounted the many failed efforts to unite the Christian churches throughout history. Reprinting documents chronicling these attempts, he declared that "the great Napoleon" could succeed where others had failed. To accomplish this signal "triumph" for humanity, the Emperor had to learn from the errors of the past, while taking advantage of present opportunities. Religious toleration was now firmly established in France, as was the "imprescriptible dogma of freedom of thought." "Enlightenment" and "liberal ideas" had replaced "fanaticism" and "superstition." Thanks to all of this, the separate Christian denominations lived peacefully side by side. These were the facts that should inform any realistic and "liberal" project of religious reunion.[112]

Like other prominent Protestants of his time, Rabaut believed that a "perfect uniformity or opinion" in religious matters was simply "impossible" to realize. It was "crazy" to think that a Christian community would suddenly agree to adopt the religious doctrines of another. This, however, need not be a problem. The differences between sects were not "essential" to "real religion" anyway. The variations concerned either "abstract" and "impenetrable" issues, or involved "indifferent matters," having nothing to do with "real piety." Modern Christians should simply focus on celebrating a cult in common "without involving themselves with the inner consciences" of their neighbors. Freedom of religion was the key to Christian unity.[113]

Such arguments were bound to frustrate and even infuriate Catholics. According to Tabaraud, they were just another manifestation of an ongoing Protestant "conspiracy"[114] against French Catholicism. In reality, Protestants had no religion at all, since they no longer cared about dogma and had given up on religious truth. Their position was akin to religious indifference and their proposed unification was only an invitation for Catholics to participate in their own destruction. Agreeing with Bonald and other ardent Catholics, Tabaraud insisted that what France needed was not religious indifference, but religious unity.

Constant was well informed on these debates. First, he was close with Charles de Villers, whose essay on Luther was at the center of the

---

[111] The full title is *Détails historiques et recueil de pièces sur les divers projets de réunion de toutes les communions chrétiennes, qui ont été conçus depuis la Réformation jusqu'à ce jour par M. Rabaut le jeune.*
[112] *Détails historiques*, pp. xj, viii–ix, xj, viii, vij.   [113] Ibid., p. 137.
[114] M. Tabaraud, *De la réunion des communions chrétiennes* (Paris, 1808), p. 450.

controversy. Constant's journal shows that after his return to Paris in December 1804, he frequently dined with Villers. Second, Constant's interests in the history of religion would have predisposed him to pay close attention to these discussions. And finally, we have specific proof that he did, since he wrote a review of Rabaut's *Détails historiques*, which he thought important enough to include in an outline of his *Principles of Politics* (1806–10).

Not surprisingly, Constant took a distinctly Protestant and liberal position on the issue of Christian unification. What Rabaut proved was that reunification on the basis of shared dogma would never work. What the Catholics were proposing was disingenuous, since they were, in effect, inviting Protestants to convert to Catholicism. This would never happen. The only *rapprochement* possible would not be based on dogma, but rather on shared sentiments felt by human "hearts."[115]

Constant also knew the arguments being made against religion by unrepentant Idéologues like Destutt de Tracy. Constant's diary shows that he was alternating between dinners with Villers and the Idéologues during this period. At the height of the controversy, Tracy reissued his *Analyse raisonnée de l'origine de tous les cultes* (1804). Tracy's book had originally appeared as a review of Charles Dupuis' *Abrégé de l'origine de tous les cultes* in the *Mercure français* and had been published as a booklet in 1799. In the new edition, Tracy reiterated his admiration for Dupuis' work, in which the renowned atheist argued that all religions, including Christianity, were nothing but variations on pagan sun worship. In typical Idéologue fashion, Tracy denied the spirituality of the soul and refused to concede that there was any social benefit to Christianity at all. To Tracy, Christianity was simply "a bad moral system based on a defective reasoning that spoils the mind."[116] To those who would argue for Christianity's political "utility," Tracy replied that it was not necessary "to deceive" uneducated men in order to rule them. People should be taught to regulate their conduct according to their "enlightened self-interest" and not according to the wishes of some "unknown being" called God. In another text written around the same time, Tracy held that "any government that wants to oppress becomes attached to priests, and works

---

[115] "Compte rendu de *Détails historiques et Recueil de pièces sur les divers projets de réunion de toutes les communions chrétiennes*," in OCBC *Œuvres*, III, 2, p. 1033.

[116] A. L. C. Destutt de Tracy, *Analyse raisonnée de l'origine de tous les cultes, ou religion universelle* (Paris, 1804), p. 147.

to make them powerful in order to be served by them."[117] Although Tracy's hostility to the Church was rather extreme even for an Idéologue, others, like Volney, Cabanis, Roederer, and Say, remained adamantly opposed to religion in general, and to Catholicism in particular. At the regular dinner parties that Constant attended in the home of Madame de Condorcet, he would have heard such arguments thoroughly discussed by all participants.

But Constant would have been equally well aware of the growing powerlessness of Idéologie. With France's transition to empire, and to a Christian one at that, the Idéologues were increasingly isolated and even irrelevant. Athough they had been instrumental to Bonaparte's rise to power, he was soon able to neutralize their political influence. By 1804, he was deriding them as "miserable metaphysicians," hopelessly out of touch with reality. Soon, he closed their section of the National Institute and forced their journal, the *Décade philosophique*, to merge with an official one. In any case, the Idéologues' concern with "ending the revolution" and with promoting social "order" made them ill-equipped to resist Napoleon's intensifying authoritarianism. Their elitism and disdain for the masses seems only to have increased during this period, helped along by the Catholic revival. Once again the French masses were showing themselves to be irrational and backward.

Over time, the elitism of the Idéologues caused them to abandon any real concern for political liberty and to focus instead on economic solutions to France's problems.[118] Jean-Baptiste Say turned to political economy as the way out of France's predicament. Prosperity, Say argued, could be achieved in any well-administered state, regardless of its political form. What French men and women needed most of all was an education in their own "enlightened self-interest." Meanwhile, in his *Commentaire sur l'Esprit des lois de Montesquieu*,[119] Destutt de Tracy argued similarly that a country should be regarded as "free" whenever its population was "happy." It was not the *form* of government that mattered, but rather how

---

[117] A. L. C. Destutt de Tracy, *Commentaire sur l'Esprit des lois de Montesquieu* (Paris, 1819), pp. 387–390. On Tracy's religious views, see J. Byrnes, "Chateaubriand and Destutt de Tracy: Defining Religious and Secular Polarities in France at the Beginning of the Nineteenth Century," *Church History*, 60, 3 (September 1991), pp. 316–330.

[118] On the Idéologues' view of political economy, see Welch, *Liberty and Utility*; Th. Kaiser, "Politics and Political Economy in the Thought of the Idéologues," *History of Political Economy*, 12, 2 (1980), pp. 141–160; L. le Van-Mesle, "La promotion de l'économie politique en France au XIX siècle," *Revue d'histoire moderne et contemporaine*, 27 (1980).

[119] Written in 1806, published in 1819.

well the country was *administered*.[120] These positions took the sting out of the Idéologues' opposition to Napoleon.

On a more personal level, one could even say that the Idéologues willingly succumbed to Bonaparte's "patronage machine" and quietly withdrew from public life.[121] Cabanis, Garat, Volney, and Tracy all accepted lucrative senatorial posts and pensions from the Emperor and, in return, no longer opposed him in any meaningful way. In other words, the Idéologues' personal comportment lent credence to Villers' conclusion that the ethics of self-interest was morally and politically corrupting.

Villers had been frustrated for some time about the moral consequences of Idéologie. In his essay on Kant he had warned French intellectuals of its debilitating effects. In his essay on Luther, he had repeated that message. Now, in the article "What is Going On on the Streets of Paris," Villers lamented the visible moral corruption.[122] Villers was convinced that both the government and Idéologie were to blame. Idéologie was fostering moral degradation and political despondence. Already frustrated with what he held to be France's intellectual elites' complicity in the country's abasement, Villers heard the National Institute present its "compliments" to the Emperor in December 1805. Villers was so sickened by the sycophantic speech that he went home and wrote an alternative speech that he wished had been delivered instead. The National Institute should have the courage to tell Napoleon that the nation had no need to extend its borders and desired no foreign conquests; rather, France needed "to cultivate itself, to perfect itself, [and] to become *truly* religious, moral and educated." To this end, the French government should respect freedom of thought and allow the ideas of "enlightened and thinking men" to circulate unrestricted. The real danger was not "the progress of philosophy" or the diffusion of enlightened ideas among the masses. Rather, it was the very opposite: the cynical attempt to keep the people of France in a state of "ignorance."[123] Villers never published his speech; but it is a clear indication of the exasperation he felt not only because of Napoleon's regime, but also because of the inability or unwillingness of French intellectuals to stand up to him.

[120] A. L. C. Destutt de Tracy, *Commentaire sur l'Esprit des Lois de Montesquieu*, in *Œuvres de Montesquieu*, vol. VIII (Paris, 1827), pp. 151–152.

[121] I. Woloch, *Napoleon and His Collaborators: The Making of a Dictatorship* (New York, 2001), pp. 50, 54.

[122] "Sur ce qui se passe dans les rues de Paris," published in *Le Publiciste*, 7 Ventose, Year XIII (1804), discussed in Wittmer, *Charles de Villers*, pp. 245–246.

[123] The episode is recounted in Wittmer, *Charles de Villers*, pp. 247–248.

In the company of Villers, Constant had ample time to ponder the interlinked moral and political corruption France was suffering, and the role that Idéologie had played in the country's decline. In the Idéologues' willingness to be silenced in return for money and prestige, Constant saw visible proof of the deleterious effects of an ethics based on self-interest. The Idéologues offered no real resistance and no viable alternative to Napoleon's despotic rule. Meanwhile, prominent Catholics were continuing to do battle against enlightened and liberal values while members of the Protestant community were bending over backwards to flatter and appease the Emperor. All of this repelled Constant as he sat down to write his *Principles of Politics* in 1806.

CHAPTER 4

Constant becomes Constant: from the Principles of Politics *(1806) to* The Spirit of Conquest and Usurpation *(1814)*

CONSTANT'S POLITICAL PRINCIPLES IN 1806

In 1806, Constant distilled all that he had learned from his travels, conversations, extensive reading, and experiences in government, and poured it into his *Principles of Politics Applicable to All Governments.* A work now regarded as one of the masterpieces of European political philosophy, it is Constant's most definitive political text. Although Constant chose not to publish it, no doubt due to a change in the political climate, it became a storehouse of ideas and phrases upon which he would draw extensively for later writings, such as the *Spirit of Conquest and Usurpation* (published in 1814) and a revised, shortened version of the *Principles of Politics* (published in 1815).

The *Principles of Politics*[1] constitutes the first and most complete example of Constant's transformation into a truly liberal political thinker. In it, he articulated for the first time what are now considered the key tenets of his mature philosophy, essential principles from which he would not deviate for the rest of his life. Certainly, however, his basic political convictions had not changed since 1795. Once again, Constant denounced arbitrary government and defended the main accomplishments of the early phase of the Revolution: civil equality, representative government, and legal safeguards protecting the rights of the individual. Now, however, he took the crucial step of declining to defend any specific type of regime or constitution. Instead, Constant wrote about the basic principles that ought to govern relations between political authority and individuals, regardless of the type of government in place. It is in the *Principles of Politics* of 1806 that Constant first articulates the tenet that it

---

[1] 1806/10, published for the first time by Etienne Hofmann in 1980, and translated into English only as recently as 2003.

is less the *form* of government that matters, than it is the *amount*. Stated another way, it is not *to whom* you grant political authority that is significant, but *how much* authority you grant. The point Constant makes repeatedly throughout the text is that political power is dangerous and corrupting; therefore it must be strictly limited. "Entrust [unlimited power] to one man, to several, to all," he writes, and "you will still find that it is equally an evil."[2] Constant was convinced that "[a]ll the ills of the French Revolution"[3] stemmed from the revolutionaries' ignoring, even subverting, this fundamental principle.

Two interrelated arguments underpin Constant's *Principles*. The first concerns the political theories of Jean-Jacques Rousseau, "the writer who has had the most influence on our Revolution." Constant begins by refuting Rousseau's contention that in any legitimate state, popular sovereignty is absolute and unbounded. Such a proposition, he maintains, is as "false" as it is "dangerous." The core principle of Constant's liberalism is precisely the opposite:

There is a part of human existence which necessarily remains individual and independent, and by right beyond all political jurisdiction. Sovereignty exists only in a limited and relative way.[4]

Constant's second argument reinforces his first. While having been led astray by their infatuation with Rousseau, Frenchmen had been equally misguided in their admiration of outmoded notions of liberty. In the *Principles of Politics*, Constant began to develop his thoughts on the distinctive nature of "modern liberty"; later, he would elaborate upon these and eventually become famous for them. "Freedom," he writes, "cannot be the same among the moderns as it was among the ancients." Ancient liberty required citizens to be constantly devoted to politics and always ready to sacrifice their personal interests for the public good. "The individual was entirely sacrificed to the collectivity." But modern men are no longer interested in, or even capable of exercising, this hyper-politicized type of liberty. Modern men want mostly to be left alone; they cherish their "independence from the government" above all. They aspire not so much to "political" as to "individual" liberty, the ability to pursue private "enjoyments"[5] with as little interference as possible.

Constant's two-pronged argument about the dangers of unbounded sovereignty and the irrelevance of ancient liberty sustains the larger point

---

[2] PoP 1806, p. 20.   [3] Ibid., p. 5.   [4] Ibid., p. 31.
[5] Ibid., pp. 361, 351, 361, 352, 361. (O'Keefe translates enjoyments as "various satisfactions.")

he wants to make in the *Principles of Politics*. Throughout the text, Constant repeatedly argues that the role of modern governments must be strictly limited, and individual rights scrupulously protected. In all matters not directly related to the maintenance of peace and order, or to the raising of taxes to pay for these, modern governments should simply *let things be* ("laisser-faire"). It is, of course, this argument that delighted Isaiah Berlin, who, in a now classic study, praised Constant as one of "the most eloquent of all defenders of freedom and privacy" and designated him as a founding father of liberalism.

What caused Constant to turn himself into an early proponent of *laissez-faire* liberalism? It has been said that Constant's political philosophy was a reaction to his own political experiences.[6] More specifically, François Furet and Marcel Gauchet have stressed the importance of the Terror in shaping his ideas. According to Furet, Constant's "entire political thought" revolves around explaining the Jacobin dictatorship,[7] while Marcel Gauchet similarly proffers that the "tyrannical derailment of the Revolution" constitutes "the center" of Constant's thought.[8]

Certainly, it would be foolish to deny the importance of the Terror in shaping Constant's liberalism. It is undoubtedly true that, like most of the intellectual and political elite, Constant reacted strongly against the Terror and wished to prevent any recurrence. But the Jacobin dictatorship was not the only form of government with which Constant had had experience by 1806, or from which he could draw conclusions. Guy Dodge has called attention to the Napoleonic regime as equally influential and, more recently, Etienne Hofmann has pointed out that Constant's *Principles of Politics* were a perfect antidote[9] to Napoleon's despotism. In this regard, it is significant that Constant was provoked by the appearance of Louis-Matthieu Molé's *Essais de morale et de politique*, in which Rousseau's political theories were used to justify Napoleon's authoritarian rule.[10] Neither should one forget that Constant's experience

---

[6] According to T. Todorov, for example, Constant "tries to theorize [his] lived reality" and, thus, what you find in the *Principles of Politics* is "a theorized practise." T. Todorov, "Benjamin Constant, penseur de la démocratie," preface to Benjamin Constant, *Principes de politiques*, ed. E. Hofmann (Paris, 1997), p. 6.

[7] F. Furet, "La Révolution sans la Terreur? Le débat des historiens du XIXe siècle," *Le Débat*, 13 (June 1981), p. 41.

[8] M. Gauchet, "Benjamin Constant: L'illusion lucide du libéralisme," in B. Constant, *Ecrits politiques*, ed. M. Gauchet (Paris, 1997), p. 28.

[9] Hofmann, *Les "Principes de politique."*

[10] Judging by the footnotes, he is also in dialogue with Ferrand, whose *Esprit de l'histoire* (1803) argues for the importance, particularly in large states and empires, of absolute sovereignty and political as well as religious laws to keep human beings in line.

with the Directory, during which he had seen at first hand a government doing the things he specifically warns against in the *Principles of Politics*. In particular, he had personally taken part in the Directory's project of national "regeneration," which was aimed at nothing less than the moral transformation of France's Catholic subjects into republican citizens through a combination of legislation and republican institutions imposed from above. For Constant, the abject failure of the regime and its policies underlined the futility of imposing moral values on a population unprepared and unwilling to receive them. Furthermore, trying to wrench the population's religion away from them had backfired miserably. Indeed, at a critical point in his argument about the dangers of government intervention into the hearts and minds of citizens, Constant comments, "One could think that the Directory was intended to give us some memorable lessons on all objects of this nature."[11]

Constant devotes long sections of the *Principles of Politics* to refute the idea that government should try to legislate moral virtue. Man, he insists, is not and never will be "a product of law"; therefore, it is neither for legislation nor for republican institutions to try to "make men." Constant recalls the institutions touted by the Directory, those "national holidays, ceremonies, periodic assemblies" that he himself had presided over as president of Luzarches. He remembers that it had not taken long before the government had had to resort to coercion.

Soon it was necessary to require the observance of these fairs, attendance at these assemblies, respect for these ceremonies, under threat of severe penalties. A duty was made of what should be voluntary. Celebration of freedom was surrounded with constraint.

Constant goes on to refute those among his contemporaries who continue to believe that laws and educational institutions imposed by the government can

excite in us the love of work, engrave in the spirit of youth respect for morality, enthuse the imagination with subtly combined institutions, and dig deep into our hearts and uproot guilty thoughts there.[12]

By 1806 Constant had come to believe that such intrusive laws, regulations, and "institutions" were not only ineffectual, but counterproductive. He was convinced that governments should remain strictly "neutral" with regard to the moral values of its citizens. On no account should governments try to "direct, improve, and enlighten" the citizen

---

[11] PoP 1806, p. 311.   [12] Ibid., pp. 47, 369, 48.

body. The widespread notion that governments should "create" or "revive" public opinion was dangerously flawed. And when it came to public education, governments should confine themselves to "simple instruction"; they should "multiply the channels and resources of instruction," enabling individuals "to get access to all proven factual truths," but always remain "neutral"[13] as to moral values.

Constant's liberalism also contained an economic component that has been noted by both his critics and admirers. Referring to the rights of private property as "sacred" and "inviolable,"[14] he advocated an "extremely limited"[15] role for governments in economic matters. He approved wholeheartedly of what he called the "proprietary spirit,"[16] which he claimed would have positive effects as it spread throughout society. But Constant's economic liberalism is perhaps best summarized by his suggestion that governments are most able to "do good" by "not acting at all."[17] Statements like these, further developed in later writings, led Karl Marx to dismiss Constant as a mere "mouthpiece" for "bourgeois society," a derogatory label that has had remarkable longevity. It has not helped matters that Constant advocated restricting full citizenship to property owners, stating categorically that "only property can render men capable of exercising political rights. Only owners can be citizens."[18] Taken together, his positions on the economy and property rights have made it easy to characterize him as an exponent of the narrow interests of the propertied middle class and an apologist for *laissez-faire* capitalism.

Such characterizations seriously distort Constant's views. Strangely, what neither his admirers, like Berlin, nor his critics, like Marx, nor even recent scholars, have noticed are the underlying reasons for Constant's small-government stance. His rationale makes it very hard to see him as an ideologist of capitalist forces or even as an advocate of the so-called "negative" type of liberalism cherished by Berlin. Constant did not advocate *laissez-faire* economic policies because he admired the bourgeoisie, valued acquisitiveness, or trusted the profit motive. He surely had no love for self-interest as a human motivation and showed no particular confidence in its ability to regulate itself. Nor can it be said that Constant was naively optimistic and simply unconcerned about the moral future of mankind. Indeed, the opposite is true. Moral apprehensions pervade the entire manuscript from start to finish. Repeatedly, Constant expresses

[13] Ibid., pp. 344, 47, 57, 311, 314.   [14] Ibid., p. 167.   [15] Ibid., p. 198.   [16] Ibid., p. 173.
[17] Ibid., p. 259.   [18] Ibid., p. 166.

concern about the "moral life of individuals."[19] It is remarkable how often he mentions the problems of moral "apathy," "lethargy," and "degradation" that are clearly weighing on his mind. He worries about the growth of "egotism," "greed," and "frivolity," as well as the problem of "vanity," the love of "luxury," and "coarse pleasures."[20] To combat these, he thinks about ways to promote "courage," the "love of generous ideas," and "ardor for the public good."[21] What readers have overlooked is that such moral concerns lie at the very heart of Constant's liberalism. Moreover, the moral vision that pervades his thought is indebted to a distinctly Protestant way of thinking. Repeatedly in his *Principle of Politics*, Constant uses language and concepts reminiscent of William Godwin, but which have deeper Protestant roots.

The reason why governments should not impose moral values on their populations was that they were likely to be ineffectual and would probably exacerbate, rather than improve, the underlying problem. First, it was highly probable that governments would make the wrong decisions. Constant had come to realize that "there is something about power which more or less warps judgement."[22] This was why "[a]ll things being equal, it is always likely that governors will have views which are *less* just, *less* sound, and *less* impartial than those of the governed." Governments would probably obstruct healthy progress due to "false ideas of stability," or they might pursue "thoughtless projects of improvement" and "premature ameliorations,"[23] equally harmful to society. In either case, government interference in the "natural" course of things was bound to be more detrimental than good.

Constant's second argument against government interference is the one most clearly indebted to William Godwin's *Enquiry Concerning Political Justice*, and to a Protestant way of thinking. It concerns the profound moral corruption promoted by intellectual tutelage, or by what Godwin refers to as man's "perpetual pupilage."[24] The argument is built on two basic principles. First, both Godwin and Constant closely link moral progress to intellectual progress; they are inextricably connected in their minds. Second, for the two types of progress to occur, individuals must be allowed to strive for the truth by themselves, in other words, to work individually and unobstructed at their own intellectual and moral self-improvement. Indeed, it is not only every individual's right but also his *duty* to strive to know what is true and just. In the words of Godwin,

---

[19] Ibid., pp. 59, 78–79.   [20] Ibid., pp. 124, 366, 364, 175.   [21] Ibid., pp. 420, 421, 422.
[22] Ibid., p. 54.   [23] Ibid., p. 340.   [24] Godwin, *Political Justice*, p. 706.

"If there be any truth more unquestionable than the rest, it is, that every man *is bound to the exertion of his faculties in the discovery of right.*"[25] When governments dictate moral and intellectual truths, and legislate in areas better left alone, the results are profoundly counter-productive. Government regulation encourages people to become mentally passive and even subservient. According to Constant, such intellectual servitude not only "perverts" human intelligence, but also corrupts man's "most delicate strands of inner feeling," thus obstructing healthy moral development.[26] Government tutelage causes "morality and inner feeling [to] undergo an unfathomable degradation."[27] It is to this problem that Constant refers when he writes that a "proliferation of laws" will have an overall harmful effect by "falsifying individual morality."[28] Too many laws prevent man from "retiring into himself, from consulting his own heart."[29] In contrast, "independent thinking"[30] is the key to moral progress. For similar reasons, Godwin had referred to the "mistaken guardianship" of government, and to the "political patronage of opinion," which in his mind caused only "torpor and imbecility" in the population.[31]

Constant's indebtedness to Godwin and a specific Protestant tradition is made evident by his adoption, at a critical point in the narrative, of a concept referred to as Godwin's "central moral principle."[32] This is the notion of "private judgement,"[33] an idea with a long history in Protestant polemics, and a concept highly valued by the school of Rational Dissent, to which Godwin belonged. Like other rational dissenters, such as Joseph Priestley, Tom Paine, and Richard Price, Godwin held the right of private judgement to be sacrosanct. Each of these men believed that moral and religious improvement depended on the progressive enlightenment of private judgement, and that the state's role in this process should be minimal. Its function should be limited to providing the necessary instruments for improvement, which meant, essentially, that the state should guarantee freedom of opinion and speech. Each individual was morally obliged to grapple with the issues on his own and to arrive at the truth independently. According to Godwin, it was "the first duty of man ... to take none of the principles of conduct upon trust, to do

---

[25] Ibid., p. 440, emphasis added.   [26] PoP 1806, p. 370.   [27] Ibid., p. 64.   [28] Ibid., p. 63.
[29] Ibid., p. 371.   [30] Ibid., pp. 100, 122.   [31] Godwin, *Political Justice*, pp. 674, 675, 671.
[32] M. Philp, *Godwin's Political Justice* (London, 1986), p. 16.
[33] I believe that L. Jaume is the first to draw attention to the idea of judgement in the thought of Constant and Madame de Staël, although he does not discuss its sources. Jaume calls the *Principles of Politics* "le grand oeuvre de Constant en matière de réflexion sur le jugement," *L'Individu*, p. 63. On Madame de Staël and the notion of private judgement, see Rosenblatt, "Madame de Staël."

nothing without a clear and individual conviction that it is right to be done."[34] Human beings must "consult [their own] judgement"[35] in all matters and know that the only valid "rule of conduct" was the "exercise of [one's own] understanding."[36] Otherwise, "degradation" would set in, turning the people in question into "mere dwarfs and mockery of men."[37]

Like Godwin, Constant had come to believe that governments should not try to dictate morality or right behavior to the public, because by so doing they would "spoil their judgement." Moral improvement was more intimately connected to the *search* for knowledge than to the mere *possession* of knowledge. "Truth is not just good to know," writes Constant, "it is good to search for." Moreover, the search for truth is a human "need," implanted in each and every individual by "providence." When individuals "make their judgement subservient to government," they abandon the "natural road to truth," which involves "reasoning, comparison, [and] analysis." They renounce the responsibility they have to improve themselves intellectually and morally, and permit themselves to become "wretchedly passive creatures." To Constant "everything imposed on opinion by government turns out to be not only useless but harmful, *truths as much as error.*" He offers an explanation of his thinking that illustrates well his interwoven intellectual, moral, and political concerns:

the adoption of an error on our own accord, because it seems true to us, is an operation more favorable to the improvement [*perfectionnement*] of the mind than the adoption of a truth on the say-so of any government whatever. In the former case, analysis is formative. If this analysis in the particular circumstance does not lead us to happy results, we are on the right track even so. Persevering in our scrupulous independent investigation, we will get there sooner or later. Under the latter supposition we are reduced to a plaything of the government before which we have humbled our own judgement. Not only will this result in our adopting errors if the dominating government gets things wrong or finds it useful to deceive us, but we will not even know how to derive from such truths as this government has given us the consequences which must flow from them. The abnegation of our intelligence will have rendered us wretchedly passive creatures. Our mental resilience will be broken.

Immediately following this explanation, Constant refers approvingly to William Godwin, calling him "[a] writer gifted with remarkable insight." He evokes Godwin's central point that people should never be made to accept truths uncritically, because that would be to "spoil their judgement."[38] Also

---

[34] Godwin, *Political Justice*, p. 672.   [35] Ibid., p. 440.   [36] Ibid., p. 120.   [37] Ibid., p. 672.
[38] All quotations in this paragraph are taken from PoP 1806, pp. 301–302, emphasis added.

like Godwin, Constant attributes a primary role in the development of judgement to the freedom of the press. It is not through government policies, but through "public opinion,"[39] as expressed by a free press, that Frenchmen's private judgement will be cultivated and refined. Only thus will there be a "free, gradual, and peaceful"[40] improvement of the intellectual and moral capacities of the population. Once again, the greatest service government can do to further enlightenment "is not to bother with it."[41] In the matter of morals and intellectual improvement, "laisser-faire" should be its entire policy.[42]

"PRIVATE JUDGEMENT" IN PROTESTANT POLEMICS

The notion of "private judgement" already had a long history in French intellectual debates when Godwin wrote his *Enquiry Concerning Political Justice*, and this history was an eminently Protestant one. French Catholics had been quick to warn of the religious and political dangers of Lutheranism when it first made its appearance. Of central concern was the Protestant doctrine of free inquiry, implicated in Luther's notion that each and every person "must decide at his own peril what he is to believe ... How he believes is a matter for each individual's conscience."[43] Catholics responded that by granting private individuals the right to examine religious matters on their own, the Reformation made each man the judge and arbiter of his own faith, in effect giving people license to believe whatever they wished. Michel Montaigne (1533–92) summarized what he and other French Catholics feared would be the inevitable consequences of Protestantism:

This incipient malady might easily degenerate into an execrable atheism because the masses, without the capacity to judge things as they really are, let themselves be swept away by the tide and are easily deceived by outward appearances ... once they have been induced to cast in doubt or leave in the balance certain key articles of faith, they will throw off every single element of their creed; from then on, they will believe nothing unless they have reached their own personal judgment in the matter and given their own private consent to it.[44]

Protestant spokesmen like Jean Claude (1617–87) responded by reaffirming the Protestant principle of free inquiry in religious matters. Men

---

[39] Ibid., p. 371.   [40] Ibid., p. 304.   [41] Ibid., p. 116.   [42] Ibid., p. 116.
[43] M. Luther, "On Secular Authority: How Far does the Obedience Owed to it Extend?" in *Luther and Calvin on Secular Authority*, ed. H. Höpfl (Cambridge, 1991), p. 25.
[44] M. de Montaigne, *Essais*, ed. M. Rat (Paris, 1958), vol. II, p. 12, p. 116.

cannot be Christians, Claude argued, because the state or church orders them to be; instead, they must arrive at the truth on their own. The Christian religion does not advocate "blind obedience"; rather, it asks each person to "judge the truths that it proposes." All Christians should accept their faith and religious commandments not just by "an act of obedience," but also by an "act of judgement." God had given all men the "admirable faculty" of being able to discern between true and false, right and wrong, and he certainly did not wish to prevent them from using it in a matter as weighty as their own salvation.[45]

But Catholics continued to argue that the great majority of people were incapable of properly judging Scripture. The simple-minded masses could not be expected to understand religion correctly on their own. Thus, society must acknowledge a "common judge" on religious matters, that is, the Church, and must promise "obedience and submission" to it.[46] Again and again it was argued that Christians could do no better than to "submit their judgement" to the Church. Not only did the Protestant doctrine of private judgement threaten to undermine religion, but it was politically subversive as well. The right of free inquiry would inevitably lead to both heresy and sedition.

Over time, and especially after the outbreak of civil wars in France, the political dangers of the Reformation were stressed. Calvinists were described not only as religious heretics but also as political subversives. Common accusations were that they had independent and rebellious spirits and that their real aim was to establish a republic in France. Of course, Protestants denied that there was anything inherently seditious or republican about their religion, but the accusation became harder to refute after the publication of Pierre Jurieu's *Lettres pastorales*. In this work, the Protestant theologian articulated a theory of resistance to political authority based on the principles of popular sovereignty and the contractual foundations of government. Even the Protestant Pierre Bayle chastised Jurieu for his "republican" ideas. By the end of the seventeenth century, the famous Catholic apologist Jacques-Benigne Bossuet (1627–1704) drew on all of this evidence to argue that Protestantism was sowing the seeds of anarchy in France. If countenanced, it would invariably lead to atheism in religion and rebellion in politics. Society would dissolve

---

[45] J. Claude, *Défense de la Réformation contre le livre intitulé préjugés légitimes contre les Calvinistes* (Paris, 1844), p. 122.

[46] P. Nicole, *De l'unité de l'église ou réfutation du nouveau système de M. Jurieu* (Paris, 1729), pp. 348, 349.

into a state of utter disorder. Such ideas lay behind the Revocation of the Edict of Nantes (1685), by which Louis XIV withdrew the right of French Protestants to practice their religion.

As previously discussed, eighteenth-century French Protestants worked hard to convince the king that they were loyal subjects and that their religion posed no threat to his political authority. They consistently maintained that the exercise of private judgement in religious matters was entirely compatible with political obedience to a lawful monarch. Nevertheless, a certain stigma of rebelliousness and sectarianism lingered on, even as attitudes towards Protestantism improved during the eighteenth century. The apparent ease with which some Protestants could extend theological concepts into the political realm did not go unnoticed by concerned observers.[47] In the *Spirit of the Laws*, Montesquieu claimed that wherever Protestantism had been established in Europe, "revolutions were made on the plane of the political state."[48] He further argued that "the Catholic religion is better suited to monarchies," while the Protestant "is better adapted to a republic."[49] Even Voltaire, the outspoken defender of Calas and religious toleration, argued that Calvinism "from its very nature" produced civil wars and "shook the foundations of states."[50] Thus, Condorcet was not proposing anything very original when, in his *Sketch for a Historical Picture of the Progress of the Human Mind* (1795), he suggested that the exercise of private judgement in the religious sphere was bound to lead to its exercise in the political sphere. Condorcet found it entirely logical that

Men, after having submitted their religious prejudices to the examination of reason, would soon expand this to political prejudices, [such that] after being enlightened about the usurpations of popes, they would end up wanting to be enlightened about the usurpations of kings.[51]

After the Revolution, reactionary theorists like de Maistre and Bonald reintroduced these arguments as a way to blame the Revolution on the Protestant Reformation. In the summer of 1806, Bonald published an

---

[47] John Locke was one such Protestant, for whom the right, and indeed duty, of individual judgement was a key concept in his defense of both religious toleration and the right of political rebellion. On this, see S. Dworetz, *The Unvarnished Doctrine: Locke, Liberalism, and the American Revolution* (Durham, NC, 1990).

[48] Montesquieu, *Spirit of the Laws*, ed. A. Cohler, B. Miller, and H. Stone (Cambridge, 1994), vol. XXIV, 5, p. 463.

[49] Ibid.   [50] *Le Siècle de Louis XIV* in *Œuvres*, ed. L. Moland (Paris, 1967) vol. XV, p. 39.

[51] Condorcet, *Esquisse d'un tableau historique des progrès de l'esprit humain*, ed. A. Pons (Paris, 1988), p. 195.

article in the *Mercure de France* that called Protestant dogmas "the leaven of all revolutions" and charged Protestants with having introduced ideas of "democracy" into the body politic. He singled out the "right of examination and interpretation" as particularly harmful and ultimately destructive of the "monarchical" principles of Catholicism.

> As soon as individuals, whose collectivity forms a people, could be judges and legislators in the religious state, even more could they be legislators and judges in the civil and political state.[52]

So, when in 1806 Constant introduced the term "private judgement" into his political writing, it was already a well-known term in French political and religious polemics. He would have been aware of the negative connotations ascribed to it by Catholic polemicists and equally aware of the positive values attributed to it by Godwin and Villers. Godwin's *Enquiry Concerning Political Justice* contained an unequivocal plea for "the universal exercise of private judgment"[53] in all realms of human existence; society's intellectual and moral improvement depended on it. Villers' writings only reaffirmed this positive assessment: all the good accomplished by the Reformation was due to its encouragement of "free inquiry." Thanks to this principle, minds had become more "scrutinizing," which, in turn, brought forth improvements in all aspects of life.

Of course a considerable change had occurred in the roughly 130-year period between Jean Claude's defense of private judgement and Constant's adoption of it. For the early Protestant apologists, the exercise of judgement was meant to lead the individual to right religion (Protestantism) and thus to salvation in the afterlife. By the late eighteenth century, the desired dynamic was almost the reverse: it was thought that Protestantism would improve individual judgement, thus leading to what Godwin referred to as "the moral improvement of the species" here on earth.

The importance that Constant accords private judgement and his indebtedness to the Protestant tradition shows how wrong it is to depict him as a mere mouthpiece for the capitalist bourgeoisie, intent on safeguarding their selfish material interests. The truth is that Constant was proffering a moral vision that stressed the right and duty of individuals to improve themselves by use of their God-given faculties. In any case, anyone who gives careful consideration to what Constant actually says about property in the *Principles of Politics* would have to reject such a mischaracterization of his views. First, Constant deliberately distinguishes

---

[52] De Bonald, "De l'unité religieuse en Europe," p. 260.   [53] Godwin, *Political Justice*, p. 440.

what he refers to as "business property" from "territorial property." Then, he argues that political power should be granted only to the latter. It is essentially for moral reasons that Constant favors a "government of landowners." While he grants that businessmen generate wealth and promote prosperity, he expresses strong reservations on moral grounds about the kinds of activities in which they engage. Constant contrasts the acquisition of "sudden wealth" through "business" with the much healthier "proprietorial spirit" encouraged by agriculture. Businessmen are more frequently exposed to "chance"; they must constantly be sensitive to the "whims, passions, pride and luxury" of their fellows. Farming, by contrast, is inherently conducive to patriotism and speaks constantly to the "moral part of man." Property in the form of land promotes a "regularity of habit" conducive to moral improvement, while "business property" does not. Obviously, property and wealth are not legitimate ends in themselves. What Constant wishes to encourage is not so much the acquisition of wealth or the accumulation of capital, and assuredly not the selfish enjoyment of these, but rather the moral consequences of a certain type of *work*. Constant favors agriculture in large part because it is an activity that demands "a sequence of observations and experiences which form and develop *judgment*."[54]

BOOK VIII: "ON RELIGIOUS FREEDOM"

The section that perhaps best illustrates Constant's transformation as a thinker is Book VIII, in which he discusses the "proper role of the government with regard to religion." Recalling his opinions when he first embarked on his book on religion, and his pronouncements on the topic during the Directory, it is striking how many positive comments he now makes. Constant's avowed purpose is no longer to "destroy" what he earlier referred to as mere "prejudices." In fact, he refers to the *philosophes'* hostility towards religion as a "bizarre fanaticism" and denounces their "thirst for destruction."[55] Constant has clearly distanced himself from the Idéologues on the topic of religion.

The Constant of 1806 has come to agree with those who speak of religion's "benefits"; and he is puzzled by the "almost ferocious hatred" still felt for something so "gentle and consoling." In particular, Constant now sees religion as an indispensable moralizing force. Calling it the "most natural" and "purest of all emotions," he credits it with inspiring "selflessness" and

---

[54] PoP 1806, pp. 174, 184, 173, 175, 176, emphasis added.   [55] Ibid., pp. 131, 134.

thus helping man to "break out of the narrow circle of his interests." Constant even suggests that *the lack* of religion might be the indication of a mind "absorbed in petty and ignoble interests." "The more one cherishes moral ideas," he writes, "the more high-mindedness, courage and independence are needed [and] the more it is necessary ... to take refuge in the belief in a God." Without religion, "the human race could never manage."[56]

If religion is such a natural and positive force, why has it so often been attacked? It is because it has been "distorted" through its association with authority or "power." In the hands of government, religion has been used as a political tool; thus it has been "transformed into a menacing institution," and has alienated many people. Persecution always provokes reaction, so any decline in religion should be blamed not on the *philosophes*, but on all those rulers and churchmen who try to manipulate religion for political reasons. Constant regrets that "atheistic governors with superstitious subjects seem to some statesmen the ideal model today." This instrumentalization of religion leads to its "abasement" and gradual decline. For the sake of political liberty as well as religion, then, governments must leave religion "perfectly independent" and never try to "make it an ally." "Religion and the state," he writes, "are two quite distinct and separate things, which, when brought together can only distort both one and the other."[57]

Constant argues that those who constantly speak of religion's "usefulness" to society, and who try to enlist it in support of a mere "common morality," are debasing religion. Here Constant's originality and distinctive view of religion becomes most apparent. "This need for utility," he writes, is an "inherent vice of the French character"; it is why France is "of all the nations the one whose writers have almost always envisaged religion in the most imperfect and narrowest way."[58] In particular, Constant denounces the "standard hypothesis" that religion is useful mainly "as a reinforcement to the penal laws." We have seen that this was a common argument at the time, used, somewhat surprisingly, by many contemporary Catholics, who saw religion as a necessary bridle on men's illicit passions. Without it, they argued, society would simply fall apart; criminality would rise, as the poor would no longer be willing to accept their inferior condition. Constant rejected this view. "This is not my

---

[56] Ibid., pp. 131, 134–135, 131, 132, 133, 134.
[57] Ibid., pp. 134, 143, 135, 146–147, quoting the liberal nobleman Stanislas Clermont-Tonnerre (1757–92), a moderate royalist in the National Assembly known for his eloquent support of the religious freedom of both Protestants and Jews. I have altered the translation here.
[58] Ibid., p. 142.

opinion," he wrote. "I place religion higher. I do not see it at all as a supplement to the gallows or the wheel." Religion was not needed to lend support to a mere "common morality" concerned with preventing crimes; rather it was needed for something far more important and uplifting:

It is for the creation of a more elevated morality that religion seems desirable to me. I do not invoke it to repress gross crimes but to ennoble all the virtues.

Once again, Constant's central goal is to release human potential. The question is not how to maintain social and political order by keeping people down, but how to improve and "ennoble"[59] them, and thereby improve society. For this loftier goal, religion is essential.

We can see that when Constant wrote these *Principles of Politics*, he had developed a distinctive position on religion. While he disagreed with Catholics and conservatives on the necessity of religion to maintain social and political order, he also disagreed with *philosophes* and Idéologues who denied the value of religion altogether. Neither tapped the power of religion to educate and moralize man.

Constant also had developed ideas on the need for religious unity, which, as we have seen, was a recurring topic of discussion at the time. Just as he disapproved of the typically French habit of searching for utility everywhere, he rejected the quest for religious unity and the obsession with a national religion. In fact, Constant argued for the exact opposite: France should amend the Concordat, and let the sects proliferate. The subdivision of sects should not be impeded in any way, and any religion should be allowed to change its dogmas without government permission. "Tolerance," he urged, "is nothing else than the freedom of all present and future religions." Moreover, the government "does harm when it wants to shore up religion against the spirit of inquiry." In any case, governments were wrong to worry about the multiplication and proliferation of religious sects, because it was a good thing, conducive to the moral progress of society. "If the government did not meddle with religion," Constant explained, "the sects would proliferate forever." A "blessed struggle" would occur between them, as "[e]ach new congregation would seek to prove the goodness of its doctrines by the purity of its morals." Competition between religious sects would further ensure that religion did not "lose its sensibility, to become a mere form."[60] To illustrate the beneficial effects caused by the proliferation of sects, Constant cited the examples of America and Scotland, where Protestantism had split into numerous branches.

---

[59] Ibid., pp. 141, 142. I have altered the translation somewhat.   [60] Ibid., pp. 144, 139, 138, 137.

CONSTANT'S OWN "CORNER OF RELIGION": FROM THE
"LETTER ABOUT JULIE" TO HIS CORRESPONDENCE WITH
PROSPER DE BARANTE

Other, more personal and autobiographical writings from this period bear witness to Constant's religious transformation since the days of his dismissive and flippant youth. In these documents, we see him approaching religion not from the perspective of a political theorist or a historian, but rather as a grieving friend, a disconsolate lover or just a suffering human being. Indeed, Constant acquired the habit of turning to religion at times of personal difficulty to seek consolation and moral fortitude, for example upon the death of a dear friend, or when he was having a particularly hard time with Madame de Staël. As the main character in his eerily autobiographical novel, *Cécile*, recounts:

> I had been very irreligious in my youth ... but since some time I had in the bottom of my heart a need to believe, either because this belief is natural to all men, or because my situation, all the more painful since I could only blame myself for what was disagreeable and bizarre about it, disposed me gradually to try to find in religion the resources against my inner agitations.[61]

Constant did not always find the comfort that he was searching for, or rather, the comfort that he found was disappointingly short-lived.

To be sure, Deguise and others are right when they argue that Constant's turn to religion never resulted in a true conversion; that is, he never embraced any specific religious doctrines.[62] Nevertheless, in his intimate thoughts about religion and correspondence with friends, Constant often reflected on the emptiness of life without a spiritual dimension. These writings evidence his altered view: he now thought of religion as something at least potentially consoling and ennobling, and repeatedly tried to experience personally its positive effects.

The "Letter about Julie"

Having determined that religious sentiment was a natural emotion, inherent in all human beings, and intimately connected to all "elevated" principles of morality, Constant must have found his dear friend Julie Talma (1756–1805) a bit of an anomaly. Although a deeply moral person,

---

[61] *Cécile*, in OCBC *Œuvres* III, 1, pp. 281–282.　　[62] Deguise and also Gouhier focus on this.

full of "noble and elevated sentiments,"[63] Julie never expressed any religious feelings. On May 5, 1805, after a prolonged illness, she died a confirmed atheist. In his "Letter about Julie," Constant tried to make sense of this apparent paradox.

Constant reasoned that "profound and sensitive" creatures like Julie normally experienced a "vague need" for religion. Julie, however, was "a remarkable exception" to this rule. He attributed this to two things. First, Julie's close ties with late eighteenth-century *philosophes* had convinced her that all religion was just "a means of domination and a pretext for intolerance." Second, she had been repelled by the "hostile and humiliating power" of Roman Catholicism, the form of religion she knew best. Too dogmatic, it repelled an "independent spirit" like Julie's. In the end, Julie's ideas were "stronger than the needs of her heart" and she remained an atheist.[64]

Adolphe *and* Cécile

Constant's two novels of this period, *Adolphe* and *Cécile*,[65] also provide insight into his more private thoughts about religion. Both are interpreted as reflecting his troubled relations with women and thus are often treated as companion pieces. Some people even believe that *Cécile* originally constituted a part of *Adolphe* that was later removed.[66]

To suggest that *Adolphe* reveals something about Constant's views on religion might sound surprising, since the novel seems to avoid the subject almost entirely. Only near the end does the principal female character, Ellénore, turn to religion to help her face death, and thereafter, Adolphe makes the simple declaration

My surprise is not that man should need a religion. What astonishes me is that he should ever believe himself sufficiently strong, sufficiently protected against misfortune to dare to reject a single one.[67]

Ironically, however, Adolphe himself is not able to subscribe to a religion.

The novel initially recounts Adolphe's seduction of Ellénore and then focuses on the destructive consequences of his inability either to commit to

---

[63] "Lettre sur Julie," in OCBC *Œuvres*, III, 1, p. 213.

[64] Ibid., pp. 220–221. The last two quotations appear to have been added to the *Mélanges de littérature et de politique* (Paris, 1829).

[65] *Adolphe* was first published in 1816 and *Cécile* in 1951.

[66] N. King's introduction to *Cécile*, in OCBC *Œuvres* III, 1, p. 229.

[67] *Adolphe*, ed. P. Coleman, trans. M. Mauldon (Oxford, 2001), p. 74.

the relationship or to end it. Despite this narrow focus, Constant presents the story in a way that encourages the reader to reflect on its broader social and political implications. More generally, the novel describes how empty and paralyzing life becomes for someone devoid of a higher sense of duty. Motivated only by self-interest tempered by sympathy, Adolphe lacks a moral compass and lives a life devoid of any real meaning. As Patrick Coleman has noted, "Adolphe lacks the inner resources needed to establish a meaningful connection with the world around him."[68] In some fragments drafted for a preface to the novel's second edition, Constant sketched the background against which he wanted his story to be understood: "everything in nature is connected," he wrote, "inconstance or exhaustion in love; in religion, incredulity in a thousand drab or frightening forms; servility in politics are symptoms that go together."[69] The novel conveys a profound sense of paralysis, as Ellénore and Adolphe become trapped in a life in which they can do no good for themselves or society. Given the author's commitment to the idea of perfectibility, and to the importance of religious sentiments, the message is startling indeed.

From the time Constant first started reading *Adolphe* in public, and then published it in 1816, people have assumed that the novel was, to some degree, autobiographical. The themes of a man struggling with his own indeciveness and trying to find his way do concur with diary entries from the period he was writing *Adolphe*. These record Constant's tendency to hesitate, doubt himself, and change his mind, behavior that his biographer concludes "borders on the neurotic."[70]

Cécile, written only a few years later, revolves around the same underlying issue: the main character's problematic relationship with a woman. This time, however, he has recourse to religion. Referred to as "I," and bearing a marked resemblance to Constant, the protagonist comes into contact with a mystic sect and, thanks to them, learns to pray and resign his will to God. This gives him considerable solace in his time of need. The problem, however, is that, in the end, their mystic precepts produce a moral paralysis not unlike Adolphe's. Constant's protagonist learns to "renounce all [his] faculties, all knowledge, all reason, all judgement." Occasionally, this engenders a "profound feeling of confidence," accompanied by a comforting sense that he is protected by God. Later, however, he realizes that what he has experienced is only "a kind of moral sleep"; having renounced "any type

---

[68] P. Coleman, "Introduction," in ibid., p. xx.   [69] Ibid., p. xix.
[70] Wood, *Benjamin Constant*, p. 183.

of direction of [his] destiny" by placing himself entirely in God's hands, he has adopted a posture of "blind and passive resignation."[71]

We now know that the encounter with a mystic sect described in *Cécile* refers to an actual event in Constant's life, but about which we have little information.[72] The novel identifies a "pietist" sect "in Lausanne" that espouses "the opinions of Fénelon and Mme Guyon."[73] Constant's reference is to a group called the "Inner souls [*Ames Intérieures*]"; it was led by Constant's cousin, Charles de Langallerie and other members of his family belonged to it as well. During the summer of 1807, while at her château near Lausanne, Madame de Staël and Constant went through what their biographers refer to as a pietist or mystic crisis. As Simone Balayé recounts, that summer, a great wave of mysticism swept over Coppet.[74] While in the midst of one of their periodic romantic crises, the couple met with Langallerie, and they read Fénelon, Madame de Guyon, and other mystics and hermetic philosophers. Madame de Staël later explained that at the time "[their] souls were tired of materialism," and they found certain mystic doctrines "appealing to the heart."[75] But not everyone at Coppet appreciated the new trend. In frustration, one member of her entourage reported that "[n]othing has changed more than Coppet ... these people are turning into Catholics, Boehmists, Martinists, Mystics"![76]

Constant, too, left behind indications that he took away something positive from his experience with the Inner Souls. On August 21, after meeting with Langallerie, he noted in his diary, "I am very struck by this new way of thinking."[77] Several years later, when he heard that Langallerie had been taken ill, he wrote to his aunt:

I am really sorry to hear about the Chevalier de Langallerie's relapse. It's one intelligent man less in the world – or it will be; a man who had very original ideas

---

[71] *Cécile*, pp. 283–284.

[72] F. Bowman "L'episode quiétiste dans 'Cécile,'" in P. Corday and J.-L. Seylaz (eds.), *Benjamin Constant: Actes du Congres de Lausanne* (Geneva, 1968), pp. 97–108.

[73] *Cécile*, p. 281.

[74] http://www.stael.org/article.php?id_article=93. On this episode see Deguise, *Benjamin Constant méconnu*, pp. 89–115; Bowman, "L'episode quiétiste," and A. Viatte, *Les Sources occultes du romantisme*, 2 vols. (Paris, 1928), vol. II, ch. 3.

[75] Ch. de Lacretelle, *Testament philosophique et littéraire*, 2 vols., (Paris, 1840), vol. II, pp. 88–89, as quoted by N. Chaquin and S. Michaud, "Saint-Martin dans le Groupe de Coppet et le cercle de Frédéric Schlegel," in S. Balayé and J.-D. Candaux (eds.), *Le Groupe de Coppet: Actes et documents du deuxième colloque de Coppet 10–13 juillet 1974* (Geneva and Paris, 1977), p. 114.

[76] Ch. V de Bonstetten to Frédérique Brun, Coppet, October 12, 1809, in *Briefe von Karl Viktor von Bonstetten an Frederike Brun* (Frankfurt am Main, 1829), vol. I, p. 282, cited in Kohler, *Madame de Staël et la Suisse*, pp. 347, 483.

[77] JI, p. 551.

on interesting subjects and a very persuasive way of expressing them. In the last analysis his system of belief is something each individual alone must judge for himself; but it has a comforting side to it, and, at certain moments, does one's soul good.[78]

Correspondence with Prosper de Barante

Constant's correspondence with Prosper de Barante (1782–1866) provides further insight into Constant's personal views on religion during this period. Barante probably met de Staël and Constant during the summer of 1804 and he became close to Constant during the winter of 1805–6. The two men would meet in the home of Suard, often in the company of Villers. Barante's *Souvenirs* contain recollections of their warm friendship and intellectual complicity. He recalls that Constant was then fast at work on his book on religion. In fact, their correspondence indicates that Constant counted on Barante as a reader.[79] A liberal-minded Catholic with Jansenist leanings, Barante went on to become a celebrated historian and statesman.

In 1808, Barante published his *Tableau de la littérature française pendant le dix-huitième siècle*. Originally submitted for an essay competition on the topic of eighteenth-century literature, *De la littérature* appears not to have pleased the jury. Constant, however, liked it very much. He appreciated it for its balanced approach to the Enlightenment and for the way it handled religion. Barante's book is both a critical overview of eighteenth-century French literature and a remarkably even-handed and nuanced analysis of the causes of the French Revolution. In Barante's mind, the Revolution should not be attributed to just one factor, but to multiple and interrelated causes. He had harsh words for key *philosophes*, like Voltaire and Diderot, because of their cynicism and lack of moderation; but the *philosophes* alone were not to blame. Indeed, they themselves were symptoms of a more general crisis. Barante also blamed the institution of absolute monarchy, the frivolity and hypocrisy of kings like Louis XIV, and the nefarious effects of a "dominating clergy." In particular, he regretted the harm done to religion and morals during the eighteenth century. It came from a multiplicity of sources: absolutist kings, the Catholic clergy, and those *philosophes* who would "reduce everything to sensations."[80]

---

[78] *Lettres de Benjamin Constant à sa famille 1775–1830*, ed. Jean-H. Menos (Paris, 1931), Letter no. CXCIX, April 20, 1813, p. 483.

[79] Letter no. III, May 16, 1806, in PB, p. 243.

[80] Prosper de Barante (1782–1866), *Tableau de la littérature française pendant le dix-huitième siècle* (Paris, 1832), pp. 5, 165.

Such a wide-ranging critique was bound to frustrate Barante's jury and many of his readers. Everyone from Catholic monarchists to Idéologues could find something at which to take offense. Constant, on the other hand, immediately praised it as level-headed and scholarly; he especially appreciated its fair treatment of sensitive topics like religion. In a letter to Barante, Constant expressed regret for the polarized intellectual climate in France and the herd-mentality that was making it impossible for the book to be properly appreciated. Everyone was expected either to attack or to defend religion; one had to be either for it or against it. On one side "there are people called *philosophes*, and when one is a *philosophe* one must be interested only in the destruction of religion, and accept everything as long as religion is destroyed." On the other, "there are people called devout and according to them doubt is a crime and religion a positive, fixed thing made up of forms well determined [*bien tracé*] ahead of time and from which one is not allowed to deviate." "In the end," he complained, "there are no individuals, but batallions who wear uniforms ... Poor devils like you and I ... don't know where to stand."[81]

His correspondence with Barante also testifies to Constant's despair over France's growing "decrepitude," political as well as moral, which he linked with the polarized intellectual climate. The moral degeneration was closely related to the unhealthy religious climate. Interestingly, Constant repeated several times his fear that day by day France was becoming more like China, the quintessential symbol of a soulless state. "China! China!," he exclaims, "We are becoming like it, we are marching towards it with big steps. Money, ceremonies, forms, that is all that remains to us."[82] Like the Chinese, the French were becoming "a mechanical species," totally predictable and uniform, like cogs in a machine.[83]

Interspersed with Constant's criticisms of France are comments on his progress with the book on religion; in Constant's mind, the two were clearly linked. In fact, he confides to Barante that his book will say plenty about France's moral decline and the litany of vices gripping it, almost all of which have something to do with religion:

I take quite some pleasure in describing, especially in the last part, the collapse of all opinions, the degeneration of the human species, skepticism reducing everything to dust, man no longer having the strength to believe in anything and puffing himself up with what is a symptom of the most incurable weakness,

---

[81] Letter no. VI, February 25, 1808, in PB, p. 250.
[82] Ibid., p. 251.   [83] Letter no. XXII (n.d), ibid., p. 538.

universal banter, authorities picking up religion, throwing it away, picking it up again, covering it with mud, then cleaning it off to use it, then breaking the instrument to make it more supple, *philosophes* turned into parasites, priests beggars one moment and courtisans the next.[84]

Of particular interest is the fact that Constant's letters do not just describe religion as a *problem*; occasionally, they present it as a *solution*. They indicate that he was beginning to believe that the ongoing religious revival might actually have favorable repercussions. In one letter, for example, Constant concludes: "only religion can revive us, just as only miracles can revive the dead."[85] In another, he proposes that France might be on the verge of some new and miraculous transformation:

Aren't you struck as I am, my dear Prosper, by the great religious impulse that seems imprinted on everyone's minds ...? Religion has left the exterior of life, but only in order better to enter the interior of man ... Is it our epoch? There is without a doubt some resemblances [between our epoch and] that which pre-ceeded and favored the establishment of Christianity. But doesn't our epoch itself have something of the miraculous about it?[86]

Under otherwise depressing circumstances, Constant's book on religion salvages his morale: "I have thrown myself entirely into my book on religion," he writes on March 20, 1808, "it is the only thing that interests me and revives me."[87]

Characteristically, Constant's letters reveal his predilection for deep introspection. He recounts that he feels sad and discouraged at times, and tells of his efforts to cure such bouts of depression with the help of religion. He confesses that he has grown "tired of incredulity."[88] One especially interesting letter discusses his exposure to the Inner Souls and the "revolution" that has occurred in him since he first met the group a year previously. Learning to abdicate one's will helps to get rid of "egoism," he explains; it can also lead to the understanding that one is "surrounded by an intelligent force." Constant adds that he can even tolerate "superstition" now, since he has come to understand the word's true meaning:

Superstition is, in fact, what survives everything ... It is nothing but applied religion, adapted to the needs we have at any moment. Religion without what is

---

[84] Letter no. VII, March 20, 1808, ibid., pp. 252–253.
[85] Letter no. XIV, November 23, 1808, ibid., p. 269.
[86] Letter no. XIII, October 21, 1808, ibid., pp. 267–8.
[87] Letter no. VII, March 20, 1808, ibid., p. 252.
[88] Letter no. XII, September 18, 1808, ibid., p. 266.

called superstition is only philosophy of another kind: and who says philosophy says something essentially dry and sterile.

Constant continues: "I don't know if you understand all this; I realize that I am describing, as a non-believer, the advantages of what is called superstition."[89]

Two months later, Constant again writes of renouncing his will and also of having read many mystics, including Madame Guyon.[90] With humor, he recounts that he even visited a fortune-teller, but remained unconvinced. Then, reflecting on his religious evolution, he claims that his views are now not so different from Barante's: "It is not religious practice that I reproach," he explains; "on the contrary, I like it and it does me good." What he opposes is only "the desire to impose [religion] on others."[91] No one should be able to force another to take any other route to religion than his own. Constant also tries to describe the nature of his own belief. "My religion consists in two things," he writes, "to want what God wants, that is, to pay him homage with my heart; [and] to deny nothing, that is, to pay him homage with my mind." Given these two things, a "road is established from earth to heaven," which allows each person to find his own private way. It is a road that provides "protection" and "consolation" and a sense of "providence" to each and every traveler.[92]

DE L'ALLEMAGNE

By 1809, Constant's and Madame de Staël's tempestuous romance had come to an end. They were no longer in love, but neither were they able to let go of each other, making for a relationship that was at times excruciating. They often fought. Quite remarkably, however, throughout their emotional turmoil, their intellectual bond remained strong. A frequent visitor to Coppet during these years observed:

No one has known Madame de Staël unless he has seen her with Benjamin Constant. He alone ha[s] the power, through an intelligence equal to hers to bring all her intelligence into play, to enhance it by competition, to kindle an eloquence, a depth of feeling and thought that she never revealed in all its brilliance except in his presence; neither was he ever truly himself except at Coppet.[93]

---

[89] Letter no. XI, July 27, 1808, ibid., pp. 262–263.
[90] Letter no. XII, September 18, 1808, ibid., p. 266.
[91] Letter no. XIV, October 23, 1808, ibid., p. 269. [92] Ibid.
[93] Sismondi to Eulalie de Saint-Aulaire, Letter no. 428 (December 13, 1830) in G. C. L. Sismondi, *Epistolario*, vol. III (Florence, 1824–35).

Therefore, in the spring of 1809, it would have been natural for
Madame de Staël to ask Constant to drop what he was doing and help her
put the finishing touches on her latest book, *De l'Allemagne*. Such was the
nature of their intellectual partnership that Constant came almost at once
and remained for a full seven weeks, this despite the fact that he had only
recently got married and was leaving his new bride alone in Paris. In a
very real sense, the finished *De l'Allemagne* reflects attitudes and ideas that
Constant and Madame de Staël shared – ideas on Napoleon, Idéologie,
and religion.

De l'Allemagne employs a discussion of Germany to criticize
Napoleonic France. Widely credited with launching romanticism in
France, the book is perhaps most of all a slashing critique of Napoleonic
despotism; however, it is also a stinging indictment of French moral
values, that de Staël sees as playing right into the hands of the dictator.
Frenchmen are "frivolous," she writes; they are "sarcastic," increasingly
egotistical, and obsessed with their material well-being. The fault for this
lies not only with Napoleon's form of rule and centuries of authoritarian
government, but also with French philosophy. Signaling her definitive
break with the Idéologues, Madame de Staël now largely blames their
ideas for the lamentable state of French morals. The influence of Villers,
whom she mentions by name, is very apparent. Like Villers, she show-
cases German literature and philosophy in order to expose the deficiencies
of France. And again like Villers, she believes that in order for France to
reform itself, it must cast off the "degrading" doctrines of Idéologie. Its
sensationalist epistemology debases human nature, while its morality of
self-interest perverts morals, making people fatalistic and egotistical. The
principles of Idéologie are just "prudent calculation"; destructive of "all
magnanimous sentiments," they favor the designs of Napoleon by helping
him to "establish the yoke of all kinds of authority."[94]

In contrast to the notions of self-interest favored by Idéologues, de
Staël proffers the religious concepts of soul, conscience, duty, and even
"enthusiasm" – all presented as express antidotes to self-interest. "Man's
destination on earth," she explains, is not mere material well-being or
"happiness." Echoing Constant, she writes that man has a "higher destiny," which concerns his "moral improvement [*perfectionnement*]." And
this improvement, she emphasizes, cannot be furthered by self-interest.
Rather, it requires precisely the opposite: self-sacrifice. It requires

[94] Ibid., pp. 90, 181, 188, 185.

generosity and "magnanimous sentiments," in other words, devotion to something larger than oneself.[95]

De Staël praises the "new German philosophy" for realizing this. Unlike the French and Idéologue variety, German philosophy affirms the moral dignity of man and respects religion. She admires Kant in particular for refuting sensationalism and the degrading morality of self-interest. Moreover, and this is a major point in the book, the Germans have the right attitude towards religion. They do not fear it as being incompatible with learning or Enlightenment, and they do not see it simply as a bridle on the people or "a penal code."[96]

Unsurprisingly, Madame de Staël's own religion appears to be almost entirely devoid of dogmas. Like Constant, she describes religion not as a set of doctrines, beliefs, or practices, but as "an inner need" or "sentiment." She praises the Germans for not espousing or rejecting any one "form" of religion; rather, they focus on the essential "sentiment of infinity" that inhabits them all. Anticipating Constant's thesis in *De la religion*, de Staël writes that "all dogmas and all cults are diverse forms that religious sentiment has assumed according to the times and according to the country." Like him, she connects religion with self-sacrifice, at times suggesting that religion and the ability to give of oneself, or rise above oneself, are the same thing. "The very premise of religious happiness," she writes, is "the sacrifice of ourselves." This is why religion "is the true foundation of morals."[97]

Unsurprisingly, de Staël also portrays Protestantism in a favorable light. She presents the Reformation as a leap forward in the progress of mankind. Why was the Protestant Reformation progressive? Because it introduced the concept of "free inquiry" into religion. As Wittmer has noted, it is not just once, but at least ten times in her book that Staël proclaims "free inquiry" to be *the* principle of Protestantism.[98] It is free inquiry that allows Protestantism to evolve and keep up to date with society's progress, while Catholicism remains frozen in the past. Protestantism makes it possible for religion and enlightenment not only to coexist in peace, but also to "serve each other mutually." Encouraging "enlightened conviction," the Protestant principle of free inquiry will allow for further improvements in the Protestant religion.[99]

---

[95] Ibid., pp. 196, 91, 196.   [96] Ibid., p. 241.
[97] Ibid., pp. 238, 266, 198–199.
[98] Wittmer, *Charles de Villers*, p. 264. For further discussion of this, see Rosenblatt, "Madame de Staël."
[99] DA, pp. 244–245.

While Madame de Staël projects an essentially pro-Protestant outlook in *De l'Allemagne*, her recent experiences with mysticism had left their mark.[100] "To resign oneself to the will of God," she writes, and "to want nothing but what He wants [is] the purest religious act of which the human soul is capable." Such comments seem to bear the imprint of the Inner Souls; as we have seen, Constant was expressing similar ideas at the time. It is perhaps also due to "the great wave of mysticism" that inundated Coppet in 1807–8 that de Staël hopefully anticipates some kind of Christian reunion. In the last part's opening chapter, she writes: "perhaps are we on the verge of some development in Christianity which would reassemble into one family all the scattered rays." Elsewhere, she speculates: "it could be that one day a cry for union rises up, and that the universality of Christians aspires to profess the same theological, political and moral religion." It is clear, however, that Madame de Staël's mysticism and yearning for Christian union are in the service of an essentially liberal and *Protestant* agenda. She states that any legitimate union could never be based on force, and even suggests that, in all likelihood, it could not happen under the present circumstances in France. "[B]efore such a miracle is accomplished," she explains, "all men who have a heart and who obey it must respect each other." Were a Christian reunification to happen, its basis would not be *doctrinal* agreement, since "it is only through *sentiment* that one can arrive at unanimity among men."[101]

In a letter written a few years later, Madame de Staël clarified what she meant by mysticism and how it related to her views on Catholicism and Protestantism, and her hopes for Christian reunification. "Liberty and religion stick together in my thought," she explained, adding that she of course meant "an *enlightened* religion" and "a *just* liberty." Mysticism meant "the religion of Fénelon," a religion "that has its sanctuary in the heart." It was an undogmatic religion based on emotions and sentiments. In so far as mysticism was all about religious *sentiments* rather than dogma, it "unites what is good in Catholicism and in Protestantism and separates religion entirely from the political influence of priests."[102] All of this was why she could refer to mysticism as "the reformation of the Reformation."[103]

---

[100] Isbell, *European Romanticism*, is very informative here.
[101] DA, pp. 264, 238, 262, 202, emphasis added.
[102] Letter to Madame Gerando, September 1815, quoted by Isbell, *European Romanticism*, p. 178, emphasis added.
[103] Ibid.

In May 1811 Constant returned to Germany, this time accompanied by his new wife, Charlotte. Arriving in Göttingen in August, Constant renewed his friendship with Villers and dedicated himself to finishing his book on religion. Diary entries testify to the singlemindedness with which he pursued his work. The journal also indicates that his marriage was not going well. Constant soon found his wife to be unintelligent and boring, and they often fought. And, as before, he found the Germans' conversation tedious and missed the social life of Paris. His frustrations help explain the frequent appearance in his journal of the initials "l.v.d.s.f", short for "May the will of God be done [*que la volonté de Dieu soit faite*]." Applying the lessons learned with the Inner Souls, Constant tried to resign his will to God's in order to obtain peace. His diary entries also record that he was reading the early Church Fathers. A February 1813 entry states that reading the Bible has "turned [his] ideas upside down."[104]

Letters to his friends Prosper de Barante and Claude Hochet[105] indicate that work on his book now involved reorganizing and rewriting what he had written before, reflecting the change in his opinions of religion since he began. The old version, begun many years ago, went in "the opposite sense" of what he now thought was "right and good." Indeed, with limited effort, he could turn his earlier manuscript into "a system of atheism" and a "manifesto against priests." But such a book no longer reflected his point of view, and thus he was "redoing" much of it. He explained to Hochet: "My book is singular proof of what Bacon says, that a little science leads to atheism and more science to religion."[106]

Other letters indicate that Constant thought it was the project itself that was causing him to alter his opinions. He wrote to Barante that in the course of his research he had discovered the value of religion "without wanting to." He was now obliged to rewrite his book according to an entirely "new plan," so that he could incorporate his "new ideas."[107] To Hochet, he reiterated a "perfectly true" comment made by a local

---

[104] JI, p. 108.

[105] Claude-Jean-Baptiste Hochet (1772–1857) met Constant and de Staël in the salon of Madame Suard. A collaborator on Suard's journal, *Le Publiciste*, he became their lifelong confidant and friend.

[106] letter no. LXXXVI, October 11, 1811, in B. Constant and G. de Staël, *Lettres à un ami: cent onze lettres inédites à Claude Hochet*, ed. J. Mistler (Neuchâtel, 1948), pp. 195, 194.

[107] letter no. XXVI, October 11, 1811, in PB, p. 546.

German professor: "it wasn't I who was making my book, but my book that was making me."[108]

"[G]radually, [and] as the facts kind of forced [him],"[109] Constant adopted ideas more favorable to religion. Once he had changed perspective, and "frankly admitted these [religious] truths," a "wonderful simplicity" came over his work. Suddenly, he found his way: "my ideas organized themselves ... great enigmas were resolved."[110] Constant recounted that "German philosophy" had helped him a lot, although he did not agree with it entirely. It was definitely superior to the "narrow and cynical" philosophy of Voltaire, Helvétius, Diderot, or Cabanis. While "a bit vague," it was "respectful of all that is religious."[111] Having been exposed to German theology fifteen years previously, Constant was now fully able to absorb its lessons in ways increasingly favorable to religion. As he wrote to Barante, "this tendency of man to improve his religion ... far from being proof that religion is nothing but a chimera ... is proof that religion is his goal and primitive destination."[112]

THE SPIRIT OF CONQUEST AND USURPATION (1814)

In late October 1813, Constant received the news of the Battle of Leipzig, and realized that Napoleon's end was near. He also received letters from Madame de Staël urging him to get involved with the rapidly changing political situation. She wanted Constant to join her in supporting the candidacy of Jean-Baptiste Bernadotte (1763–1844) to the French throne. A former marshal under Napoleon, Bernadotte was now the Crown Prince of Sweden.[113] The moment was just right, Madame de Staël thought, to make France a constitutional monarchy with Bernadotte as king. "What I don't understand," she wrote to Constant on April 17, 1813, "is why your taste for letters has not manifested itself earlier and why it won't manifest itself now? ... What are you doing with your rare genius?"[114]

Once again, Constant responded to Madame de Staël's call. He put aside his book on religion and threw himself into the political battle. On November 6, he met with Bernadotte in Hanover and offered his services;

---

[108] letter no. XCVIII, December 2, 1812, in *Lettres à un ami*, p. 229.

[109] letter no. XXVI, October 11, 1811, in PB p. 546.

[110] letter no. XXVII, December 2, 1811, ibid., p. 549.

[111] Ibid.   [112] letter no. XXVI, October 11, 1811, ibid., p. 546.

[113] He was also a recent convert to Protestantism. He became King Karl XIV Johan of Sweden in 1818.

[114] letter no. 57, April 17, 1813, Madame de Staël to Benjamin Constant, in KK, p. 146.

simultaneously he began work on an essay to support Bernadotte's bid for the throne. Soon, however, it became evident that he would not be a viable candidate after all; the crowned heads of Europe would only accept a Bourbon on the French throne. Constant therefore made a few changes to his essay, but published it anyway. It quickly went through several editions and became recognized as a classic of its genre.

Constant's hastily written pamphlet, *The Spirit of Conquest and Usurpation*, was the product of his long and deep reflections. His main argument, for which he now became famous, was that governments, in order to be successful, had to be in keeping with their country's "stage of social development." Despotism was impossible in modern times. Thus, the Napoleonic dictatorship had been doomed from the outset. Given France's "stage of civilization," authoritarian types of government bent on military conquest were anachronisms, bound to fail. France had "reached the age of commerce," a stage of development that required peace and a maximum level of personal liberty for its citizens. It was a great tragedy for France that Napoleon had been so fundamentally wrong "about what [was] actually possible." His form of rule was entirely out of synch with the present "stage of our civilization."[115]

Constant also made public many ideas on modern liberty that he had already expressed in his as yet unpublished *Principles of Politics*. If despotism was no longer possible in modern times, neither was the hyper-politicized form of liberty practiced by the ancients. The liberty of ancient republics, Constant explained, consisted in the "active participation in collective power." The people in its entirety contributed to the making of laws, and, for this, individual citizens had to make considerable personal sacrifices. Modern men were simply not ready to make such sacrifices. They aspired not to political participation, but to "peaceful enjoyment of individual independence." This was the inevitable result of the "commercial tendency of the age." What modern men wanted most was "repose," and along with repose, the ability to engage in "industry," "peaceful work," and "regular exchange."[116] For these reasons, modern governments were obliged to guarantee the rights of individuals to everything from property to privacy and free expression.

First and foremost, however, Constant's pamphlet was a sweeping indictment of Napoleon's despotic regime. Constant even used a special word for it: he called it "usurpation," which he said was "more hateful" than despotism, in the way that it "trampled" on principles and employed

[115] SCU, pp. 51, 53, 48, 140.   [116] Ibid., pp. 102, 54.

"treachery, violence and perjury" to accomplish its goals. Pervading the entire pamphlet is Constant's deep moral outrage over the corruption fostered by Napoleon's despotism. Large parts read more like a dissertation on moral decline than a treatise on constitutional monarchy. If the liberal principles Constant had articulated in his *Principles of Politics* were designed to unlock human potential and allow for the improvement of individuals, Napoleon's despotism had accomplished precisely the reverse. The despot's rule had encouraged only the "moral degradation and evergrowing ignorance"[117] of the French population.

The despicable "military spirit" that Napoleon had instilled in the population was only one part of a much larger problem. Long before the arrival of "the age of commerce," soldiers had fought for "nobler motives." Then, they were motivated by "ideal[s]" and "conviction[s]." Under modern conditions, however, such lofty goals were no longer possible. The true impetus behind present-day military expansionism was only "a base greed for present and material enjoyments." This was also why military expansionism was now inherently anachronistic. All that modern armies really accomplished was to "turn ... the progress of civilization against civilization itself." Dedicated only to the principle of self-interest, they entirely destroyed "learning, delicacy, rightness of mind and that tradition of gentleness, nobility and elegance that alone distinguishes us from the barbarians."[118]

Constant had scathing words for Bonaparte and what he had done to France:

Surely, Bonaparte is a thousand times more guilty than those barbarous conquerors who, ruling over barbarians, were by no means at odds with their age. Unlike them, he has chosen barbarism; he has preferred it. In the midst of enlightenment, he has sought to bring back the night. He has chosen to transform into greedy and bloodthirsty nomads a mild and polite people.

But it was not just the military expansionism promoted by Napoleon that was so profoundly corrupting, it was also the nature of his rule. While he "dazzl[ed]" the people with his military conquests, he abolished freedom of the press, banished all political discussion, and turned France into a "vast prison." Arbitrary power "destroys morality," Constant explained, because it instills fear in everyone. Since everyone is frightened, no one dares to contest or even to criticize the regime. This is also why men under despotic regimes "plunge into selfishness." They turn inwards, focusing on themselves and

---

[117] Ibid., pp. 95, 6.   [118] Ibid., pp. 60, 56, 57, 56, 57, 68.

their material comforts, because that is all they dare concern themselves with. The simple truth, Constant insists, is that "there is no morality in the absence of security"; "everyone marches, his eyes lowered, on the narrow path which is to lead him safely towards his grave." Over time, moral "apathy" and "stupor" set in, and ideas simply "dr[y] up."[119]

Napoleon did not just silence the population. To say that would be to deny the distinctively modern and pernicious nature of his rule. Napoleon's style of government reached a new level of despotism by the unprecedented extent of its intrusiveness into the lives of private individuals. Crucially, the Emperor also managed to mobilize popular support in new and insidious ways: he "extorted or paid for acclamation" and he "counterfeit[ed] liberty" in innumerable ways. Thus, he was able to enlist the population in his hypocrisy and deceit, in effect making the French people "participate . . . in their own subjugation." This new kind of popular mobilization was the distinguishing factor between mere "despotism" and Napoleonic "usurpation":

Despotism, in a word, rules by means of silence, and leaves man the right to be silent; usurpation condemns him to speak, it pursues him into the most intimate sanctuary of his thoughts, and by forcing him to lie to his own conscience, deprives the oppressed of his last remaining consolation.[120]

Although Constant blamed Napoleon for what happened to France, he alone was not responsible; there were accomplices. There were the intellectuals who advised and encouraged him, and the population that willingly bowed down to him. Indeed, one of the main points of the *Spirit of Conquest and Usurpation* was to identify the underlying conditions that had made Napoleon's rise and despotism possible. Beyond the individuals who collaborated with him and the population who willingly submitted to him, Constant pointed the finger of blame at specific intellectual trends that had helped Napoleon to subjugate the country. In particular, Constant identified the French Enlightenment's attack on religion and the Idéologues' morality of self-interest. By denying the value of religion and trumpeting a philosophy of self-interest, French intellectuals had unwittingly encouraged Napoleon's despotic designs.

When he first arrived here, alone, out of poverty and obscurity, and until he was twenty-four, his greedy gaze wandering over the country around him, why did we show him a country in which any religious idea was the object of irony? When he listened to what was professed in our circles, why did serious thinkers

---

[119] Ibid., pp. 161–162, 91, 45, 118, 126, 118, 117, 122, 121.   [120] Ibid., pp. 95, 162, 96–97.

tell him that man had no other motivation than his own interest? ... Finally, when in a France torn apart, tired of suffering and lamenting, and demanding only a ruler, he offered to become that ruler, why did the multitude hasten to solicit from him their enslavement? When the crowd is pleased to show its love for servitude, it would be too much for it to expect its master to insist on giving it liberty instead.[121]

The Napoleonic episode had caused religion a great deal of harm. Here again, Constant blamed not only Napoleon, but also his willing accomplices. Napoleon had tried to "humiliate" religion by turning it into his political "slave"; thanks to a favorably disposed clergy, he had almost succeeded:

Oh shame! We have seen [the French clergy] ordering invasions and massacres in the name of a religion of peace, soiling the sublimity of holy books with the sophisms of politics, disguising their sermons as manifestos, blessing heaven for the triumphs of crime and blaspheming against the will of God by accusing it of complicity.

On the other hand, French intellectuals were also culpable: by denying the value of religion altogether, they had encouraged selfish, materialistic, and politically servile behavior. They had helped to create a country of

incredulous lackeys docilely crawling, bustling zealously about, denying God and trembling before a man, moved by nothing but fear, having no motive other than the salary which their oppressor throws to them.

Constant then added glumly: "a race that, in its voluntary degeneration has no illusions to raise it up, such a race has fallen from the rank which Providence has assigned to mankind."[122] The *philosophes* and Idéologues had irresponsibly attacked the "uplifting illusions" of the French people causing them to become selfish and servile.

The truth was, however, that these intellectuals were wrong. Man was not motivated by self-interest alone, and religion was not a chimera that could either be dismissed disdainfully or simply ignored. In France, "not all religious sentiment had been destroyed"; nor did "egoism ... reign alone." And, most importantly, "the national desire was *not* for servitude." Moreover, the French intellectuals' underlying morality of self-interest was fundamentally mistaken. Human beings did not only need "rest, industry, domestic happiness" or "private virtues" in order to be satisfied. Perhaps if they did, they could live relatively happily under conditions of despotism. But in reality human beings also needed "the

[121] Ibid., p. 162.   [122] Ibid., pp. 127, 127–128, 129.

activity of the mind"; they aspired to "the development of [their] intellectual faculties." And for this most basic need of human nature, they required freedom of thought and religion, freedoms that authoritarian regimes were unwilling to grant. "Man's intelligence cannot remain stationary," and neither can it be restricted to the menial tasks imposed on it by regimes like Napoleon's: "[the mind's] most noble need is not the ingenious adornment of frivolous subjects, adroit flattery, sonorous declamation upon different objects." Rather, "heaven and its own nature have made it an eternal tribunal, where everything is analyzed, examined and ultimately judged." To fulfill its purpose as "an eternal tribunal," ascribed to it by its "divine origins," the mind must be allowed complete freedom. When it is restricted, morality immediately suffers: "everything sinks, everything degenerates and is degraded."[123]

Constant's *Spirit of Conquest and Usurpation* is rightly celebrated as a powerful critique of despotism and an insightful plea for a new kind of liberty suited to a modern and commercial age. Once again, however, it is important to appreciate the moral concerns that pervade Constant's liberalism. Liberty is of inestimable value, he writes, "because it gives soundness to our mind, strength to our character, elevation to our soul."[124]

---

[123] Ibid., pp. 162, 120–121, 124, 121, 125. [124] Ibid., p. 110.

CHAPTER 5

Politics and religion during the Restoration (1814–1824)

KEEPING POLITICAL LIBERTY ALIVE

Constant's vacillations

Constant's vacillations during the early phases of the Restoration have been well scrutinized. First, upon the collapse of Napoleon's regime, Constant rallied to the constitutional monarchy of Louis XVIII; he even produced the outline of a constitution for such a monarchy, which he published in May 1814.[1] Then, upon Napoleon's return less than a year later, Constant switched allegiances, accepting a position in Napoleon's Council of State, and producing a constitution for him as well. After Napoleon's second abdication and the re-ascension of Louis XVIII, Constant once again rallied to this government, eventually becoming one of its staunchest defenders. Such rapid turn-abouts elicited charges of inconsistency, opportunism, and hypocrisy that dogged Constant for the rest of his life and which have made a lasting imprint on scholars. His adversaries called him, at worst, an unprincipled turncoat or, at best, a wavering fool, someone so desperate for a political position in government that he would sacrifice his most basic principles for a spot in the limelight. It was suggested that the real reason for his erratic behavior involved one of his last great "extravagances," an intensely passionate and rather bizarre infatuation with the legendary beauty, Juliette Récamier (1777–1849). At the time, Récamier had three other suitors, all of whom Constant, in fits of jealous despair, challenged to duels. Meanwhile, his love for Récamier remained unrequited, making him seem all the more pathetic. Thus did the "inconstant Constant" become the butt of many snide remarks, derisive jokes, and contemptuous epithets.

---

[1] *Réflexions sur les constitutions, la distribution des pouvoirs et les garanties dans une monarchie constitutionnelle*, in OCBC *Œuvres* VIII, 2, pp. 951–1061.

In retrospect, however, it is his consistency, rather than his inconsistency, that is noteworthy during these controversial episodes. To understand this, one must return to Constant's breakthrough of 1806: it was not the "form" of a government that mattered, nor *who* held the reins of power, but *how much* power and what kind of power was held. During the First Restoration, Louis XVIII committed many blunders that bespoke of his lukewarm attitude to the principles of constitutional monarchy. This alienated him from large portions of the population who had not been enthusiastic about him in the first place. Constant, however, remained part of the loyal opposition and only withdrew his support after the king himself had relinquished the reins of power and fled the country.

Thereafter, Constant's collaboration with Napoleon during the Hundred Days focused on getting the former emperor to accept a constitution that was more liberal than Louis XVIII's. Upon his return, Napoleon painted himself as a savior of the Revolution, who would prevent a return to the Old Regime. Constant tried to hold him to this task by drawing up the "Additional Act to the Constitutions of the Empire"; this document, very similar to Louis XVIII's Charter, was the most liberal constitution France had ever seen. Surely, Constant's effort to get Napoleon to acquiesce and rule by such a constitution evidences Constant's idealism and, perhaps, naivety more than any cynical opportunism or hypocrisy on his part.

In response to those who accused him of being without scruples in politics, Constant published his *Principles of Politics* in May 1815, meant as a companion piece to the new constitution. He drew his main points from his manuscript of 1806, presenting his ideas so as to educate the French reading public and answer any concerns they may have had in the troubled political climate.

On the opening page of this text, readers found an unambiguous statement followed by an equally unambiguous endorsement: "Our present constitution formally recognizes the principle of the sovereignty of the people ... this principle cannot be contested." Of course, Constant knew very well that, at the time, royalists who wished to restore the Old Regime were contesting it. But Constant also clarified his position: by supporting the principle of popular sovereignty, he was no Jacobin disciple of Rousseau; rather, he was a liberal, who believed that sovereignty could legitimately have "only a limited and relative existence." "No authority upon earth is unlimited," he declared, "neither that of the people, nor that of the men who declare themselves their representatives, nor that of the kings." Besides the principle of popular sovereignty, he was also committed to the need for a "distribution and balance of powers" and the general project of "sheltering individuals from governments." Individuals have rights that are independent of all social and political authority. Constant listed them as "Individual freedom, religious freedom, freedom of opinion, which includes the freedom to express oneself openly, the enjoyment of property."[2]

After Waterloo and Napoleon's second abdication, Constant left the country. But a memoir explaining his conduct under Napoleon was so convincing that Louis XVIII allowed him to return to France. An expanded version, *Mémoires sur les cent jours*, was published in 1820. In it, Constant explained why his collaboration with Napoleon was not a betrayal of his principles:

I have always believed, and the belief has been the rule of my conduct, that in matters of government it is necessary to start from the point where one is; that liberty is possible under all forms; that liberty is the end and the forms [of government] are the means.[3]

Constant thus began the slow process of shedding his reputation as an unprincipled opportunist. Gradually, he rose in the French public's esteem. He became a leading figure of liberal constitutionalism, tirelessly defending the principles he had laid out in his *Principles of Politics*. He did this as an elected deputy and gifted speaker in the Chamber (1819–22, 1824–30), and as a prolific journalist and writer.

Under Constant's guidance, the liberals' principal aim was to protect the revolutionary settlement – civil equality, representative government, and individual freedoms – while steering France towards a British-type constitutional monarchy they thought would suit it. The Charter, or constitution by which Louis XVIII ruled, was vague and even contradictory on several key issues, allowing for conflicting interpretations. The challenge was to defend it, while giving it as liberal an inflection as possible under the circumstances. Constant did this by fighting for the expansion of the franchise and by resisting the royalists' repeated attempts to restore a territorial aristocracy through the imposition of primogeniture and entailments. He also advocated increased powers for the legislature, the election of local government officials, the liberalization of press laws, and the expansion of the jury system. He fought to maintain and fortify the rule of law and constitutional procedures. He lobbied for

---

[2] PoP 1815, pp. 175, 180, 183, 179, 180.
[3] *Mémoires sur les cent jours, en forme de lettres* (Paris, 1820), p. 61.

liberal economic principles such as free trade and the end to unnecessary restrictions and prohibitions on business. In countless speeches delivered in the Chamber of Deputies, and in an astounding number of pamphlets and articles published in opposition newspapers, Constant defended liberal principles and warned against the abuse of power wherever he saw it. Only a constitutional government abiding by liberal laws could provide the "positive safeguards" necessary to guarantee the liberty of individuals. "What prevents arbitrary power," he insisted, "is the observance of procedures ... it is to them alone that the oppressed may appeal."[4]

As Robert Alexander has shown, Constant also rendered invaluable services to the liberal cause through his work as a grassroots organizer. By participating in banquets, petitions, and subscriptions across the country, he helped not only to encourage the politicization of the French electorate, but equally to build the political networks and organizations that liberals needed to succeed in elections. During the Restoration, Constant proved himself to be "a great constituency man."[5]

The problem of industrie

Constant's main adversaries during this period were the Ultraroyalists, men like Louis de Bonald and Joseph de Maistre, whose openly professed goal was to undo the Revolution and restore the Old Regime. They would bring back the authoritarian and Catholic monarchy, overthrow the principle of civil equality, and rid France of Constant's cherished freedoms. Heading the list were freedoms related to religion and opinion, which they viewed as conducive to "anarchy" and moral decline. Both Bonald and de Maistre denounced liberalism as an "antisocial" and immoral doctrine responsible not only for the "satanic" Revolution but also for what they held to be France's steady decline ever since. In numerous articles and speeches, Constant warned against their extremist views, which, he insisted, were as absurd as they were dangerous.

Less well known are Constant's other political adversaries during the Restoration, for instance, the more moderate royalists.[6] But perhaps even more importantly, during the 1820s, serious disagreements began to manifest themselves within Constant's own liberal left. The "liberals"

---

[4] PoP 1815, p. 292.
[5] R. Alexander, *Re-Writing the French Revolutionary Tradition* (Cambridge, 2003), p. 274.
[6] See Annelien de Dijn, *French Political Thought from Montesquieu to Tocqueville: Liberty in a Levelled Society?* (Cambridge, 2008).

were not an actual party yet, at least not in the modern sense of the term, and considerable differences of opinion existed among Constant's friends and allies.[7] Throughout the Restoration period, and with the growing strength of reactionary forces during the mid-1820s, Constant worked hard to convince liberals to remain committed to their constitutional principles. He tried to educate them, fortify them, and he even chastised them when he detected dangerous tendencies in their way of thinking. What distinguished Constant from other liberals was his moral vision, his constant promotion of the moral "self-improvement [*perfectionnement*]" of individuals. In some ways, Constant's moral concerns only grew more acute as the reactionaries ascended and France seemed to be heading backwards.

We already know about Constant's growing disenchantment with the Idéologues' morality of self-interest. We have seen that Madame de Staël was taking her distance from the Idéologues in *De la littérature* (1800) and that by *De l'Allemagne* (1810), her breach with them was very much in the open. As for Constant, the *Spirit of Conquest and Usurpation* identified the morality of self-interest as an important contributing factor in France's subjugation by Napoleon, and the *Principles of Politics* insisted on the need for religious sentiments precisely in order "to stimulate man to step *beyond the narrow circle of his interests*."[8]

During the Restoration, Constant began to worry about a new trend that was an offshoot of Idéologie. This new trend was a liberal social theory that eventually became known as "industrialism."[9] Important proponents of it were Charles Dunoyer (1786–1862), Charles Comte (1782–1837), and Claude Henri de Saint-Simon (1760–1825), all of whom started out as liberals with an orientation similar to Constant's. Over time, however, they began to change direction. Disillusioned by the upheavals of the revolutionary period and the succession of constitutions, none of which seemed to solve France's fundamental problems, they turned to the economic realm for what they hoped would be more lasting solutions. Adopting the Idéologues' language of self-interest, they abandoned faith in political and constitutional liberalism, and argued increasingly that *work* and production would cure France's ills. In the

---

[7] Alexander, *Re-Writing*. [8] PoP 1815, p. 277, emphasis added.
[9] The best introductions are E. Allix, "J.-B. Say et les origines de l'industrialisme," *Revue d'économie politique*, 24 (1910), pp. 303–313, 341–363; idem, "La méthode et la conception de l'économie politique dans les oeuvres de J.-B. Say," *Revue d'histoire des doctrines économiques et sociales*, 4 (1912), pp. 321–360; M. James, "Pierre-Louis Roederer, Jean-Baptiste Say, and the Concept of Industrie," *History of Political Economy*, 9 (1977), pp. 455–475; and Kaiser, "Politics and Political Economy."

journal *Le Censeur européen* (1817–18) and in other publications of the
1820s, they espoused a philosophy that has alternatively been described as
"militant economic liberalism" or "libertarianism."[10]

Early in their careers, Comte and Dunoyer had been activists in the
campaign for liberal constitutionalism, promoting freedom of speech,
trial by jury, and the rule of law. In fact, at one point they became famous
for their aggressive court cases, which challenged the abuses of the regime.
Around 1817–18, however, they began to abandon such battles. In the
writings of Dunoyer, the idea of a spontaneously self-regulating society
increasingly displaced politics as his main interest and hope. The future of
France, he argued, lay in *de*politicization; he looked forward to a complete withering away of the state, a time when all aspects of social and
economic life would be regulated by supply and demand. Dunoyer
believed that society would reach the height of perfection when everyone
worked and no one governed.[11]

A text by Dunoyer recounts his group's intellectual pilgrimage from
constitutional liberalism towards *industrie*.[12] It was through exposure to
political economy that they had begun to see the light. Two sources had
been fundamental to their intellectual development. One was Constant,
the first writer to have called attention to the "goal" society was moving
towards and which should be the true "purpose" of politics. Approvingly,
Dunoyer cited the passages in the *Spirit of Conquest and Usurpation* that
hail France's arrival in the "age of commerce" and proclaim the goals of
"industry," "peaceful work," and "regular exchange." The other source
was Jean-Baptiste Say, who, in the second edition of his *Traité d'économie
politique*, confirmed his intention to stop thinking about what should be
the right form of government. *Industrie* was society's true goal. Dunoyer
reviewed this work enthusiastically in *Le Censeur européen*.

Reading Constant and Say had caused a "revolution" in Dunoyer's
thinking. He suddenly realized that economic writers had a way of getting
to the "bottom" of things. They knew that an effective politics had to be
about more than constitutions. They focused on the "goal of social
activity," in other words, the prosperity and happiness of society, and did

---

[10] Welch, *Liberty and Utility*, p. 158.
[11] On Dunoyer, see D. Hart, "Class Analysis, Slavery and the Industrialist Theory of History in
French Liberal Thought, 1814–1830: The Radical Liberalism of Charles Comte and Charles
Dunoyer," unpublished Ph.D., King's College Cambridge, 1994. Online version available at
http://www.arts.adelaide.edu.au/personal/DHart/ClassicalLiberalism/ComteDunoyer/index.html
[12] C. Dunoyer, "Esquisse historique des doctrines auxquelles on a donné le nom d'Industrialisme,
c'est-à-dire, des doctrines qui fondent la société sur l'Industrie," *Revue encyclopédique*, 33 (1827),
p. 378.

not waste time on futile constitutional engineering.[13] Armed with this realization, Dunoyer used *Le Censeur européen* to promote the doctrine of *industrie*. The first edition announced his conviction that liberals should adopt "a new direction." A succession of transient political regimes had proved that good constitutions were not what made a people free. Given the deplorable moral state of the French people, its "vices," its "ignorance," and its political "incapacity," it was no wonder that the constitutions had failed. The cure did not lie in constitution-making;[14] rather, *industrie* held the keys to France's future. *Industrie* would reconcile the aims of economic and moral progress with social stability. Therefore, the focus of liberals should be on the promotion of productive work and wealth creation. "The first need of man," wrote Dunoyer's colleague, Charles Comte, "is to provide for his subsistence," to which Dunoyer added:

We've said it twenty times already, and we'll repeat it a thousand times more. The goal of man is not government; government should be just a very secondary thing ... [man's] goal is industry; it is work, it is the production of all the things necessary to his happiness.[15]

Dunoyer's other associate, Saint-Simon, was clearly on the same wavelength. In his own journal, appropriately entitled *L'Industrie*, he praised Jean-Baptiste Say for having suggested that "political economy is the real and only foundation of politics."[16]

As their commitment to *industrie* deepened, these young liberals became ever more disenchanted with the whole idea of political liberty. A notable change occurred in their attitude towards the English political system. Comte and Dunoyer began to speak less reverently about it. Instead, they praised England's recently adopted *laissez-faire* economic principles. The secret of that country's success, they now claimed, was not its form of government, but rather a culture dedicated to science and industry. France would be wise to adopt England's economic policies and refrain from emulating its political institutions. Dunoyer's recollections show his frustration with Constant, who was refusing to abandon an old-fashioned view of politics and embrace the program of *industrie*. Dunoyer noted that, after the *Spirit of Conquest*, "none of M. Benjamin Constant's writings showed that he understood the consequences of his own

---

[13] Ibid., pp. 374, 375, 370.   [14] *Le Censeur européen* (Paris, 1817), vol. I, pp. llj, 5, 71, and passim.
[15] *Le Censeur européen*, vol. II, pp. 1, 102.
[16] 'L'Industrie, in *Œuvres de Claude-Henri de Saint-Simon*, 6 vols. (Paris, 1966), vol. I, p. 185.

observations ... Most of his writings revolved around the kind of political questions quite correctly called metaphysical."[17]

Constant was, to be sure, still focused on educating the French in the liberal principles of *politics*. While his younger colleagues were abandoning political liberty and embracing the principles of *industrie*, Constant was giving lectures at the Athénée Royal[18] on the British constitutional system, which he obviously believed was still an instructive model for France. Between 1818 and 1820, Constant published, in four volumes, his *Collection complète des ouvrages publiés sur le Gouvernement représentatif et la Constitution actuelle de la France, formant une espèce de Cours de politique constitutionnelle*. He also ran for office; he was elected deputy for La Sarthe in 1818, and remained a deputy fighting for constitutional, liberal principles for most of the Restoration. In other words, Constant remained firmly committed to defending political liberty, while other liberals turned to the economy.

On the Liberty of the Ancients

The tensions within the liberal party form the immediate context of Constant's most famous and often-quoted text, "On the Liberty of the Ancients Compared with that of the Moderns." First delivered in 1819 as a lecture at the Athénée Royal,[19] where Constant was teaching his course on British constitutionalism, it was subsequently published separately as a pamphlet. In succinct terms, Constant reiterated what he, Madame de Staël, and others had been saying for some time, and that had inspired his younger liberal colleagues: France had reached the age of commerce. This age required a new form of liberty. The hyperpoliticized type of liberty practised by the ancients was no longer viable. "Since we live in modern times," Constant declared, "I want a liberty suited to modern times." Uninterested in and incapable of exercising the kind of liberty practiced in antiquity, modern men aspired only to "individual liberty" and "independence" from government. They wanted to live in peace and security, and to dedicate themselves to the pursuit of "private pleasures."[20]

---

[17] Dunoyer, "Esquisse," pp. 373–374.
[18] Originally founded as the Paris Lycée in 1785, and renamed the Athénée in 1802, this education center offered courses to adults. It became a liberal haven during the Restoration. See B. Haines, "The Athénée de Paris and the Bourbon Restoration," *History and Technology*, 5, (1988), pp. 29–271 and H. Guénot, "Musées et lycées Parisiens (1780–1830)," *Dix-huitième siècle*, 18 (1986), pp. 249–267.
[19] On this institution, see Haines, "The Athénée de Paris."
[20] "Liberty of the Ancients Compared with that of the Moderns," in PW, pp. 323, 317.

All of this was music to the ears of the budding political economists in his audience – those new young liberals attracted to the principles of *industrie*. They must have appreciated Constant's unequivocal endorsement of *laissez-faire* economic principles. Government intervention in the economy, he asserted, was "always a trouble and an embarrassment": "Every time governments pretend to do our own business, they do it more incompetently and expensively than we would."[21] These statements on commerce and modern liberty are what have made Constant's essay famous. Isaiah Berlin, no doubt, read them as the quintessential endorsement of the "negative" variety of liberalism he so admired. More recently, Pierre-Henri Tavoillot has quoted them to make the same point.[22] Constant did indeed say that modern men desired, above all, to be left alone and free from government interference so that they could pursue their own "private pleasures."

Surely, however, it would be wrong to read Constant's essay as a simple reiteration of these principles, which he had articulated in earlier writings and for which he had already become well known. To do so would be to ignore the importance of the last section, which, in all likelihood, he designed to be a climactic conclusion. Having reiterated the main principles of modern, "individual" liberty – principles with which his audience was familiar – Constant went on to insist that only *political* liberty could make modern liberty secure. He warned his fellow liberals against their recent tendency to economize liberty and to downplay the importance of political engagement.[23] "The danger of modern liberty," Constant lectured them, was that "absorbed in the enjoyment of our private independence, and in the pursuit of our particular interests, we should surrender our right to share in political power too easily." Such depoliticization, he warned, suits the "holders of authority," who "are only too anxious" to encourage it. Constant's point was that both types of liberty, "individual" *and* "political," were necessary, and that his audience should "learn to combine the two." He tried to make sure that nobody could possibly misinterpret what he was saying: "As you see, Gentlemen," he emphasized, "my observations do not in the least tend to diminish the value of political liberty."[24]

---

[21] Ibid., p. 315.
[22] P.-H. Tavoillot, "Fondation démocratique et autocritique libérale: Sieyès et Constant," in A. Renaut (ed.), *Histoire de la philosophie politique*, vol. IV: *Les critiques de la modernité politique* (Paris, 1999.)
[23] Others have called attention to Constant's concern for political liberty; see S. Holmes, *Benjamin Constant and the Making of Modern Liberalism* (New Haven, CT, 1984); Dijn, *French Political Thought*.
[24] "Liberty of the Ancients," pp. 326, 327, 323.

Constant reaffirmed what he saw as the indispensable *moral* component to modern liberty. Once again addressing the young liberals who were turning to economics as the answer to France's problems, and who were proposing economic prosperity and the "happiness" it generated as man's all-important goal, Constant asked: Was "happiness" really "the only aim of mankind"? His answer to the question merits being quoted in full:

in that case our course would be narrow indeed, and our destination far from elevated ... There is not one single one of us who, if he wished to abase himself, restrain his moral faculties, lower his desires, abjure activity, glory, deep and generous emotions, could not demean himself and be happy. No, Sirs, I bear witness to the better part of our nature, that noble disquiet which pursues and torments us, that desire to broaden our knowledge and develop our faculties. It is not to happiness alone, it is to self-improvement [*perfectionnement*] that our destiny calls us.

As if to complete the circle, Constant then added: "and political liberty is the most powerful, the most effective means of self-improvement that heaven has given us."[25]

The Commentaire sur l'ouvrage de Filangieri

Keeping political liberty alive became even more urgent to Constant after 1820. On February 13 of that year, the presumptive heir to the throne, the Duc de Berry, was assassinated by a Bonapartist fanatic, triggering a strong political reaction throughout the country. The Ultraroyalists were swept to power in the Chamber. A growing number of people blamed the assassination on liberalism, whose lax morals and *laissez-faire* principles were creating a state of "anarchy." In the name of "order" and "public safety," the government resorted to emergency laws, censorship, and, in several cases, outright repression. Newspapers were shut down, lecture courses were terminated, and prominent liberals were prosecuted in the courts. A so-called "double vote" was introduced for the richest part of the electorate and the government further manipulated tax qualifications to eliminate liberal voters.

Constant fought these measures as best he could with speeches in the Chamber, but he was vastly outnumbered. In 1822, he lost his bid for re-election, and soon the reactionary turn had reduced the liberals to only nineteen seats. Miraculously, Constant was returned to the Chamber in 1824. These were difficult times for liberals, some of whom, in frustration

[25] Ibid., p. 327.

with electoral politics, turned to illegal conspiratorial organization and planning insurrections to accomplish their aims.[26] Constant, however, remained committed to legal methods of resistance. He continued fighting the Ultraroyalists with speeches in the Chamber, and by writing articles and pamphlets. Along with liberal activists like Goyet de la Sarthe (1770–1833),[27] Constant worked to build the networks and to encourage the "genuine politicization"[28] needed for the liberals to recover from their electoral losses.

These setbacks only served to confirm the disenchantment some leftists were feeling about constitutional liberalism and electoral politics. This was a watershed moment in the intellectual evolution of previously liberal activists, men like Saint-Simon and his disciple, Auguste Comte. The liberal defeat caused both men to give up hope in political liberty. In reaction to the disheartening events, Saint-Simon began using the word "crisis" with increasing frequency. It enabled him to explain why he ultimately had to reject the liberal approach to government. France was in a desperate state of "disorganization."[29] Although liberals had been effective in destroying the feudal and theological system of the Old Regime, they had been less successful in establishing a much-needed "new system of order." Increasingly, Saint-Simon worried about anarchy, his tone becoming more emphatic over time. He distanced himself from "jurists and metaphysicians" – in other words liberals, like Constant, who obsessed about the "forms" of government, while they forgot about its "goal."[30] Government, Saint-Simon insisted, was more about ends than means. The goal of society being the general public's prosperity and happiness, only managerial action should be required to create the industrial system and to keep it going.

Gradually, Saint-Simon came to avoid the word "government" altogether, preferring instead to speak of "administration." What was needed to achieve an enlightened social order was a regime dominated not by "jurists and metaphysicians," but by entrepreneurs and scientists devoted to economic expansion. An effective industrial organization required the social leadership of experts, a hierarchy of talent, and an appropriate

---

[26] See A. Spitzer's study on the French Carbonari, *Old Hatreds and Young Hopes* (Cambridge, MA, 1971). Robert Alexander (*Re-Writing*) also discusses this in some detail.

[27] See their correspondence: *Benjamin Constant et Goyet de la Sarthe: Correspondance 1818–1822*, ed. E. Harpaz (Geneva, 1973).

[28] Alexander, *Re-Writing*, p. 339.   [29] *L'Industrie*, May 1817, in *Œuvres*, vol. I, p. 174.

[30] *Du système industriel*, in *Œuvres*, vol. III, p. 10.

community of ideas and values.[31] A scientifically rational system, he began to repeat, was one in which the most "capable" citizens "directed" public affairs.

Once an admirer of the British constitution, Saint-Simon now became increasingly hostile to it. Referring to Britain's "bastard constitution," he argued that its political system was "radically vicious" and should not be taken as a model for France. "The political state of England is a state of illness, a state of crisis," he wrote in 1821. During the years before his death in 1825, Saint-Simon labored to differentiate what he now referred to as industrialism from what he regarded as the overly metaphysical, "vague," and, interestingly enough, *sentimental* ideas associated with liberalism.[32] "Liberal" became an ugly word for him, and he encouraged his followers no longer to call themselves by that name.

Manifestly, Constant's brand of constitutional liberalism was now under attack from both left and right. On the right were the Ultraroyalists, represented by Bonald and de Maistre, who wanted to bring back an authoritarian, Catholic monarchy. On the left were those liberals who were losing their respect for constitutional principles and their faith in political liberty. Constant's *Commentaire sur l'ouvrage de Filangieri*, published in 1822 and 1824, answered adversaries on both sides, by proffering his own independent liberal line. In between the publications, he first ran and lost the election of November 13, 1823, and then won on February 26, 1824.

Once again, it is ironic that this text, though mostly neglected, is typically cited as evidence of Constant's primary commitment to *economic*, or *laissez-faire* principles.[33] This misses its principal point. While it is certainly true that Constant endorses *laissez-faire*, economic freedom is only part of Constant's message. The *Commentaire* also contains an urgent plea to fellow liberals of all stripes to keep the political spirit alive.

There was much in the *Commentaire* to please the advocates of *industrie* and to annoy royalists, whether moderate or Ultra. Constant insisted that there could be no turning back the clock. Once again, he repeated his positions: France had reached the age of commerce; the goal of modern men was not the same as those of antiquity; modern men aspired most of all to rest and ease, both of which depended on industry. Governments, Constant again argued, should play only a very limited role in the economy. But the

---

[31] Here I borrow the words of G. Iggers, *The Cult of Authority: The Political Philosophy of the Saint-Simonians, a Chapter in the Intellectual History of Totalitarianism* (The Hague, 1958), p. 20.

[32] *Catéchisme des industriels*, in *Œuvres*, vol. IV, pp. 178–203.

[33] Exceptions to the rule are Kloocke (in *Benjamin Constant*) and A. Laurent, "Preface," in B. Constant, *Commentaire sur l'ouvrage de Filangieri*, ed. A. Laurent (Paris, 2004).

Commentaire contains another argument that would have made an impression on liberal readers. Constant emphasized the need for liberal constitutions. It is certainly no accident that the words "constitution" and "constitutional institutions" are repeated numerous times. What a state needs to prosper, or even to survive, is a good and well-protected constitution.

Constant's comments on England are particularly enlightening, given that, while he was writing, certain aspects of the English socio-economic system were being held up as models. On the one hand, industrialists and Saint-Simonians were saying that France should stop trying to imitate England's political system, but rather adopt its *laissez-faire* economic principles. On the other hand, in admiration of England's large land-owning class, moderate royalists were arguing that France should restore its own territorial aristocracy, for both political and economic reasons.[34] In response to these arguments, Constant stated that it was neither England's socio-economic policies nor its aristocracy that should be emulated. The survival of England, despite its many industrial and commercial *errors*, its huge debt and widespread poverty, was due to nothing else but its *political institutions*.

The constitutional institutions of the English protect them from the results of their industrial and commercial errors. The point is that the political institutions, parliamentary discussions and freedom of the press that England has enjoyed without interruption for one hundred and twenty six years have counterbalanced the vices of its laws and of its government. The energy of the character of its inhabitants has maintained itself, because they have not been disinherited of their participation in public affairs.

Constant went on to attack the *dirigisme* of governments, whether it be in the guise of Old Regime restrictions and prohibitions or in the form of industrialist policy.

That time is over when one used to say that everything should be done for the people and not by the people. Representative government is nothing else but the people's entry into participation in public affairs. It is therefore by them that everything for them is carried out ... It is not from authority that improvements should stem.

Constant insisted that governments had no special knowledge superior to that of the citizens. Repeating an insight expressed years earlier, he claimed that "there is something in power that falsifies judgement."

---

[34] Dijn, *French Political Thought*.

Therefore, laws decreed from above should always be greeted with a good deal of suspicion:

Let us beware today more than ever of all efforts to distract our attention away from politics and onto legislation. When governments offer the people legislative improvements, the people should answer by demanding constitutional institutions.

Constant's *Commentaire* called for a rebirth of public spirit. He thought political activity ennobling; he thought it necessary to guarantee man's individual liberty. For these reasons, the focus on economics and mere administration should be resisted. It was crucial "to preserve interest in public affairs."[35]

KEEPING RELIGIOUS LIBERTY ALIVE

Along with keeping political liberty alive after the assassination of the Duc de Berry in 1820, there was the need to address what was increasingly being referred to as France's religious and moral crisis. To many, France seemed to have lost its moral compass. The Revolution had unleashed harmful passions; selfishness, pride, and ethical disorders were on the rise. The loudest voices declaiming France's decline were those of Catholic conservatives and Ultraroyalists. To them, Enlightened philosophy, liberalism, and the decline of religion were to blame. Their only remedy was firm government allied with a fully restored Catholic Church.

The "crisis" of the Catholic Church

When Catholic traditionalists spoke about the religious crisis, they were not exaggerating; from their perspective, there truly was cause for worry – despite the ongoing revival. The Revolution had seriously weakened the Church, and Napoleon had done little to improve the situation. The most acute problem was probably the shortage of personnel. In 1814, there were only 36,000 priests in France, about half the number of 1789.[36] This meant that there were 3,345 vacancies. And these numbers continued to decline, so that by 1828, there were close to 5,000 vacancies.[37] Moreover,

---

[35] Constant, *Commentaire*, pp. 90, 23, 69, 45, 84–85.
[36] G. Bertier de Sauvigny, *La Restauration* (Paris, 1974), p. 307.
[37] M. Faugeras, *La reconstruction catholique dans l'ouest après la Révolution. Le Diocèse de Nantes sous la Monarchie censitaire*, 2 vols. (Fontenay-le-Comte, 1964), vol. II, pp. 5–8, as noted by E. Berenson, "A New Religion of the Left: Christianity and Social Radicalism in France,

many of the active priests were old and poorly trained; according to one account, 42 percent of the French clergy in 1814 was over the age of sixty.[38]

Further complicating the problem was the Church's finances. When its property was sold off during the Revolution, the Church lost its main means of support; it now lacked sufficient funds to rebuild destroyed or damaged churches and to open the seminaries needed to train new priests. Episcopal circulars testify to the Church leadership's anxieties about the poor state of services in many parishes, the irregularities in liturgical and sacramental life, and, more generally, the inadequate teaching of religion and Christian morals. In many parts of France, there had been no Mass and no catechism taught for years. One of the more concrete effects of the French Revolution, therefore, was "the disappearance of the official Church from the lives of French men and women throughout the country."[39]

As we have seen, however, this disappearance of the official Church did not mean that there was a corresponding decline in religiosity. On the contrary, recent studies have shown that the vacuum of clerical power actually triggered a revival of popular religion. A new kind of popular piety, awakened during the radical phases of the Revolution, continued to grow during the early years of the Restoration. Indications are that this was a simple, non-dogmatic religion focused on the person of Jesus Christ.

Expressing itself without the direction of ordained priests, this popular religiosity seemed only to compound the problems of the Church authorities. When Ultra spokesmen like Bonald and de Maistre wrote about the growing anarchy in the country, this is what they were talking about. Increasingly alarmed at the resurgence of "superstition" and even "paganism," Church leaders felt an ever more pressing need to re-Catholicize the country.[40] It was urgent that they take control of the religious sentiments of the population and channel them in the right direction.

This was the purpose of the Mission movement, which was launched in full force during the early Restoration and soon became very

---

1815–1848," in F. Furet and M. Ozouf (eds.), *The French Revolution and the Transformation of Modern Political Culture*, vol. III (New York, 1989), p. 551.

[38] G. Cholvy and Y.-M. Hilaire, *Histoire religieuse de la France contemporaine* (Toulouse, 1990), vol. I, p. 14.

[39] E. Berenson, "A New Religion of the Left," p. 541.

[40] On this popular religiosity, see G. Cholvy, "Réalités de la religion populaire dans la France contemporaine," in B. Plongeron *et al.* (eds.), *La religion populaire dans l'occident chrétien* (Paris, 1976); and Y.-M. Hilaire, "Notes sur la religion populaire au XIXe Siècle," in Y.-M. Hilaire (ed.), *La religion populaire: aspects du christianisme populaire à travers l'histoire* (Lille, 1981). Also see E. Berenson, *Populist Religion and Left-Wing Politics in France, 1830–1852* (Princeton, NJ, 1984).

controversial.[41] Its principal aim was to instill properly Catholic values in the population. Compensating for the shortage of personnel, specialized priests, trained in innovative conversion techniques, were sent to villages to offer mass instruction in Catholic doctrine. Using accessible and often fiery language designed to move people and win converts, these missionaries stressed the need for confession, sacrifice, and penitence. They staged spectacular ceremonies designed for maximum effect: mass confessions in the open air, elaborate processions along heavily decorated streets, sermons delivered at night in graveyards, and dramatic re-enactments of the crucifixion involving gigantic crosses. Between 1815 and 1830, there were more than 1,500 such missions all over France.[42]

The revivalist missions purveyed a distinct political message: having sinned during the Enlightenment, and having been punished by the Revolution, France was now being offered a chance of deliverance by the return to power of the Bourbon kings and the Catholic Church. While they preached obedience to the Bourbons, the Mission priests relentlessly attacked the Revolution, particularly key principles such as popular sovereignty and individual rights. Often, the ceremonies involved casting the works of famous *philosophes*, such as Rousseau and Voltaire, into the flames of giant bonfires. Understanding the Mission's political utility, Louis XVIII, who was otherwise known as a religious skeptic, lent them his backing and even offered state funding.[43]

Indeed, it was not long before Louis' support for Roman Catholicism's return to dominance became known, but it was obvious that it was based on political expediency. Louis had become convinced that a union of throne and altar was necessary to strengthen his position and stabilize France. On their side, the bishops rallied to the king, sure that he would favor Catholicism with all his might. "Let us not doubt," wrote one bishop to his diocese, "that the king whom heaven has just recalled . . . will protect the Catholic religion." The bishop was confident of Louis XVIII's awareness

---

[41] Abbé E. Sevrin, *Les missions religieuses en France sous la Restauration, 1815–1830* (St. Maudé, 1948); J. M. Phayer, "Politics and Popular Religion: the Cult of the Cross in France, 1815–1840," *Journal of Social History*, 2, 3 (Spring, 1978), pp. 346–365; M. Riasanovsky, "The Trumpets of Jericho: Domestic Missions and Religious Revival in France, 1814–1830," 2 vols., unpublished Ph.D. dissertation, Princeton University, 2001; S. Kroen, *Politics and Theater: The Crisis of Legitimacy in Restoration France, 1815–1830* (Berkeley, 2000), esp. ch. 2, and "Revolutionizing Religious Politics during the Restoration," *French Historical Studies* 21, 1 (Winter, 1998), pp. 27–53; M. Lyons, "Fires of Expiation: Book-Burnings and Catholic Missions in Restoration France," *French History*, 10, 2 (June, 1996), pp. 240–266.

[42] Sevrin, *Missions*, vol. I, p. 5; Kroen, *Politics*, p. 40.

[43] Riasanovsky, "The Trumpets of Jericho," pp. 30–33; Kroen, *Politics*, pp. 84–85.

that Catholicism was "a veritable prop for his throne."[44] France's bishops were devoted to the Bourbons and felt it their right and duty to support the politics of the legitimists against any opposition.

In principle, the Charter of 1814 guaranteed freedom of religion; in reality, however, it was ambiguous, even contradictory on the question. Article 5 held that "Everyone may profess his own religion with equal liberty and receive the same protection for his religious worship." Article 6 then added that "the Apostolic, Roman and Catholic religion is the state religion." Article 7 finally explained that "only the ministers of the Catholic, Apostolic and Roman religion, and those of other Christian cults are to receive payments from the Royal Treasury."

From the outset, Louis XVIII's government openly and, at times ostentatiously, favored the Catholic Church. It did so not only through legislation and funding, but also with symbolism carefully orchestrated for maximum effect. Thus, for example, the King chose May 3, 1815, to enter Paris and reclaim his throne. In the liturgical calendar of the Catholic Church, May 3 corresponded to the festival of the Finding of the Holy Cross.[45] Soon, long-forgotten Catholic customs and ceremonies were reintroduced underscoring Catholicism's role as the state religion. Meanwhile, Louis' regime also devoted itself to erasing the Revolution on the symbolic plane.[46] One way was to hold expiatory ceremonies to commemorate the deaths of Louis XVI, Marie-Antoinette, Madame Elisabeth, Louis XVII, and the Duc d'Enghien. These were accompanied by processions and sermons clearly meant not just to restore the Catholic Church to its pre-revolutionary prominence, but to enhance its power and prestige even further.

With these goals in mind, a series of measures were instituted and police ordinances passed. Work on Sundays and religious holidays was declared against the law. All householders, regardless of religious affiliation, were required to decorate their homes on certain Catholic holidays. Bishops were permitted to open an ecclesiastical school in each department, and this school would be exempt from university control. Reversing a revolutionary trend, gifts to ecclesiastical institutions were now encouraged, and clerical salaries raised. Perhaps most indicative of the King's stance on religion was his intention to abrogate the Napoleonic Concordat and re-establish the one of 1516. By this move, he would have

---

[44] "Mandement de M., l'évêque de Troye," quoted in *L'Ami de la religion, et du Roi*, vol. I, p. 101.
[45] Phayer, "Politics and Popular Religion," p. 347.   [46] Kroen, *Politics*, esp. ch. 1.

given the Church more power than it had had in 300 years. To many, he seemed to be trying, quite literally, to turn back the clock. Negotiations with Pius VII began, but the plan provoked a storm of protest and had to be abandoned.

These serious blunders, when combined with the arrogance of the returning emigrés and clergy, provoked a backlash. Fear and resentment grew among many sectors of the population. Protestants, of course, had special reasons to be afraid, but the measures also sparked Gallican fears of ultramontanism. It was impossible not to notice the increasing Jesuit presence in France and their heavy involvement in the Mission movement. In many parts of France, the missions were deeply resented by the local populations. Young people booed, whistled, and hissed during religious services; stink bombs were set off in churches; and performances of Molière's anticlerical comedy *Tartuffe* were demanded whenever missionaries were expected.[47]

This mood of alarm and resentment greatly facilitated Napoleon's return to power during the Hundred Days. He cleverly presented himself as the savior of the Revolution and a bulwark against the power of priests. As he marched to Paris, he recited powerful anticlerical rhetoric:

I have come to save Frenchmen from the slavery in which priests and nobles wish to plunge them ... Let them take guard. I will string them up from the lamp posts.[48]

In return, Napoleon was greeted with shouts of "Down with the priests! Down with the aristocrats! Hang the Bourbons! Long live liberty!"

Protestants were especially inclined to welcome the return of Napoleon. In fact, like Constant, a considerable number accepted offices in his new administration, thereby exposing themselves to the revenge reprisals that followed his second abdication.

Religion in the *Principles of Politics of 1815*

The new constitution that Constant wrote for Napoleon made his views on church–state relations very clear. The *Acte additionnel* reversed the Charter of 1814's recognition of Catholicism as France's state religion. Article 62 of the *Acte* simply stated that "freedom of religion [*la liberté des cultes*] is guaranteed to all." In essence, Constant demoted Catholicism to

---

[47] Ibid.
[48] R. Alexander, *Bonapartism and the Revolutionary Tradition in France: The Fédérées of 1815* (Cambridge, 1991).

one of several competing religions. In his *Principles of Politics* of 1815, published as a commentary and elucidation of the *Acte*, Constant clarified why. "The present constitution has returned to the only reasonable view on the subject of religion," he wrote, "that of sanctioning freedom of worship without restriction, without privilege."[49] Alert readers could not have missed the Protestant bias of his chapter on religion; in it he adapted many arguments being made by other liberal Protestants in France.

Constant presented his argument as a friend, not a foe, of religion. Openly declaring his disagreements with Idéologie and the traditional thinking of the French Enlightenment, and expressing his deep respect and admiration for religion, he redefined religion in ways that certainly would have displeased many readers, especially traditional Roman Catholics. Lifting entire sentences from his unpublished 1806 *Principles*, Constant declared that religion was not a set of dogmas and practices prescribed by a given church, but rather a natural "emotion" or "sentiment" experienced by individuals. It was these religious emotions and feelings that he valued as "favourable to the development of morality," since they "stimulate man to step beyond the narrow circle of his interests." Religious "sentiment," whenever it occured, inspired within human beings "a momentary disinterestedness" and awakened " the power of sacrifice," making human beings capable of greater generosity, courage, and sympathy. It raised men above the "habits of common life" and the "petty material interests that go with it."[50] Such statements were bound to displease not just the Idéologues, but also Christians who regarded dogmas and ceremonies as intrinsic to religion.

Constant was well aware that his definition of religion would frustrate and repel some individuals for its lack of specificity. But its vagueness was precisely the point; it was his attempt to find a basis upon which all religions could agree. Religious "sentiment" was the common denominator of *all* religions. As many liberal Protestants in France had been saying, and Madame de Staël had written in *De l'Allemagne*, Christians would never come to agreement on dogmas. If diverse religious sects were ever to unite, it would be through people's *hearts*. Thus, Constant asks:

How would you define the impression of a dark night, of the ocean stretching beyond our sight? How would you define the emotions caused by the songs of Ossian, the Church of St. Peter, meditation upon death, the harmony of sounds or forms? How would you define reverie, that intimate quivering of the soul, in

---

[49] PoP 1815, p. 274.
[50] Ibid., pp. 277 and 278. I have altered the translation of *sentiment religieux* from religious "feeling" to religious "sentiment."

which all the powers of the senses and thought come together and lose themselves in a mysterious confusion? There is religion at the bottom of all these things. All that is beautiful, all that is intimate, all that is noble, partakes of the nature of religion.[51]

This definition of religion accorded well with his own "corner of religion," which was, as he admitted, somewhat "vague" and all about "sentiments."

Additionally, Constant wanted to define what religion was not. It was not "[d]ogmatic religion" that he defended and admired, and which he regarded as only a "hostile and persecuting power." It was also not what "authority" continually tried to make of religion, in other words, "a useful tool" or "an institution of intimidation." Religion should not be seen or used as a simple "re-enforcement of the penal laws." "I place religion higher than this," he wrote, repeating the words from his earlier manuscript; "I do not regard it as a supplement to power and to the wheel."

To those who called for government protection and encouragement of religion in an irreligious age, Constant demanded precisely the opposite. Throughout history, alliances between religion and authority had always proven counter-productive; they alienated people and turned religion into an object of derision and scorn. Instead, had religion been left "perfectly independent," "it would never have been other than an object of respect and love." A perfectly free religion, that is one not controlled by any political authority, would have been able to create "a more elevated morality," a morality not just concerned with "repress[ing] gross crimes," but with "ennobl[ing]" man.[52]

Here, Constant cited the Count of Clermont-Tonnerre, a liberal nobleman and moderate royalist deputy in the National Assembly during the early phase of the Revolution. "Religion and the state," Clermont-Tonnerre had said,

Are two perfectly distinct, perfectly separate things, the union of which can only denature both of them. Man has relations with his creator; he forms or receives such and such a set of ideas about these relations; this system of ideas is called religion. Everyone's religion is therefore the opinion that everyone has of his relationship with God. Because every man's opinion is free, he may accept or not accept a given religion. The opinion of the minority can never be subjected to that of the majority. No opinion can therefore be commanded by the social pact. Religion belongs to all times, to all places, to all governments. Its sanctuary is in man's conscience, and conscience is the only faculty that man could never

---

[51] Ibid., p. 279.   [52] Ibid., pp. 279, 284, 279, 283, 281, 283.

sacrifice to social convention. The social body must never impose any cult; it must never reject any.[53]

Constant now also made public his ideas on the desirability, or rather the undesirability, of religious unity. We have seen that Christian reunion was a recurring topic of discussion in France at the time. Here he put forth many of the arguments being made by French Protestant leaders. The "multitude of sects," he wrote, was precisely what was "most healthy for religion." It was healthy because it ensured that religion "remains a feeling and does not become a mere formality." A proliferation of sects also had great advantages for morality.[54] As proof of this, Constant argued that the appearance of Protestantism had been good for Catholicism in that it had reformed the habits of the Catholic clergy.

A beneficial consequence of ending the state's "meddl[ing]" in religion would be that "the sects would multiply themselves indefinitely"; a "happy struggle" and "honorable rivalry" would result, with innumerable advantages for society as a whole. As proof, Constant offered the example of America and Scotland, where "tolerance is far from being perfect but where nevertheless Presbyterianism has divided into numerous branches." If the multiplication of sects had had disruptive effects in France until now, it was only because "authority has meddled with it." A plurality of religion posed absolutely no danger for society or for religion itself – on the contrary. In sum, Constant advocated the "complete and utter freedom of *all* forms of worship."[55]

In fact, Constant's *Principles of Politics* went quite a bit further than the Organic Articles, indicating that Napoleon's new religious policies would be more liberal than before. From now on, there would be no restricting sects from subdividing themselves. The only way to prevent religious subdivision, explained Constant, was to prevent man from reflecting upon his religion. When this happens, religion becomes "external" to him and he loses all interest in it. It becomes "an almost mechanical habit," "degenerates" and "loses all its influence over morality."[56] Therefore, the government should not limit the number of sects recognized by law.

On the issue of the state financing of religion, Constant also expanded the principles of Napoleon's original settlement. The state should maintain the religions by paying the priests' salaries "of *all those communions which are at all numerous.*" Any time a new sect gained a "substantial number" of adherents, the state should simply pick up its

[53] Ibid., p. 288.   [54] Ibid., p. 285.   [55] Ibid., pp. 286, 276, my italics.   [56] Ibid., p. 285.

costs. Constant explained: "It is with religion as with main roads. I would like the state to maintain them, provided that it lets everyone free to choose the smaller paths."[57]

Published during the Hundred Days, Constant's chapter on religion would have seemed designed to annoy his Catholic adversaries. In fact, it was probably interpreted as blatantly anti-Catholic and pro-Protestant. Constant was saying, in effect, that moral progress would come from more freedom and diversity; the answer to France's moral and political dilemmas lay not only in a liberal constitution based on popular sover- eignty and widespread individual freedoms, but also in a liberal Prot- estant culture. His defense of "religion" would, of course, have been rejected by those who used the word as a synonym for Catholicism; they would also have dismissed Constant's notion that "[t]he complete and utter freedom of all forms of worship" was "favorable to religion." Instead, Ultraroyalist spokesmen like Bonald and de Maistre argued that liberalism was not only not the solution to France's problems, it *was* the problem. Recognizably *Protestant*, Constant's type of thinking was the root cause of France's moral crisis. To Ultraroyalists, his Protestantism and his liberalism were inextricably connected, two faces of the same coin.

Catholic–Protestant wars

The Second Restoration once again recognized Roman Catholicism as the state religion of France. Rejoicing, many Catholics turned revengeful and aggressive. A wave of reprisals punished those who had served Napoleon during the Hundred Days. A brutal "White Terror" broke out in the south, particularly in the Gard around Nîmes, where many Protestants lived. From September through November 1815, Catholic Ultraroyalists attacked French Protestants and their churches, ostensibly for having supported Napoleon. According to contemporary reports, as many as 1,000 Protestants were killed in the rampage; hundreds more were imprisoned and many were forcibly re-baptized.

In the Chamber, Bonald now insisted that it was necessary to replace talk of the "rights of man" with an emphasis on the "rights of God":

Without a doubt, Sirs, the re-establishment of religion [i.e. Catholicism] is the most pressing need of the people, and the first wish of its deputies; our duty is to return to religion its consideration and its influence, to return it to the habits and

---

[57] Ibid., p. 289, my italics.

the sentiments of the people and to make of it, in one word, the most powerful auxiliary of the administration.[58]

Lamennais

In 1817, a relatively unknown priest named Felicité de Lamennais stepped on to the scene with his *Essai sur l'indifférence en matière de religion*. The first volume was a spectacular success: 40,000 copies were sold within a few weeks, and Lamennais' talents were soon compared to those of Pascal and Bossuet. With both precision and flair, Lamennais took aim at Constant's entire liberal agenda, from the principle of popular sovereignty to the idea of religious toleration. Ultraroyalists were ecstatic; recognizing an ally, they invited him to contribute to their journals.

Lamennais has fascinated many scholars, who have lavished attention on his remarkable political evolution, from staunch supporter of a Catholic monarchy buttressed by a strong state religion to "liberal" Catholic believing in the separation of church and state. In so doing, however, they have neglected a critical vein running through all of Lamennais' work: his almost visceral hatred for Protestantism. Indeed, modern readers might be surprised by the extent to which the *Essai*'s diatribe against liberalism is also a diatribe against Protestantism. Lamennais interwove attacks on liberal political principles with broadsides against Martin Luther and the Reformation, arguing that France's return to moral and spiritual health required the extinction of Protestantism.

At the same time, it is clear that what compelled Lamennais to write his essay were not primarily theological issues; rather, he felt an urgent need to save France, and even civilization itself, from what he saw as the growing threat of dissolution. A society's situation was dire, he wrote, when it no longer accepted the principle of authority in religion, that is, when it no longer cared about the "truth," and allowed itself to become religiously "indifferent," in other words, "atheist."[59]

It was obvious to Lamennais that France's lamentable predicament was due to the pernicious influence of the Protestant Reformation. Europe had been improving steadily until "the Reformation suddenly arrested its progress." Thanks to Luther, Europe was exposed to "the abyss into which she is sinking every day." The main error of Protestantism was that it replaced the "principle of authority" with the "principle of inquiry"; the

---

[58] "Proposition faite à la Chambre des Députés, séance du 26 décembre 1815," in *Œuvres de M. de Bonald*, vol. VII: *Pensées sur divers sujets, et discours politiques* (Paris, 1817), p. 65.

[59] F. de Lamennais, *Essai sur l'indifférence en matière de religion* (Paris, 1843), vol. I, p. 270.

only possible outcome of such a move was "an anarchic system of philosophy" which would lead to atheism "sooner or later." For Protestants, Christianity was nothing more than a matter of "opinion." Due to them, the sects multiplied and Christian unity was forever shattered.[60]

Calling it "Protestant," Lamennais denounced the liberal principle of religious toleration; he did the same with the principle of popular sovereignty and social contract. The idea of a pact between a ruler and his people was "absurd, harmful, degrading," and the idea of popular sovereignty was "a disastrous principle." Both could be traced back to Luther, who, along with his disciples, "justified rebellion" and "encouraged it by their writings." The Protestants persuaded parts of Europe that sovereignty resided in the people; "soon the blood of kings flowed on the scaffold." In passing, Lamennais noted the "perfect conformity" of Protestant doctrine with that of the Jacobin terrrorists: "The fanaticism of religious freedom gives birth to the fanaticism of political liberty." Only Roman Catholicism could save France from the looming danger. "Unity" and "immutability" of doctrine were necessary to establish "order."[61]

Such arguments did not go unanswered. Madame de Staël's *Considérations sur la Révolution française*, published posthumously in 1818, was defiantly unapologetic. De Staël denounced the French Catholic clergy's meddling in politics, and the fact that "it has constantly preached, and still preaches, intolerance."[62] On the question of Protestantism, she added:

Far from concealing the fact that freedom of conscience is closely related to political liberty, it seems that Protestants should pride themselves on this analogy. They have always been and will always be the friends of liberty; the spirit of inquiry in religious matters leads necessarily to representative government.[63]

France needed "a religion based on inquiry,"[64] in other words, a religion that fostered the development of the kind of mentally alert and responsible citizenry needed in a liberal polity.

Sadly, however, Madame de Staël had now passed away, and Constant was obliged to continue the fight without her. For reasons that remain somewhat unclear, their relationship had become increasingly strained during the last few years of her life. No doubt, she was jealous and disappointed when Constant married Charlotte, and annoyed when he failed to repay money she lent him. It is also likely that she was embarrassed when, in the midst of Constant's grand passion for Juliette Récamier, he held public

---

[60] Ibid., pp. 52, 261. [61] Ibid., pp. 365, 374, 381, 481, 381. [62] De Staël, *Considérations*, p. 217.
[63] Ibid., p. 73. [64] Ibid., p. 146.

readings of *Adolphe* in the salons of Paris and London. Rightly or wrongly, many people assumed that the heroine was modeled on her, and that the novel described Constant's pathetic attempts to extricate himself from her grip.[65]

In any case, as Madame de Staël lay dying in the summer of 1814, she refused to allow Constant to pay her his last respects. He was made to feel estranged, not only from her, but also from her entourage and family, including their daughter, Albertine.[66] Nevertheless, he wrote de Staël a moving obituary in the *Mercure de France* and, twelve years later, he wrote an even longer and more impressive tribute.[67] Undeterred, de Staël's family's resentment remained unabated until he died; indeed, it lasted throughout the nineteenth century, causing considerable damage to his reputation.

Constant's lectures on religion at the Athénée Royal[68]

In early 1818, before his lecture series on the English constitution and his famous speech "Liberty of the Moderns Compared to the Ancients," Constant had focused on religion in another series of lectures at the Athénée Royal. Although of critical importance, this little-known fact has been neglected by scholarship.[69] It shows, once again, how seriously Constant took his work on religion and how pertinent he thought it was to politics.

As a topic, the history of religion must have seemed a bit odd to the audience, since the Athénée Royal was primarily known for its lectures on science and political economy.[70] Indeed, at the outset, Constant made a point of anticipating criticism from those who might regard religion as irrelevant to politics. Under present circumstances, he began, the most important topics were undoubtedly those having to do with "constitutional

---

[65] See p. Delbouille, "Les contemporains devant Adolphe," in *Genèse, structure et destin d'Adolphe* (Paris, 1971), pp. 385–412.

[66] Wood, *Benjamin Constant*, p. 224.

[67] "De Madame de Staël et de ses ouvrages," in *Portraits, Mémoires, Souvenirs*, ed. E. Harpaz (Paris, 1992) pp. 212–254. See also his article in the *Journal générale de France*, reproduced by S. Balayé in *Cahiers Staëliens*, 9 (December, 1969), pp. 17–38.

[68] B. Constant, "Fragment de la copie des lectures à l'Athénée Royal sur la religion," Bibliothèque cantonale et universitaire de Lausanne, Fonds Constant.

[69] An exception to this rule is Bryan Garsten, who was working on this very topic when I was writing this section of my book and who generously shared with me his (then) unpublished paper, "A Religion for Liberals?: Benjamin Constant's Other Lectures." See Garsten's essay, "Constant and the Religious Spirit of Liberalism," in Rosenblatt (ed.), *Cambridge Companion to Constant* (forthcoming).

[70] Haines, "The Athénée de Paris."

liberty." To distract his audience from that subject would be very wrong. However,

[a]mong all people religious institutions have always had a close rapport with political liberty ... To occupy oneself with the religious institutions of various peoples is thus not to leave the sphere of politics.

Unfortunately, all that remains of Constant's Athenée lecture series on religion are some notes, and from these we cannot be sure what he ended up reading to his audience. Many sentences and entire paragraphs are struck out with a thin line, indicating that Constant changed his mind and probably deleted them. Nevertheless, based on the sentences and paragraphs that Constant left intact, one can perceive the themes he covered and the points he made.

First, Constant presented the argument that he had made in *Principles of Politics*: religion was "inherent to man" and worthy of respectful consideration. The source of religion was not just "fear" or "calculation," as some people were saying; nor was it the product of naive "hopefulness." Rather, religion was a profound and inextirpable "need of the soul," "inherent to the nature of man." It was also "indestructible," in other words, there to stay. His point was, once again, to defend a certain definition or conception of religion that was compatible and supportive of liberal values.

Throughout history, religion had certainly been a party to numerous "vices" and had served "as a pretext for many crimes." But this, Constant insisted, only happened when it was turned into the "monopoly" and exclusive "privilege" of a small group of people bent on denying other people their rights. "Authority degrades religion," Constant declared, when it tries to "fashion it according to its own designs." He had particularly harsh words for "sacerdotal corporations" who kept civilization back, causing "everything to remain immobile, petrified." He denounced the priests who "invent a language unintelligible to the people" and devise "somber and lugubrious ceremonies" for their own sinister purposes. Because of the respect Constant professed for religion, he thought that "no foreign authority" should be allowed to "command it by force or degrade it by calculation." Although he was careful to repeat, several times, that his intention was not to attack Roman Catholicism, the disclaimer would not have fooled his audience. And although he ostensibly spoke about pre-Christian religions, it would have been evident to everyone that his lectures were really about France and its throne-and-altar alliance.

Some of Constant's lecture notes indicate that he was making public, apparently for the first time, what would become the main thesis of his multi-volume book on religion: when left free of "sacerdotal" interference, religions will always be beneficial to society and will, moreover, naturally improve over time. Thus, it seems that Constant lectured on the principle of progressive revelation or, as he put it at the Athénée, "the doctrine of religious perfectibility." He may even have included a section (struck through with a line) on liberal German Protestant theology, perhaps using parts of his Brunswick manuscript. Constant's declared aim was to prove that

every religious form follows a progressive march, by which it modifies itself, perfects itself, and when it is no longer susceptible to improvement, gives way to another form.

Constant's political message was obviously strongly anti-Catholic, no matter how many times he claimed otherwise. At the very least, it was an attack on Catholicism as described by its most zealous defenders in France. Clearly, Constant advocated "liberating" religion from the control of both priests and political authorities so as to allow it to evolve "naturally" towards ever more enlightened forms. He preferred those religions "independent of a sacerdoce" in which "everything is individual." Again, one sees Constant's bias for Protestantism, the religion of northern Germany, which, in his mind, was "independent," advocated "free inquiry," tolerated others, and, most importantly, evolved with the times.

De Maistre's Du pape

In *Du pape* (1819), Joseph de Maistre made the Ultraroyalist argument against Protestantism even more explicit. Stressing the "gravity of the circumstances" in France, de Maistre thought it imperative to understand the "true causes of general commotion that is causing the authority of governments to waver." The instability of the French government was due to Protestantism and the blame rested with the "monstrous dogma" of popular sovereignty, a doctrine that Protestantism had "transported from religion into politics." Thanks to its system of "universal independence" and the immense "pridefulness" that had infested society, every man now wanted "to fight, judge, write, administer, govern." "Help us," de Maistre wrote, "to make Protestantism disappear." In order to re-establish morals, and to strengthen the throne, it was necessary to "erase from the European dictionary that fatal word 'Protestantism.' "[71]

---

[71] J. de Maistre, *Du pape* (1819), pp. 3, 5, 133, 238, 351.

Vincent

Samuel Vincent (1787–1837), pastor of Nîmes in the region of Gard,[72] objected vehemently to such ideas, and the inflammatory language with which they were expressed. A region known for religious hostilities, the Gard had been the scene of brutal Protestant massacres during the recent White Terror. Vincent complained that Lamennais' arguments were dangerous and likely to re-ignite hostilities; also, they were anachronistic. The espousal of anti-Protestantism was incompatible with the values of modern France. What characterized the present century, he wrote, was "the spirit of tolerance and support."[73] Vincent's *Observations sur l'unité religieuse* shows how closely allied liberal Protestantism was to the form of political liberalism advocated by Constant, and that a recourse to history and the notion of historical progress was a crucial element of both. Vincent's arguments are often indistinguishable from those of Constant and Madame de Staël.

Vincent urged people not to be duped by Lamennais' defense of "religion" and morality, supposedly for the benefit of France. With all his talk of unity and authority, what Lamennais really wanted was to "impose ignorance on humanity." If man has one "sacred right," Vincent argued, it is "to use his faculties for his own improvement [*perfectionnement*]." The "noble faculties of the human mind," he continued, were the "most beautiful present that man has received from his creator." To deny man the use of those faculties was to ignore "the clearest wish" of God and to "commit at the same time an injustice and an impiety." All Lamennais' talk of authority was contrary to the spirit of true Christianity.[74]

Anyway, where was the Scriptural support for Lamennais' position? Did Christianity, according to "its authentic documents," really wish to keep humankind "forever in tutelage"? Did it really prohibit "inquiry, reflection, judgement"? On the contrary, Vincent insisted, Jesus Christ made using one's faculties not only "a right" but a sacred "duty": "He call[ed] on his disciples to reflect; he trie[d] to develop their minds; he invite[d] them to understand what they [saw]."[75] Protestantism was therefore truer to Jesus' own principles than Catholicism was; Protestantism

---

[72] B. Reymond, "Redécouvrir Samuel Vincent," *Etudes théologiques et religieuses* 54, 3 (1979), pp. 411–423.

[73] J. L. S. Vincent, *Observations sur l'unité religieuse en réponse au livre de M. de La Mennais, intitulé: Essai sur l'indifférence en matière de religion, dans la partie qui attaque le protestantisme* (Paris, 1830).

[74] Ibid., pp. 20, 21.

[75] Ibid., pp. 21–23. Vincent provides biblical support (Luke XI. 52, John V. 39.41, I Cor X. 15.27) for the right and duty of judgement. According to Vincent, Saint Paul wanted his disciples to

conformed more closely to the "primitive purity" that "God intended." "True Christianity," by which Vincent meant liberal Protestantism, proposed "human improvement" as its goal. It did not condone the "subjugation of people's minds by use of prejudice."[76]

With regard to France's moral crisis, Vincent vehemently maintained that it had nothing to do with religious toleration. Denouncing the Catholic "mania for unity of faith," he countered: "today you find more piety and purer morals in those places where religious freedom is most complete." As examples, Vincent pointed to America, England, and Protestant Germany. Protestants do not think that "a perfect conformity of opinions" is necessary in religion. Nor do they think it desirable or even possible "to bind one another" through religion. And certainly, they do not believe that one generation should "bind" the ones that follow, "to the detriment of Holy Scripture and the progress of truth."[77]

On the contrary, Protestants believe in the spirit of inquiry, which they hold responsible for a great number of benefits, such as an "ennobling" kind of Christianity, a "great zeal" in religion, and "a great love for humanity." The spirit of inquiry has engendered "a progressive and rapid march towards all that is great, beautiful and true." True Christianity thrives in conditions of liberty and variety; this is also why "it will always favor wise and liberal institutions."[78]

Lamennais' proposals, Vincent contended, would have only nefarious results for France, on morals, on "social institutions," on politics and even on religion itself. With all its doctrinal "scaffolding," the mental subordination it promoted, and the intolerance it preached, Lamennais' brand of Catholicism was really in opposition to "true Christianity" and even a hindrance to "the development of religious sentiments." Vincent warned that it was also dangerous politically, because of its connection with Rome. Once Catholicism had subjugated the minds of the people, it was certain that it would aim to subjugate kings as well. Soon, France would become subject to "a foreign power." Protestantism, by contrast, "does not recognize an exterior authority; it obeys civil power."[79]

One can see why Catholics saw Protestantism and liberalism as two sides of the same coin. Vincent was fleshing out ideas found in both Constant and Madame de Staël. The goal of Vincent's Protestantism was

---

"examine and judge what he proposed to them"; I Cor X. 15 states: "I speak to you as men of sense. Form your own judgement on what I say."
[76] Vincent, *Observations*, pp. 123, 100.   [77] Ibid., pp. 69, 131.   [78] Ibid., pp. 135, 176.
[79] Ibid., pp. 109, 69, 123, 61, 100, 109.

the same as Constant's liberalism: the development of man's faculties. To both, all good things would come from encouraging the activity of the mind. Based on the spirit of free inquiry, and the rights of private judgement, Protestantism favored what Constant referred to as "that noble disquiet" in man, that "better part of our nature" that pushes him towards "self-improvement."[80] In this endeavor, the purpose of "true" Christianity was to be "a salutary guide" and not "a chain that weighs man down." It should be less a bridle holding him back, than a "spur" that "raises up and ennobles his nature."[81]

Lamennais again

In the second volume of the *Essai sur l'indifférence* (1820), Lamennais replied directly to Vincent. People should make no mistake: the only religion that could save France from the present chaos was Roman Catholicism, not the "vague" religion of Protestants like Vincent, in which "everything becomes individual." To them, dogmas were nothing but "opinions" destined to change. What France needed was the re-establishment of "order"; for that to occur, the "anarchy of opinions" had to cease and one unifying faith be accepted. Lamennais repeated the idea that without authority, society would dissolve; submitting religion and the laws of morality to the mere "opinions" or "sentiments" of individuals would create a "horrible disorder." In any case, religion was not a matter of "opinion" or "sentiment." Religion was "law." And because it was law, it depended upon authority.[82]

Lamennais also responded to Madame de Staël, whose *Considérations* had annoyed him. Madame de Staël "adopts this [Protestant] doctrine," Lamennais wrote, "and even applies it to politics, so that each person must search within himself ... which is the best religion, the best morals, the best legislation and the best form of government." He then cited her "curious" or bizarre principles:

there are no morals [and] no politics in which one must admit what is called authority. The conscience of men is a perpetual revelation within them, and their reason an inalterable fact. What constitutes the essence of the Christian religion is the agreement between our intimate sentiments and the words of Jesus Christ.[83]

---

[80] Constant, "Liberty of the Ancients," p. 327.
[81] Vincent, *Observations*, p. 174.   [82] Lamennais, *Essai*, vol. II, pp. xxiv, 127, v, lxxi, lxxiv, 178.
[83] Lamennais cites *Considérations*, vol. III, p. 15; the quote is on p. 138 of Lamennais, *Essai*, vol. II.

Lamennais was reflecting the mood of Catholic Ultraroyalists, who, after the Duc de Berry's assassination, swept into power on a reactionary wave. Soon, they implemented measures to "protect religion." A bishop was placed at the head of the university and given the portfolio for a newly created Ministry of Ecclesiastical Affairs and Public Instruction. Legislation was passed allowing for the suspension of newspapers whose "spirit" was deemed disrespectful to religion.[84] Repressive measures were also taken against individual rights. Saint-Simon was put on trial, *Le Censeur européen* ceased publication, and Guizot's lecture course at the Athénée Royal was cancelled. As mentioned earlier, many liberals were so disheartened by the events taking place that they turned to conspiracy, or withdrew from politics. The election of February 1824 was a landslide in favor of the government, with 410 royalist deputies gaining seats, and only nineteen liberals.

Catholic dissensions

Although the years 1821–7 have been called "triumphalist" ones for intransigent Catholics, their victory proved illusory. Instead of helping them to consolidate their domination, their measures provoked a severe backlash. Popular anticlericalism exploded throughout France.[85] This in turn contributed to the return of the liberals to power in the elections of 1827, and the collapse of the Bourbon monarchy in 1830.

One of the main problems was that the measures taken to shore up "religion" were unpopular not just with Protestants and non-believers, but with many Catholics as well. The liberal Abbé de Pradt (1759–1837), for example, wrote several books deploring the wrong direction the Catholic clergy had taken since 1814. In his mind, the French Church had lost touch with the people of France. By attacking the Revolution, and constantly favoring the throne-and-altar alliance, the clergy was alienating many people and was showing itself favorable to the interests of the nobility. Tragically, these actions were against its own interests. For the first time in history, de Pradt declared, a country's clergy had entirely "lost connection" with the "spirit and language of its country."[86]

What the French clergy seemed not to understand was that, due to the Revolution, "everything today ha[d] changed," and it was necessary to adapt to these changes. In general, the French people liked their priests, but abhorred their involvement in politics, the always harmful "mixing of

---

[84] Kroen, *Politics*, p. 112.   [85] Ibid.   [86] D. de Pradt, *Les quatre concordats* (Paris, 1818), pp. 23, 224.

the spiritual with the temporal," as de Pradt put it. Moreover, the sad picture of religion in France that people like Lamennais were painting, was not true: "Never before has France been more religious than at present." What the Ultraroyalist clergy apparently could not comprehend was that people could retain "religious sentiment" while declining to practice their "exterior cult." The problem with the Catholic Church was that it was focusing on the "exterior" part of religion, while ignoring the moral side. This, too, was alienating people. "The people are religious," insisted de Pradt, "but enlightened."[87] What they needed, therefore, was a more enlightened form of religion than their church was offering them.

De Pradt's views were fairly common among liberal Catholics, many of whom were certain that their church was headed in the wrong direction. The Catholicism being promoted by the missionaries was seen as too superstitious, too preoccupied with dogmas and ceremonies, and too closely connected to the reactionary politics of the Ultraroyalists. Other Catholics also denounced the co-mingling of church and state, the atmosphere of inquisition, and the stridency of the Restoration Church. Increasingly, they felt that it was out of synch with the values of modern France.

The Society for Christian Morals

The "triumphalist" years for intransigent Catholicism brought with them a feeling of vulnerability among French Protestants, but they were not without resources. Protestant journals were launched with the express purpose of educating the public on the nature of Protestantism and defending its values and goals. Moreover, starting around this time, a loose network of Protestant associations was established with several interrelated religious, social, and political aims. In 1818, Parisian Protestants founded a Biblical Society, which included an auxiliary society for women. Soon thereafter, a Society of Evangelical Missions was established in Paris. Through these voluntary associations, French Protestants worked both to spread Protestant values and to protect their right to religious liberty.

French Protestants also reached out to liberal-minded Catholics. In 1821, a group of Protestants, who were already on the administrative committee of the Biblical Society, formed an inter-confessional association that brought together Protestants and willing Catholics. This

---

[87] Ibid., pp. 211, 111, 197, 199, 221.

society, called the Society for Christian Morals,[88] attracted a considerable number of liberal politicians and intellectuals, and would go on to have a rather high profile in Restoration politics. Two of its presidents during this time would be Catholics. In 1822, the society could count 111 members. By January 1824, the number had grown to 291, and in January 1827, it was 373. Benjamin Constant joined the society in 1825, and became its president in 1830.

The stated goal of the Society for Christian Morals was to promote "Christian morals" irrespective of dogma. Its members would work towards "the encouragement of all that is morally good, of all that can hasten and spread the progress of civilization." In his opening address, the first president of the society, the Catholic Duc de la Rochefoucauld-Liancourt, declared that it was entirely possible to promote Christian morals without getting bogged down in theological controversy. "In its debates and writings," he promised, "the Society for Christian Morals will carefully avoid all that could arouse controversy or become a subject of doubt in religious matters." Over the years, the society went on to engage in a variety of charitable works, among which were endeavors to abolish gambling and lotteries, to reform prisons, and to end the slave trade. It also published a journal and sponsored essay competitions.[89]

Notably, the members of the society, whether Catholic or Protestant, did not agree with the pessimistic prognosis of Lamennais and others, who decried France's religious "indifference" and/or "atheism." The people of France, they responded, *were* religious. The influence of religion was still great; in fact it was the "most powerful motor" affecting the population. In their minds, the vitality of religion was the reason why public morals were actually *improving*; this visible progress was due to the "religious sentiments" that characterized the period. For the Society for Christian Morals, the problem in France was neither "atheism" nor "anarchy"; rather, it was "ignorance." It was ignorance that "paralyzed" man, ignorance of the right moral principles. Hence the task the society assigned itself: the propagation of Christian moral values.[90]

The society clearly defined itself in opposition to those on the right, who claimed that only Catholicism could cure the country's ills. Significantly, it also defined itself against those on the left, who thought no religion

---

[88] See C. Duprat, *Usages et pratiques de la philanthropie: Pauvreté, action sociale et lien social, à Paris, au cours du premier XIXe siècle*, 2 vols. (Paris, 1996) and M. Sacquin, "Catholicisme intégral et morale chrétienne: un débat sous la Restauration entre le *Mémorial catholique* et le *Journal de la Société de la morale chrétienne*," *Revue historique*, 286, 2 (1991), pp. 337–358.

[89] *Journal de la Société de la morale chrétienne*, 1, 1 (1822), pp. 3, 8, 2.   [90] Ibid., p. 3.

necessary. To those who believed that "political science" alone could create a moral society, the members replied that they did not share this "exaggerated confidence in the effects of the social mechanism." Rather, France needed charitable associations like theirs. It was essential to "apply" Christian morals to "social relations," and to make morals "penetrate more and more into all parts of the public economy."[91] Moreover, the members believed in the "spirit of association" and wished to "extend its domain." "Everything which gives men the opportunity to join together to reconcile and publish ideas together" was salutary in a constitutional regime. Private associations like theirs could help moralize France.[92]

The Mémorial catholique

Lamennais was appalled by the society's agenda. Like the French government, he considered it a religious, political, and social threat. A police report of January 1824 confirms their view that "The Society of Christian Morals [was] a vast league recently formed by Protestants and our liberals, born Catholics, to *decatholicize* France."[93] Lamennais responded to the perceived danger by creating his own society, the Association for the Defense of *Catholic* Morals. Prior to that, he founded the Catholic journal the *Mémorial catholique*, whose *raison d'être* was to attack, in every issue, directly or indirectly, the liberal and ecumenical agenda of the Society for Christian Morals.

The *Mémorial catholique* incessantly repeated Lamennais' dire predictions about Protestantism and religious toleration; it warned that society was perishing due to the "anarchy of opinions." Outside of the one, unifying and true Catholic faith there could only be "particular opinions" of no moral or religious value. Governments needed to know that society's current problems were a direct result of the principles set in motion by the Protestant Reformation. Protestantism was an "individual" and "essentially independent" form of Christianity; for this reason it was "necessarily anarchic" and would invariably lead to atheism. Indeed, it was not really a religion at all, but rather a "system of destruction," a "purely negative thing."[94] Modern Protestantism no longer respected any laws or dogmas; thus it fomented "the revolt against all superiors" and a

---

[91] Ibid., pp. 7, 5.   [92] *Journal de la Société de la morale chrétienne*, 5, 34 (1824), p. 215.

[93] Quoted in Duprat, *Usages et pratiques*, vol I, p. 489, emphasis added. See also Sacquin, "Catholicisme intégral," pp. 342, 353–355.

[94] *Mémorial catholique*, March 1824, pp. 165 and 213.

system of complete "spiritual freedom and equality." As such, it was bound to lead to nothing but anarchy and continuing revolution.[95] Catholicism, on the other hand, was an "eminently social" religion, because it gave people common beliefs and duties and preached "obedience to spiritual authority." Such obedience was the very basis of the political order. Catholicism and Protestantism could not coexist; one had to choose between them. It was necessary to work towards the "unity," not the "nullity," of dogmas.[96]

The first issue of the *Mémorial catholique* contained seven pages full of attacks on the Society for Christian Morals and its ecumenical message. The author was the Swiss Charles Haller, a recent convert to Catholicism. According to Haller, the society could not claim to be truly Christian, since it was, in fact, theologically "indifferent." As such, it was exacerbating the malady afflicting France. Another author concurrred: "an immense doubt" now threatened society; everywhere people were "tormented by uncertainty," unaware of their origins or true "destination." It was no wonder that, in the midst of such incertitude, society was crumbling. It was perishing "through disputation." "Mental anarchy" was threatening to "dissolve" everything.[97]

Only a couple of years earlier, Haller had published his reasons for converting to Roman Catholicism in an open letter to his family.[98] Such accounts of conversions were frequently seen in the Catholic press.[99] Haller's reasons were mainly social and political. He had been horrified by the French Revolution, and was certain that Protestant principles were to blame. Catholic unity was now necessary to bring order back to the country; it was essential to have a "stable" and "uniform" religion to which every individual subscribed. In Protestantism, "each one frames a religion to himself," leading to a "multitude of ridiculous sects." Moreover, Protestants believe that "religion should continually reform and modify itself." Haller could not live in the state of "confusion" created by such principles. He was convinced that Protestantism would produce more "dreadful convulsions"[100] and, ultimately, the end to all religion.

---

[95] Ibid., pp. 213–216.   [96] *Mémorial catholique*, March 1824, "Introduction," pp. 5–14.

[97] Ibid., pp. 77–81.

[98] *Letter of Mr. Charles L. Haller, Member of the Supreme Council of Berne, in Switzerland, to his Family, announcing his Conversion to the Catholic Faith*, trans. J. Norris (London, 1821).

[99] The most famous conversion account of the period is recounted by C. Ford, "Private Lives and Public Order in Restoration France: The Seduction of Emily Loveday," *American Historical Review*, 99, 1 (February 1994), pp. 21–43. On the longer tradition of conversion accounts, see S. Rosa, "'Il était possible aussi que cette conversion fût sincère': Turenne's Conversion in Context," *French Historical Studies*, 18, 3 (Spring 1994), pp. 632–666.

[100] *Letter of Mr. Charles L. Haller*, pp. 27, 24, 22, 23, 26, 23.

Protestant responses

To these arguments, Protestants responded as best they could, but they did not renounce their commitment to the principle of free inquiry. On the contrary, they publicized it ever more vocally, repeating that an enlightened religion based on free inquiry was exactly what France needed. Thus, in the first issue of the Protestant journal *Archives du christianisme* appeared the rhetorical question: "who wants a religion to which one arrives by ignorance?" Where religion was more "enlightened," it was also more "firm."[101] Similarly, the first issue of *La Revue protestante* hailed the spirit of inquiry as the source of "most of the great benefits that have improved Europe in modern times." Significantly, the journal's very subtitle announced that its aim was to handle "Christian Questions by the Method of Free Inquiry."

Protestants tended to view the religious condition of France more favorably than conservative Catholics, who bemoaned the decline of "religion," and often spoke of a "crisis." To Catholics, France was in need of aggressive re-Catholicization; hence the need for the Missionary campaign. In contrast, the first issue of the Protestant *Archives du christianisme* announced optimistically that "people are returning to religion."[102] All that was needed to strengthen the religious revival was to provide bibles and to encourage people to read them. In fact, Protestant leaders may have considered the supposed religious "crisis" an opportunity.

This seems to have been the conviction of Charles Coquerel, the editor-in-chief of *La Revue protestante*. In 1823, Coquerel published a book entitled *Tableaux de l'histoire philosophique du christianisme*, a copy of which he sent to Constant. After surveying the history of Christianity, Coquerel felt certain that religious conditions in France were finally just right for Protestantism to take hold and thrive. The "march of civilization" had given French men "new needs," both political and religious. Modern men "want[ed] to believe," but they wanted "an enlightened religion, reasonable and free." If presented with a clear and unobstructed choice, Frenchmen would certainly choose a "system of free examination" over a "system of authority." "Everywhere," Coquerel thought, "people [were] calling for a reasonable religion." Moreover, a "severe theology," such as that being preached by certain Catholics, would never be able to vanquish the dreadful materialism of recent years. Rather, the present need was for "a simple and understandable religion"

---

[101] *Archives du christianisme au dix-neuvième siècle*, 1 (1818), p. 224.   [102] Ibid., p. 9.

with "clear and evident doctrines." Such a religion would not only "guarantee civil liberties," but would also "serve as their foundation."[103]

On May 18, 1823, Constant wrote Coquerel to thank him for the gift copy of his book. Constant's letter is worth quoting at length as it shows the confluence of the two men's perspectives:

> I have received, with much gratitude, the book you were kind enough to send me. What I have already read persuades me that you have approached the subject from a new and important point of view. In the state of decrepitude to which the excess of civilization has brought us, without religious sentiment there will be no regeneration of the human race. But the worn-out forms that are being imposed on it have the double inconvenience of impeding its developments and of furnishing arms to its enemies. It is a consolation to see the new generation avoiding both the barrenness of incredulity and the slavery of dogmatic beliefs ... Continue, Sir, to use your talents to serve the cause of humanity.[104]

---

[103] C. Coquerel, *Tableaux de l'histoire philosophique du christianisme, ou études de philosophie religieuse* (Paris, 1823), pp. 221, 55, 222, 306, 55, 222.

[104] V. Glachant, *Benjamin Constant sous l'oeil du guet d'après nombreux documents inédits* (Paris, 1906), p. 152.

CHAPTER 6

"The Protestant Bossuet": De la religion
in political context (1824–1830)

The first volume of Constant's *De la religion* appeared in the highly polarized context just described. A book of remarkable erudition, based on years of research, it had gone through major transformations over the course of Constant's life. While writing it, his perspective had evolved from one inspired by the French Enlightenment and hostile to religion, to one inspired by the German Enlightenment and favorable to religious *sentiments*, if and when left free. At the height of his career during the second Restoration, and as his health steadily declined, Constant worked feverishly to get his tomes to press, quite literally "exhausting himself to death"[1] in the process. Volume I appeared in May 1824, volume II in October 1825, and volume III in 1827. Volumes IV and V were published posthumously in 1831.

Constant knew that his book would be controversial. Coming in the midst of a period of Catholic triumphalism and royalist reaction, it offered an essentially Protestant view of history meant to undergird his liberal politics. To his friend Sismondi, he confided:

I have decided to attempt to publish my book, even though we live under Jesuit rule, but I shall publish it in installments, because the first, which I don't think will alarm anyone, will I hope establish its reputation sufficiently for no one to dare stop me later on.[2]

After the first volume's appearance, in September 1824, he wrote to his cousin, Rosalie:

thank you for approving of my book. I am hard at work on the second volume which is more shocking than the first. It's impossible to foresee or calculate

---

[1] E. Hofmann, in DLR, p. 1122.
[2] N. King and J.-D. Candaux, "La correspondance de Benjamin Constant et de Sismondi (1801–1830)," ABC, 1 (1980), p. 152

today what it will be permissible to print or say, but I must work on in the meantime.[3]

Ostensibly, *De la religion* was a scholarly book recounting the history of polytheism, but its political purpose was obvious to anyone who read it. On every page, Constant refuted the Catholic and Ultraroyalist agenda. Notably, however, Constant also aimed his lessons at Idéologues and industrialists – in fact, at anyone who might dismiss, ignore, or undervalue religion as a force for good. Thus, he charted an independent course that earned him very little praise and few disciples.

Indeed, the preface to the first volume gave the impression that Constant's primary purpose was less to refute the Ultraroyalists than it was to lambast the Idéologues and industrialists. Constant zeroed in on their ethics of self-interest, denouncing it as demeaning, demoralizing, and dangerously depoliticizing. To subscribe to their system of morality was to deny humankind's "true destination" and to condemn it to moral "degradation." This, he argued, was the tragic lesson learned over the past twenty years. What France had witnessed was the nefarious effects of a morality of self-interest. It was true that self-interest caused people to work and tend to their private lives. Thus it maintained a certain "order." But at what cost? In France, it had led to political "indifference" and even "servility" in the population. People had come to practice only "domestic virtues," while "the cause of the fatherland was deserted." A society based on self-interest alone was like a society of "industrious beavers" or "well-organized bees"; ruled by nothing but "prudence" and an "arithmetic morality," it had no moral content.[4]

Addressing himself repeatedly to the "Friends of Liberty," Constant admonished them that this was not the way to preserve freedom. "No," Constant insisted, "nature did *not* place our guide in our self-interest"; rather, man's true guide to morality lay in his "inner" or "religious sentiment." And this sentiment was favorable to morals precisely because it "pushe[d] man out of himself," thus enabling *dis*interested behavior. Describing religious sentiment much as he had in the *Principles of Politics*, he called it "a universal" and "fundamental law of man's nature,"[5] the indispensable attribute that enabled self-sacrifice and generosity between human beings. As such, it deserved people's respect, and even their veneration.

---

[3] As quoted by Wood, *Benjamin Constant*, p. 238.	[4] DLR, pp. 29, 31, 32, 33, 32.	[5] Ibid., p. 39.

Repeating another favorite theme, Constant added that religious sentiment encouraged a "higher" type of morality than the Idéologues' pedestrian focus on mere "happiness" and "well-being."

All moral systems can be reduced to two: one assigns interest as our guide and well-being as our goal. The other proposes improvement [*perfectionnement*] as our goal and inner sentiment, the abnegation of ourselves and the faculty of sacrifice as our guide.

Constant chastised those among his liberal colleagues who ignored, devalued, or attacked religious sentiment. In so doing, they were endangering the one true principle capable of keeping human beings on the right track.

Consider man dominated by his senses, besieged by his needs, softened by civilization, and all the more enslaved by his pleasures because civilization makes them easier. Don't destroy the one disinterested motive in him that fights against so many causes of degradation.

"Liberty is nourished by sacrifices," Constant insisted. He begged his friends and allies on the left not to "snuff out the convictions that are the foundations of citizenly virtues [and] that create heroes."[6]

France's new generation was being held back, Constant wrote, because of its simplistic and one-sided ideas about religion. On the one hand, there was the "tradition of incredulity," which had become entrenched and "dogmatic." On the other was "the unfortunate alliance between religion and politics." Neither alternative was helpful. In Protestant Germany, however, theologians had been able to avoid these extremes and reconcile the Enlightenment with religion. Having already made many of these points before, Constant added something new: he explained the principle of progressive revelation, and applied it to the history of religion. In other words, he put in place his theory of "religious perfectibility," which he had referred to in his Athénée lectures. Constant did not hide the fact that he owed the idea to Protestant Germany, where there existed a religious "system" that was "consoling," "noble," and "eminently just."[7]

Constant's denunciation of France's religious failings and intellectual culture, as well as his praise of Protestant Germany, certainly irritated many readers, especially since his own "Frenchness" was questionable. Constant claimed that the Germans understood what Frenchmen had trouble grasping: "that everything is progressive in man." The French

[6] Ibid., pp. 30, 33, 34.   [7] Ibid., pp. 74, 77.

were too "arrogant" and "self-satisfied" to realize this; each generation was sure that it, and it alone, had reached the point of perfection. In contrast, the Germans, who were "less pleased with themselves," understood that all human ideas, including religious ones, are subject to "modifications" and "essential improvements" over time, such that each generation pre-pares the ground for the next. They knew that "social, political [and] religious forms ... are indispensable aids to man, but which must modify themselves as he himself modifies himself."[8]

Making public ideas he had acquired in Germany, Constant explained that religions were composed of both "form" and "sentiment." Religious sentiment stemmed from the need human beings have to communicate with invisible powers, while the form derived from the need to give that communication some regularity and permanence.[9] There could be no religious sentiment without a form; one could not exist without the other. The point was, however, that the form of a religion was always adapted to a stage of civilization, and thus was good only "for a time." Gradually, the form would develop a "dogmatic and stationary character";[10] it would become oppressive as it refused to adapt to the evolution of human intelligence. Religious sentiment, reacting against the confinement imposed by a superannuated form, would therefore separate itself from it and begin to look for a new form, better suited to the needs of a new epoch.

Constant's account of the religious form/sentiment dynamic allowed him to do two things. First, it allowed him to argue that religions were meant to adapt to, and evolve with, the times, in other words, to keep pace with the progress of civilization. Thus, he delivered a blow to Roman Catholicism, which claimed to be immutable and timeless. But Constant's perspective produced a second consequence as well: it enabled him to explain the upsurge of incredulity and anticlericalism that France was experiencing. According to Constant's theory, anti-religious senti-ments appeared at times of great intellectual advance. During such periods, religious sentiment chafed at the restrictions imposed on it by a petrified form, a form destined soon to give way to a more enlightened, and thus more suitable, one. France's polarized, even "anarchic," religious culture was therefore perfectly normal and understandable, since the country was poised to embrace a new, more enlightened form of religion.

As a rather provocative example of how this dynamic worked, Con-stant referenced the period just prior to Christ's appearance.[11] French

---

[8] Ibid., p. 74.   [9] Ibid., p. 52.   [10] Ibid., p. 53.   [11] Ibid., p. 65.

Catholics often evoked this age in comparison with their own. Chaos and incredulity reigned then, they said, as it did now. The "anarchy" threatened society with dissolution, but then order was imposed by the appearance of Jesus Christ and his unifying message. Now, in the similarly anarchic conditions of Restoration France, they reasoned that the government should again impose order by reinstating and fortifying Roman Catholicism as the country's national religion.

Constant, however, saw history differently. His research showed that it was impossible to stop the natural "march of religion" by trying to resurrect an old religion after it had lost its appeal. The story of Christ's appearance proved this to be true. Despite the fact that polytheism had the strong support of Rome's rulers, religious sentiment could not be prevented from choosing Christianity instead. If conditions were now similar in France, Constant intimated, the authorities should not try to prop up an ossified and superannuated religion. Rather, it signaled that Frenchmen's religious sentiments were searching for a newer, purer form of religion that was better suited to the current stage of civilization. In this transition, the authorities should "remain neutral": man's God-given intelligence would "take care of the rest."[12]

To those on both the right and the left who maintained that religion supports "authority," fosters "immobility," and thus helps to maintain social and political "order," Constant replied that they had their facts wrong. First of all, the "fundamental principles of all religions" were "always in agreement" with "the most expansive principles of liberty." The problem was that religions tend to create "authorities" who then work together with governments to "destroy liberty." France had witnessed this recently, Constant wrote in reference to Napoleon: "The most complete despotism that we have ever known grabbed hold of religion as an auxiliary." During "fourteen years of servitude," religion became "a humble dependent, a timid organ" which "prostrated itself before power . . . offering flattery in return for disdain."

But new religions, within which religious sentiment was fresh and powerful, were always good for liberty. The epochs during which religious sentiment triumphed were also those in which liberty triumphed. Here again, Constant proffered a controversial reading of early Christianity: The first Christians, he argued, "revived the noble doctrines of equality and fraternity between all men." Later on, Protestantism had been favorable to liberty as well. Indeed, Constant proposed that "all

---

[12] Ibid., p. 82.

religious crises have done good ... even if constituted religions ... have often done harm."[13]

To interpret early Christianity in this way was, of course, to offer a distinctly Protestant version of its history. Astute readers would not have missed Constant's claim that the early Christians used the weapon of free inquiry to great effect against reigning polytheism, nor his reference to the early Church Father, Tertullian, who "did not want a sacerdoce," because he believed that "[w]e are all priests." In fact, Constant's entire philosophy of history, with its principle of "religious perfectibility," had a pronounced Protestant bias. As the latest religious form assumed by Christianity, it was by necessity also the best and purest one available. However, Constant did not believe that early nineteenth-century Protestantism constituted the culmination and endpoint of religious evolution; rather, "additional improvements [would] one day further reform the Reformation."[14]

Constant was well aware that his perspective on religion would both "dissatisfy the devout" and "displease the *philosophe*," and this was especially true of his view of revelation.[15] Neither denying it outright nor accepting an orthodox view of it, he put forward his own version of the German and Protestant idea of progressive revelation. "There is a revelation," Constant contended, "but this revelation is universal, it is permanent [and] has its source in the human heart." Further on, he clarified this by adding that "to assume that the germ of religion is to be found in the heart of man is surely not to give this gift from heaven a purely human origin. The infinite being deposited this germ in our breast." Constant specified that he was not suggesting that a new religious form could not be communicated to man in a supernatural manner. Putting his statements together, it seems that Constant saw revelation as a communication between God and man that takes place through his religious sentiment; without doctrinal content, it was composed, rather, of generous "emotions" and uplifting "feelings." It was a "gift from heaven" that allowed man continuously to improve over time. Notably, Constant included a statement claiming that he did not think that the "main idea of my book" contradicts "the Protestantism that I profess."[16]

---

[13] Ibid., pp. 58, 61, 62.   [14] Ibid., pp. 66, 58, 76.

[15] On this topic, see also F. Bowman, "La révélation selon Benjamin Constant," *Europe*, 46, 467 (March, 1968), pp. 115–127; J.-R. Derré, "L'auteur de *De la religion* et le christianisme," in P. Corday and J.-L. Seylaz (eds.), *Actes du congrès Benjamin Constant (Lausanne, octobre 1967)* (Geneva, 1968), pp. 85–95.

[16] DLR pp. 76, 43, 581, 582.

Reviews of volume I

Reviews of *De la religion* were highly critical. On the left and the right, readers were surprised, if not dismayed, that such a brilliant and effective deputy could produce such a "vague" and awkward book. According to readers across the political spectrum, it was boring and superficial, full of errors and contradictions. They predicted that it would be a complete failure, soon consigned to the dustbin. One reviewer called on Constant's friends to convince him not to publish more volumes, since they would likely further harm his reputation.

The Catholic and royalist paper, *L'Etoile*, immediately declared *De la religion* "nothing but a long profession of Deism," in other words, "disguised atheism."[17] *L'Ami de la religion et du Roi* warned that the book was particularly "dangerous" because of Constant's reputation and because of the "religious varnish" he used to disguise his "antichristian system."[18] With obvious sarcasm, the *Gazette de France* first noted Constant's "politeness" and "reserve" towards Catholicism, and then pummeled him for countless "errors" and "misinterpretations."[19]

More rigorous and respectful was the analysis by *Le Mémorial catholique*, which identified Constant's position as recognizably Protestant. It was typical these days, the reviewer wrote, to "systematically reduce religion to individual sentiment." But this was particularly true of Protestantism, since it "openly declares its indifference for dogmas" and restricts itself to "a vague sentiment of respect for the Bible." Protestants were only Deists in disguise. The reviewer noted that Protestant spokesmen, like Samuel Vincent, argued that religion was just "an affair of the heart." However, even Protestants realized that religion was necessary to society, and thus they tried to think of one that did not involve an obligation to believe anything. This was the explanation behind Constant's "religion of sentiment."[20]

Perhaps the most damaging critique, over the long run, came from Baron d'Eckstein (1790–1861). A recent convert to Catholicism, he was regarded as somewhat of an expert on both religion and German scholarship.[21] In *Le Drapeau blanc*, Eckstein launched a veritable campaign of

---

[17] *L'Etoile*, June 19, 1824. Constant responded to this review in *Le Constitutionnel* (June 24, 1824). He insisted that he was not a Deist and that he held primitive Christianity to be a "divine doctrine of peace and love." The article is reproduced in *Recueil d'Articles 1820–1824*, ed. E. Harpaz (Geneva, 1981), pp. 342–346.

[18] *L'Ami de la religion et du Roi*, September 25, 1824.   [19] *Gazette de France*, June 24, 1824.

[20] *Le Mémorial catholique*, November, 1824.

[21] N. Burtin, *Le baron d'Eckstein: un semeur d'idées au temps de la Restauration* (Paris, 1931).

defamation that went on for several years. His criticism was particularly galling to Constant, who responded angrily to it in later volumes of *De la religion.*[22]

In his first review, Eckstein dismissed *De la religion* as just one more in the vast array of "literary infirmities" that, thankfully, would soon be forgotten. To begin, however, he congratulated Constant for his attack on the Enlightenment, noting, with pleasure, that he inveighed against the *philosophes* and proponents of the ethics of self-interest. In the process, Constant occasionally sounded a bit like Jean-Jacques Rousseau, although he never quite rose to the Genevan's level. When it came to religion, however, Eckstein accused Constant's research of being superficial and flighty. It was clearly not the work of a serious scholar; rather it was the product of a "man of the world," who was too busy with politics to read his sources carefully and had made many mistakes. Moreover, Constant's own religion was nothing more than a "gentle mysticism." His "sentimentalist" God was too "individual," and his religion too watered down to amount to anything concrete.[23] In any case, the obvious point of the whole book was to attack Catholicism, despite the author's many disingenuous disclaimers.

On the left, reviews ranged from being mildly complimentary, although these were always mingled with some incomprehension, to being outright hostile and dismissive. In *Le Globe*, the book was described as elegantly written, and full of "clear ideas, elevated, profound [and] new."[24] The compliments ended there. Constant's "doctrine" was too "vague," wrote the reviewer, and the book lacked a clear "psychological theory."[25] The explanations and descriptions of the nature of religious sentiment were neither precise nor weighty enough for the readers of *Le Globe*; nor were Constant's ideas particularly original. In the end, he was "but the elegant interpreter of a common opinion."[26]

Even more critical was the *Mercure de France*. Yet again, the reviewer began by acknowledging the importance of the subject and praising Constant's literary style; but then he, too, went on the attack. Although Constant had some "talent," he was wrong on the essentials. Many of his "vague assertions" were unsubstantiated, and he failed to acknowledge properly the work of important French *philosophes* like Condorcet, Voltaire, and Montesquieu. What particularly annoyed the reviewer was

---

[22] See, for example, Book VI, ch. V, p. 797; Book X, ch. IV, p. 877; Book XII, ch. XI, p. 944; Book XV, ch. II, p. 975; Book XV, ch. III, p. 977.
[23] *Le Drapeau blanc*, June 21, 1824, p. 4.   [24] *Le Globe*, October 4, 1824, p. 40
[25] Ibid., October 6, 1824, p. 44.   [26] Ibid.

Constant's criticism of French eighteenth-century philosophy. He had misrepresented the *philosophes* and distorted the morality of self-interest. The *Mercure's* critic could not understand why Constant chose to "humiliate" French pride by vaunting Germany. There was something dishonorable about this undertaking, especially for a foreigner: "Foreigners who accuse us of arrogance are truly ungrateful." And, quite simply, it was ridiculous to suggest that France had something to learn from Germany on the subject of progress ... had Constant not read Condorcet?[27]

A reviewer for the *Revue encyclopédique* concurred with the *Mercure*. It was hard to understand Constant's need to attack the Enlightenment, and his "hot-headed hatred" for the *philosophes*. The pursuit of self-interest was not degrading as Constant maintained, and he should be more sensitive to the dangers of criticizing its proponents. Whose cause did Constant think he was serving?[28]

Perhaps the most cutting of all was the review by Stendhal (1783–1842), who published a running commentary on *De la religion* in his *Courrier Anglais*. A liberal with industrialist sympathies, Stendhal had admired Constant's *Spirit of Conquest and Usurpation*, but he was terribly disappointed in *De la religion*. The book was full of "conjectures," while nothing essential was "positively proved"; moreover, it was "horribly boring" and badly written.[29] Like the others, Stendhal took particular umbrage at Constant's "frivolous" and "presumptuous" attacks on French philosophy. Obviously, he was trying to refute the French Enlightenment with the help of "mystical" arguments "borrowed from the miserable Germany philosophy." This philosophy, Stendhal claimed, was "the laughing-stock of Europe." In the end, *De la religion* belonged to the category of books written by "society people" who had no profound ideas and did not know how to argue. A better title might have been *The Mistake of a Talented Man*. Constant should stick to making speeches and give up on philosophy.[30]

This disdain and mockery from someone who was, after all, a political ally serves to highlight the very different reception the book was accorded by the Protestant community of Paris. According to Philippe Stapfer, the Swiss and Protestant editor of the *Archives du christianisme*, Constant should be congratulated for the "justness," "fairness," and "profundity" of

---

[27] *Mercure de France*, vol. V, pp. 575–581; vol. VI, pp. 56–63.
[28] *Revue encyclopédique*, vol. XXIV (1826), pp. 63–74.
[29] *Courrier Anglais*, vol. II (September, 1824), p. 195.
[30] *Courrier Anglais*, vol. IV (November, 1824), pp. 29, 31, 11, 31.

his book. Stapfer, who had known Constant since around 1800, was an admirer of German philosophy and a good friend of Charles de Villers. After reading the first volume, Stapfer wrote a letter in which he professed his complete agreement with its argument and expressed his "sentiments of gratitude, admiration and high esteem":

I have just finished reading, or rather devouring, the volume that I owe to your goodness, and I can't tell you what exquisite enjoyments it has given me. Your work is an immense benefit in the present state of society. It is made to fill the sad gap which has, for too long, in France separated philosophy from belief, religion and liberty. You fulfill a glorious mission, that of contributing to end a divorce which is against nature.[31]

A similarly enthusiastic response came from *La Revue protestante*, a journal recently founded by a group of prominent French Protestants and pastors, one of whom was Samuel Vincent. The journal's chief editor was Charles Coquerel, whose *Tableaux de l'histoire philosophique du christianisme* Constant had praised in 1823. The first issue of the *Revue protestante* referred glowingly to "the important work by Benjamin Constant, whose last volumes are so impatiently awaited." The editors were thrilled that Constant "openly professes Protestantism" and were proud to count him among their own. "Our religious faith participates in the progress of the human mind," they boasted, and "we do not want to remain immobile while everything marches around us." Protestants do believe in revelation, "but it is not a pope [or] a council that obliges us; it is free inquiry, the feeling of evidence, the force of our reason." As believers in "free inquiry" and "religious sentiment," the editors of the *Revue protestante* had only good things to say about *De la religion* and recommended it highly. Constant sent a copy of volume II directly to Coquerel, accompanied by a letter saying that he would be "very happy to associate himself with the *Revue protestante*."[32]

CHARLES X AND "THE INVASION OF THE PRIESTS"

On September 16, 1824, Louis XVIII died. At heart a Voltairian skeptic and a realist, he had supported religion for reasons of political expediency. Several times during his reign, he had tried to chart a moderate course. His brother Charles X (1757–1836), who now ascended the throne, was very

---

[31] As quoted by G. Rudler, "Benjamin Constant et Philippe-Albert Stapfer," in *Mélanges de philologie, d'histoire et de littérature offerts à Joseph Vianey* (Paris, 1934), pp. 326–327.
[32] As quoted by Deguise, *Benjamin Constant méconnu*, p. 223.

different. The Revolution and a long period of exile had turned him into a devout Catholic and a fanatic counter-revolutionary. His aim, it soon became clear, was to roll back the consequences of the Revolution and fully restore *ancien régime* Catholicism. During his elaborate coronation cere-mony at Rheims Cathedral, he prostrated himself on the ground to show his submission to the Catholic Church. Soon, rumors began to circulate that the King was a Jesuit in disguise.

There followed a series of laws that shocked the nation. One of the most controversial was a measure to compensate former emigrés for property lost during the Revolution. Severe press laws were also passed, and, finally, there was a bill to restore primogeniture. Most provocative of all, however, was the Law on Sacrilege of 1825, which introduced capital punishment for blasphemy. Constant fought bravely against all these measures with impassioned speeches in the Chamber. Simultaneously, he worked hard to get the second volume of *De la religion* ready for pub-lication.

The Law on Sacrilege stated that thefts committed in churches would lead to solitary confinement in prison or hard labor for life. It further decreed that the profanation of the sacred vessels or the Host would be punishable by the same sentence given to criminals convicted of parricide. The condemned person would be made to walk barefoot to his execution with his head covered with a black cowl. Before being executed, his right hand would be amputated.

Supporters of this law justified it on the grounds that "religion" (i.e. Catholicism) needed protection. According to some reports, vandalism and thefts committed in churches were increasing at alarming rates. Church officials also felt besieged by the barrage of anticlerical pamphlets and books that were circulating throughout the country. The Catholic journal, *Tablettes du clergé et des amis de la religion*, reported that Vol-taire's complete works were available "everywhere," causing the Church immeasurable "shame" and "outrage." Religion, conservative newspapers argued, was needed to strengthen monarchy.[33]

In retrospect, it is easy to see that the Law on Sacrilege was a big mistake. It was very unpopular with the public and caused a tremendous backlash against the regime. Fantastic rumors of a "priestly plot" spread; they claimed that Jesuits were infiltrating every part of the country in a plan to establish a theocracy. Once again, then, the government's

---

[33] See for example, *Le Conservateur* I, pp. 351–2, cited by G. Venzac, *Les origines religieuses de Victor Hugo* (Paris, 1955).

measures to prop up the Church were largely counter-productive. Proponents of the bill miscalculated the mood of the country.

Liberals seized upon the error and cleverly exploited it. Having lost the elections of 1824, they now sensed the possibility for a comeback. Capitalizing on the fears of a Jesuit plot, they magnified the threat in their journals and newspapers. Liberal papers like *Le Constitutionnel* and *Le Courrier français* harped on the Jesuit theme,[34] repeatedly denouncing the "sacerdotal invasion." New editions of Voltaire, Rousseau, the Civil Constitution of the Clergy of 1790, and Molière's *Tartuffe* were published. Liberals also flooded the country with political pamphlets, cartoons, songs, and cheap books aimed at discrediting the Church. Pamphlets publicized speeches made by liberals in the Chamber of Deputies, while others sensationalized trials involving liberal newspapers.[35] Selling in the tens of thousands, the propaganda offensive was a great success. It has been estimated that over a span of seven years, 2,700,000 "antireligious" books were published.[36] The campaign was in no small measure responsible for the liberals' return to power in 1827 and the subsequent fall of the Bourbon monarchy in 1830.

Liberal journals and newspapers eagerly fed the mounting anticlericalism, often pointing out the political purposes of the re-Christianization campaign. The *Courrier français*, for example, ran the rather typical warning:

You want a representative government, institutions that protect the rights of all, an active commerce, a flourishing industry? Well then, all of this is incompatible with the influence of the Catholic clergy. This clergy is the enemy of liberal constitutions, of social guarantees, of all that emancipates human intelligence, of all that gives man the sentiment of his dignity.[37]

The Law on Sacrilege also contributed to the growing hostility to the Mission movement. Increasingly, the missionaries' attacks on the Revolution and their efforts to resurrect the Old Regime provoked "cross troubles" throughout the country. Crosses were removed, damaged, or destroyed. In churches, priests were hissed and booed, and services rudely interrupted. As before, audiences throughout the country demanded performances of Molière's anticlerical comedy *Tartuffe* to coincide with the arrival of

---

[34] See *Le Constitutionnel*, January 12, 1825, February 6, 1825, April 9, 1825 (on the sacrilege bill), February 16, 1825 (on indemnity), and February 10, 1826 (on primogeniture).
[35] Kroen, *Politics*, p. 185.
[36] C. Pouthas, *L'Eglise et les questions religieuses sous la monarchie constitutionelle*, (Paris, 1961) p. 255.
[37] *Courrier français*, February 14, 1826.

missionaries. Liberal publications, such as *Le Constitutionnel* and *L'Ami de la Charte*, reported enthusiastically on such anticlerical incidents, deriding the missionaries and advertising the availability of more cheap editions of Voltaire and Rousseau.[38] In Lyons, Rouen, and Brest, protests against the missionaries degenerated into riots, some of which had to be put down by government troops. Cumulatively, these events contributed to a growing feeling of religious "anarchy" in the country.

Particularly ominous for the Church and its allies in government was the fact that attacks on "Jesuitism" did not just come from staunch secularists or the extreme left wing. Even royalists and observant Catholics were becoming disaffected. Anticlericalism was growing exponentially across the country, as French men and women felt growing "dissatisfaction, distrust and outright disgust" for the missionary movement.[39] Many began referring to the austere, dogmatic and frightening version of Christianity it disseminated as "New Catholicism," and they rejected it.[40]

One of the most incendiary attacks on the government's religious policies came from the Comte de Montlosier (1755–1838), a devout Catholic and royalist nobleman. A liberal aristocrat in 1789, he had emigrated in 1791. Ironically, Montlosier's fame rested upon his passionate defense of the French clergy during the Revolution. However, beginning in 1815, he spoke out against the Jesuits, who, he thought, represented the worst tendencies in the French clergy. Then, enraged by the Law on Sacrilege, he began a full-scale onslaught with five articles in the *Drapeau blanc*, followed by a book. Clearly striking a nerve, Montlosier's "little masterpiece of political propaganda"[41] quickly ran through eight editions. In just three months, it sold more than 10,000 copies.[42]

Montlosier denounced the "vast conspiracy" orchestrated by "Jesuits and by congregations,"[43] who were using "religion as a political tool, and politics as a religious tool." Their methods deliberately confused religion and politics, creating a nefarious "politico-sacerdotal system." Calling himself "a simple Christian" who was repelled by the Church's "spirit of domination," Montlosier's attacks were particularly effective because he

---

[38] Kroen, *Politics*, p. 185.   [39] Ibid., p. 10.   [40] Sevrin, *Missions*, vol. I, p. 175.

[41] S. Mellon, *The Political Uses of History: A Study of Historians in the French Restoration* (Stanford, CA, 1958), p. 168.

[42] G. Cubitt, *The Jesuit Myth: Conspiracy Theory and Politics in Nineteenth-Century France* (Oxford, 1993), p. 70.

[43] This was an alleged kind of Catholic Freemasonry controlled by the pope with secret agents strategically placed throughout the government and administration.

had the long-established credibility of a sincere believer. He now accused wrong-minded priests of turning people away from religion. If atheism was growing in France, it was their own fault. The missions were producing "ignorance and barbarism" in the population, while "Jesuitism" was fomenting the abandonment of religion. In sum, the "invasion of the priests" had to stop.

Montlosier's writings show that the Church itself was becoming polarized. Another critic was the liberal Abbé de Pradt, who now issued a second edition of his *Les quatre concordats*, and supplemented it with *Du jésuitisme ancien et moderne*. In his new book, de Pradt lambasted the religious "fever," "illness," and "mania" that had infected people like de Maistre, Bonald, and Lamennais, and repeated his denunciation of the "sacrilegious mixing" of religion and politics. The Jesuits themselves were an anachronism and Jesuitism was nothing but "organized intolerance," thus contrary to the natural rights of man. De Pradt found it ironic that intransigent Catholics worried about defections to Protestantism, since they themselves were to blame. "It is from *you* people are fleeing,"[44] insisted this frustrated abbé.

Constant's article "Christianity"

In April 1825, while the debate over the Law on Sacrilege was raging, Constant published an article in the *Encyclopédie moderne* entitled "Christianity," or "On the Human Causes which Contributed to the Establishment of Christianity."[45] A month later, *Le Globe* published long excerpts from it. Once again, Constant used his view of religious history to address the political situation in France and to refute the Ultraroyalist agenda. Here, Constant described in much greater detail what he had only hinted at in the first volume of *De la religion*: the religious and political context when Christianity made its first appearance. His account of the transition from a decaying and corrupt polytheism to a vibrant and free Christianity delivered a barbed political message: the government's efforts to resuscitate Roman Catholicism were pointless and bound to fail. A new and more enlightened religion was on its way.

---

[44] *Du jésuitisme ancien et moderne* (Paris, 1825), pp. 8, 23, 10, 75, 307, 65, 67, 308, emphasis added.
[45] The article appears to be an abbreviated version of his two-volume book published posthumously, *Du polythéisme romain, considéré dans ses rapports avec la philosophie grecque et la religion chrétienne*, ed. J. Matter (Paris, 1833.) I am quoting from G. Ripley's translation in PhM, pp. 320–345.

Constant depicted the period of Christ's appearance in a manner that invited parallel with his own. He described a situation in which a great "disproportion" existed between the reigning religion and the period's "condition of intelligence." As a result of this disjunction, there was widespread skepticism and disrespect for religion. "Brutal incredulity" coexisted with mindless "superstition." Having outlasted its usefulness, polytheism was for all intents and purposes a "fallen religion." No doubt motivated by the threat this situation posed to their power, the authorities stepped in to attempt to revive a religion that had lost its appeal. They tried to "bring under [their] yoke the rebellious spirits" who had so irreverently applied "examination" to the "holy traditions of the past."[46]

Of course, the defenders of polytheism were unsuccessful: "Man does not recover his respect for that which has ceased to appear respectable." A new religion was called for, one "more youthful and vigorous." Christ's appearance was a "memorable revolution" and "an extraordinary circumstance." Constant did not hesitate to use language evocative of a miracle; he volunteered that he was not averse to attributing "supernatural cases" to the "important revolution" that brought Jesus Christ to the world.[47]

Constant described early Christianity in a way that jelled with his liberal and Protestant purposes. In contrast to "the multiplicity of rites, of ceremonies, and of practices" then in existence, Christianity favored "simple" and "modest" ceremonies. It proclaimed "a direct communication with the Divinity" and thus, presumably, had little need for a sacerdotal corps. Notably, early Christianity also "presented relief to the poor, justice to the oppressed, liberty to the slave, *as their natural rights.*" It was in this sense that the new religion was "a vast system of amelioration." Unfortunately, it had to suffer the enmity of powerful forces, especially the established authorities and priests.[48]

Professions of Protestantism

During the last years of his life, Constant frequently referred to himself as a Protestant. During the debate about the Law on Sacrilege in the Chamber, Constant spoke against it from the perspective of a concerned Protestant. The law was clearly Catholic in inspiration, he noted, and, as

---

[46] "On the Human Causes which have Contributed to the Establishment of Christianity," in PhM, pp. 320, 321, 322, 323.
[47] Ibid., pp. 324, 326, 330.   [48] Ibid., pp. 333, 335, 334, 335, 341, emphasis added.

such, it was a threat to religious toleration in general, and Protestants in particular:

It is sad, gentlemen, to see the barriers going up again between two Christian churches to which the general softening of attitudes, the advances in learning, and the Charter seemed to have brought genuine concord. But since the language of thirteenth-century Catholic theologians is now being spoken in this Chamber, I am forced in my turn to speak that of the leaders of the Reformation to whom your respect for freedom of worship allows me to express my gratitude. I owe to those reformers the inestimable privilege of being all the more persuaded of the truth of our sacred books because they gave me the right to study the scriptures and to be convinced by them myself.[49]

A few months later, again identifying himself as a Protestant, Constant vehemently defended the rights of French Protestants to equal treatment under French law. This time, the occasion was the controversy over the recent conversion to Protestantism of a man named Mollard-Lefèvre and the publishing of his reasons in the *Courrier français* on July 31, 1825. As mentioned earlier, Catholic newspapers frequently published letters by Protestant converts to Catholicism, and, for example, had recently celebrated the conversion of Charles Haller.[50] However, when it came to reporting a conversion to Protestantism, the government clamped down immediately: the issue was seized the day after the article was published. This provoked an uproar among liberal defenders of both the freedom of the press and religion.

Infuriated by the government's actions, which were somewhat predictable, the editor of the *Courrier français*, Count Kératry,[51] responded with a brochure accusing the government of favoring a "false" and "miserable" brand of Catholicism entirely out of synch with the age. The government's policies were counter-productive and were alienating the "enlightened classes" of France. The ultramontanism of people like Lamennais was a "degradation" of Christianity; if people were becoming indifferent to religion, Catholics had only themselves to blame. Worst of all was the "invasion of religion into politics and politics into religion." The "thinking people" of France had become embittered by this; Kératry thought it high time to "bring them back." A new direction was needed in

---

[49] As quoted by D. Berthoud, *Constance et grandeur de Benjamin Constant* (Lausanne, 1944), pp. 86–87.
[50] M. Saquin, *Entre Bossuet et Maurras: L'Antiprotestantisme en France de 1814 à 1870* (Paris, 1998), pp. 21–27.
[51] Auguste Hilarion, comte de Kératry (1769–1859).

religious matters, and a reform of Catholicism was long overdue. Catholicism could no longer be left in the hands of "Jesuits."[52]

In its August 5 issue, Constant intervened in defense of the *Courrier français'* right to publish Mollard-Lefèvre's letter. Constant pointed out that the authorities were standing idly by while people like Lamennais were permitted to write the most atrocious things about Protestants. In contrast, Mollard-Lefèvre had said nothing derogatory about Catholicism; he had simply explained his preference for Protestantism. Constant also called attention to the Catholic newspaper *L'Etoile's* freedom to refer to Protestants as religious "heretics" and to describe Protestantism as a religion that favored "insubordination, egoism and cupidity." And even though *L'Etoile* went so far as to claim that Lutheranism favored rebellion and that Protestantism was akin to "anarchy," nothing was done to restrain it. However, the moment a simple confession of faith by a Protestant convert was published, the government leaped into action. Whatever happened to the equal protection of religion that was promised in the Charter?

Declaring himself a "deputy, citizen and Protestant," and repeatedly referring to Protestantism as "our faith" and "our religion," Constant defended the rights of his co-religionists. He also described his religion in a way designed to appeal to liberal-minded Catholics, those "thinking classes" who were repelled by "Jesuitism" and the "invasion of priests." In Protestantism, Constant explained, "all nuances of Christianity" were thought to be "equally agreeable to its divine author." As a Protestant, he thought of Catholics as his Christian "brothers," separated from Protestants only "by a few dogmas" and by a different "exterior organization." To Protestants, Constant was keen to say, "every Christian who professes his cult in good faith professes a cult of truth." Protestants also did not require any special treatment, assistance, or protection from the government, only the right to express their faith openly and freely as guaranteed by the Charter: "We believe our religion to be true, and our laws give us the right to say so."[53]

Stendhal, who was following the stir created by Mollard-Lefèvre's letter, took note of Constant's very public intervention in the affair. He regretted that religion was back "in fashion" in France and, in so doing, continued his criticism of Constant's tack towards religion. In a letter to a friend, Stendhal sarcastically suggested that Constant was just trying to

---

[52] A.-H. de Kératry, *Du culte en général et de son état, particulièrement en France* (Paris, 1825).

[53] *Courrier français* article of August 5, 1825, reproduced in *Recueil d'Articles 1825–1829*, ed. E. Harpaz (Paris, 1992), pp. 20–27.

make a name for himself. His ambition was obvious: he wanted to make himself out to be "the Bossuet of the Protestants."[54]

DE LA RELIGION, VOLUME II (OCTOBER 1825)

"Dependent" vs. "independent" forms

In the first volume of *De la religion*, Constant had focused on the religious form/sentiment distinction. In the second volume, he posited a new distinction, that between two types of religious forms: the "dependent" variety, whose dogmas were controlled by a priesthood, and the "independent" variety, whose dogmas were free from priestly control. According to Constant, only one people had managed to liberate itself from the power of priests and to establish a truly "independent" religion: the ancient Greeks of the fifth century BC. Because of this, they should serve as a model to all modern men, who owed them a debt of gratitude.

It was "lucky for the human race" that the Greeks had been able to preserve their "freedom of intelligence," since it was precisely this freedom that enabled crucial "improvements [*perfectionnements*]" in both religion and morals. Because of its independence from priestly control, the Greek religion had been able to evolve according to the "natural march of religious ideas." Its dogmas gradually changed over time, as "an effect of the progress of Enlightenment and of the natural development of thought."[55]

While admiring the religious independence of the Greeks, volume II also had harsh words for "sacerdotal corporations." By this, Constant meant the priesthood of antiquity, which had done "great harm" to man. Their immense power had been universally pernicious. Writing in a scholarly tone, Constant nevertheless referred to their "usurpations" in ways that invited pointed comparisons with his own times. Priests, he noted, always tend to "seek a power without limits." For that purpose, they deliberately strive to "enslave" people's minds. The sacerdotal corporations of antiquity set themselves up as the "privileged intermediaries" between man and God. By claiming to be the "exclusive favorites of heaven" and the "dispensers of supernatural favors," they exploited the gullible and became "all-powerful."[56]

---

[54] Letter of August 18, 1825, in Stendhal, *Lettres de Paris* (Paris, 1983), as quoted by Saquin, *Entre Bossuet et Maurras*, p. 30.
[55] DLR, pp. 244, 243, 242.   [56] Ibid., pp. 145, 197.

Never satisfied with religious power, priesthoods sought to become politically dominant as well. Inevitably, this led to conflicts with governments, which were always won by the priests. Throughout history, the basis of sacerdotal power was a "monopoly" over thought; they acquired "exclusive possession of the sciences" and fought hard "to keep people in ignorance." The sacerdotal spirit, Constant insisted, was "the enemy" of "the prosperity and progress of the people," since such prosperity and progress would inevitably "lead to independence." As "dominating" corporations, priesthoods caused everything they controlled to become "monotonous" and "immobile."[57]

Mankind should be grateful to the one people who had freed itself from the empire of priests. The Greeks had left behind a precious inheritance. At the end of the second volume, Constant concluded that

we owe to the Greeks the life of thought and moral force ... Let us carefully guard this precious deposit: ancient Greece knew how to conquer it, let modern Europe know how to defend it.[58]

In an effort to tone down his anticlericalism somewhat and avoid alienating liberal Catholics, Constant included a few strategically placed disclaimers, as he had in his Athénée lectures and in the first volume of *De la religion*. His preface stated that "[n]othing I have written can be misinterpreted, by those with good intentions, as an attack on priests." Rather, what he was really against was "the alliance of despotism and the priesthood," an alliance that subverted the principles of some of the Church's own most prominent and respected representatives:

Our reprobation of this alliance of despotism and the sacerdoce does not apply to the church in whose name Fénelon,[59] Massillon[60] and Fléchier[61] never ceased to repeat to kings that the laws were the foundation and limit of their power.

While statements such as these mitigated Constant's attacks on Catholicism, others declared unequivocally his Protestant perspective on religious history. His position was recognizably pro-Protestant and anti-Catholic. For example, Constant explained that his research into religion had been pursued according to "the right conferred to us by our belief."

---

[57] Ibid., pp. 165, 212, 203, 167.   [58] Ibid., p. 244.

[59] François de la Salignac de la Mothe (1651–1715), Archbishop of Cambrais, celebrated bishop and author, opposed Bossuet, and is widely regarded as having spoken truth to power.

[60] Jean Baptiste Massillon (1663–1742), celebrated preacher and bishop, suspected of Jansenist sympathies due to his severe moralism.

[61] Esprit Fléchier (1632–1710), next to Fénelon regarded as one of the greatest orators of his century.

The right in question was, of course, that of free "inquiry."[62] This right, as we have seen, was recognized by Protestants at the time, but not by Catholics, even liberal ones.[63] Elsewhere, Constant spoke respectfully about the need for religious "ministers," who provide "guidance" and "instruction," while he pointedly rejected the notion of "infallible *priests*."[64]

More generally, Constant's notion of "religious perfectibility" and his related idea of progressive revelation had a strong Protestant bias, although these views were clearly not orthodox. Inspired by the liberal Protestant Germans, Constant's version of progressive revelation was rather vague and diffuse. For him, revelation seems not to have had any connection to the person of Jesus Christ or to any particular dogma. "For those who believe in God," he wrote, "all light comes from him ... and revelation is everywhere there is something true, something noble and something good."[65] Elsewhere, Constant explained:

if one believes in revelations, then one must consider these revelations as aids granted by a powerful and good being to an ignorant and weak one, when his own forces are not enough.[66]

Again, Constant seems to have regarded revelation as a kind of "light" that God imparts to man periodically in order to encourage his moral improvement, but without restricting his will.

Although the "goal of man is improvement [*le perfectionnement*]," God wants man to perfect himself "by his own efforts, by the use of his faculties, by the energy of his free will." God wants to "enlighten [man] without enchaining him," always leaving him free to choose what is right and good. Indeed, the battle to find truth and freely choose it is the very "means of man's improvement." If his will were to be enslaved, then man would be reduced to being a mere "machine" and there would be "nothing moral" about his improvement.[67]

Constant claimed, yet again, that he had no aversion to the idea that there was something miraculous about revelation or that a supernatural force might intervene at critical times in history. He employed Judaism as an example: the apparition and longevity of the Jewish religion was something "impossible to explain by reasoning." Like the German Protestants, Constant saw revelation as a progressive and educational process that stretched out over history, and by which God providentially oversaw man's gradual improvement.

---

[62] DLR, p. 189.   [63] See for example, the beginning of Abbé de Pradt's book, *Du jésuitisme*.
[64] DLR p. 198, emphasis added.   [65] Ibid., p. 191.   [66] Ibid., p. 189.   [67] Ibid.

Constant's philohellenism

To praise the independent spirit of the Greeks, and to hold them up as an example for the world, was more than an academic exercise in 1825. Since 1821, when they had risen up against their Ottoman rulers, the Greeks were in the midst of a desperate struggle for independence. Supporting their cause well before 1825,[68] Constant was one of the first and the most vocal advocates of Greek independence in France. He wrote at least five articles on the topic and made several speeches in the Chamber of Deputies.[69] In September of 1825, just one month before the second volume of De la religion came out, he had published an "Appel aux nations chrétiennes," in which he begged true Christians to intervene to help their Greek brothers liberate themselves from the Turks.

At the time, however, the major European powers expressed little sympathy for the Greeks and had no desire to get involved. The so-called Holy Alliance viewed the war as an internal Ottoman matter; in their eyes, the sultan was a legitimate sovereign and the Greeks were simply rebels. Apparently, this was also how the Ultraroyalists viewed the Greeks. Some observers say that the French were more interested in seeking commercial benefits from Turkey than in aiding their Christian brothers.[70] Although it became harder to remain passive after the Massacre of Chios in 1822, the French government was extremely slow to respond.

For a long time, all of France's aid to the Greeks came from private initiatives like the Society for Christian Morals, of which Constant became a member in 1825. Constant had an uphill struggle to convince his government to come to the aid of the Greeks. In this campaign, he tried to coerce it by exposing the hypocrisy of an ostensibly Christian government refusing to come to the aid of fellow Christians. On the floor of the Chamber he exclaimed:

Sirs, do not deliver the Christians to the Turks and you will better defend Christianity than with all your processions, ceremonies and exterior acts.[71]

His brochure "Appel aux nations chrétiennes" also tried to shame the government into action. First of all, Constant published his appeal on

---

[68] See B. Anelli, "Benjamin Constant et la guerre pour l'indépendance de la Grèce (1821–1830)," ABC, 23–23 (2000), pp. 195–203; and idem, "Benjamin Constant et la guerre pour l'indépendance de la Grèce: deux lettres inédites (1824 et 1825)," ABC, 20 (1997), pp. 153–161.

[69] Four in the *Courrier français* and one in *Le Temps*.

[70] J. Puryear Vernon, *France and the Levant* (Berkeley, CA, 1941).

[71] *Archives parlementaires*, quoted by B. Anneli.

behalf of the Society for Christian Morals; he repeated the society's name *nine* times in this relatively short piece. As Constant described it, the Society for Christian Morals was devoted to "religion and humanity" and those two things were "inseparable."[72] In his brochure, Constant said that all Christians should be shocked by the atrocities being committed against the Greeks, and he listed a litany of outrages:

> Our altars profaned, objects of our veneration the butt of execrable insults, the ministers of our cult butchered in the sanctuary, martyrs punished for professing our faith, the name Christian an entitlement to insults, chains and death.

To abandon the Greeks under these circumstances would be an "apostasy" and a "sacrilegious hypocrisy."[73]

Among his reasons for advocating French intervention was also the fact that Greece served as a buffer against the Turkish Empire. Europeans should not flatter themselves with the idea that they had adequate forces to resist the Turks, should they wish to expand further. According to Constant, the Europeans of his day were "softened, incredulous, degraded by pleasures, disarmed by industry, incapable of conviction and sacrifice." What the Greeks had, and what French had lost, was the ability "to believe and to die." The Greeks' faith animated their pursuit of liberty; this was the Christianity Constant admired. Because of their courage in the face of despotism, their devotion and enthusiasm as they fought oppression, and their disdain for death in the pursuit of freedom, the Greeks were a model for Frenchmen.

Joseph de Maistre's view of the Greek "character"

Not surprisingly, Ultraroyalists had a starkly different view of the Greeks, one that informed their foreign policy. An inkling of it can be glimpsed in Joseph de Maistre's *Du pape*, which came out only two years before the Greek uprising began. According to de Maistre, a distinguishing characteristic of the Greeks was their "inaptitude for any great political or moral institutions." Indeed, they had never even had the honor of "being a people" in the full sense of the word. The core problem was their "spirit of division and opposition." It made the Greeks "superficial" like children and "ferocious" like beasts. Comparable to "enraged sheep," the Greeks were naturally prone to "devour their shepherds."[74]

---

[72] "Appel aux nations chrétiennes en faveur des Grecs," in E. Harpaz (ed.), *Benjamin Constant Publiciste 1825–1830* (Paris and Geneva, 1987), p. 59.
[73] Ibid., p. 62.   [74] *Du pape*, p. 328.

Du pape reminds its readers of the trouble the Greeks had caused the Christian church during its first centuries, "possessed" as they were by "the demon of pride and argumentation." They tried to be simultaneously philosophers and Christians, a disastrous combination that only led them astray. What the Greeks had not realized was that by separating themselves from the Mother Church, they in effect "became Protestants," in other words, "separate and independent."[75] And like the later Protestants, the Greeks were "dividers" of religion, unwilling to recognize the need for Christian unity. Their "spirit of division and opposition" had by now acquired such deep roots that they had even "lost the very idea of unity."[76]

De Maistre's comments testify to a French awareness of the rumblings of a Greek national resistance movement well before 1821. *Du pape* registers the "fermentation . . . a new spirit, an ardent enthusiasm for national glory" smoldering in Greece. But de Maistre warns against seeing this in a favorable light. People living in Greece, who know its inhabitants, also know that "it will never be possible to establish a Greek sovereignty." If the Greeks were to rebel, all that would happen is that they would "change masters"; they would always remain subjugated because of their divisive character.[77]

Constant's conclusions could not have been more different. The Greeks' independent spirit was a model to the world. Inspired by their Christian faith, they were energetically and heroically confronting despotism, while the French turned away, quite literally minding their own businesses, oblivious or insensitive to the suffering of their Christian brothers. By showcasing the Greeks' courage, heroism, and independent spirit, Constant was not only imploring the French in general to support their war of independence, but also urging French liberals in particular to be as heroic and self-sacrificing in the face of despotism as the Greeks. Elsewhere, Constant exhorted the "friends of liberty" in France to be "the first Christians of a new Byzantine Empire."[78]

Reviews of volume II

With the publication of volume II, Catholic reviewers stepped up their criticism of Constant's book. Eckstein published a 95-page review in the first issue of his new journal, *Le catholique*. He repeated what he had said in *Le Drapeau blanc* and then piled on top of that. Once again, then,

---

[75] Ibid., p. 336.   [76] Ibid., p. 333.   [77] Ibid., pp. 337, 338, 339.   [78] Preface to DLR, p. 34.

Constant was accused of shoddy scholarship. While Eckstein acknowledged that Constant had read a vast amount, he had read it too quickly
and thus had misunderstood many of the sources he cited. The result was
an incoherent argument full of contradictions.[79] Echoing Stendhal's
equally poor impression, Eckstein described the scholarship as "superficial," typical of "a man of the world" who was dabbling in research. *De la
religion* was the work of "a simple amateur."[80]

Beyond this devastating criticism, Eckstein accused Constant of
allowing himself to be "carried away" by political objectives.[81] An ardent
adversary of "any nobility and any priesthood," Constant's real purpose,
despite his disclaimers, was obvious: he wished to wound Catholicism. A
major part of the problem was his being Protestant; he could not properly
understand Catholicism, preoccupied as he was with establishing "an
exclusively popular cult."[82] At heart, Constant was a "partisan of democracy in religion as in politics," a perspective that would eventually spell
the end of both religion and society.[83]

Unsurprisingly, *De la religion* received accolades in the *Revue protestante*. Responding to the Catholic press, the reviewer said that Constant
was clearly not attacking religion itself; nor was he hostile to priests in
general. Rather, he was against "theocracy"; he was denouncing the
"monopoly" of an "invasive sacerdoce" – which was precisely what was
being promoted by journals like *Le Drapeau blanc* and the *Mémorial
catholique*. Praising Constant for delivering a powerful blow to the
reigning "mania for theocracy," the *Revue protestante* was delighted that
he had arrived at his views by applying his "right of free inquiry," and that
he was now openly professing his Protestantism. The journal also highlighted, and reproduced, long passages from "the beautiful chapter xi," in
which Constant discussed Judaism and defined revelation.[84]

However, more harsh criticism came in the form of Lamennais' *De la
religion considérée dans ses rapports avec l'ordre politique et civil*. In contrast to
Eckstein's attack on superficial scholarship, Lamennais focused entirely on
Constant's Protestantism. In fact, Lamennais' book appears at times to be
just one long diatribe against Protestantism, in which he singles out Constant and the *Revue protestante* for special rebuke. If France was in a
deplorable state, it was in large part due to people like Constant. The country

---

[79] Constant counter-attacked in volume III of his work, accusing Eckstein of poor scholarship and
superficial understanding.
[80] *Le Catholique*, October 1827, p. 29.   [81] Ibid., p. 21.   [82] Ibid., p. 38.   [83] Ibid., p. 33.
[84] *Revue protestante*, vol. II (October 1825), pp. 179–188.

had turned into a "vast democracy," a mere "assemblage of thirty million individuals," with no real bond nor moral connection between them.[85] The idea of popular sovereignty had brought along in its train "an extreme cupidity" and an "insatiable thirst for gold." France's dismal situation was, of course, caused by the Revolution, but, as Ultraroyalists and intransigent Catholics were fond of saying, it had an earlier source: the Protestant Reformation. Once the principle of authority in religion was denied, it was bound to be denied in politics as well, and the individual's will would be substituted for the will of God. "The painful anxiety" and "convulsive movements" that France was presently experiencing were nothing but the result of a battle between Protestantism and Catholicism. Thanks to the Protestant heresy, "atheism and its consequences" were manifest everywhere.

Once again, Lamennais explained that Catholicism was founded on authority; to Catholics, religion was a "divine law," which prescribed "what one must believe" and "how one must practice." Catholics believed that Jesus Christ came to establish unity by bringing all individuals together into one family. What could be "more noble," "more generous," and "more useful to humanity" than that? Protestantism, by contrast, was founded on the principle of private judgement. Protestants claimed that Jesus' teachings could be reduced to "the freedom from all authority and the right of each individual to deny all dogmas." Such principles were clearly "destructive of all bonds," not just in the spiritual domain but throughout "human society." Citing the *Revue protestante*, Lamennais derided how the Protestants defined their religion: it was nothing but "the act of independence of human reason." Referring to Constant's *De la religion* and its favorable reception by the Protestant community, Lamennais expressed dismay that

religion is reduced to an undefinable sentiment which manifests itself in different forms according to the time and place, and Protestants applaud this, they praise it, they openly adopt this doctrine.

Their attitude was a great "misery" for society since it meant that there would no longer be any bond between individuals. Lamennais staunchly defended the idea that only Roman Catholicism could keep society from disintegrating:

without a pope [there is] no Church; without a Church, no Christianity; without Christianity, no religion and no society.[86]

---

[85] F. de Lamennais, *De la religion considérée dans ses rapports avec l'ordre politique et civil* (Paris, 1825), pp. 331, 108.

[86] Ibid., p. 181.

THE PROBLEM WITH *INDUSTRIE*: CONSTANT AND RELIGION SEEN FROM THE LEFT

Unquestionably, the throne-and-altar alliance committed a major mistake with its regressive legislation, and especially with the infamous Law on Sacrilege. The country was in no mood for theocracy. Liberals were able to capitalize on the discontent and soon the government appeared doomed. It was only a matter of time before Ultraroyalists and intransigent Catholics would be swept from power.

However, *De la religion* did not just attack intransigent Catholicism and the throne-and-altar alliance; it also contained timely warnings to all those *philosophe*-inspired intellectuals and politicians who thought that France could do without religion. Constant criticized Voltairean-styled liberals who were pursuing a vendetta against Christianity. This, Constant thought, was also the wrong way to proceed and would cause the country harm. On the eve of his second volume's appearance, he vented his frustrations in a letter to his cousin, Rosalie:

We are at a moment in time when everything that isn't positive, everything that doesn't produce something material, seems to be just a mind-game and a waste of time ... Everything that isn't a steam engine is [regarded as] a reverie.

Under the circumstances, Constant worried about how his second volume would be received: "I am not finding a public which might sympathize with my ideas."[87]

One can understand why he felt that way; his first volume had been criticized by the left because many liberals did not understand his attack on the French Enlightenment and the morality of self-interest. Some, as we have seen, were angered by his "humiliation" of France and his praise of Germany. Moreover, people were puzzled by what they thought was a mixed message: was Constant *for* civilization or was he against it? Did he believe in progress, or did he believe that France was in a state of decline? Both *De la religion* and the "Appel aux nations chrétiennes" contained somber passages that suggested he had ambivalent feelings on the question. "The *threat* in modern civilization," he warned in volume I, was that human beings might become so saturated in material pleasures that they became "slaves of their pleasures."[88] Then, in the "Appel aux nations chrétiennes," he described the French as "softened," "degraded by pleasures," "disarmed

---

[87] Letter no. CXCII (Benjamin to Rosalie, October 6, 1825) in KK, p. 268.
[88] DLR, p. xxxviii, emphasis added.

by industry," and incapable of conviction and sacrifice.[89] His solution for this problem was religion, but the religion he described appeared "vague" and unsatisfactory to many people. In the polarized context of the mid-1820s, no one could quite understand or appreciate Constant's stance, except, of course, some Protestants.

In volume II, Constant continued down the same path. France needed religion now more than ever. "Let us not flatter ourselves," he warned, "that despite the brilliant epoch our civilization is presently in, we do not still have perils to fear." "Egoism" and "luxury" were growing problems, as was a general sense of "fatigue" in the population. France was suffering from an "excess of civilization." And neither industry nor philosophy could provide solutions. Under the circumstances, "only religion can save us"; religion was France's one, all-important "means of improvement."[90]

As Constant was defending religion, he wanted to make it perfectly clear that he was simultaneously, and perhaps most of all, defending the people's right to religious *freedom*. Any attempt to control and direct the religious sentiments – by either a self-interested priesthood or a self-interested government, of whatever political orientation – was a tragic mistake. Constant demanded state neutrality in matters of religion.

If the independent religion of the ancient Greeks constituted a model to be emulated, the modern Chinese state-controlled religion served the opposite purpose. In China, Constant explained, the priesthood had lost its battle with the temporal authorities, and the emperor had set himself up as the uncontested "master" of religion. The result was deplorable for religion: an emphasis on "frivolous and fastidious ceremonies" at the expense of "religious sentiment," a tendency towards "irreligious abstractions" in the enlightened classes and "stupid superstitions" in the populace. "Magic" replaced religion as China turned into a "theocracy of atheists."[91]

Thus, the Chinese were made to suffer "the most heavy oppression" and a "frightful immobility."[92] They were simultaneously civilized and oppressed. Constant's point was that human faculties were as badly stunted by the Chinese government's control over religion as they were elsewhere, under the power of priests. Constant was eager to stress that none of this should be blamed on religion itself; rather, the problem lay with those who tried to *control* religion and, through religion, rule the people. This applied to *all*: priests, governments, elitist intellectuals, etc.

---

[89] "Appel aux nations chrétiennes," p. 67.   [90] DLR, pp. 244, 245, 244, 246.
[91] Ibid., pp. 220–201.   [92] Ibid., p. 200.

Advocating state neutrality in religion did not mean that Constant was without a preference. While Constant proposed Christianity as a valid and necessary response to France's predicament, he redefined it in a distinctly Protestant way. He referred people to the period of Christ's appearance. "We have already said it," he emphasized, "the present crisis is the same that menaced human nature when Christianity was established." The difference in 1825, however, was that France already had Christianity: "today we are in possession of Christianity; and, of all the forms that religious sentiment can assume, Christianity is the most satisfying and pure."[93]

Although Christianity was "unalterable" in the "essential truths" it "engraved on the heart," it was also "flexible" in the forms that it took over the course of history. In everything coming from God, Constant explained, "Christianity is not progressive, for it is perfect." However, in its external forms, and especially in the diverse "opinions" of various sects, there was "ample room for improvement."[94] This was Constant's point: Christianity was meant to participate in the process of religious perfectibility and thus remain forever relevant.

Charles Dunoyer's L'industrie et la morale considérées dans leurs rapports avec la liberté *(1825)*

Despite Constant's warnings and suggestions, in the winter of 1825–6, the *industrialiste* Charles Dunoyer delivered a series of lectures at the Athénée Royal in which he largely ignored the topic of religion. His subject was the relationship between industry, morals, and liberty. Religion played no positive role in Dunoyer's theory of human progress; instead, he described history as an evolution through various economic stages. Beginning with savagery, mankind passed through nomadism, slavery, feudalism, and mercantilism, all of which prepared it for *industrie,* the final and future stage. Each stage was heavily dependent on its mode of production, such that any non-economic influences on human progress appeared derivative.

Around 1817, Dunoyer had started to distance himself from Constant's constitutional brand of liberalism. In the *Censeur européen*, Dunoyer instead began advocating the principles of *industrie.* The answer to all of France's problems, he now argued, lay in productive work. And work should no longer be seen as just a means to some other end, but as the true goal of social activity. Since all good things came from industry, production, and exchange, Dunoyer advised liberals to reorient their

[93] Ibid., pp. 246, 247.   [94] Ibid., p. 247.

priorities and focus on the economy. One had to liberate the economy from the shackles that were impeding it. In effect, Dunoyer evolved into what one expert has called a "hardcore advocate of pure laissez-faire."[95]

Dunoyer's lectures at the Athénée Royal constituted a plea on behalf of the principles of *industrie* and were published as a book the same year. Claiming not to have abandoned the fight for liberty, the motto on the title-page summed up his new position: "We can only become free by becoming industrious and moral." And while Dunoyer repeatedly invoked the need to encourage morality, he implied that good morals would come, almost reflexively, from industry and the prosperity it engendered. Industry, he wrote, "is the foster-mother of virtue."[96]

It is clear that Dunoyer had read Constant, and had been disturbed by him. Dunoyer had been annoyed by *De la religion*'s warnings about "excessive" civilization and by its suggestion that material improvement might lead to moral decline. In his plea for *industrie*, Dunoyer was anxious to refute even the possibility that such an idea was logical. Rather, he maintained that work and the wealth it engendered would always foster better taste, more habits, and morals.[97] In short, work made men more moral and, therefore, more free.

The search for a new doctrine: from Jouffroy to Saint-Simon

Dunoyer was not alone in ignoring, or even denying, religion as a factor in human progress. Destutt de Tracy and Jean-Baptiste Say remained committed to their Idéologue principles and hostile to religion to the very end. As staunch secularists, they found "religious sentiments" anathema to their socio-economic and political theories; to them, moralization involved teaching people how to identify their real interests, and nothing more. By the late 1820s, Say was openly deriding what he referred to as the "Germanic sect," which based its ideas on the so-called "truths of sentiment."[98]

Not all liberals, however, were non-believers. Even more worrying than the die-hard Idéologues, from Constant's perspective, was the growing tendency among some liberals to seek an entirely new religious doctrine for France. Increasingly, they attacked *both* Catholicism *and* Protestantism as outmoded religions that had outlived their usefulness. In fact, a

---

[95] Hart, "Class Analysis."
[96] *L'industrie et la morale considérées dans leurs rapports avec la liberté* (Paris, 1825), p. 340.
[97] Ibid., pp. 99, 106.
[98] R. Whatmore, *Republicanism and the French Revolution: An Intellectual History of Jean-Baptiste Say's Political Economy* (Oxford, 2000), p. 208.

growing chorus on the left now described Protestantism as an entirely "negative" religion that needed to be replaced with something more "positive." During the last years of his life, as Constant became ever more concerned about this trend, he consistently advised liberals, as he had previously advised Ultraroyalists, to *let religion be*. Intellectual elites should resist the temptation to set themselves up as formulators of religious dogmas.

The article "Comment les dogmes finissent" by Theodore Jouffroy, published in *Le Globe* in May of 1825, testifies to this new tendency. *Le Globe* was very much a liberal journal, utterly opposed to the Ultraroyalist agenda. A valiant fighter in the battle for freedom of religion, it consistently fought for the neutrality of the state in religious matters.[99] Earlier in the month it had printed long excerpts of Constant's article "On the Human Causes which have Contributed to the Establishment of Christianity." So, when Jouffroy's article appeared, it seemed to come as a rejoinder.

Ostensibly, the article posed an abstract, even academic question: What happens when a dogma "is over"? In reality, however, the question went right to the core of sensitive debates going on at the time in France. What would happen to Roman Catholicism, whose time had passed? What would replace it? Jouffroy did *not* view Constant's brand of Protestantism as the answer.

When, over the centuries, a religion became "corrupted" by countless "errors" and "absurdities," Jouffroy argued that it was only a matter of time before people stopped believing in it. The spirit of examination would be awakened and a new faith would appear, drawing people even further away from the old. In turn, the old religion would try to fight back, denying people the right of inquiry and reinforcing its old "superstitions" and dying "formulas." But these reactions would not work, because there was no way to save a religion when it was "over."

On the other hand, the new religion, having been born in combat against the old, would not satisfy people either. The reason was that it had "nothing positive" to contribute; it was "just the negation" of the old. This skepticism, however, would not last for ever, because people "have a need to believe" something "positive." Everyone feels a bit "empty" when the old religion is gone; a "vague anxiety" prevails. People need a "new doctrine" around which to rally.

---

[99] Jean-Jacques Goblot, *La jeune France libérale: Le Globe et son groupe littéraire 1824–1830* (Paris, 1995).

Saint-Simon's "New Christianity" (1825)

Saint-Simon responded to the call for a new religion when he published his "New Christianity" in 1825. Because he died shortly thereafter, the book came to be regarded as a *quasi* last will and testament to his disciples. It was around this time that Saint-Simonianism started to become popular in France, possibly thanks to the new book. The movement seems to have been especially popular among Jouffroy's young students.[100]

Originally a solid member of the liberal camp, Saint-Simon had drifted away due to his frustration with the liberals' inability to solve France's many problems. He became particularly sensitive to the deplorable condition of the working classes and what he held to be the rampant egoism of their employers. By 1823–4, Saint-Simon was openly attacking what he now derisively called the liberal "bourgeoisie," who were proving to be incapable of establishing the industrial regime so desperately needed. What was urgently required, Saint-Simon now claimed, was a union of bankers and the government *against* the liberals. "Order" and the rule by "experts" should be established.

Some of Saint-Simon's ideas made him sound eerily similar to counter-revolutionaries and Catholic conservatives. Like them, he worried increasingly about establishing order and promoting social cohesion. Also like them, he was now convinced that the core of France's crisis lay in the realm of ideas. To cure these problems, Saint-Simon determined that a new religious doctrine was needed. This, however, is where he radically diverged from the Catholic conservatives and Ultraroyalists: Saint-Simon's "New Christianity" was certainly *not* Catholicism, which, he concluded, was completely out of touch with modern society's needs. Neither did he favor a variety of Protestantism, no matter how modernized or improved. Indeed, Saint-Simon's "New Christianity" seems to have been designed expressly to counter the "New Protestantism" advocated by people like Constant.

The goal of Saint-Simon's religion was to make men "behave as brothers to one another." Neither Catholicism nor Protestantism had proved to be up to that task. More specifically, his new form of Christianity would "direct society towards the great goal of the most rapid improvement possible of the lot of the poorest class." In so doing, it would promote a "doctrine" truly appropriate to France's "stage of civilization."[101]

---

[100] Ibid., p. 523.

[101] H. de Saint-Simon, *Le nouveau christianisme et le écrits sur la religion*, ed. H. Desroche (Paris, 1969), pp. 149, 174, 160.

Saint-Simon was highly critical of Protestantism, calling it an "incomplete" religion, vastly "inferior" to his New Christianity. Protestants were overly concerned with studying the Bible and not enough with aiding their neighbors. Moreover, Protestantism was incompatible with Saint-Simon's political vision, because it led to political views "contrary to the public good." It encouraged people to establish "an equality that is absolutely impracticable" and stopped them from creating a system where "the most capable governed."

Like Jouffroy, Saint-Simon was willing to concede that, historically, Protestantism had served a pivotal role. Luther had rendered "a capital service to civilization" by attacking the Catholic Church. However, the dogmatic part of Luther's reform was entirely inadequate and "incomplete." In fact, because it lacked a proper "doctrine," Protestantism was now *impeding* progress. It was contributing to the rise of egoism in the modern world – and egoism, to Saint-Simon, was the "political malady" of the century. Although it had been a necessary stage in the religious evolution of mankind, Protestantism should now be superceded by a new religion that was more binding and truly moralizing. Notably, Saint-Simon made a point of denouncing the "vague" ideas and sentiments emanating from northern Germany.[102]

Auguste Comte, Le Producteur, *and the search for a new "spiritual authority"*

Like Saint-Simon, starting around 1817, Auguste Comte expressed growing anxiety that society was "disorganized" and that a "great crisis" was gripping post-revolutionary France.[103] He deplored the "profound moral and political anarchy" which he saw all around and which was threatening society with "iminent and inevitable dissolution."[104] Liberalism, he now began to think, was the problem and not the solution to the crisis. Placing too much emphasis on the rights of the individual, it was dissolving and atomizing. By 1819, Comte was mocking what he called "the ridiculous prejudice" that "any man is capable ... of forming a just political opinion and ... of setting himself up as a legislator."[105] Indeed, Comte was certain that the profound "social malaise" gripping his contemporaries was due to intellectual or spiritual

---

[102] Ibid., pp. 160, 181, 180.
[103] Essay 3: "Plan of the Scientific Work Necessary for the Reorganization of Society" (1822–4), in H. Jones (ed.), *Early Political Writings* (Cambridge, 1998), p. 85.
[104] Ibid., p. 49.
[105] Essay 1: "General Separation between Opinions and Desires"(originally submitted to *Le Censeur* in July 1819), in *Early Political Writings*, p. 1.

anarchy caused by the so-called right of private judgement.[106] A new "general doctrine"[107] was needed to unify minds and re-establish order.

As he turned his attention to the spiritual reasons for France's crisis, Comte found that he had much in common with thinkers of the reactionary school: de Maistre, Bonald and Lamennais. Like them, Comte began to portray Enlightenment philosophy and liberal principles as destructive of the social order, while he described medieval Europe with its binding ethos of Catholicism in an increasingly positive light. He singled out two principles that were obstructing the re-establishment of order. One was popular sovereignty. The other was freedom of conscience, or, as Comte also called it, "the right of private judgement," which he linked closely with Protestantism.[108] In agreement with the Ultraroyalists, Comte denounced the isolation, confusion, and skepticism promoted by freedom of conscience. "The sovereignty of each individual mind," Comte complained, "tends essentially to prevent the uniform establishment of any system of general ideas."[109] Also like the Ultraroyalists, he came to see both Protestantism and liberalism as antisocial doctrines, that were aggravating the spiritual and moral chaos of France.

For all these reasons, Comte was naturally drawn to collaborate with the new Saint-Simonian journal, *Le Producteur*. Launched in October 1825, soon after the philosopher's death in 1825 and almost simultaneously with volume II of *De la religion*, *Le Producteur* was a perfect venue for Comte, who quickly became the journal's leading light. Its first issue announced "the need for a [new] doctrine" that would "direct all of man's knowledge and sentiments towards a common goal."[110] Soon thereafter, the journal attacked freedom of conscience as having outlived its usefulness. It was only "partisans of the past"[111] who clung to this principle of destruction,[112] which was fomenting anarchy and chaos in society. Under present circumstances, the notion that each individual should be allowed "to judge, according to his own personal reason"[113] was only an impediment to society's progress, ensuring that nothing gets "reorganized."[114]

The journal also published a critical review of Dunoyer's *L'industrie et la morale*.[115] In one of the first recorded uses of the word "individualism," the author of the review took issue with Dunoyer's "exaggerated"[116] emphasis on the individual and his rights and needs. Such a perspective was adapted to

---

[106] Essay 3, p. 72.   [107] Ibid., p. 62.   [108] Ibid., p. 65.   [109] Ibid., p. 55.
[110] *Le Producteur, journal de l'industrie, des sciences et des beaux-arts*, vol. I (1825), pp. 4 and 10.
[111] Ibid., pp. 399, 401.   [112] Ibid., p. 409.   [113] Ibid., p. 410.   [114] Ibid., p. 538.
[115] Ibid., vol. II (1825), pp. 158–170.   [116] Ibid., p. 162.

the goal of destroying the Old Regime, but not to building anew. It was now more important "to coordinate" than "to dissolve," and to focus more on society than on the individual. A "positive" theory had to replace a merely "critical" one if France was to be pulled out of the current impasse.[117]

Constant's "Overview of General Trends"

Returning to the Athénée Royal on 3 December 1825, Constant delivered a lecture entitled "A Rapid Overview of General Trends in Nineteenth Century Thought." In it, he identified the current trends of thinking and gave his opinion on them. He directed his lesson to those young people who had been attracted by the principles of *industrie*, and who were now flirting with Saint-Simonianism. The lecture indicates that Catholicism was no longer his only or even main concern; the danger confronting France was less the traditional authoritarianism of the right than the peculiar authoritarianism of the left.

Constant began by acknowledging the general "fermentation" that everyone was feeling. There was something in the air: "a new order of things" seemed eminent. He acknowledged the critical importance of *industrie*. "Today," he declared, "industry is *the* principal thought – perhaps the unique thought of the century." Constant then clarified his own point of view. Industry, one should never forget, was "the signal of a new era favorable to [*public* and . . .] *political liberty*." Taking issue with the Saint-Simonians and Comtians, he insisted that "the dominant need of our epoch" was *both* industry *and* freedom of conscience. Man's thought was his "most sacred property," and the expression of this thought, his "most inviolable right." Authorities had no right to meddle with an individual's thoughts, whether true or false.[118]

In a similar vein, friends of religion should always make sure to protect freedom of conscience. Religion must never be allowed to become the instrument of "greedy" groups of people wishing to impose a "monopoly" on mankind.[119] Here, Constant singled out the Saint-Simonians in what appears to have been a diatribe. Although this section of his speech was not printed in the newspaper, we know that he severely berated them because of the spirited responses that were subsequently published in other journals. For example, two days later, Leon Halévy, a frequent contributor to

---

[117] Ibid., p. 163.
[118] "Coup d'oeil sur la tendance générale des esprits dans le dix-neuvième siècle", in *Benjamin Constant publiciste*, pp. 70, 73, 74, 75.
[119] Ibid., p. 75.

Le Producteur, wrote a letter to *L'Opinion* objecting vehemently to Constant's characterization of Saint-Simonianism and insisting that he had no rational reason to be so alarmed. Constant immediately responded; in a letter reprinted in both the *Journal du Commerce* and *Le Producteur*, he clarified and reinforced his disapproval of Saint-Simonianism.

Le Producteur included its own response to Constant's critique, which, in its editors' minds, was an overreaction. Perhaps Constant was afraid of losing disciples? But whatever his reasons were for attacking their school of thought, he was wrong to frighten the public. He should not imply that the Saint-Simonians wished to impose a new "Inquisition." Such grave accusations were terribly unfair.[120] Notably, Constant's warnings did not change *Le Producteur's* positions. On the contrary, it continued to deplore the "complete chaos of ideas, opinions, interests, sentiments and actions" that people like Constant thought belonged to "the natural order" of society. Again, the editors lamented "the state of anarchy" in France and argued that it was time for society to be "reorganized." A "general principle" was needed to "bind" people.[121]

In the following issues, *Le Producteur* published a series of articles by Auguste Comte that were bound to alarm Constant further. Entitled "Considerations on the Spiritual Power," they argued for the need to institute a new "spiritual authority" that would put an end to the present crisis by imposing a collective purpose on society. Given the present state of France, it was imperative to "unite minds" and "settle [people's] ideas." The "Considerations" also reveal Comte's growing aversion to liberal economic principles and his concern for the commercialism and "material spirit" taking hold. More specifically, he feared the isolation and disorder caused by the division of labor. He thought that as the economy expanded, hostilities between employers and workers were bound to increase. Thus, Comte distanced himself not just from political liberalism, but also from economic liberalism, which he now blamed for encouraging egoism and materialism. If anyone wanted to see the horrifying example of a place where the "material spirit" was "completely dominant" and where "spiritual disorganization" had been "pushed infinitely further than anywhere else," he need only look at the United States.[122]

The fundamental problem confronting France was "spiritual disorganization"; and the solution lay in a new "spiritual authority." This new

---

[120] See *Le Producteur*, vol. I (1825), pp. 482–484, 536–540, in which the letters in question are reproduced.

[121] Ibid., p. 539.

[122] Essay 5, "Considerations on the Spiritual Power," in *Early Political Writings*, p. 198.

power would "impose reciprocal duties on employers and workers" and "prepare individuals for the social order in which they are to live." Thus, it would institute the social consensus and harmony so desperately needed. If anyone needed clarification as to the kind of spiritual authority Comte had in mind, he referred them to Joseph de Maistre's *Du pape*. The new spiritual authority would be "analagous" to the Catholic clergy at the height of its glory in the Middle Ages. "Dogmatism," Comte explained, is "the natural state of human intelligence," while skepticism is just "a state of crisis." What all this boiled down to was "ending the revolutionary period," all the "anarchy" and "chaos" that Comte saw all around him, through "the government of opinion" by a new spiritual and scientific elite.[123]

Constant's review of Charles Dunoyer and the article on religion for the Encyclopédie progressive

Two articles published in 1826 illustrate Constant's efforts to respond to the Saint-Simonian and Comtian tendencies of the left. The first was a review of Dunoyer's book, *L'industrie et la morale considérées dans leurs rapports avec la liberté*, published in La *Revue encyclopédique*;[124] the second was an article on religion submitted to the *Encyclopédie progressive*. Both articles reaffirmed Constant's commitment to a liberal and recognizably Protestant perspective on the "tendencies of the age" and the course of human progress. He proffered the need for a "higher morality" than industrialism proposed, and he pleaded for the freedom of conscience that alone could produce such a morality.

Constant's review of *L'industrie et la morale* was a friendly one. He acknowledged Dunoyer's services to the liberal cause, his courageous battle for constitutional guarantees, and his invaluable aid in assuring France's liberties. In particular, Constant highlighted the author's differences from a certain "school," whose aim was to found an "industrial theocracy." Pointedly, he refused even to mention the name of this school; rather, he attacked it as "the enemy of all inquiry" and denounced it as harmful to both industry and liberty.[125]

---

[123] Ibid., pp. 220, 205, 214, 203, 201, 205.
[124] "De M. Dunoyer et de quelques-uns de ses ouvrages" appeared first in the *Revue encyclopédique* on February 1, 1826, and then was republished in slightly altered form in the *Mélanges de littérature et de politique* (Paris, 1829.)
[125] The review appeared first in the *Revue encyclopédique*, vol. XXIX (February, 1826); Constant revised it and republished it as part of his *Mélanges* in 1829. The quotations are from the *Revue encyclopédique*, pp. 417, 418.

Constant then clarified what he had said about civilization in *De la religion.* He reassured Dunoyer that he was "a partisan" of civilization; however, he needed to warn people about some of its effects. There was nothing intrinsically wrong with modern civilization procuring many "pleasures" for man; rather, the problem was that those pleasures were making men more conservative and less willing to take risks. In that sense, civilization was favoring a political resignation harmful to the maintenance of liberty. The present state of civilization, explained Constant, "tends towards stability [. . . and] order more than moral virtue." To combat this tendency, one should not lose track of "all the generous emotions" and view human beings merely as "industrious animals."[126]

Constant hoped that Dunoyer and others of a similar persuasion would reject "the narrow systems which only offer physical well-being as mankind's goal." Man had a higher purpose: he was created "to instruct himself, enlighten himself, and in that way, to soften and improve himself." In sum, it was important to "counterbalance" the depoliticizing and dehumanizing effects of civilization by encouraging "noble and disinterested sentiments." Only then could one hope to "preserve civilization itself from the dangers resulting from its own tendencies."[127]

Constant again took aim at Saint-Simon's disciples, who, in a recent review, had criticized Dunoyer's book for its "individualism." In fact, one of the first recorded uses of the term "individualism" occurred in an issue of *Le Producteur* in which its reviewer regretted that Dunoyer had tried to reduce political economy to the "narrow proportions of individualism."[128] In response, Constant defended Dunoyer's individualism, calling it "the only just system, [and] the only one favorable to the improvement of humankind." Its first principle was that each and every person should "develop his faculties to his full extent" and never "subordinate himself to any intellectual authority outside himself." What others referred to as "moral anarchy" was a necessary part of the intellectual, spiritual, and moral process. There was no need for a "spiritual authority"; on the contrary, such an authority would only create "apathy" and "torpor" in the population. Instead, "freedom of inquiry" should be respected – for the sake of civilization, for the sake of industry, and for the sake of liberty.[129]

126 Ibid., p. 420.   127 Ibid., pp. 424, 421.
128 See K. Swart, "Individualism in the Mid-Nineteenth Century (1826–1860)," *Journal of the History of Ideas,* 23, 1 (January–March, 1962), pp. 77–90.
129 *Revue encyclopédique,* vol. XXIX (February, 1826), pp. 432, 434.

Constant's article in the *Encyclopédie progressive* summarized the main arguments of *De la religion* in ways designed to drive his main political points home. It explained the difference between religious forms and religious sentiment, between dependent and independent forms, and placed great emphasis on religious perfectibility. Religion was not "rigid and immutable"; rather, it was "progressive." Any evils allegedly caused by religion should be attributed to those "theocratic corporations" who "perverted" people's religious sentiments and tried to hinder the natural evolution of religion.[130]

Constant warned his readers that believing that religion should remain immobile could lead to "great and dangerous errors." Whenever human thought was shackled, the result was only superstition. The mind, he explained, has "an invincible propensity to inquiry and examination"; remove this propensity and you reduce man "to the rank of a mere machine."[131]

Constant regretted that some Frenchmen were still under the influence of eighteenth-century thinking. There remained a fair amount of "frivolous incredulity" among the young, some of whom continued to see the present situation as just a simple battle between philosophers and priests. Obviously, such people could neither comprehend the progress of religion nor even perceive the differences between a "rigid Catholicism" and the "most improved Protestantism." But they were wrong. The Protestant reformers had distinguished themselves from Catholics by asserting "the rights of mental independence." This was why, ultimately, Protestantism would be the best religion for France. Protestantism was Christianity "restored at once to its ancient purity and to its progressive advancement." This is how it could be "contemporaneous with every age, because it keeps pace with every age."[132]

On this issue, Constant held up America as a model for France. In America, thanks to freedom of religion, religious sentiments were flourishing peacefully, alongside industry.

America covers the ocean with its flag; it surpasses every nation in its application of physical resources; and yet, such is the authority of the religious sentiment in that country, that a single family is often divided among several sects, with no interruption of domestic affection and peace.[133]

France must "leave religion to itself." Freedom of conscience alone could ensure that religion played a positive role in the progress of civilization. Accompanied by free inquiry, it would guarantee that religion kept pace with society and continually improved over time.

---

[130] B. Constant, "The Progressive Development of Religious Ideas," in PhM, pp. 313, 315.
[131] Ibid., pp. 292, 298   [132] Ibid., pp. 317, 311, 303.   [133] Ibid., p. 318

A letter from his liberal-minded and pious cousin, Rosalie, verbalized the convictions of Constant's closest supporters. Rosalie wrote to express her whole-hearted approval of excerpts she had read from his article and her support for his efforts on behalf of religion. Now, she was eagerly awaiting the third volume of *De la religion*. What "consoled" her when contemplating France's present situation was that

the Reformation, sooner or later, must follow ... I see in the near future the Reformation gradually establish itself. May God wish that it be without a battle, [and] with only the weapons of persuasion! You can contribute to it.[134]

Rosalie pressed her cousin repeatedly for the third volume; but she was obliged to be patient. Constant's rapidly declining health, combined with his political obligations, slowed down his scholarly work considerably; nevertheless, he continued to prepare the last three volumes of *De la religion* for publication: volume III appeared in 1827, and volumes IV and V posthumously in 1831.

De la religion, *volumes III, IV, V*

The last volumes of *De la religion* reaffirmed the principles of the first two, each successive volume in effect reasserting the same basic message in different words. Thus, it is not without some justification that Constant was accused of repetitiveness in his later years. As he had said many times before, he said again: religious sentiment is an inherent factor of human nature, and here to stay. If left free to evolve naturally, it will always be beneficial to man and society. Religion is "perfectible" and destined to participate in the progress of civilization; therefore, as the understanding and general condition of human beings improve, so should their religion. Indeed, when left entirely free, religion will always "march along with ideas"; it will "enlighten itself with reason, purify itself with morals, and, at each epoch, sanction all the best things."[135] In this way, religion will also "regenerate itself indefinitely,"[136] continually bestowing its benefits on society.

History proved, however, that priesthoods tended to obstruct this process and to "falsify morality" by turning religion into a political tool.[137] Together with political authorities, they tried to utilize people's religious sentiments as a "means of power." Constant dismissed the idea that he proffered such criticism out of a hatred for priests. It was "imposed religions," "stationary dogmas," and the political *use* of religion that he abhorred. Neither did his

---

[134] Letter no. CCVIII "Rosalie à Benjamin," October 27, 1826, in KK, p. 294.
[135] DLR, p. 576.   [136] Ibid., p. 574.   [137] Ibid., p. 566.

critique imply a rejection of revelation; on the contrary, he was open to the
idea of "supernatural communications" between God and man:

The more one believes in the goodness and justice of a Providence that has
created man and that serves him as a guide, the more it is natural to believe that
this benevolent providence proportions its teachings to the level of intelligence of
those destined to receive it.[138]

In fact, Constant saw the interconnected ideas of progressive revelation and
religious perfectibility as the only way to reconcile the existence of a
benevolent God with the nature of the human mind. It was impossible to
deny that freedom of inquiry was an "invincible penchant"[139] of human
nature. Why would God endow man with it only to decree its exercise a
crime? Asking man to sacrifice his right of free inquiry would be to reduce
him to the rank of a mere "machine"; it would be equivalent to "moral
suicide."[140]

As usual, his views on religion were meant to deliver a political message.
Rushing his final volumes to print, Constant hoped to convince his readers
that they had before them a unique opportunity. Roman Catholicism was a
spent religion that had been destroyed by the Revolution; now, forty years
later, it was impossible to revive it. Constant declared: "All that is worn-out
perishes [and] what is dead cannot be reborn." "Religious sentiments" were
another matter, and they were all around; "everywhere" there was "a mysterious agitation, a desire to believe, a thirst for hope."[141] France's present
generation was protesting against "the material tendency,"[142] and yearning
for a new religion. In answer to this sense of anticipation, it was crucial "to
leave religion to God and to itself."[143] Religious sects were cropping up
everywhere,[144] and if left alone they would soon bestow their benefits on
society. Constant reassured his readers that the religion that would eventually emerge from the competing sects would resemble "Christianity,
returned to its primitive simplicity and combined with free inquiry."[145] In
short, it would resemble the "new and improved" Protestantism he had been
promoting for some time.

In other venues, articles, and speeches of the time, Constant continued
to profess his personal preference for Protestantism. He consistently argued
that while Christianity was eternal, its "inseparable ally" must be
"free inquiry." And while the young needed religion, they also "want[ed] to
examine." The present generation was "serious," "studious," and a bit

[138] Ibid., p. 575.   [139] Ibid.   [140] Ibid.   [141] Ibid., p. 565.   [142] Ibid.   [143] Ibid., p. 576.
[144] Ibid., p. 565.   [145] Ibid., p. 909.

"skeptical"; it rightly wanted "to know before it judge[d]." Like many liberal Protestants, Constant felt certain that if allowed to make a reasoned choice, people would select "new and improved" Protestantism over Catholicism or any other strictly "dogmatic" religion.[146]

Constant's final words

While bringing the final volumes of *De la religion* to press, Constant also published a collection of essays under the title *Mélanges de littérature et de politique* (1829). Most of these essays had been published before, but Constant now revised them slightly and presented them in one volume with a new preface. It is often said that during the last years of his life Constant wished to be elected to the Académie française, and that his final publications, including the *Mélanges*, were related to this effort. This may very well be true, but it should not distract us from the actual contents and moral message of his last publications. The *Mélanges* included texts that expressed the very essence of Constant's moral and religious ideas. Constant chose to include essays such as his "Letter about Julie," "The Progressive Development of Religious Ideas," "On the Human Causes which have Contributed to the Establishment of Christianity," and his review of Charles Dunoyer's book. In the preface, he professed to have fought his whole life for the same principles, and clarified what his brand of liberalism was about:

For forty years I have defended the same principle, liberty in everything, in religion, in philosophy, in literature, in industry, in politics: and by liberty I mean the triumph of *individuality*, as much over [state] authority which would wish to govern by despotism, as over the masses which claim the right to subject the minority to the majority.[147]

Constant's use of the word "individuality" is interesting. In his 1826 review of Dunoyer, he had defended "individualism" against the attacks of the Saint-Simonians, but now he preferred to use a word that perhaps had not acquired as many pejorative connotations.[148] As early as 1820, de Maistre had

---

[146] See his article of June 10, 1829 in the *Courrier français*, reproduced in *Recueil d'articles 1825–1829*. References to his allegiance to Protestantism can be found in many places; see, for example pp. 22, 26, 87, 88. See also his article of September 30, 1829, reproduced in *Recueil d'articles 1829–1830*, ed. E. Harpaz (Paris, 1992), in which he suggests that although the French in general are a "tired race" (p. 35), they are also suffering a religious crisis (p. 34) during which the young have a "thirst for investigation and improvement" (p. 35.)

[147] Constant's preface to his *Mélanges de littérature et de politique*, in *Ecrits politiques*, ed. M. Gauchet (Paris, 1997), p. 623.

[148] On "individualism," see Swart, "Individualism"; S. Lukes, "The Meanings of Individualism," *Journal of the History of Ideas*, 32, 1 (1971), pp. 45–66; G. Clacys, "'Individualism,' 'Socialism,' and 'Social Science': Further Notes on a Process of Conceptual Formation, 1800–1850," *Journal of the*

associated individualism with "political protestantism," in his words, "this deep and frightening division of minds, this infinite fragmentation of all doctrines."[149] Thereafter, Auguste Comte and the Saint-Simonians used "individualism" to designate the pernicious and "negative" ideas they thought were destroying France. In article after article, they contrasted "disorder, atheism, egoism and individualism" with "order, religion, association and devotion." By using the word "individuality" rather than "individualism," Constant no doubt intended to distance himself from the criticism that his brand of liberalism favored selfishness or socially dissolving behavior; rather, he meant to stress that it fostered intellectual and moral self-improvement. Vindication of Constant's semantics followed during the 1830s and 1840s, when the Swiss Protestant theologian, Alexandre Vinet, a fellow member of the Society for Christian Morals, went on to emphasize the differences between individualism and individuality. He called them "two sworn enemies; the first an obstacle and negation of society; the latter a principle to which society owes all its savor, life and reality."[150]

Constant also reaffirmed, yet again, his view that a liberal constitutional regime needed a "new and improved" Protestantism to sustain it. Only a "perfectible" and pure religion, one that could "keep pace with intelligence" and respected "the rights of mental independence" could accomplish the moral reform France so desperately needed. In Constant's view, it was "from the bosom of the Protestant Church, that Christianity, restored at once to its ancient purity and to its progressive perfectibility ... [was] a doctrine contemporaneous with every age, because it keeps pace with every age."[151]

History of Ideas, 47, 1(1986), pp. 81–93; and M.-F. Piguet, "Benjamin Constant et la naissance du mot 'individualisme,'" ABC, 29 (2005), pp. 101–124.

[149] "Extrait d'une conversation," *Œuvres complètes*, vol. XIV, p. 286, as quoted by Lukes, "Meanings," p. 46.

[150] A. Vinet, *Etudes sur Blaise Pascal* (Paris, 1904), p. 112, as quoted by Swart, "Individualism," p. 85. See E. Koehler, "Religious Liberty and Civisme Morale: Alexandre Vinet, French Protestantism and the Shaping of Civic Culture in Nineteenth-Century France," unpublished Ph.D. dissertation, University of California, Davis, 2002.

[151] "The Progressive Development of Religious Ideas," in PhM, pp. 302, 303. I have altered the translation slightly, preferring "perfectibility" to "advancement."

CHAPTER 7

Constant's legacy

THE 1830 REVOLUTION

The years surrounding the Law on Sacrilege (1824–5) were a watershed moment in French history. The stubbornly rightward thrust of Charles X's policies and his support of "Jesuitism" alienated large sections of the population; increasingly, it became evident that his reign was doomed. Starting with the November 1827 elections, the liberals made dramatic gains. Charles' response to the expressed will of the voters was to take even more drastic steps to reinforce his rule. Eventually, during the so-called Three Glorious Days of July 27–29, 1830, the people of Paris rose up and replaced him with his more pliable cousin, Louis-Philippe d'Orléans.

Constant's contribution to these events, and thus to the survival of constitutional government in France, was critical. Throughout the Restoration, he had tirelessly advocated liberal causes in the Chamber of Deputies and in his copious writings. He had also been an excellent tactician for the liberal opposition and an effective grassroots organizer.[1] Constant was prodigious. While parliamentary work took up most of his time, he also wrote an extraordinary number of articles for liberal newspapers. From January to August 1828, he made forty-nine speeches in the Chamber; then, between April and June 1829, he published twenty-four articles in the *Courrier français* alone. During the denouement leading to Charles' ultimate ouster, Constant's participation was significant as well: he rejected the conciliatory decrees offered by Charles X; he wrote an address to Duke of Orléans offering him the position of Lieutenant-General of France; and he prepared a proclamation justifying the overthrow of the Bourbon king.

---

[1] Alexander, *Re-Writing*, and idem, "Benjamin Constant as a Restoration Politician," in H. Rosenblatt (ed.), *Cambridge Companion to Constant*.

The Revolution of 1830 is often described as a "bourgeois revolution." From this perspective, the liberals who organized and led it are frequently described as defenders of "middle-class interests," and Louis-Philippe's reign is labeled the "bourgeois monarchy." Such characterizations are misleading on two accounts: (1) they downplay the alliance between the common people and the liberals that ensured the Revolution's success and (2) they overlook the role that anticlericalism played in its outbreak. The overthrow of Charles X's government was made possible by the abhorrence liberals and workers jointly felt for "Jesuitism," and their common desire to put an end to it.[2]

This alliance between liberals and workers had been forged during the Restoration, when the working classes of France began to read and become educated by liberal newspapers. Indeed, it was *Le Constitutionnel*'s expanding working-class readership that turned it into France's largest selling newspaper. In some parts of the country, liberals also helped to organize anticlerical demonstrations, which were then reported on in their newspapers. Coverage was also given to the proceedings in the Chamber of Deputies; summaries and excerpts of speeches by liberal deputies were often included, causing some of them to become popular heroes.

Well aware of this liberal–working-class alliance, French police reports complained that liberal newspapers were "regulating the spirit of the multitude."[3] In the minds of Ultraroyalists, the liberal press was fomenting dissent and disorder. To them, newspapers like *Le Constitutionnel* were engaged in a despicable "political protestantism,"[4] which is one of the reasons why Charles X attempted to impose censorship on them in 1827. As we know, however, this maneuver backfired; it only served to embitter people further, and drew the workers and liberals even closer together.

As one of the most vocal deputies in the Chamber, and one of the most prolific of all liberal journalists, Constant was crucial to the liberal–working-class alliance. His popular influence merited constant police surveillance during the final years of the Restoration.[5] A letter from his

[2] E. Newman, "The Blouse and the Frock Coat: The Alliance of the Common People of Paris with the Liberal Leadership and the Middle Class during the Last Years of the Bourbon Restoration," *Journal of Modern History*, 46, 1 (March, 1974), pp. 26–59.
[3] An, F7 3881, March 19, 1827, as quoted by Newman, "The Blouse," p. 48.
[4] Villèle family papers, as quoted by S. Kent, *The Election of 1827 in France* (Cambridge, MA, 1975), p. 8.
[5] Glachant, *Benjamin Constant*.

electoral agent, Goyet de la Sarthe, testifies not only to how popular Constant's newspaper articles had become, but also to the breadth of his readership, which included both workers and the better-off:

You have written a lot in the *Minerve* for the last three weeks; continue, it is necessary. All the subscribers, upon initial reception, search for your articles ... Your piece in the 78th edition has been read and re-read with the greatest interest in all the [reading] societies. Do not neglect the *Renommé*, between you and me, most people think that it needs you ... Here there are meetings of twenty to thirty workers solely to listen to readings of the *Minerve* and other journals. It is the same among the wealthier class of patriots. These societies have subscriptions with the bookstores; a single copy suffices for 100 people.[6]

Meanwhile, Constant's speeches in the Chamber had become legendary; excerpts and reports about them appeared regularly in liberal newspapers, and a two-volume collection of them came out in 1827 and 1828. Constant's brilliance as an orator was widely acknowledged, as was the wit, sarcasm, and dogged tenacity with which he pursued his political objectives. He also had a very special style of delivery. All of this earned him many admirers, as well as enemies. The following is an eye-witness account:

One saw him arrive at the Chamber always a few minutes before the sitting, dressed in his gold-embroidered deputy's uniform so as to be ready to address the House from the tribune where it was obligatory to wear this formal dress. His hair was blond and turning white, and on his head he wore an old round hat. He carried under his arm a coat, books, manuscripts, printer's proofs, a copy of the budget and his crutch. Once he had got rid of all these impediments and was seated on his bench, on the far left, he began to write and to send off an unbelievable quantity of letters and notes to people, to the great annoyance of the gentlemen ushers of the Chamber. Then – or rather at the same time – he corrected the proofs of his latest book, took notes to enable him to reply to the person speaking from the tribune, answered the questions of all those crowding around him to ask for information on different subjects and tried to attract attention so as to be allowed to speak himself. And when it was his turn to address the Chamber, he picked up seemingly at random a few scraps of paper from the mass of documents around him and he made his way slowly up to the tribune ... His pale forehead and long face, so like that of a Puritan, were not well suited to expressing emotion, and his slow and monotonous delivery at first surprised those whom his reputation for eloquence had drawn to the Chamber. But gradually his voice grew louder, became impassioned and filled the room. His great blue eyes flashed with sudden brilliance, and the most lucid reasoning, irony, wit and well-chosen quotations all poured forth in abundance in his

---

[6] From *Benjamin Constant et Goyet de la Sarthe: Correspondance 1818–1822*, p. 132.

improvised speeches. One could listen to him for hours without tiring of hearing him speak. It was a delight to see him calmly drive his opponents into a fury and then, as if it were merely an amusement for him, meet the paroxysms of rage on the right-wing benches with cold and cutting politeness – which only exasperated his adversaries all the more. He was quite untroubled by other deputies insolently calling him a blackguard, a fomenter of sedition, a revolutionary, or by the loud shouts of many of them claiming that he was out of order. He carried on speaking as if he were in a quiet drawing room, and more than once he disconcerted his enemies by a witticism so apt that it completely disarmed them by provoking their laughter.[7]

In 1827, Constant stood for election simultaneously in Alsace and Paris; after winning in both places, he chose to represent the predominantly Protestant Alsace. Regular police reports document Constant's enormous popularity with crowds there; but he remained a favorite with Parisians as well. At midnight on April 17, 1827, a large crowd made up of hundreds of workers marched through the streets of the capital paying visit to their favorite deputies. After cheering outside Lafayette's door, they made their way to Constant's home, where they shouted:

> Long Live the Charter! Long Live Benjamin Constant!
> Long Live Casimir Perier![8] Long Live Chateaubriand![9]
> Down with the skull-cap! Down with the Jesuits!
> Long Live Freedom of the Press![10]

For all the above reasons, Constant played an indispensable role in the downfall of the Bourbon regime. Recognizing this, King Louis-Philippe d'Orléans offered him a post in his new Council of State. He also gave Constant a considerable sum of money to help pay off his gambling debts. Constant accepted the king's donation, but not before making a statement that sent an unwelcome signal to the new government. "Sire," Constant declared,

> I will accept this generosity, but liberty comes before gratitude. I want to remain independent and if your government commits errors, I will be the first to rally the opposition.

To his credit, Louis-Philippe responded, "That is how I see it as well," but other liberals would not be so understanding.

---

[7] Quoted in D. Berthoud, *Constance et grandeur*, pp. 70–1; quoted and translated by Wood, *Benjamin Constant*, p. 229.

[8] Casimir Perier (1777–1832) was a popular opposition deputy from Paris.

[9] François-René de Chateaubriand (1768–1848) had gone over to the opposition in 1824.

[10] An, F7 3881, April 18, 1827, as quoted by Newman, "The Blouse," p. 47.

The Revolution of 1830 brought to power the so-called Doctrinaires, men like Pierre-Paul Royer-Collard (1763–1845) and François Guizot (1787–1874),[11] who went on to dominate the next eighteen years. Evidence suggests that after the uprising, these liberals sought only minimal changes to the constitution and the manner in which France was governed. Now that they were in power and had a friendly king with whom to work, they set about trying to "end the revolution" as quickly as possible. Unlike them, however, Constant was dissatisfied with the status quo and wanted additional reforms.

During the first months of the new regime, Constant allied himself with what is loosely referred to as the "party of movement" against the Doctrinaire's "party of resistance."[12] Opposing the new government on several issues, he spoke out in favor of lowering property qualifications for the vote, greater liberty in education, a freer press, and even the right of workers to form associations. These positions put him in direct conflict with François Guizot, the rising star of French liberalism. Constant's interventions show that he thought the liberalism of some Doctrinaire leaders "insufficiently liberal" and that he wanted to "shake up the inertia of the [liberal] government."[13]

Haunted by the fear of further revolutionary upheavals, Guizot proposed to close down workers' associations by applying an emergency provision of the Penal Code. Speaking on behalf of the so-called "needs," "interests," and "wishes" of France, he denounced the associations as displaying "revolutionary" traits that threatened the new government's survival.[14] Constant picked up the gauntlet in defense of the workers' right to assemble and debate politics:

These men, according to an entirely natural impulse, without any bad intention whatsoever, saw that they were promised [new] institutions, and they assembled to discuss established institutions and the promises made. In theory, they had the right; otherwise why did you consecrate freedom of the press? You did it so that any citizen might communicate his opinions to an immense number of citizens, and [yet] you would like to prevent a handful of citizens from verbally

[11] On the Doctrinaires, see P. Rosanvallon, *Le moment Guizot* (Paris, 1985); A. Craiutu, *Liberalism under Siege: The Political Thought of the Doctrinaires* (Lanham, MD, 2003); and Jaume, *L'Individu.*
[12] H. A. C. Collingham (with R. Alexander), *The July Monarchy: A Political History of France 1830–1848* (London and New York, 1988), p. 31.
[13] On this period see P. Bastid, *Benjamin Constant et sa doctrine* (Paris, 1966); Alexander, "Benjamin Constant"; and J.-P. Aguet, "Benjamin Constant parlementaire sous la monarchie de Juillet (juillet–décembre 1830)," *ABC*, 2 (1982), pp. 3–45.
[14] As quoted by Aguet, "Benjamin Constant parlementaire," p. 24.

communicating their opinions to a few others. This seems entirely contradictory to me.

Sustaining his defense, Constant continued: in July, the people of Paris could have committed great disorders, but did not. Instead they comported themselves with "virtue" and "disinterestedness." Without the slightest indication that they were revolutionary or wished to overthrow the constitutional monarchy, why should they now be treated with such distrust?[15]

Likewise, Constant fought Doctrinaire attempts to limit the freedom of the press, denouncing the new government's efforts to "concentrate in the hands of a few wealthy men the right to have an opinion and to express it freely." He admonished liberals to stop worrying so much about the politicization of the masses; it was wrong-headed to worry "constantly about anarchy, which doesn't exist, [and about] demagoguery, which is visible nowhere." The "admirable people of Paris" posed no political threat; actually, the danger to France's constitutional government was coming from the right.[16] To his cousin, Rosalie, Constant also expressed his high regard for the "excellent population of Paris," about whom there was no reason to be anxious.[17] Simultaneously, he spoke out in defense of the right of the young to participate in politics.[18] But nobody was listening to him any longer.

Constant's more democratic, even populist, leanings and his deep disappointment over the conservatism of the liberal government were later recognized in newspapers and in the memoirs of key politicians. In its article announcing Constant's death, the *Courrier français* reported that "since the July Revolution, his opinions and his character seemed reinvigorated by the popular enthusiasm [*semblaient s' être retrempés par l'élan populaire.*]"[19] The *Tribune politique et parlementaire* reported that Constant had died "exhausted by recent battles, discouraged by fruitless efforts, deeply hurt to see so many dashed hopes."[20] Indeed, in one of his last speeches on the floor of the Chamber, Constant admitted to feeling "a profound sadness."[21] He was very disappointed that the Revolution of 1830 was not living up to its promises.

Constant's opposition infuriated Guizot, who could not, or perhaps would not, understand. After all, Constant had accepted money from the

---

[15] Ibid., p. 25. [16] Ibid., p. 30.
[17] Letter no. CCXXV, (Benjamin to Rosalie end of August, 1830), B & R, p. 321.
[18] As quoted by Aguet, "Benjamin Constant parlementaire," p. 21.
[19] Ibid., p. 38. [20] Ibid., p. 4. [21] Ibid., p. 3.

king and a position in his Council of State. Guizot interpreted the behavior as sheer disloyalty from a man who had no principles and who, moreover, engaged in the most despicable kind of demagoguery. In his *Mémoires* Guizot wrote:

He had received, from the new government, positions, honors and favors ... Nevertheless, Mr. Benjamin Constant involved himself more and more in the opposition, and in the least worthy of oppositions, the subtle flattery of revolutionary and popular passions.[22]

Constant's criticism of the liberal government confounded other Doctrinaires as well. Charles de Rémusat's *Memoirs*, though more friendly than Guizot's, record his frustration that Constant kept harping on the same worn-out themes: "he didn't bother to think anything new ... his speeches were nothing but clever and facile repetitions."[23] Lest one think that Constant's repetitiveness was due to mental decline, a comment he made to his cousin Rosalie around this time is illuminating:

Despite all the interest which politics must and do inspire in me in my present situation, I sometimes get terribly tired of my job as a schoolteacher, having to repeat again and again the same ideas.[24]

Rémusat also recoiled at Constant's "mocking demeanor," which was no longer appropriate; "blasé" as always, and now visibly aged as well, he was "neither liked nor esteemed" by his more conservative colleagues.[25] Given this antipathy, it is not surprising that Constant's colleagues passed him over for the post of Minister of Public Instruction, a position he very much wanted. Instead, they chose a man named Mérilhou, who Rémusat described as a "babbling idiot." No doubt, the episode further weakened Constant's morale.[26]

Moreover, Constant's physical health was now steadily declining. The illness he was suffering from remains a mystery, but paralysis was slowly spreading throughout his body. In July 1830, he underwent a painful operation, from which he may never have fully recovered. Not long thereafter, he reported to Rosalie that his legs were swelling and that "old age" was invading his body, creeping up from his toes to his stomach and even to his face, making it difficult to eat.[27] Towards the very end, he could only ingest soup and sometimes had trouble speaking. Nevertheless, due to his

---

[22] F. Guizot, *Mémoires pour servir à l'histoire de mon temps*, vol. II (Paris, 1859), p. 143.
[23] C. de Rémusat, *Mémoires de ma vie*, ed. C. Pouthas (Paris, 1959), vol. II, p. 422.
[24] Letter no. CLXIII September 1820 in B&R, p. 230.   [25] Rémusat, *Mémoires*, vol. II, p. 422.
[26] As reported by Rémusat, ibid., p. 423.
[27] Letter no. CCXXV, approx. August 20,–September 27, 1830, B&R, pp. 321–322.

extraordinary will and strength of purpose, he continued to participate in Chamber debates, until late in November, when his condition suddenly worsened. He died on December 8.

Among his many friends, disciples and admirers, the news of Constant's death was met with a profound sense of sadness. On the eve of his funeral, Victor Hugo wrote to Constant's widow:

Your private grief is also a public calamity. The loss that strikes you strikes us all. Allow me to tell you that tomorrow, in the midst of that tearful public that will join the procession for this distinguished man, there will be a sorely afflicted heart. It will be mine, Madame ... He has left two widows, you and France.[28]

But perhaps the best indication of Constant's enormous popularity, and the political stature he had achieved, was the imposing state funeral that he received on December 12, 1830. Moving descriptions of it can be found in liberal newspapers and in the memoirs of several participants. The city of Paris turned out *en masse* to bid farewell; huge crowds made up of people "from all classes"[29] lined the streets to watch the funeral cortège as it made its way from the Protestant church in the Rue Saint Antoine to the Père Lachaise cemetery. Surrounded by twelve legions of the National Guard, the coffin was carried by students, who at one point cried out "To the Pantheon!" But the police prevented this. One observer, who was close to the ruling circle, later revealed that the authorities had feared a popular insurrection.[30] At the graveside, prominent politicians, including Lafayette, delivered emotional eulogies highlighting Constant's immeasurable services to France.

According to the *Courrier français*, France owed Constant "eternal gratitude," because,

no other writer has contributed as much to her political education; no other writer has been better at popularizing constitutional questions and rendering them familiar to all classes of citizens.[31]

In the same vein, *Le Constitutionnel* wrote:

It is impossible to overstate how much Benjamin Constant contributed to our memorable victory in July, by his unreserved affection for the people, and for the young, whom he enlightened, sustained, and unceasingly inspired.[32]

---

[28] V. Hugo, *Œuvres complètes*, vol. IX: *Lettres à la fiancée: correspondance*, I (Paris, 1947), pp. 483–484, quoted by Kelly, *Humane Comedy*, p. 17.
[29] *Courrier français*, December 9, 1830.   [30] Rémusat, *Mémoires*, vol II, p. 423.
[31] *Courrier français*, December 9, 1830, p. 569.   [32] *Le Constitutionnel*, December 13, 1830.

Two days later, *Le Constitutionnel* underscored the theme: "Benjamin Constant admired, honored, and cherished the people."[33]

The pastor presiding at Constant's funeral, Athenase Coquerel,[34] was effusive in praise. Referring to Constant's "noble," "elevated," and "generous" soul, he paid homage to his "religious love of liberty" and patriotism. Coquerel reminded the mourners that if he was able to speak openly and freely in a Protestant church, it was largely due to the indefatigable efforts of Benjamin Constant, who had devoted his life to the defense of "all the sacred causes on which the future of humanity depends." Constant knew that "liberty is the will of God" and believed in liberty "the way you believe in a religion." He never lost hope and never despaired.

Notably, Coquerel spoke admiringly of Constant's *De la religion*. This lifelong work was the result of "tranquil courage" and the laudable product of "a good man." The pastor also took pride that, in his research, Constant had "liberally used our holy right of free inquiry, the fundamental basis of the Reformed Church." Indeed, Coquerel suggested that it was Constant's research that had led him to religion, such that he was being buried as a full member of the Protestant community. And finally, after acknowledging Constant's fidelity to his principles, Coquerel predicted that France would never forget Benjamin Constant and the great services he had rendered to the cause of liberty.

But, of course, Coquerel was wrong. Constant's contributions to liberalism *were* soon overlooked, and a very different picture of him came to predominate. According to P. Thureau-Dangin, a Catholic royalist, Constant was quickly forgotten because of his many "vices," "lack of character," and "moral inconstancy." Although the "selfish" and "corrupt" Benjamin Constant had achieved a modicum of "popularity" during his lifetime, he never received any real "esteem" or "consideration." He certainly "did not deserve glory after his death."[35] On this question, both sides of the political spectrum soon agreed. In his *Histoire de dix ans 1830–1840* (1842–4), the early socialist thinker Louis Blanc (1811–82) emphasized Constant's "light-weight morals," "skepticism," and moral "indifference." Constant had a "feeble temperament" and a "cold heart."[36] Not long thereafter, Karl Marx dismissed Constant as nothing more than a pathetic "mouthpiece" of "bourgeois society."[37]

---

[33] Ibid., December 15, 1830.   [34] The brother of Charles Coquerel.
[35] P. Thureau-Dangin, *Le parti libéral sous la Restauration* (Paris, 1876).
[36] L. Blanc, *Histoire de dix ans 1830–1840* (Paris, 1877), pp. 175–176.
[37] In *The Eighteenth Brumaire of Louis Bonaparte* (1852). This despite the fact that he had Constant's *The Spirit of Conquest and Usurpation* and the *Principles of Politics* – and even *De la religion*. On this, see P. Higonnet, "Marx, disciple de Constant?" ABC, 6 (1986), pp. 10–16.

It is customary to blame the disparaging image of Constant on Charles-Augustin Sainte-Beuve (1804–69), the foremost literary critic of his time. For reasons that are still somewhat unclear,[38] Sainte-Beuve took an intense personal dislike to Constant, about whom he began writing in 1835 and continued for many years. Each piece Sainte-Beuve published became progressively more vindictive and nasty. Those who have studied these texts agree that he pursued Constant "like a dog does his prey."[39] Sainte-Beuve's acrimony was "bitter," "virulent," and "personal."[40]

Actually, however, the campaign of character assassination and career destruction began well before Sainte-Beuve, and was, in all likelihood, politically motivated. Like other politicians, Constant had been denigrated in the press: labeled a hypocrite during the Directory, he was called an opportunist and a turncoat during the Hundred Days.[41] Curiously, however, the most damaging blows came later; they were struck by some of his liberal allies, who turned against him after the July Revolution, because they no longer appreciated or had use for his oppositional and individualistic brand of liberalism.

As we have seen, Guizot's *Mémoires* expressed his deep antipathy: Constant was nothing but a "skeptical and mocking sophist, with no convictions, no consideration." His soul was "blasé" and his life "worn-out"; if he engaged in any political battles it was only because he was "bored" and looking for some kind of "amusement."[42] Rémusat later echoed this characterization of Constant as "blasé" and further rebuked his penchant for sarcasm. Notably, however, Rémusat refused to participate in what he referred to as an ongoing campaign for Constant's "depreciation." He observed that Constant was being disparaged although there was "nothing very serious that could be alleged against him." In fact, Rémusat felt that the resentment towards Constant was mostly coming from people of "ordinary" and "mediocre" intelligence well beneath him.[43]

The pinnacle of nastiness was reached with Sainte-Beuve; but here, again, political motivations played a crucial role. Sainte-Beuve's essays show

---

[38] The question has been studied by Rudler in his preface to *La jeunesse de Benjamin Constant* and Deguise, *Benjamin Constant Méconnu.*

[39] M. Faguet, as quoted by Rudler, *La jeunesse de Benjamin Constant*, p. 9.

[40] Rudler, *La jeunesse*, p. 9.

[41] He was in good company. On this, see A. Spitzer, "Malicious Memories: Restoration Politics and a Prosopography of Turncoats," *French Historical Studies*, 24, 1 (Winter 2001), pp. 37–61.

[42] In fact, Constant did sometimes refer to his political career as an antidote to "discouragement" and "apathy." See for example, Constant to Madame de Nassau, January 20, 1800, cited in Holmes, *Benjamin Constant*, pp. 45–46.

[43] Rémusat, *Mémoires*, vol. II, p. 422.

bitterness over Constant's politics of "perpetual opposition." At a critical time for France, Constant refused to do the right thing and become "a man of the government." Instead, he continued to oppose and to criticize. Such behavior could only be attributed to a lack of principle. And thus, Sainte-Beuve set about showing what a cynic, a libertine, and a *roué* Constant was. "I am not presenting a brief for the prosecution," wrote Sainte-Beuve, before launching into a no-holds-barred character assassination. It was important to let people know why Constant was not worthy of any "consideration." It was "natural and legitimate to enter his private life into the record."[44]

Due largely to Sainte-Beuve, then, the French public's attention was diverted from Constant's political achievements and refocused on the perceived vices of his personal life, mainly his gambling and problems with women, which were interpreted as clear and unambiguous evidence of his lack of morals. It goes without saying that this widely disseminated image of Constant helped his political enemies.

In 1844, Sainte-Beuve procured some of the private correspondence between the young Constant and Isabelle de Charrière.[45] (Some of this correspondence was cited in chapter 1 of this book as evidence of Constant's emotional crisis while at Brunswick.) Sainte-Beuve published these letters selectively, accompanying them with a commentary that portrayed Constant as a bored and self-absorbed egotist, who, already as a young man, possessed neither principles nor beliefs. According to Sainte-Beuve, Constant's "weakness for women," visible at an early age, doomed him to political mediocrity. One should bear in mind the important influence women had had on Constant's political career; the fact that he had been led around by women throughout his life constituted further evidence of his weak and unmanly character.[46]

Sainte-Beuve reasoned that once people had access to details about Constant's private life, they would easily conclude that he did not merit their esteem. Here was a man who wrote a novel on love, but was incapable of loving, and who wrote a book on religion, but was incapable of believing. Highlighting Constant's supposed tendency to mock everything, Sainte-Beuve detected a "secret disdain for men"[47] in all his writings. During the last few years, Constant's disheveled appearance and, particularly, his

---

[44] C.-A. Sainte-Beuve, *Nouveaux lundis* (Paris, 1884), p. 428.
[45] See his use of this correspondence in his *Portrait de femmes* (Paris, n.d.).
[46] Sainte-Beuve, *Nouveaux lundis*, p. 425.
[47] Sainte-Beuve, in *Revue des Deux Mondes*, vol. VI (1844), p. 196.

"emaciated" face and "unkempt" hair, were just the outward manifestations of a "worn-out" person with nothing new or profound to offer France.[48] Of course, it was much easier for Sainte-Beuve to disparage Constant's appearance and character than to confront his ideas. Indeed, it has been observed that as Sainte-Beuve's political views became more conservative, his animosity towards Constant increased.

This is not to suggest that Guizot and Sainte-Beuve were not genuinely repelled by Constant's morals or lack of them. He was unquestionably a gambler who accumulated debts, and the previously divorced husband of a German divorcée. Furthermore, his novel, *Adolphe*, which he published in 1816 (after private readings in the salons of Paris and London), did not enhance his reputation.[49] In it, he seemed to engage in a bizarre act of exhibitionism and self-flagellation; he portrayed himself as a self-centered and vacillating man lacking in moral fortitude and direction. Meanwhile, the details of Constant's numerous love affairs with society women had become part of the public record, thus encouraging many to regard him as a socialite; a "man of the world" was how critics of *De la religion* labeled him. On top of this, there is evidence that Constant frequented prostitutes, although it is hard to tell how many people knew this.

Finally, Constant was fond of making self-deprecating jokes and sarcastic remarks. When, towards the end, an acquaintance encountered him at a gambling house and inquired what he was up to, Constant responded: "these days, all I think about is religion."[50] Sainte-Beuve was probably not the only person to interpret this comment to mean that Constant's interest in religion was insincere. On another occasion, when asked how he was coping with his health problems, Constant replied: "I eat my soup and go gambling [*au tripot*]."[51] Such irreverent musings did not sit well with the Doctrinaires, who interpreted them as yet more evidence of his bad character and lack of principles. No doubt, it was reservations about his morals that blocked Constant's election to the Académie française, despite his repeated and somewhat pathetic attempts to be admitted during the last years of his life. When a place finally became available, the Académie ignored him; instead, it honored a nonentity named Guillaume Viennet. Announcing the news to a shattered Constant, Royer-Collard poured salt into his wounds by declaring: "be well assured,

---

[48] Sainte-Beuve, *Nouveaux lundis*, p. 428.
[49] Delbouille, *Genèse*; see especially the chapter entitled "Les contemporains devant Adolphe," pp. 385–412.
[50] Recounted by Sainte-Beuve in *Revue des Deux Mondes*, vol. VI (1844) p. 212.
[51] An often repeated story, apparently originally attributed to Molé.

Sir, that the Academy did not for one moment compare Mr. Viennet's talents to yours."[52]

While Constant's personality and private life may have provoked the Doctrinaires' distaste, the venom of their attacks, which went on well after his death, suggests an underlying political animus. This was certainly the conclusion of Constant's young friend and disciple, Jean Jacques Coulmann. As early as 1831, Coulmann felt the need to defend Constant's reputation in a speech before the Society for Christian Morals, which he subsequently published. One should recall that only a few months earlier, the Society had elected Constant president, which, in itself, was not an insignificant endorsement of his moral standing. According to Coulmann, the systematic disparagement of Constant's character was the work of his political enemies. In his defense, Coulmann endorsed Constant's much-deserved "glory" and paid homage to his admirable "private qualities," such as his "character" and "charitable nature." Constant's soul was "true," "good," and "proud," his love of liberty constant. "Always faithful to his principles," he was animated by "a profound sentiment of the equality of all men" and a "sincere love of the people."[53]

Unable to stem the tide of insulting portrayals, Coulmann tried again a few years later in his *Reminiscences*. Once more, he wrote of Constant's goodness, generosity, and steadfast devotion to the cause of liberty. The ongoing character assassination was the work of "political adversaries," "jealous colleagues," and "pedants" who were angered by Constant's so-called betrayal after the July Revolution.[54] According to Coulmann, Constant had been "profoundly discouraged" by the Doctrinaires' political conservatism.[55] Ironically, it was one of Constant's particular qualities, his penchant for self-critique, that his enemies were using against him. He never posed, Coulmann explained, and "he enjoyed speaking ill of himself." Lesser men were turning Constant's own words against him.[56]

While they disparaged his character and publicized his supposed lack of principles, Constant's political opponents, whether on the left or right, avoided any mention of his deep moral and religious convictions, or, for that matter, his lifelong devotion to his work on religion. During his lifetime, they had maligned his ideas for being conducive to moral and

---

[52] Rémusat, *Mémoires*, vol. II, p. 423.
[53] J.-J. Coulmann, *Notice sur Benjamin Constant lue à la séance générale de la Société de la morale chrétienne, April 1831* (Paris, n.d.).
[54] J.-J. Coulmann, *Reminiscences* (Paris, 1862–69), vol. III, p. 37.   [55] Ibid., p. 219.
[56] Ibid., p. 37.

intellectual anarchy, as well as to selfish, materialistic behavior. This denigration of his political theories now dovetailed with the unattractive personal image that was being circulated. In the same breath, his theories and character were belittled as cynical, self-interested, and fundamentally immoral.

According to Emile Faguet, Constant was fundamentally an "egoist," and this "was the foundation for his entire political system." Constant had invented liberalism, but it was a very "dry" and "cold" philosophy; in reality, it was "nothing but a perpetual need for personal autonomy."[57] No wonder his ideas never caught on in France. As Henri Michel wrote in his influential *L'idée de l'état*, there was nothing "grand" nor "generous" about Constant's liberalism. Like that of the economists, it was an essentially "negative" philosophy concerned only with the individual's "calculation of self-interest." Moreover, it lacked "metaphysical support."[58]

During Louis-Philippe's July Monarchy (1830–48), the Doctrinaire's more elitist and conservative kind of liberalism prevailed. The nineteenth century would show that France preferred "a liberalism *by* the state" to one based on the rights of the individual. Indeed, after Constant, the dominant strain of French liberalism was hostile to individualism and deeply suspicious of market forces.[59] And, following the country's so-called "republican moment"[60] in the 1870s, the very term "liberalism" disappeared from the canon of the left, falling victim to the endemic weakness of the French liberal tradition.[61] Along with liberalism, Constant's political and religious writings faded from view. Hardly anyone read, or even knew of, *De la religion*. Instead, his admirers and critics focused on *Adolphe*, which allowed them to praise his literary talents while deploring his character.

Thankfully, the recent resurgence of interest in Constant's political writings has revived his reputation as a liberal thinker and he is finally getting the attention he deserves. The "intellectual sea change" that took place in France during the 1970s and 1980s brought liberalism back in vogue.[62] Suddenly, Constant re-emerged as one of the most articulate

[57] E. Faguet, *Politiques et moralistes du dix-neuvième siècle* (Paris, 1891), pp. 194, 213.
[58] H. Michel, *L'idée de l'état* (Paris, 1898), pp. 334, 340.   [59] Jaume, *L'individu, emphasis added.*
[60] Ph. Nord, *The Republican Moment. Struggles for Democracy in Nineteenth-Century France* (Cambridge, MA, 1998).
[61] T. Judt, *Past Imperfect: French Intellectuals, 1944–1956* (Berkeley, CA, 1992), pp. 238, 230. S. Hazareesingh speaks of its "endemic" weakness in *Political Traditions in Modern France* (Oxford, 1994), p. 225.
[62] M. Lilla, "The Other Velvet Revolution: Continental Liberalism and its Discontents," *Daedalus*, 123, 2 (Spring, 1994), p. 148. On this moment in French history, see M. S. Christofferson, "An

early defenders of an individual's rights against the encroaching power of the state. He was admired for having unmasked the "illusion of politics"[63] and championed a "liberalism of opposition."[64] Ironically, then, the position for which his liberal contemporaries had criticized him now became Constant's crowning glory: his "negative," "skeptical," and "oppositional" stance. Meanwhile, his religious writings continued to be ignored, and along with them, his more affirmative, optimistic, and constructive side. A partial and skewed understanding of his liberalism was handed down to modern readers – one in large part constructed by his enemies.

Giving Constant's religious and moral vision its due is not just about getting history right. And it is certainly not just an issue of antiquarian interest. For when his liberalism is understood in all its multi-dimensional complexity, it addresses issues that are as relevant today as in his lifetime. Constant invites us to ponder carefully the relationship between politics and religion, church and state, liberal democracy and moral values. Perhaps most importantly, he reminds us that the liberal insistence on state neutrality in religious matters is not a sign of moral indifference, but the very opposite. It is only when religious sects are allowed to proliferate freely, and when people are encouraged to develop their "right to examine," that they can aspire to the "more elevated" form of morality so deeply valued by Constant.

Antitotalitarian History of the French Revolution: François Furet's *Penser la Révolution française* in the Intellectual Politics of the Late 1970s," *French Historical Studies*, 22, 4 (Fall, 1999), pp. 557–611 and S. Khilnani, *The Intellectual Left in Postwar France* (New Haven, CT, 1993).
[63] M. Gauchet, "Benjamin Constant."
[64] P. Manent, *An Intellectual History of Liberalism*, trans. R. Balinski (Princeton, NJ, 1995), p. 84.

Select bibliography

1. BY CONSTANT

PUBLISHED TEXTS

Adolphe, trans. M. Mauldon, ed. P. Coleman (Oxford, 2001)

"Appel au nations chrétiennes en faveur des Grecs," in E. Harpaz (ed.), *Benjamin Constant Publiciste 1825–1830* (Paris and Geneva, 1987), pp. 59–68

"A Charles His, rédacteur du *Républicain français*," in OCBC *Œuvres* I, pp. 295–300

"Aux citoyens représentans du peuple composant le Conseil des Cinq-cents," in OCBC *Œuvres* I, pp. 395–399

Commentaire sur l'ouvrage de Filangieri, ed. A. Laurent (Paris, 2004)

"Compte rendu de *De la littérature*, de Mme de Staël," in OCBC *Œuvres* III, 2, pp. 905–916

"Compte rendu de *Détails historiques et Recueil de pièces sur les divers projets de réunion de toutes les communions chrétiennes*," OCBC *Œuvres* III, 2, pp. 69–81

"Coup d'oeil sur la tendance générale des esprits dans le dix-neuvième siècle. Extrait du discours prononcé par M. Benjamin Constant, dans la Séance d'ouverture de l'Athénée royale de Paris, le 3 décembre 1825," in E. Harpaz (ed.), *Benjamin Constant publiciste 1825–1830* (Paris, 1987)

De la force du gouvernement actuel de la France et de la nécessité de s'y rallier, in OCBC *Œuvres*, I, pp. 327–380

De la religion considérée dans sa source, ses formes et ses développements, ed. T. Todorov and E. Hofmann (Arles, 1999)

"De la restitution des droits politiques aux descendans des religionnaires fugitifs," in OCBC *Œuvres* I, pp. 407–411

Des effets de la terreur, in OCBC *Œuvres*, I, pp. 509–529

Des réactions politiques, in OCBC *Œuvres*, I, pp. 455–506

Des suites de la contre-révolution de 1660 en Angleterre, in OCBC *Œuvres* I, pp. 645–679

"Discours d'installation prononcé à Luzarches le 23 brumaire an VI (November 13, 1797)," OCBC *Œuvres* I, pp. 575–577

"Discours prononcé au Cercle constitutionnel pour la plantation de l'arbre de la liberté, le 30 fructidor an V (September 16, 1797)," in OCBC *Œuvres* I, pp. 551–562

Du moment actuel et de la destiné de l'espèce humaine, ou Histoire abrégée de l'
   égalité, in OCBC *Œuvres* III, 1, pp. 367–389
Du polythéisme romain, considéré dans ses rapports avec la philosophie grecque et la
   religion chrétienne, ed. J. Matter (Paris, 1833)
"Fragments d'un essai sur la perfectibilité de l'espèce humaine," in OCBC
   Œuvres III, 1, pp. 439–453
Fragments d'un ouvrage abandonné sur la possibilité d'une constitution républicaine
   dans un grand pays, in OCBC *Œuvres* IV, pp. 397–761
Journal intime (1811–1816), in OCBC, *Œuvres* VII, pp. 47–289
Journaux intimes (1804–1807), in OCBC, *Œuvres* VI, pp. 47–576
"Lettre sur Julie," in OCBC *Œuvres* III, 1, pp. 205–223
"Liberty of the Ancients Compared with that of the Moderns," in PW,
   pp. 308–328
"De Madame de Staël et de ses ouvrages," in *Portraits, Mémoires, Souvenirs*, ed.
   E. Harpaz (Paris, 1992), pp. 212–254
Ma vie, in OCBC *Œuvres* III, 1, pp. 303–358
Mélanges de littérature et de politique (Paris, 1829)
Mélanges de littérature et de politique, in B. Constant, *Ecrits politiques*, ed.
   M. Gauchet (Paris, 1997), pp. 624–755
Mémoires sur les cent jours, en forme de lettres (Paris, 1820)
"On the Human Causes which have Contributed to the Establishment of
   Christianity," in G. Ripley (ed.), *Philosophical Miscellanies translated from*
   the French of Cousin, Jouffroy, and B. Constant (Boston, 1838), pp. 320–345
"On the Perfectibility of the Human Race," in PhM, pp. 346–368
Positions de combat à la veille de juillet 1830. Articles publiés dans le Temps, ed.
   E. Harpaz (Paris, 1989)
"Prière au créateur du monde," in OCBC *Œuvres* I, p. 55
Principles of Politics Applicable to All Governments (1806–1810), ed. E. Hofmann,
   trans. D. O'Keeffe (Indianapolis, 2003)
Principles of Politics Applicable to All Representative Governments (1815) in PW,
   pp. 169–305
"The Progressive Development of Religious Ideas," in PhM, pp. 292–319
Recueil d'articles 1820–1824, ed. E. Harpaz (Geneva, 1981)
Recueil d'articles 1825–1829, ed. E. Harpaz (Paris, 1992)
Recueil d'articles 1829–1830, ed. E. Harpaz (Paris, 1992)
Réflexions sur les constitutions, la distribution des pouvoirs et les garanties dans une
   monarchie constitutionnelle, in OCBC *Œuvres* VIII, 2, pp. 951–1061
The Spirit of Conquest and Usurpation and their Relation to European Civilization,
   in PW, pp. 44–167

MANUSCRIPTS

"D'une nouvelle espèce de rapports que les théologiens modernes voudraient
   introduire dans la religion," Bibliothèque cantonale et universitaire de
   Lausanne, Fonds Constant

"Fragment de la copie des lectures à L'Athénée Royal sur la religion," Bibliothèque cantonale et universitaire de Lausanne, Fonds Constant

CORRESPONDENCE

Benjamin Constant et Goyet de la Sarthe: Correspondance 1818–1822, ed. E. Harpaz (Geneva, 1973)

Constant, B. and I. de Charrière, *Correspondance 1787–1805*, ed. J.-D. Candaux (Paris, 1997)

Constant, B. and R. de Constant, *Correspondance, 1786–1830*, ed. A. and S. Roulin (Paris, 1955)

Lettres à un ami: cent onze lettres inéaites à Claude Hochet, ed. J. Mistler (Neuchâtel, 1948)

"Lettres de Benjamin Constant à Prosper de Barante," *Revue des Deux Mondes*, 34 (1906), pp. 241–272, 528–567

Madame de Staël, Charles de Villers, Benjamin Constant, *Correspondance*, ed. K. Kloocke *et al.* (Frankfurt am Main, 1993)

OCBC *Correspondance générale* III (1795–1799), ed. C. P. Courtney, B. Anelli, and D. Wood, with P. Rickard and A. Tooke (Tübingen, 2003)

OCBC *Correspondance générale* IV (1800–1802), ed. C. P. Courtney, D. Wood, A. Tooke, and P. Rickard (Tübingen, 2003)

2. OTHER PRIMARY SOURCES

L'Ami de la religion et du Roi

Annales de la religion

Archives du christianisme

Le Censeur européen

Le Constitutionnel

Courrier français

La Décade philosophique, littéraire et politique

Le Drapeau blanc

Le Globe

Journal de la Société de la morale chrétienne

Journal des Débats

Mercure de France

Le Producteur

Le Publiciste

La Revue encyclopédique

La Revue protestante

Barante, A.-G.-P.-B. de, *Souvenirs du Baron de Barante de L'Académie française, 1782–1866*, ed. C. de Barante, 8 vols. (Paris, 1890–1901)

de, *Tableau de la littérature française pendant le dix-huitième siècle* (Paris, 1832)

Blanc, L., *Histoire de dix ans 1830–1840* (Paris, 1877)

Bonald, L. de, "De l'unité religieuse en Europe," in *Œuvres complètes*, vol. X: *Mélanges littéraires, politiques et philosophiques* (Geneva, 1982), pp. 229–283
"Proposition faite à la Chambre des Députés, séance du 26 décembre 1815," in *Œuvres de M. de Bonald*, vol. VII: *Pensées sur divers sujets, et discours politiques* (Paris, 1817)
Théorie du pouvoir politique et religieux, ed. C. Capitan (Paris, 1966)
Chateaubriand, R., *Génie du christianisme*, ed. M. Regard (Paris, 1978)
Claude, J., *Défense de la Réformation contre le livre intitulé préjugés légitimes contre les Calvinistes* (Paris, 1844)
Comte, A., *Early Political Writings*, ed. H. Jones (Cambridge, 1998)
Condorcet, *Esquisse d'un tableau historique des progrès de l'esprit humain*, ed. A. Pons (Paris, 1988)
Coquerel, C., *Tableaux de l'histoire philosophique du christianisme, ou études de philosophie religieuse* (Paris, 1823)
Coulmann, J.-J., *Notice sur Benjamin Constant lue à la séance générale de la Société de la morale chrétienne, April 1831* (Paris, n.d.)
Reminiscences (Paris, 1862–9)
Daunou, P.-C.-F., *Essai sur l'instruction publique* (Paris, 1793)
Destutt de Tracy, A. L. C., *Analyse raisonnée de l'origine de tous les cultes, ou religion universelle* (Paris, 1804)
Commentaire sur l'Esprit des lois de Montesquieu (Paris, 1819)
Commentaire sur l'Esprit des Lois de Montesquieu, in *Œuvres de Montesquieu*, vol. VIII (Paris, 1827), pp. 151–152
Détails historiques et recueil de pièces sur les divers projets de réunion de toutes les communions chrétiennes, qui ont été conçus depuis la Réformation jusqu' à ce jour par M. Rabaut le jeune (Paris, 1806)
Discours Prononcé par Cen Portalis, orateur du Gouvernement, dans la séance du Corps législatif du 15 germinal an X, sur l'organisation des cultes (Paris, Year X)
Discours qui a remporté le prix d'Histoire proposé par l'Institut national de France, décerné dans sa séance publique du 15 vendémiaire an 9 sur cette question: Par quelles causes l'esprit de liberté s'est-il développé en France, depuis François Ier jusqu'en 1789? Par le citoyen Nicolas Ponce (Paris, Year IX)
Dunoyer, C., "Esquisse historique des doctrines auxquelles on a donné le nom d'Industrialisme, c'est- à-dire, des doctrines qui fondent la société sur l'Industrie," *Revue encyclopédique*, 33 (1827)
L'industrie et la morale considérees daus leurs rapports avec la liberté (Paris, 1825)
Fiévée, Joseph, *De la religion considerée dans ses rapports avec le but de toute legislation* (Paris, 1795)
Garat, D.-J., *Mémoires historiques sur la vie de M. Suard, sur ses écrits, sur le XVIIIe siècle* (Paris, 1820)
Godwin, W., *An Enquiry Concerning Political Justice, and its Influence on General Virtue and Happiness*, in OCBC *Œuvres* II, 1
Guinguené, P.-L., *Coup-d'oeil rapide sur le Génie du christianisme, ou quelques pages sur les cinq volumes en-8* (Paris, Year X)
Guizot, F., *Mémoires pour servir à l'histoire de mon temps* (Paris, 1859)

Helvétius, C.-A., *De l'homme* (Paris, 1989)

Kératry, A.-H. de, *Du culte en général et de son état, particulièrement en France* (Paris, 1825)

La Harpe, J. F. de, *Du fanatisme dans la langue révolutionnaire, ou De la persécution suscitée par les barbares du dix-huitième siecle, contre la religion chrétienne et ses ministres* (Paris, 1797)

Lamennais, F. de, *De la religion considérée dans ses rapports avec L'ordre politique et civil* (Paris, 1825)

   Essai sur l'indifférence en matière de religion (Paris, 1843)

La Réveillère-Lépaux, L.-M., *Réflexions sur le culte, sur les cérémonies civiles et sur les fêtes nationales lues à l'Institut le 12 floréal an V dans la séance de la classe des sciences morales et politiques* (Paris, Year VII)

Las Cases, E.-A.-D., *Le Mémorial de Sainte-Hélène*, ed. M. Dunan (Paris, 1951)

Laverne, L. M. P. Tranchant de, *Lettre à M. Charles Villers relativement à son Essai sur l'esprit et l'influence de la Réformation de Luther* (Paris, 1804)

Lessing, G., "The Education of the Human Race," in *Lessing's Theological Writings*, ed. and trans. H. Chadwick (Stanford, CA, 1983)

Letter of Mr. Charles L. Haller, Member of the Supreme Council of Berne, in Switzerland, to his Family, announcing his Conversion to the Catholic Faith, trans. J. Norris (London, 1821)

Luther, M., "On Secular Authority: How Far does the Obedience Owed to it Extend?" in *Luther and Calvin on Secular Authority*, ed. H. Höpfl (Cambridge, 1991)

Mackintosh, J., *Memoirs of the Life of the Right Honourable Sir James Mackintosh*, ed. R. Mackintosh (London, 1835)

Maistre, J. de, *Considerations on France*, ed. and trans. R. Lebrun (Cambridge, 2000)

   Du pape (Paris, 1819)

The Marx–Engels Reader, ed. R. Tucker (New York, 1978)

Masson, P.-H., *Discours sur le rétablissement de la religion; prononcé dans le temple des protestans de Paris, le Dimanche 5 Floréal, an X (April 25, 1802)* (Paris, n.d.)

The Mind of Napoleon: A Selection from his Written and Spoken Words, ed. and trans. J. C. Herold (New York, 1955)

Montaigne, M. *Essais*, ed. M. Rat (Paris, 1958)

Montesquieu, *Spirit of the Laws*, ed. A. Cohler, B. Miller, and H. Stone (Cambridge, 1994)

Necker, J., *Cours de morale religieuse* (Geneva, 1800)

   De la Révolution française, in *Œuvres complètes de M. Necker publiées par M. le Baron de Staël, son petit fils*, vol. X (Paris, 1820–21)

Nicole, P., *De l'unité de l' église ou réfutation du nouveau système de M. Jurieu* (Paris, 1729)

Pradt, D. de, *Du jésuitisme ancien et moderne* (Paris, 1825)

   Les quatre concordats (Paris, 1818)

Projet de réunion de toutes les communions chrétiennes ... par M. de Beaufort, Jurisconsulte (Paris, 1806)

Rémusat, C. de, *Mémoires de ma vie*, ed. C. de Pouthas (Paris, 1959)

Rivarol, A. de, *De la philosophie moderne* (n.p., n.d.)

Robertson, W., *History of America* (London, 1796)

> *History of the Reign of the Emperor Charles V* (New York, 1838)

> *The Situation of the World at the Time of Christ's Appearance, and its Connexion with the Success of his Religion, Considered* (Edinburgh, 1759)

Roederer, P.-L., *Œuvres du Comte P.-L. Roederer* (Paris, 1853–1859)

Rousseau, J.-J., *Discourse on Political Economy*, in *The Basic Political Writings*, ed. and trans. D. Cress (Indianapolis, 1987)

> *The Geneva Manuscript*, in *On the Social Contract*, ed. R. Masters (New York, 1978)

> *On the Social Contract*, in *The Basic Political Writings*, ed. and trans. D. Cress (Indianapolis, 1987)

Sainte-Beuve, C.-A., *Nouveaux lundis* (Paris, 1884)

> *Portrait de femmes* (Paris, n.d.)

Saint-Simon, Cl.-H. de, *Le nouveau christianisme et les écrits sur la religion*, ed. H. Desroche (Paris, 1969)

> *Œuvres de Claude-Henri de Saint-Simon*, 6 vols. (Paris, 1966)

Sismondi, G. C. L. *Epistolario*, vol. III (Florence, 1824–35)

Staël, G. de, *De l'Allemagne*, ed. S. Balayé (Paris, 1968)

> *Des circonstances actuelles qui peuvent terminer la Révolution et des principes qui doivent fonder la république en France*, ed. L. Omacini (Geneva, 1979)

> *Considérations sur la Révolution française*, ed. J. Godechot (Paris, 2000)

> *Correspondance générale*, vol. III, part 1, ed. J. J. Pauvert, notes and commentary by B. Jasinski (Paris, 1962)

Delphine, trans. A. H. Goldberger (Dekalb, IL, 1995)

"Lettres sur J.-J. Rousseau," in *Œuvres de jeunesse*, ed. S. Balayé and J. Isbell (Paris, 1997)

De la littérature, ed. G. Gengembre and J. Goldzink (Paris, 1991)

Suard, J.-B., "Avertissement du traducteur," in *Histoire du règne de l'empereur Charles-Quint, Précédée d'un Tableau des progrès de la Société en Europe, depuis la destruction de l'Empire Romain jusqu'au commencement du seizième siècle* (Amsterdam, 1771)

Tabaraud, M., *De la nécessité d'une religion de l'état* (Paris, 1803)

> *De la réunion des communions chrétiennes* (Paris, 1808)

Thibaudeau, A.-C., *Mémoires sur le Consulat 1799–1804* (Paris, 1827)

Villers, Ch. de, *Essai sur l'esprit et l'influence de la Réformation de Luther. Ouvrage qui a remporté le prix sur cette question proposée dans la séance publique du 15 germinal an X, par l'Institut national de France: "Quelle a été l'influence de la réformation de Luther sur la situation politique des différens Etats de l'Europe, et sur le progrès des lumières?"* (Paris, 1804)

> *Philosophie de Kant, ou principes fondamentaux de la philosophie transcendentale* (Metz, 1801)

Vincent, J. L. S., *Observations sur l'unité religieuse en réponse au livre de M. de La Mennais, intitulé: Essai sur l'indifférence en matière de religion, dans la partie qui attaque le protestantisme* (Paris, 1830)

Voltaire, *Political Writings*, ed. D. Williams (Cambridge, 2000)

Le Siècle de Louis XIV in *Œuvres*, ed. L. Moland (Paris, 1967)

3. SECONDARY SOURCES

UNPUBLISHED

Carlsson, E., "Johann Salomo Semler, The German Enlightenment, and Protestant Theology's Historical Turn," Ph.D. dissertation, University of Wisconsin-Madison, 2006.

Christofferson, M. S., "The Anti-Totalitarian Moment in French Intellectual Politics, 1975–1984," Ph.D. dissertation, Columbia University, 1998

Coleman, D., "The Foundation of the French Liberal Republic: Politics, Culture and Economy after the Terror," Ph.D. dissertation, Stanford University, 1997

Evans, H., "Les idées et les sentiments religieux de Benjamin Constant," Ph.D. dissertation, Université de Bordeau, 1958

Hart, D., "Class Analysis, Slavery and the Industrialist Theory of History in French Liberal Thought, 1814–1830: The Radical Liberalism of Charles Comte and Charles Dunoyer," Ph.D. dissertation, King's College Cambridge, 1994

Jainchill, A., "Republicanism and the Origins of French Liberalism, 1794–1804," Ph.D. dissertation, University of California, Berkeley, 2004

Kaiser, T., "The Ideologues: From the Enlightenment to Positivism," Ph.D. dissertation, Harvard University, 1976

Koehler, E., "Religious Liberty and Civisme Morale: Alexandre Vinet, French Protestantism and the Shaping of Civic Culture in Nineteenth-Century France," Ph.D. dissertation, University of California, Davis, 2002

Lee, J., "The Moralization of Modern Liberty," Ph.D. dissertation, University of Wisconsin–Madison, 2003

Riasanovsky, M., "The Trumpets of Jericho: Domestic Missions and Religious Revival in France, 1814–1830," 2 vols., Ph.D. dissertation, Princeton University, 2001

PUBLISHED

Adams, G., *The Huguenots and French Opinion, 1685–1787: The Enlightenment Debate on Toleration* (Waterloo, Ontario, 1991)

"Monarchistes ou républicains," *Dix-huitième siècle*, 17 (1985)

Aguet, J.-P., "Benjamin Constant parlementaire sous la monarchie de Juillet (juillet–décembre 1830)," ABC, 2 (1982), pp. 3–45

Agulhon, M., preface to J. Lalouette, *La Libre pensée en France, 1848–1940* (Paris, 1997)

Alexander, R., "Benjamin Constant as a Restoration Politician," in H. Rosenblatt
(ed.), *Cambridge Companion to Constant*, forthcoming
Bonapartism and the Revolutionary Tradition in France: The Fédérées of 1815
(Cambridge, 1991)
Re-Writing the French Revolutionary Tradition (Cambridge, 2003)
Allison, H. E., *Lessing and the Enlightenment: His Philosophy of Religion and its
Relation to Eighteenth-Century Thought* (Ann Arbor, MI, 1966)
Allix, E., "J.-B. Say et les origines de l'industrialisme," *Revue d'économie politique*,
24 (1910)
"La méthode et la conception de l'économie politique dans les *Œuvres* de
J.-B. Say," *Revue d'histoire des doctrines économiques et sociales*, 4 (1912),
pp. 321–360
Anelli, B., "Benjamin Constant et la guerre pour l'indépendance de la Grèce
(1821–1830)," ABC, 23–23 (2000), pp. 195–203
"Benjamin Constant et la guerre pour l'indépendance de la Grèce: deux lettres
inédites (1824 et 1825)," ABC, 20 (1997), pp. 153–161
Aner, K., *Die Theologie der Lessingzeit* (Hall, 1929)
Aston, N., *Religion and Revolution in France 1780–1804* (Washington, DC, 2000)
Azouvi, F., "L'Institut national: une encyclopédie vivante?," in F. Azouvi (ed.),
L'Institution de la raison: La Révolution culturelle des Idéologues (Paris, 1992)
(ed.), *L'Institution de la raison: La Révolution culturelle des Ideologues* (Paris,
1992)
Azouvi, F. and D. Bourel, *De Königsberg à Paris: La réception de Kant en France
(1788–1804)* (Paris, 1991)
Baczko, B., *Ending the Terror: The French Revolution after Robespierre*, trans.
M. Petheram (New York, 1994)
Baelen, J., *Benjamin Constant et Napoléon* (Paris, 1965)
Balayé, S., "A Propos de Benjamin Constant lecteur de *Delphine*," in *Cahiers
staëliens*, 26–27 (1979) pp. 26–27
"Delphine, roman des Lumières: pour une lecture politique," in Ch. Mervaud
and S. Menant (eds.), *Le Siècle de Voltaire: Hommage à René Pomeau*
(Oxford, 1987)
"*Delphine* de Madame de Staël et la presse sous le Consulat," *Romantisme*, 51
(1986), pp. 39–47
Madame de Staël: Lumières et liberté (Paris, 1979)
"Unemissaire de Bonaparte, Fiévée critique de Madame de Staël et de
Delphine," *Cahiers staëliens*, 26–27 (1979), pp. 99–116
Bastid, P., *Benjamin Constant et sa doctrine* (Paris, 1966)
Baubérot, J., *Histoire de la laïcité en France* (Paris, 2000)
Benin, S., *The Footprints of God: Divine Accommodation in Jewish and Christian
Thought* (Albany, NY, 1993)
Berenson, E., "A New Religion of the Left: Christianity and Social Radicalism in
France, 1815–1848," in F. Furet and M. Ozouf (eds.), *The French Revolution
and the Transformation of Modern Political Culture*, vol. III (New York,
1989)

Populist Religion and Left-Wing Politics in France 1830–1852 (Princeton, NJ, 1984)

Bertho, J.-P., "Naissance et élaboration d'une 'théologie' de la guerre chez les évêques de Napoléon (1802–1820)," in J.-R. Derré *et al.* (eds.), *Civilisation chrétienne: Approche historique d'une idéologie* (Paris, 1975)

Berthoud, D., *Constance et grandeur de Benjamin Constant* (Lausanne, 1944)

Bertier de Sauvigny, G., *La Restauration* (Paris, 1974)

Bien, D., *The Calas Affair* (Princeton, NJ, 1960)

Boudon, J.-O., "Bonaparte et la réconciliation religieuse," in *Terminer la Révolution?: Actes du colloque ... 4 et 5 décembre, 2001* (Paris, 2003)

Napoléon et les cultes (Paris, 2002)

Bowman, F., "L'episode quiétiste dans 'Cécile,'" in P. Corday and J.-L. Seylaz (eds.), *Benjamin Constant: Actes du Congrès de Lausanne* (Geneva, 1968)

"La révélation selon Benjamin Constant," *Europe*, 46, 467 (March, 1968), pp. 115–125

Boyer, A., "De l'actualité des anciens républicains," in S. Chauvier (ed.), *Libéralisme et républicanisme* (Caen, 2000)

Breyer, S., *Active Liberty: Interpreting Our Democratic Constitution* (New York, 2005)

Brown, S., "William Robertson (1721–1793) and the Scottish Enlightenment," in S. Brown, (ed.), *William Robertson and the Expansion of Empire* (Cambridge, 1997)

Burnand, L., *Necker et l'opinion publique* (Paris, 2004)

Burtin, N., *Le baron d'Eckstein: un semeur d'idées au temps de la Restauration* (Paris, 1931)

Byrnes, J., "Chateaubriand and Destutt de Tracy: Defining Religious and Secular Polarities in France at the Beginning of the Nineteenth Century," *Church History*, 60, 3 (September 1991), pp. 316–330

Carpenter, C., "Ethics and Polytheism in Constant's Early Writings: The Influence of Hume, Smith and Gillies," ABC, 29 (2005), pp. 73–100

Chadwick, O., *The Popes and European Revolution* (Oxford, 1961)

Chaquin, N. and S. Michaud, "Saint-Martin dans le Groupe de Coppet et le cercle de Frédéric Schlegel," in S. Balayé and J.-D. Candaux (eds.), *Le Groupe de Coppet: Actes et documents du deuxième colloque de Coppet, 10–13 juillet 1974* (Geneva, 1977)

Chartier, J.-L., *Portalis: Le père du Code civil* (Paris, 2004)

Cholvy, G., "Réalités de la religion populaire dans la France contemporaine," in B. Plongeron *et al.* (eds.), *La religion populaire dans l'occident chrétien* (Paris, 1976)

Cholvy, G. and Y.-M. Hilaire, *Histoire religieuse de la France contemporaine* (Toulouse, 1990)

Christofferson, M. S., "An Antitotalitarian History of the French Revolution: François Furet's *Penser la Révolution française* in the Intellectual Politics of the Late 1970s," *French Historical Studies*, 22, 4 (Fall, 1999), pp. 557–611

Clacys, G., "'Individualism,' 'Socialism,' and 'Social Science': Further Notes on a Process of Conceptual Formation, 1800–1850," *Journal of the History of Ideas*, 47, 1 (1986), pp. 81–93

Clarke, I., "From Protest to Reaction: The Moderate Regime in the Church of Scotland, 1752–1805," in N. T. Phillipson and R. Mitchison (eds.), *Scotland in the Age of Improvement* (Edinburgh, 1996)

Coleman, P., "Introduction," in B. Constant, *Adolphe*, ed. P. Coleman, trans. M. Mauldron (Oxford, 2001)

Collingham H. A. C. (with R. Alexander), *The July Monarchy: A Political History of France 1830–1848* (London and New York, 1988)

Cordey, P., "Madame de Staël et les prédicants lausannois," *Cahiers staëliens*, N S, 8 (1969), pp. 7–21

Courtney, C. P., "Isabelle de Charrière and the 'Character of H. B. Constant': A False Attribution," *French Studies*, 36, 3 (July 1982), pp. 282–289

Craiutu, A., *Liberalism under Siege: The Political Thought of the French Doctrinaires* (Lanham, MD, 2003)

Crowley, R. A., *Charles de Villers: Mediator and Comparatist* (Berne, 1978)

Cubitt, G., *The Jesuit Myth: Conspiracy Theory and Politics in Nineteenth-Century France* (Oxford, 1993)

Daiches, D., "The Scottish Enlightenment," in D. Daiches, P. Jones and J. Jones (eds.), *The Scottish Enlightenment 1730–1790: A Hotbed of Genius* (Edinburgh, 1996)

Daiches, D., P. Jones, and J. Jones (eds.), *The Scottish Enlightenment 1730–1790: A Hotbed of Genius* (Edinburgh, 1996)

Dansette, A., *Histoire religieuse de la France contemporaine: De la Révolution à la Troisième République* (Paris, 1948)

Darnton, R., *The Literary Underground of the Old Regime* (Cambridge, MA, 1982)

Déchery, M., "Benjamin Constant à Luzarches," in D. Verrey and A.-L. Delacrétaz (eds.), *Benjamin Constant et la Révolution française, 1789–1799* (Geneva, 1989)

Deguise, P., "Benjamin Constant a-t-il été dénonciateur? L'affaire Oudaille," *Mercure de France*, 343 (Sept.–Dec., 1961), pp. 75–92

Benjamin Constant méconnu: Le livre "De la religion" avec des documents inédits (Geneva, 1966)

Delbouille, P., *Genèse, structure et destin d'Adolphe* (Paris, 1971)

Derré, J.-R., "L'auteur de *De la religion* et le christianisme," in P. Corday and J.-L. Seylaz (eds.), *Actes du congrès Benjamin Constant (Lausanne, octobre 1967)* (Geneva, 1968)

Desan, S., *Reclaiming the Sacred: Lay Religion and Popular Politics in Revolutionary France* (Ithaca, NY, 1990)

Dickey L., "Saint-Simonian Industrialism as the End of History: August Cieszkowski on the Teleology of Universal History," in M. Bull (ed.), *Apocalypse Theory and the Ends of the World* (Oxford, 1995)

Dijn, A., de, *French Political Thought from Montesquieu to Tocqueville: Liberty in a Levelled Society?* (Cambridge, 2008)

Dodge, G., *Benjamin Constant's Philosophy of Liberalism: A Study in Politics and Religion* (Chapel Hill, NC, 1980)

Dupont, A., *Rabaut Saint-Etienne, 1743–1793: Un protestant défenseur de la liberté religieuse* (Geneva, 1989)

Duprat, C., *Usages et pratiques de la philanthropie: Pauvreté, action sociale et lien social, à Paris, au cours du premier XIXe siècle.* 2 vols. (Paris, 1996)

Dworetz, S., *The Unvarnished Doctrine: Locke, Liberalism, and the American Revolution* (Durham, NC, 1990)

Ellis, G., "Religion According to Napoleon: The Limitations of Pragmatism," in N. Aston (ed.), *Religious Change in Europe, 1650–1914* (Oxford, 1997)

Encrevé, A.,"La Réception des ouvrages de J. Necker sur la religion, d'après sa correspondance privée," in L. Burnand (ed.), *Jacques Necker (1732–1804): Banquier, ministre, écrivain* (Geneva, 2004)

Faguet, E., *Politiques et moralistes du dix-neuvième siècle* (Paris, 1891)

Fontana, B.-M., *Benjamin Constant and the Post-Revolutionary Mind* (New Haven, CT, 1991)

"The Shaping of Modern Liberty: Commerce and Civilisation in the Writings of Benjamin Constant," ABC, 5 (1985), pp. 3–15

Ford, C., "Private Lives and Public Order in Restoration France: The Seduction of Emily Loveday," *American Historical Review*, 99, 1 (February 1994), pp. 21–43

Furet, F., "La Révolution sans la Terreur? Le débat des historiens du XIXe siècle," *Le Débat*, 13 (June 1981), pp. 40–54

Garsten, B., "Constant and the Religious Spirit of Liberalism," in H. Rosenblatt (ed.), *Cambridge Companion to Constant*, forthcoming.

Gauchet, M., "Benjamin Constant: L'illusion lucide du libéralisme," in B. Constant, *Ecrits politiques*, ed. M. Gauchet (Paris, 1997)

"Constant," in F. Furet and M. Ozouf (eds.), *A Critical Dictionary of the French Revolution*, trans. A. Goldhammer (Cambridge, MA, 1989)

Giblein, J., "Note sur le protestantisme de Mme de Staël," in *Bulletin du protestantisme français* (Paris, 1954)

Glachant, V., *Benjamin Constant sous l'oeil du guet, d'après nombreux documents inédits* (Paris, 1906)

Goblot, J.-J., *La jeune France libérale: Le Globe et son groupe littéraire 1824–1830* (Paris, 1995)

Gordon, D., *Citizens without Sovereignty: Equality and Sociability in French Thought, 1670–1789* (Princeton, NJ, 1994)

Gouhier, H., *Benjamin Constant: devant la religion* (Paris, 1967)

Grange, H., *Benjamin Constant: Amoureux et républicain, 1795–1799* (Paris, 2004)

Guénot, H., "Musées et lycées Parisiens (1780–1830)," *Dix-huitième siècle*, 18 (1986), pp. 249–67

Hahn, R., *The Anatomy of a Scientific Institution: The Paris Academy of Sciences, 1666–1803* (Berkeley, CA, 1971)

Haines, B., "The Athénée de Paris and the Bourbon Restoration," *History and Technology*, 5 (1988), pp. 29–271

Hales, E. E. Y., *Napoleon and the Pope* (London, 1962)

Hartman, M., "The Sacrilege Law of 1825 in France: A Study in Anticlericalism and Mythmaking," *Journal of Modern History*, 44, 1 (March, 1972), pp. 21–37

Hazareesingh S., *Political Traditions in Modern France* (Oxford, 1994)

Herold, J., *Mistress to an Age: A Life of Madame de Staël* (New York, 1958)

Hesse, C., *Publishing and Cultural Politics in Revolutionary Paris 1789–1810* (Berkeley, CA, 1991)

Higonnet, P., "Marx, disciple de Constant?" ABC, 6 (1986), pp. 10–16

Hilaire, Y.-M., "Notes sur la religion populaire au XIXe siècle," in Y.-M. Hilaire (ed.), *La religion populaire: aspects du christianisme populaire à travers l'histoire* (Lille, 1981)

Hofmann, A., "The Origins of the Theory of the *Philosophe Conspiracy*," French *History*, 2, 2 (1988), pp. 152–172

Hofmann, E., "Histoire de l'ouvrage," in B. Constant, DLR, pp. 1111–1122

"Histoire politique et religion: essai d'articulation de trois composantes de l'oeuvre et de la pensée de Benjamin Constant," *Historical Reflections*, 28, 3 (Fall, 2002), pp. 397–418

Les "Principes de politique" de Benjamin Constant: la genèse d'une oeuvre et l'évolution de la pensée de leur auteur, 1789–1806 (Geneva, 1980)

Hogue, H., *Of Changes in Benjamin Constant's Books on Religion* (Geneva, 1964)

Holmes, S., *Benjamin Constant and the Making of Modern Liberalism* (New Haven, CT, 1984)

Hufton, O., "The Reconstruction of a Church, 1796–1801," in G. Lewis and C. Lucas (eds.), *Beyond the Terror: Essays in French Regional and Social History, 1794–1815* (Cambridge, 1983), pp. 21–52

Iggers, G., *The Cult of Authority: The Political Philosophy of the Saint-Simonians, a Chapter in the Intellectual History of Totalitarianism* (The Hague, 1958)

Isbell, J., *The Birth of European Romanticism: Truth and Propaganda in Staël's "De l'Allemagne," 1810–1813* (Cambridge, 1994)

James, M., "Pierre-Louis Roederer, Jean-Baptiste Say, and the Concept of Industrie," *History of Political Economy*, 9 (1977), pp. 455–475

Jasinski, B., "Benjamin Constant tribun," in E. Hofmann (ed.), *Benjamin Constant, Mme de Staël et le groupe de Coppet: Actes du deuxième Congrès de Lausanne et du troisième colloque de Coppet* (Oxford, 1982)

L'engagement de Benjamin Constant: amour et politique, 1794–1796 (Paris, 1971)

Jaume, L., *L'Individu effacé ou le paradoxe du libéralisme français* (Paris, 1997)

Jovicevich, A., *Jean-François de la Harpe, adepte et renégat des lumières* (South Orange, NJ, 1973)

Juden, B., "Accueil et rayonnement de la pensée de Benjamin Constant sur la religion," in E. Hofmann (ed.), *Benjamin Constant, Madame de Staël et le groupe de Coppet: Actes du deuxième congrès de Lausanne et du troisième colloque de Coppet* (Oxford, 1982)

Judt, T., *Past Imperfect: French Intellectuals, 1944–1956* (Berkeley, CA, 1992)

Kafker, F. J. Laux and D. Gay Levy (eds.), *The French Revolution: Conflicting Interpretations* (Malabar, FL, 2002)

Kaiser, Th., "Politics and Political Economy in the Thought of the Idéologues," *History of Political Economy*, 12, 2 (1980), pp. 141–160

Kelly, G. A., *The Humane Comedy: Constant, Tocqueville, and French Liberalism* (Cambridge, 1992)

Kent, S., *The Election of 1827 in France* (Cambridge, MA, 1975)

Khilnani, S., *The Intellectual Left in Postwar France* (New Haven, CT, 1993)

King, N. and J.-D. Candaux, "La correspondance de Benjamin Constant et de Sismondi (1801–1830)," ABC, 1 (1980)

Kitchin, J., *Un journal "philosophique": La Décade (1794–1807)* (Paris, 1965)

Kloocke, K., *Benjamin Constant: Une biographie intellectuelle* (Geneva, 1984)

"Le concept de la liberté religieuse chez Benjamin Constant," ABC, 10 (1989), pp. 25–39

"Les écrits de Benjamin Constant sur la religion: quelques réflexions hermeneutiques et méthodologiques," in *Huit études sur Benjamin Constant. Cahiers de l'Association internationale des études françaises*, 48 (1996)

"Religion et société chez Benjamin Constant" in L. Jaume (ed.), *Coppet, creuset de l'esprit libéral: Les idées politiques et constitutionnelles du groupe de Madame de Staël* (Paris and Aix-Marseille, 2000)

Kohler, P., *Madame de Staël et la Suisse* (Payot, 1916)

Kroen, S., *Politics and Theater: The Crisis of Legitimacy in Restoration France, 1815–1830* (Berkeley, 2000)

"Revolutionizing Religious Politics during the Restoration," *French Historical Studies*, 21, 1 (Winter, 1998), pp. 27–53

Kuhn, F., "La vie intérieure du protestantisme sous le premier empire," *Bulletin de l'histoire du protestantisme français*, 51, 2 (February, 1902), pp. 57–73

Ladous, R., "Catholiques libéraux et union des églises jusqu'en 1878," in *Les catholiques libéraux au XIXe siècle* (Grenoble, 1974)

Latreille, A., *L'eglise catholique et la Révolution française: Le pontificat de Pie VI et la crise française (1775–1799)* (Paris, 1946)

Napoléon et le Saint-Siège: 1801–1808, l'ambassade du cardinal Fesch à Rome (Paris, 1935)

Latreille, A., J.-R. Palanque, E. Delaruelle, and R. Rémond, *Histoire du catholicisme en France: La période contemporaine* (Paris, 1962)

Laurent, A., *La philosophie libérale: Histoire et actualité d'une tradition intellectuelle* (Paris, 2002)

Lee, J., "An Answer to the Question: What is Liberalism? Benjamin Constant and Germany," ABC, 29 (2005), pp. 127–141

Lefebvre, G., *The Thermidorians & the Directory*, trans. R. Baldick (New York, 1964)

Ligou, D., "Franc-maçonnerie et protestantisme," *Dix-huitième siècle*, 17 (1985), pp. 41–51

Lilla, M., "The Other Velvet Revolution: Continental Liberalism and its Discontents," *Daedalus*, 123, 2 (Spring, 1994)

Livesey, J., *Making Democracy in the French Revolution* (Cambridge, MA, 2001)

Lukes, S., "The Meanings of Individualism," *Journal of the History of Ideas*, 32, 1 (1971), pp. 45–66

Lyons, M., "Fires of Expiation: Book-Burnings and Catholic Missions in Restoration France," *French History*, 10, 2 (June, 1996), pp. 240–266

Madelin, L., *Le Consulat et l'empire* (Paris, 1932–3)

Mandrou R. *et al.*, *Histoire des protestants en France* (Toulouse, 1977)

Manent, P., *An Intellectual History of Liberalism*, trans. R. Balinski (Princeton, NJ, 1995)

Mathiez, A., *La Révolution et l'Eglise* (Paris, 1910)
 La Théophilanthropie et le culte décadaire 1796–1801 (Paris, 1903)

McMahon, D., *Enemies of the Enlightenment: The French Counter-Enlightenment and the Making of Modernity* (Oxford, 2001)

McManners, J., *Church and Society in Eighteenth-Century France* (New York, 1998)

Mellon, S., *The Political Uses of History: A Study of Historians in the French Restoration* (Stanford, CA, 1958)

Michel, H., *L'idée de l'état* (Paris, 1898)

Mortier, R., "Philosophie et religion dans la pensée de Mme de Staël," *Rivista de letterature moderne e comparate* (September–December 1967)

Newman, E., "The Blouse and the Frock Coat: The Alliance of the Common People of Paris with the Liberal Leadership and the Middle Class during the Last Years of the Bourbon Restoration," *Journal of Modern History*, 46, 1 (March, 1974), pp. 26–59

Nord, Ph., *The Republican Moment: Struggles for Democracy in Nineteenth-Century France* (Cambridge, MA, 1998)

Omacini, L., "Benjamin Constant, correcteur de Mme de Staël," *Cahiers staëliens*, NS, 25 (1978), pp. 5–23

Omacini, L. and R. Schatzer, "Quand Benjamin Constant travaille sur les papiers de Mme de Staël: le cas de la 'Copie' des *Circonstances actuelles*," in F. Tilkin (ed.), *Le Groupe de Coppet et le monde moderne: Conceptions – Images – Débats. Actes du VIe Colloque de Coppet* (Liège, 1998), pp. 59–82

Ozouf, M., *Festivals and the French Revolution*, trans. A. Sheridan (Cambridge, MA, 1988)
 "Revolutionary Religion," in F. Furet and M. Ozouf (eds.), *A Critical Dictionary of the French Revolution*, trans. A. Goldhammer (Cambridge MA, 1989)

Palmer, R. R., *The Improvement of Humanity: Education and the French Revolution* (Princeton, NJ, 1985)

Perrochon, H., "Les sources suisses de la religion de Mme de Staël," in *Madame de Staël et l'Europe, Colloque de Coppet* (Paris, 1970)

Perry, E. I., *From Theology to History: French Religious Controversy and the Revocation of the Edict of Nantes* (The Hague, 1973)

Pettit, Ph., *Republicanism: A Theory of Freedom and Government* (Oxford, 1997)

Phayer, J. M., "Politics and Popular Religion: the Cult of the Cross in France, 1815–1840," *Journal of Social History*, 2, 3 (Spring, 1978), pp. 346–365

Phillipson, N., "Providence and Progress: An Introduction to the Historical Thought of William Robertson," in Stewart Brown (ed.), *William Robertson and the Expansion of Empire* (New York, 1997)

Philp, M., *Godwin's Political Justice* (London, 1986)

Picavet, F., *Les Idéologues* (Paris, 1891)

Piguet, M.-F., "Benjamin Constant et la naissance du mot 'individualisme,'" ABC, 29 (2005), pp. 101–124

Pitassi, M.-C., "Le catéchisme de Jacob Vernes ou comment enseigner aux fidèles un 'christianisme sage et raisonnable,'" *Dix-huitième siècle*, 34 (2002)

Plongeron, B., "L'Eglise et les déclarations des droits de l'homme au XVIIIe siècle," *Nouvelle revue théologique*, 191 (May–June, 1979), pp. 360–377

"Les projets de réunion des communions chrétiennes, du Directoire à l'Empire," *Revue d'histoire de l'Eglise de France* 66 (1980), pp. 17–49

Pocock, J. G. A., *Barbarism and Religion* (Cambridge, 1999)

"Conservative Enlightenment and Democratic Revolution: The American and French Cases in British Perspective," *Government and Opposition*, 24, 1 (1989), pp. 81–105

Poland, B., *French Protestantism and the French Revolution: A Study in Church and State, Thought and Religion, 1685–1815* (Princeton, 1957)

Popkin, J., *The Right-Wing Press in France, 1792–1800* (Chapel Hill, NC, 1980)

Pouthas, C., *L'Eglise et les questions religieuses sous la monarchie constitutionnelle* (Paris, 1961)

Reill, P., *The German Enlightenment and the Rise of Historicism* (Berkeley, CA, 1975)

Reymond, B., "Redécouvrir Samuel Vincent," *Etudes théologiques et religieuses*, 54, 3 (1979), pp. 411–423

Robert, D., "Court de Gébelin et les églises," *Dix-huitième siècle*, 17 (1985)

Les églises réformées en France (1800–1830) (Paris, 1961)

Rosa, S., "'Il était possible aussi que cette conversion fût sincère': Turenne's Conversion in Context," *French Historical Studies*, 18, 3 (Spring 1994), pp. 632–666

Rosanvallon, P., *Le moment Guizot* (Paris, 1985)

Rosenblatt, H., "The Christian Enlightenment," in T. Tackett and S. Brown (eds.), *The Cambridge History of Christianity*, vol. VII: *Enlightenment, Revolution and Reawakening (1660–1815)* (Cambridge, 2006)

"Eclipses and Revivals: The Reception of Constant in France and America," in H. Rosenblatt (ed.), *Cambridge Companion to Constant*, forthcoming

"Madame de Staël, the Protestant Reformation, and the history of 'private judgement,'" ABC, 31–32 (2007), pp. 143–154

"Reinterpreting Adolphe: The Sexual Politics of Benjamin Constant," *Historical Reflections*, 3, 3 (Fall 2002), pp. 341–360

Rousseau and Geneva: From the First Discourse to the Social Contract, 1749–1762 (Cambridge, 1997)

"Why Constant? A Critical Overview of the Constant Revival," *Modern Intellectual History*, 1, 3 (2004), pp. 439–453

Rudler, G., "Benjamin Constant et Philippe-Albert Stapfer," in *Mélanges de philologie, d'histoire et de littérature offerts à Joseph Vianey* (Paris, 1934)

La jeunesse de Benjamin Constant (1767–1794): Le disciple du XVIIIe siècle, utilitarisme et pessimisme, Mme de Charrière d'après de nombreux documents inédits (Paris, 1908)

Sacquin, M., "Catholicisme intégral et morale chrétienne: un débat sous la Restauration entre le *Mémorial catholique* et le *Journal de la Société de la morale chrétienne*," *Revue historique*, 286, 2 (1991), pp. 337–358
    Entre Bossuet et Maurras: L'Antiprotestantisme en France de 1814 à 1870 (Paris, 1998)
Saltet, M., *Benjamin Constant historien de la religion* (Geneva, 1905)
Schmidt, P., *Court de Gébelin à Paris (1763–1784): Etude sur le protestantisme français pendant la seconde moitié du XVIIIe siècle* (St. Blaise, 1908)
Sepinwall, A., *The Abbé Grégoire and the French Revolution: The Making of Modern Universalism* (Berkeley, CA, 2005)
Sevrin, E., *Les missions religieuses en France sous la Restauration, 1815–1830* (St. Maudé, 1948)
Sher, R., *Church and University in the Scottish Enlightenment: The Moderate Literati of Edinburgh* (Princeton, NJ, 1985)
Simon, J., *Une Académie sous le Directoire* (Paris, 1885)
Skinner, Q., *Liberty before Liberalism* (Cambridge, 1998)
Spitzer, A., "Malicious Memories: Restoration Politics and a Prosopography of Turncoats," *French Historical Studies*, 24, 1 (Winter 2001), pp. 37–61
    Old Hatreds and Young Hopes (Cambridge, MA, 1971)
Starobinski, J., *Blessings in Disguise; or, The Morality of Evil*, trans. A. Goldhammer (Cambridge, MA, 1993)
Staum, M., *Minerva's Message: Stabilizing the French Revolution* (Buffalo, NY, 1996)
Sutherland, D. M. G., *The French Revolution and Empire: Quest for a Civic Order* (Malden, MA, 2003)
Swart, K., "Individualism in the Mid-Nineteenth Century (1826–1860)," *Journal of the History of Ideas*, 23, 1 (January–March, 1962), pp. 77–90
Tackett, T., *Religion, Revolution and Regional Culture in Eighteenth-Century France: The Ecclesiastical Oath of 1791* (Princeton, NJ, 1986)
Tambour, E., "Benjamin Constant à Luzarches," *Revue de l'histoire de Versailles et de Seine-et-Oise* (Feb.–Nov. 1906), pp. 333–335
    Etudes sur la Révolution dans le Département de Seine-et-Oise (Paris, 1913)
Tavoillot, P.-H., "Fondation démocratique et autocritique libérale: Sieyès et Constant," in A. Renaut (ed.), *Histoire de la philosophique politique* (Paris, 1999), vol. IV: *Les critiques de la modernité politique*
Thompson, P., "Benjamin Constant: l'allégorie du polythéisme," ABC, 12 (1991), pp. 7–18
    La religion de Benjamin Constant: Les pouvoirs de l'image: essai de mise en perspective d'une situation (Pisa, 1978)
Thureau-Dangin, P., *Le parti libéral sous la Restauration* (Paris, 1876)
Todorov, T., "Benjamin Constant, penseur de la démocratie," preface to Benjamin Constant, *Principes de politiques*, ed. E. Hofmann (Paris, 1997)
Van Kley, D., "The Abbé Grégoire and the Quest for a Catholic Republic," in J. and R. Popkin (eds.), *The Abbé Grégoire and His World* (Dordrecht, 2000)

Van-Mesle, L. le, "La promotion de l'économie politique en France au XIX siècle," *Revue d'histoire moderne et contemporaine*, 27 (1980)

Venzac, G., *Les origines religieuses de Victor Hugo* (Paris, 1955)

Vermale, V., "Les origines des *Considérations sur la France* de Joseph de Maistre," *Revue d'histoire littéraire de la France*, 33 (1926), pp. 521–529

Vernon, J. P., *France and the Levant* (Berkeley, CA, 1941)

Viatte, A., *Les Sources occultes du romantisme*, 2 vols. (Paris, 1979)

Vincent, K. S., "Benjamin Constant, the French Revolution, and the Origins of French Romantic Liberalism," *French Historical Studies*, 23, 4 (Fall 2000), pp. 607–637

"Benjamin Constant, the French Revolution, and the Problem of Modern Character," *History of European Ideas*, 30 (2004), pp. 5–21

Vuilleumier, H., *Histoire de l'Eglise réformée du Pays de Vaud sous le régime bernois*, vol. III: *Le refuge, le piétisme, l'orthodoxie libérale* (Lausanne, 1930)

Welch, C., *Liberty and Utility: The French Idéologues and the Transformation of Liberalism* (New York, 1984)

Whatmore, R., *Republicanism and the French Revolution: An Intellectual History of Jean-Baptiste Say's Political Economy* (Oxford, 2000)

Wittmer, L., *Charles de Villers 1765–1815: Un intermédiaire entre la France et l'Allemagne et un précurseur de Mme de Staël* (Geneva, 1908)

Woloch, I., *Napoleon and His Collaborators: The Making of a Dictatorship* (New York, 2001)

The New Regime: Transformations of the French Civic Order, 1789–1820 (New York, 1994)

"'Republican Institutions,' 1797–1799," in C. Lucas (ed.), *The French Revolution and the Creation of Modern Political Culture*, vol. II: *The Political Culture of the French Revolution* (Oxford, 1988)

Wood, D., *Benjamin Constant: A Biography* (New York, 1993)

"Constant in Edinburgh: Eloquence and History," *French Studies*, 40 (April 2, 1986), pp. 150–166

Woronoff, D., *La République bourgeoise 1794–1799 de Thermidor à Brumaire* (Paris, 1972)

Index

266

IDEAS IN CONTEXT

Edited by Quentin Skinner and James Tully